The TIMELINE HISTORY *of* ENGLAND

The **TIMELINE HISTORY** *of* **ENGLAND**

ROBIN EAGLES

Series Editor Justin Wintle

BARNES & NOBLE

NEW YORK

Acknowledgements

This book has been from the outset a joint effort, and much of the credit truly belongs to the series editor, Justin Wintle, and to Andy Dickson. I must say a special word of thanks also to my friends and family, but most of all to Beverly Adams, Sarah Morpeth, Jonathan and Laura Eagles, and my parents. I am forever in their debt.

ISBN 0-7607-7974-0

Printed in Thailand

CONTENTS

MODERN ENGLAND

Feet
3000
2000
1500
1000
500
250
0

N

SCOTLAND

Edinburgh

NORTHERN
IRELAND

Isle of
Man

REPUBLIC
OF IRELAND

IRISH
SEA

Douglas

Carlisle

Newcastle-upon-Tyne

Tyne

Tees

York

Bradford

Leeds

Liverpool

Manchester

Mersey

Chester

Nottingham

Leicester

NORTH
SEA

Trent

E N G L A N D

Norwich

Birmingham

Severn

Avon

Great Ouse

Cambridge

WALES

Oxford

Cardiff

Bristol

Thames

LONDON

Dover

Southampton

Portsmouth

Brighton

Exeter

Plymouth

Isle of
Wight

0   50 miles

Scilly
Isles

Penzance

ENGLISH CHANNEL

INTRODUCTION

ENGLAND FORMS PART OF THE PRESENT-DAY UNITED KINGDOM, along with Scotland, Wales and Northern Ireland. Sometimes the union is called "Great Britain," sometimes just "Britain." Formally it is known as the "United Kingdom of Great Britain and Northern Ireland." Within the UK, England is the dominant partner in terms of geographical size, population and influence. Some fifty million of the current United Kingdom's sixty million live in England; until very recently England's government and parliament provided the political hub for the entire UK; economically it continues to dominate its immediate neighbors.

But these modern details and distinctions belie the long history of the British Isles. In the beginning, of course, there was no England, no Scotland, Wales or Ireland. In the period of prehistory (about which little is known), first man's ancestors—the hominids—then *homo sapiens sapiens*, colonized the British Isles, creating settlements that were loosely and only locally confederated. The first tangible evidence of wider societies is provided by the remarkable remains at Stonehenge, whose scale and construction history suggest that it was a ritual center for people living miles around. Yet despite Stonehenge's advanced design—first erected around 2000 BC, it is one of the great monuments of the European Neolithic era—its precise use and significance remain veiled, as does the identity of those who built it.

In all probability there must have been many waves of invaders and settlers over the centuries after the construction of Stonehenge. Of these many immigrants, it was the metal-working Celts who eased Britain out of prehistory into history proper. Although they left no early written records, they were observed, then overrun, by the

Romans—who did. Following expeditions undertaken by Julius Caesar in 55 and 54 BC, the Romans attempted wholesale subjugation under the emperor Claudius almost a hundred years later. But they were unable to tame the Scottish highlands, made only marginally greater progress in the mountainous territory that was to become Wales, and Ireland—known as Hibernia ("winter quarters")—was left largely untouched. In the fertile lowlands, however, the Romans succeeded in transplanting their advanced civilization, and it is from Roman times that England, known then as "Britannia," began to take shape as a territorial and political entity.

The same area formed the major part of kingdoms established by the Anglo-Saxons from the mid-5th century onwards. These soon converted to Christianity, and eventually became a single kingdom ruled by the House of Wessex. It is from this period that the name "England" (Land of the Angles) derives. But England's identity remained in near-constant flux. The Anglo-Saxons were invaded on numerous occasions, first by the Vikings and then, in the 11th century, by the Normans.

The Norman Conquest was critical to England's evolution. In the two centuries before 1066 England had been increasingly influenced by Scandinavia—indeed much of northern England was for a time a Viking kingdom known as the "Danelaw." But the Normans realigned their new territories with a different area of the continent, and it was this involvement that would shape the next stage of England's history. Throughout the Middle Ages, English and French fortunes were closely entwined—politically, militarily, and through royal and aristocratic bloodlines. France sought to conquer England, and England France. The result was a patchy and uncertain conflict, the Hundred Years War, that extended the tug-of-war between the two powers over some four generations.

Gradually, though, the kingdom of England emerged as a clear force in its own right. It was this kingdom, which grew in prosperity and influence under the Plantagenets and continued to do so under the Tudors, that began to make headway internationally in both trade and military power. The eventual result was the acquisition of an extraordinary empire, which at its 19th-century zenith extended across Canada, India, the Far East, Australasia and Africa.

Closer to home, too, the English tried to establish colonies. Union with Wales was negotiated in 1536; Scotland joined in 1707; Ireland was brought into the fold in 1801. Despite some benefits for these three individual countries, England's own interests remained the reason for a united Britain. Divisions remained, and during the course of the 20th century separatist forces within the union began to make themselves heard. Ireland was partitioned shortly after World War I, forming a southern (mainly Catholic) republic and six northern (mainly Protestant) counties that remained within the UK. Some eighty years later, regional legislatures were established in Scotland and Wales in an attempt to give people in both countries more control over their politics.

All this, it has been said, leaves Britain—and with it the dominance of the English—looking more fragile now than ever before. Some doubt that the United Kingdom will still be united, still less a kingdom, in years to come. By the same token, though, this fragmentation has encouraged some historians to concentrate their efforts on the study of national and regional identity, considering both ideals of Britain and Britishness as well as what it might mean to be English.

But who are the English? Racially as well as politically, the answer is complex. England is—and always has been—a melting pot. Today, the descendants of Celts, Romans, Angles, Saxons, Jutes, Vikings, Normans and other European peoples mix with those from further afield—in particular immigrants from former colonies, many of whom arrived in the latter half of the 20th century to supply low-wage labor for the postwar British economy. England is now more multi-cultural and multi-ethnic than ever before.

This long assimilative tradition is just one of many that continues to influence life in 21st-century England. The monarchy, of course, still looms large. Despite criticism of it in sections of society, the royal family continues to provide a popular national focus and—its defenders often claim—a much-needed center of political stability around which the country's parliamentary democracy functions. Though England is often accused of being hidebound, obsessed by history, perhaps it is truer to say that its culture is continually involved in a dialogue between the past and the present—especially as the nation struggles to adapt to a world in which it is no longer one of the most powerful players.

In many ways the ongoing debate over "Europe"—whether or not England should engage more fully with the European Union—embodies these kinds of anxieties, perhaps because it has such a long pedigree. England has always had a tempestuous and involved relationship with the rest of Europe, and the present-day arguments rehearse older ones too: whether it is better to function as a fully European country, or to remain in insular isolation (bolstered, of course, by a so-called "special relationship" with the United States and by remaining close to former colonies through the British Commonwealth). At the cusp of the third millennium, that decision looks like one of the most momentous England and its people have had to face.

CHAPTER ONE

Prehistoric, Early and Roman Britian
{UP TO **c.450 AD**}

THE BRITISH ISLES ORIGINALLY FORMED PART of the Eurasian landmass before breaking off to form an archipelago. They did not remain separate, however: when sea-levels fell during the Ice Ages, a land bridge re-appeared between Britain (the largest of the British Isles) and the northwest of what was to become the continent of Europe. It was probably across this land bridge that ***homo erectus***, then **Neanderthal** man and finally ***homo sapiens*** sapiens traveled in search of new lands to settle.

In time, the land bridge became permanently submerged, but the inhabitants of mainland Europe gradually learned to build boats capable of navigating the waters around Britain. Fresh waves of settlers continued to arrive and make the most of its fertile and hospitable terrain—particularly in the low-lying southern and central sections of the island.

But Britain's north and west are dominated by highlands, which probably proved less hospitable to early settlers. While the precise circumstances surrounding the island's separation into three territories—**England**, **Scotland** and **Wales**—are naturally a matter of debate, it seems likely that its topography has a great deal to do with it: England is mainly low-lying, while Scotland and Wales are largely mountainous. Since the "English" territory was more accessible and fertile, and capable of sustaining a greater population, it tended to dominate its two neighbors. However, England continued to attract the attention of European predators. Right up until the **Norman Conquest** of 1066 and beyond its history is one of conquest and attempted conquest.

While it is clear that waves of sea-borne migration continued to replenish Britain's human population once the European land bridge became submerged around 7500 BC, little is known about the early settlers. **Stonehenge** and other megalithic monuments indicate that by as early as 3000 BC powerful tribal kingdoms had formed, but these did not last and no trace remains of the language or languages they spoke. Only with the arrival of the **Celts** in the centuries preceding the Roman Conquest does linguistic evidence become available— albeit in a confusing way. Two variants of what is assumed to have been a common Celtic language, related to the widely diffused Indo- European language group, have survived into contemporary times. The first and oldest is called **Q-Celtic** or **Goidelic**, and forms the basis of modern Irish, Scottish Gaelic and Manx (spoken on the Isle of Man). The second and younger tongue is **P-Celtic**, known also as **Brythonic**: the basis of modern Welsh, Breton and Cornish.

That these languages share Celtic roots suggests that the Celts sep- arated from the original Indo-European population in the Black Sea region, then moved into central Europe—possibly as a result of pres- sure from further east. In due course they inhabited parts of Britain, most of France and sections of the Iberian peninsula. But the exact sequence of their movements is uncertain. A remarkable feature of western Europe c.1000 BC is the existence of a lively sea-based trade along the Atlantic coast, stretching from southern Ireland and Cornwall down to the Straits of Gibraltar, and connecting with Greek and Phoenician trading communities in the Mediterranean. This extended trade network enabled the startling pan-European cultural transformation known as the **Bronze Age** to happen. Significant deposits of tin in Cornwall and copper in Ireland were integral to its development and, given that the Celts were renowned as fine metallurgists, it seems almost certain that the Irish and Cornish ends of the trade were already Celticized. In the case of

Ireland, this must certainly be so—otherwise the survival there of the Q-Celtic language is difficult to explain.

Because Q-Celtic also survives in Scotland, it is widely assumed that the whole of Britain must have seen **Goidelic Celtic** communities at this relatively early stage. Whether this was in fact the case, or whether the early Celts were less thorough in their occupation, is not known for sure. The evidence merely suggests that there was a gap of some kind between this earliest settlement and a second wave of immigration, which arrived from middle Europe from the 8th century BC onwards. This secondary expansion, which coincided with the onset of the **Iron Age** in northern and western Europe, is usually divided into two cultural phases, named after the archeological sites in Germany and Switzerland where contrasting artifacts were discovered: Hallstatt culture and **La Tène** culture. Although very few **Hallstatt** artifacts have been excavated in England and Britain, more sophisticated La Tène artifacts have been found in abundance.

Taking all of this fragmentary evidence into account, the most likely scenario is that an early Celtic settlement of England was followed by a hiatus during which the various Celtic communities of western Europe ceased having very much to do with their parent peoples. Then a second Celtic settlement from the 4th century BC onwards largely swallowed up the first, at least on the British mainland.

By about 150 BC it is clear that a Celtic people called the **Belgae** dominated southern England while East Anglia, the north and the west were split between Brythonic-speaking tribes such as the **Iceni** and **Brigantes**. All formed separate kingdoms and all regularly fought against each other—something that greatly contributed to the ease with which the Romans managed to dominate in the 1st century AD. Although some Celtic tribes collaborated on defense—the **Catevellauni** and **Silures**, for instance—others like the Brigantes made their own bargains with the imperial invaders. This inherent lack of unity meant not only that the Celts of Britain were subjugated by the Romans in the lands south of the Scottish Highlands, but that they were to suffer much the same fate when the Anglo-Saxons arrived four centuries later.

The inhabitants of Britain's lowlands enjoyed the benefits of Roman civilization, or at least the spectacle of it, in a way that those in the hills simply couldn't or didn't. Yet too much can be made of the newly "European" development of southern Britain by Roman rule. Though they set about it less overtly, the Celts too had brought the British Isles closer to mainland Europe. Nor was the Roman occupation unchallenged: a succession of uprisings showed that even the warring Celts could sometimes unite against a common enemy. And when it came down to it, the style of Roman government was predominantly one of strategic control, operating out of fortified camps and townships. Britain itself—and British society—remained decidedly tribal. It was Rome's inability to consolidate its control in the Welsh and Scottish highlands that marked the beginning of England as a distinct entity.

At the end of the Roman period, it is hard to know quite how "Romanized" most Britons were, but there was undoubtedly a profound impact. Some British chieftains were heavily influenced by continental culture and became **Romano-Britons**, adopting Roman habits and dress and living in specially commissioned villas; one such may have been the client-king **Cogidubnus**, for whom the palace at **Fishbourne** in Sussex was probably built. The Britons who faced the Anglo-Saxon onslaught also seem to have employed Roman tactics to face off the invaders: the myths that surround **King Arthur** or **Ambrosius Aurelianus** most probably derive from a Romano-British leader, perhaps a holder of one of the military offices created by the Roman authorities. Arthur's knights employed the kind of cavalry tactics typical of Roman auxiliaries, which suggests that some of the civil and military structures survived the Roman departure. Significantly, too, most of the Britons living in what had been Roman Britain were **Christian**. Christianity was slow to take root, and it was probably not until the 3rd century that many urban British began to adopt its practices. By the time of the Roman withdrawal, however, the religion was firmly established, and it was only the incursion of the Saxons that forced it into the hinterlands. There it continued as a distinctive Celtic Christianity—later to be challenged and eventually overwhelmed by continental missionaries sent to convert the very people they had fled from.

c.300,000 BC Britain is colonized by *homo erectus*, taking advantage of an interglacial period of the Ice Age during which the island is joined to the European continent. Primitive humans hunt the mammoth and hippopotamus species prevalent in southeast England using simple wooden spears.

c.400,000 BC **Swanscombe Woman**, a member of this *homo erectus* community, lives in Kent. Hers are the oldest surviving human remains found in Europe.

c.70,000 BC The first **Neanderthals** settle in England. They inhabit caves and hunt wild animals for food and clothing.

c.35,000 BC The last Neanderthals are displaced by the ancestor of modern humans, *homo sapiens sapiens*, who begins settling in Britain.

c.12,000 BC The last **Ice Age** comes to an end.

c.7500 BC The land bridge connecting Britain with Europe is covered by the sea and Britain is separated from the Continent.

c.4300 BC **Causeway** settlements and **long barrow** burials are developed by Stone Age Britons. The causeways may lead to burial chambers of high-ranking members of these communities or sites of ritual significance.

STONEHENGE

*D*escribed by the 18th-century antiquarian William Stukeley as "that most noble and stupendous piece of Antiquity," Stonehenge is Europe's outstanding megalithic monument. It has also teased generations of researchers: the 17th-century architect and designer Inigo Jones reckoned it to be of Roman origin, while some Arthurian myths ascribe its construction to the wizard Merlin. Modern archeology, at any rate, shows it to be the outcome of three discrete stages of construction between around 2800 and 2000 BC, known as Stonehenge I, II and III.

Its precise function is still disputed, but it seems to be a ritual circle of great importance, its alignment with the rising sun of the summer solstice no accident. There is little more than speculation about the kind of worship that occurred there, though, nor is it clearly understood how the huge standing stones were transported to the site or raised. The discovery of similar stones off the coast of southern England have led some scholars to conclude that these were pieces intended for the Stonehenge complex lost at sea while en route. And strong claims have been put forward in favor of Preseli, two hundred miles away in southwest Wales, as the quarry from which the "bluestones" for Stonehenge II would almost certainly have had to have been carried by sea. The stone is certainly not local to Wiltshire, and this suggests that social and trading relations extended across wide swathes of Neolithic Britain. It may even be that Stonehenge was a ritual center for a number of British tribes, not just the vision of one local people.

c.3500 BC The first circular ritual monuments, or **henges**, are built, important both as temples for local religious cults and as clear indicators of where tribal boundaries lie.

A prehistoric dolmen, or megalithic tomb, in Cornwall

c.2800 BC The first work is undertaken at **Stonehenge** in Wiltshire.

c.2750 BC The **Beaker People**, possibly early Celtic migrants from Germany and the Low Countries, begin settling in Britain, bringing with them a metal-working technology that makes use of Irish copper and Cornish tin to make bronze. They derive their name from their custom of burying their dead with pottery jars or beakers in the long **barrows** or **tumuli** that still dominate the West Country landscape.

c.2600 BC The ritual complex at **Avebury** and the man-made hill at **Silbury** are developed by the "Wessex People."

c.2100 BC The Bluestone circle at **Stonehenge II** is erected.

THE CELTS

*T*he term Celtic is used in two main ways: to denote specific peoples and languages and to describe a style or styles of culture (political and artistic as well as material) that dominated central, northwestern and western Europe during the 1st millennium AD and before. But Celtic studies is a field rife with dispute. Even the distinguished historian Barry Cunliffe has struggled to come up with a watertight interpretation, commenting that "perhaps the only real definition of a Celt, now as in the past, is that a Celt is a person who believes him or herself to be Celtic." If we allow, though, that "Celtic" can broadly describe the Germanic peoples who colonized Britain prior to the Roman invasion, then the final Celtic intruders into Britain were the several **Belgic** tribes that, originating beyond the Rhine, had already invaded northeastern Gaul during the 4th and 3rd centuries BC. The most powerful of these Belgae were the **Catevellauni** and **Atrebates**. These overran the south, displacing the tribes already settled there.

c.2000 BC The Sarsen circle is added to **Stonehenge III**.

c.1000 BC As the Atlantic seaboard trade establishes itself, **hill forts** become a common feature of the southern British landscape, reflecting the prevalence of tribal structures and the growing wealth of a warrior aristocracy.

c.750 BC As new Celtic migrations originating in central Europe push westwards, **iron** begins to displace bronze as the principal metal used for making tools and weapons in Britain.

c.500 BC **Trade** between southern Britain, Ireland and Brittany in northern France flourishes.

c.325 BC The Greek adventurer and geographer **Pytheas of Massilia**

Warfare was a regular feature of Celtic society: complex hill fort defenses and the use of the chariot emphasize the investment made by a warrior aristocracy in military security and offensive capability. The Celts were more than fighters, though. Their arrival in Britain led to a diversification of agriculture and trade and the developments of arts such as metallurgy, pottery, ornamented stone-cutting and jewelry. The term Celtic Art is most often applied to the finely crafted late La Tène artifacts associated with the Belgic warrior aristocracy. These pieces form the high-point of Celtic bronze production and indicate real prosperity, featuring intricate curvilinear engraving and enamelwork. Objects like the **Snettisham torc** and bracelet and the oblong shield recovered from the Thames near Battersea, London (all now in the British Museum) lend credence to the image of a cultured people able to spend surplus wealth on luxury items.

(Marseille) circumnavigates Britain and visits tin mines in Cornwall. Although his findings are treated with suspicion by contemporaries, his visit coincides with a period when southern Britain and the Mediterranean are coming into renewed and increasing contact. His estimates of the British coastline and of the distance between Britain and Massilia are generally accurate.

c.300 BC As Celtic **La Tène** culture continues to spread through western Europe, the British are actively engaged in human sacrifice as part of their religious ceremonies.

c.200 BC An aggressive Celtic people called the **Belgae** begin to raid and colonize Britain, forcing earlier Celtic arrivals such as the **Iceni** out of the southeast—where the Belgae now form kingdoms of their own.

55 BC Julius Caesar, commanding the Roman armies in Gaul and concerned by the assistance given to his opponents by "Britons," sends Commius, king of the Gaulish Atrebates, to Britain to persuade the Belgae and other tribes to submit to Rome's authority. Commius is captured and imprisoned. Caesar mounts his first **armed reconnaissance** of Britain, landing on the south coast with a force of around 2000 troops. He frees Commius, who returns with him to Gaul.

54 BC Caesar revisits Britain with a greater force, again accompanied by Commius, and "pacifies" some of the tribes in the southeast. The British over-king **Cassivelaunus** is forced to surrender. As well as agreeing to pay tribute to Rome, Cassivelaunus is compelled to refrain from interfering with the neighboring Trinovantes who enter into an alliance with the Romans. Caesar is ill-equipped for a sustained occupation, however, and returns to Gaul.

50 BC Commius, having rebelled against Rome with the Gaulish chieftain Vercingetorix in 53, flees to Britain, where he becomes king of a British kingdom of Atrebates.

34 BC A projected invasion of Britain by **Octavius** (the future **First Emperor Augustus**) is abandoned as civil war breaks out inside the Roman empire.

26 BC Invasion of Britain is again suspended, this time because of local rebellions in Spain and the Alps that force Augustus to change his plans.

LINDOW MAN

*I*n 1984 peat cutters working in Lindow marsh in Cheshire were astonished to discover a foot protruding from their equipment. Suspecting foul play, the police were summoned to investigate and unearthed a human body missing only part of its lower limbs, which had been severed by the cutting apparatus.

Subsequent carbon dating indicated that the naked, bearded victim (who became known as Lindow Man and who now resides in the British Museum in London) was reckoned to be of Iron Age vintage. Archeologists working on the corpse discovered a number of gruesome features that must have contributed to his death. He had been hit over the head with a mercy blow, garrotted and his throat had been slashed. He had then been pushed face-first into a pool. This "triple death" of the knife, the noose and the drowning—a feature of Druidic ritual and associated with the death of Merlin in some romances—possibly identifies him as a sacrificial victim. Some researchers connected his death with the fall of the Druids' stronghold at Anglesey and the defeat of Boudicca, although more precise carbon-14 dating has since suggested that he died later, possibly as late as 119 AD. The fact that he had rare mistletoe pollen in his stomach has been taken to imply that the sacrifice could have been part of the feast of Beltain and his execution an offering to a god such as Belenos, rituals in whose honor Caesar describes in his account of the Roman campaign. Ultimately, though, it seems unlikely that the mystery of Lindow Man's death will ever be fully solved.

c.10 AD Cunobelinus (Cymbeline) of the Catevellauni secures his position as over-king of much of southeast England.

c.20 Around this time the individual known as **Lindow Man** is killed and offered to a lake deity.

c.40 Cunobelinus banishes his son **Adminius**, who flees to the Continent with a small band of followers and surrenders to the Romans. The emperor **Gaius Caligula** plans an invasion of Britain, but calls it off at the last moment. Cunobelinus dies soon afterwards.

c.41 Cunobelinus is succeeded by his sons **Togdumnus** and **Caratacus**. Verica of the Atrebates is exiled by the Catevellauni and flees to the court of the new Roman emperor **Claudius**.

43 Responding to Verica's plea, Claudius orders the **invasion** of Britain. An army of four legions is led by the capable **Aulus Plautius**, who becomes the first Governor of the new Province of Britain. The first year of conquest meets with considerable success: eleven British kings, clearly happier to accept Roman rule rather than subjugation by the Catevellauni, offer their submission. The Catevellauni hold out, though, and there is heavy fighting around the River Medway in Kent. The British retreat to the Thames, where a further battle is fought and **Togodumnus** is killed. It takes the arrival of Claudius himself later in the year to inspire the Romans to complete their operations against the Catevellauni by seizing **Camulodunum** (Colchester), although they fail to capture Caratacus.

44 The Romans divide their forces and pursue campaigns against the Durotriges of Devon and Dorset; there is fierce fighting at the hill forts of **Hod Hill** and **Maiden Castle**. **Vespasian**, a young commander and future emperor, is thought to have been responsible for overcoming a number of British fortifications.

45 The Durotriges are defeated, and most of southern Britain comes under Roman control.

47 Claudius's armies extend the Roman occupation to the **River Severn** in the west and the **Trent** in the midlands. The new governor

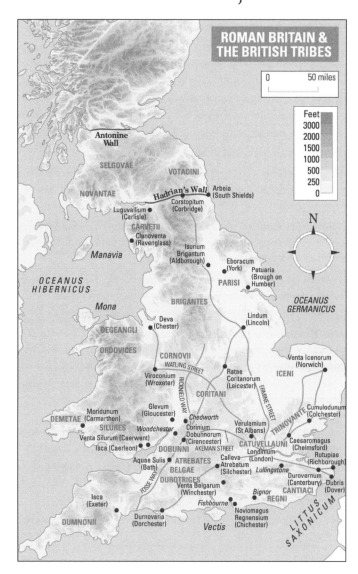

**ROMAN BRITAIN &
THE BRITISH TRIBES**

0   50 miles

Feet
3000
2000
1500
1000
500
250
0

N

Antonine
Wall

SELGOVAE

VOTADINI

NOVANTAE

Hadrian's Wall   Arbeia
(South Shields)

Corstopitum
(Corbridge)

Luguvallium
(Carlisle)

CARVETII

Glanoventa
(Ravenglass)

Isurium
Brigantum
(Aldborough)

Eboracum
(York)   Petuaria
(Brough on
Humber)

Manavia

OCEANUS
HIBERNICUS

PARISI

Mona

BRIGANTES

Lindum
(Lincoln)

OCEANUS
GERMANICUS

DEGEANGLI

Deva
(Chester)

ORDOVICES

CORNOVII

WATLING STREET

Viroconium
(Wroxeter)

Ratae
Coritanorum
(Leicester)

ICENI

Venta Icenorum
(Norwich)

CORITANI

Moridunum
(Carmarthen)

Glevum
(Gloucester)

Chedworth

Corinium
(Cirencester)

Verulamium
(St Albans)

Cumulodunum
(Colchester)

DEMETAE

SILURES   Woodchester

Venta Silurum (Caerwent)

Isca (Caerleon)

DOBUNNI

Dobunnorum

AKEMAN STREET

Caesaromagus
(Chelmsford)

Aquae Sulis
(Bath)

ATREBATES

BELGAE

Calleva
Atrebatum
(Silchester)

Londinium
(London)

Lullingstone

Rutupiae
(Richborough)

DUROTRIGES

Venta Belgarum
(Winchester)

Bignor

Durovernum
(Canterbury)   Dubris
(Dover)

CANTIACI

Isca
(Exeter)

DUMNONII

Durnovaria
(Dorchester)

Fishbourne

Vectis

Noviomagus
Regnensium
(Chichester)

REGNI

LITTUS
SAXONICUM

ERMINE STREET

TRINOVANTE

CATUVELLAUNI

FOSSE WAY

RICKNIELD WAY

Ostorius Scapula provokes a rising among the Iceni and other peoples of Norfolk by attempting to disarm them.

48 The revolt of the Iceni and others continues.

49 Greater resistance is offered by **Caratacus**, now operating from the territory of the Silures and Ordovices in Wales. A colony of Roman veterans is established at the old Catevellaunian capital of **Colchester**.

50 A new township is founded at **Londinium** (London) to provide merchants with a safe deep-water port on the Thames.

51 Scapula **defeats** Caratacus who, betrayed by the Brigantes, is taken to Rome in chains. There he impresses Claudius with his "noble bearing" and his death sentence is revoked.

58 Suetonius Paulinus is appointed governor of Britain. He continues the process of conquest, undertaking a major campaign against the tribes of South Wales.

61 Perhaps in order to undermine Celtic morale, Suetonius Paulinus attacks a fortified Druid center on the island of **Anglesey** in northwest Wales and slaughters several hundred Druidic priests.

King Prasutagus of the Iceni dies, leaving half of his property to the emperor. Agents of the Roman procurator flog his widow **Queen Boudicca** (Boadicea) and rape his daughters. Led by

> The Britons took no prisoners, sold no captives as slaves and went in for none of the usual trading of war. They wasted no time in getting down to the bloody business of hanging, burning and crucifying. It was as if they feared that retribution might catch up with them while their vengeance was only half-complete.
>
> —**Tacitus**, *Annals*,
> **trans. Peter Salway**

Boudicca, the Iceni and neighboring Trinovantes revolt and brutally sack **Camulodunum** (Colchester), **Londinium** (London) and **Verulamium** (St Albans). Suetonius Paulinus, returning from Wales, is forced to take on Boudicca's troops despite being heavily outnumbered. But the overconfident British are defeated, perhaps near **Mancetter** (in present-day Warwickshire), and Boudicca flees. According to legend she and her two daughters subsequently poison themselves.

Around this time construction begins of an impressive Roman pleasure complex at **Aquae Sulis** (Bath), a city whose modern name refers to the hot mineral springs tapped by the Romans.

70 The future governor of Britain, **Gnaeus Julius Agricola**, is given command of the 20th Legion at Wroxeter in acknowledgment of his support for the new Emperor Vespasian (69–79). He arrives in Britain at a time of renewed unrest—the northern border is no longer secure, the Brigantes having recently **rebelled**.

The current governor of Britain, Vettius Bolanus, is replaced by the more dynamic **Petillius Cerialis**, who is determined to pursue an active policy of "pacification."

74 Sextus Julius Frontinus, succeeding Petillius as Governor, turns his attention to the problem territory of Wales, and is successful in subduing the **Silures**.

77 Agricola, having repeatedly shown military prowess, becomes governor. Immediately he is confronted by crisis as the **Ordovices** of north Wales revolt, wiping out a Roman cavalry detachment. He responds swiftly and decisively: overcoming the Ordovices, he seizes the opportunity to pacify the whole of **Wales**.

78 Moving his forces to the north, Agricola defeats the troublesome **Brigantes** and prepares for a campaign against the peoples of what is now Scotland. At the same time he seeks to consolidate Rome's hold over the territories already controlled, encouraging **Roman dress** among his Celtic subjects and the use of the **Latin** language.

80 Agricola begins campaigning in **northern Britain** (Scotland), in line with the expansionist policies of the new emperor, **Domitian**.

The British client king **Cogidubnus**—possibly the builder of **Fishbourne**, a palace near Chichester—dies. His territory is taken over and reorganized by the Romans into three new **civitates** (districts) administered from **Chichester**, **Silchester** and **Winchester**.

83-4 Agricola defeats a coalition of northern British tribes at **Mons Graupius**, an unknown battle site perhaps at Bennachie in Aberdeenshire. According to the historian **Tacitus** he achieves a complete rout, with the Romans suffering only 360 dead to the Britons' 10,000. Agricola is awarded triumphal decorations and a stat-

BOUDICCA (d.C.60 AD)

*B*oudicca (Boadicea), widow of King Prasutagus of the Iceni tribe, was the leader of just one of several local rebellions against Roman rule in Britain—a short-lived revolt distinguished mainly by the atrocities committed by the troops under her command.

Boudicca's protests at Roman taxes after her husband's death led to her being flogged and her daughters raped. Perhaps because these events coincided with news of Suetonius Paulinus's onslaught against the Druids of **Anglesey**, Boudicca was able to mobilize both her own Iceni and the nearby Trinovantes against **Colchester**, with its detested temple built in honor of "the god" Claudius; they burnt it to the ground, massacring everyone in their path.

Suetonius hurried back from Wales ahead of his main force, but his appeal to the commander of the 2nd Legion for assistance was ignored and, unable to muster sufficient strength to hold Londinium, he abandoned it and

ue by Domitian, then recalled to Rome for other duties. Although he leaves Britain "peaceful and secure" for his successor, in reality he has only succeeded in pushing the Roman frontier further north: the Scottish Highlands remain out-of-bounds.

85 Pressure on the **Danube** forces Rome to withdraw its troops from northern Britain. Its most northerly forts are dismantled.

90 A new **colonia** (colony) is established at **Lincoln**.

96 A new colonia is begun at **Gloucester**.

98 The historian **Tacitus** completes the ***Agricola***, an account of his father-in-law's life and campaigns. The new emperor **Trajan**

Verulamium to Boudicca's followers. In **Londinium** alone the Iceni are reputed to have slaughtered some 70,000 inhabitants. Suetonius retreated to a position possibly near **Mancetter**, which may have had sacred significance for the Britons. Although heavily outnumbered, the legionaries' disciplined defense devastated Boudicca's army, which was trapped by their own baggage wagons.

Despite missing such a crucial military opportunity—and the brutality of her forces—Boudicca has passed into legend as the model of heroic British womanhood, even British nationhood: brave, resilient, proud. And despite the exaggerations and distortions of mythmakers, she was clearly an imposing person. The Greek historian Dio Cassius wrote: "She was huge of frame, terrifying of aspect, and with a harsh voice. A great mass of bright red hair fell to her knees: she wore a great twisted golden torc, and a tunic of many colors, over which was a thick mantle, fastened by a brooch."

Agricola had to deal with people living in isolation and ignorance, and therefore prone to fight; and his object was to accustom them to a life of peace and quiet by the provision of amenities. He therefore gave private encouragement and official assistance to the building of temples, public squares, and good houses. He praised the energetic and scolded the slack; and competition for honor proved as effective as compulsion. Furthermore, he educated the sons of the chiefs in the liberal arts, and expressed a preference for British ability as compared with the trained skills of the Gauls. The result was that instead of loathing the Latin language they became eager to speak it effectively. In the same way, our national dress came into favor and the toga was everywhere to be seen. And so the population was gradually led into the demoralizing temptations of arcades, baths, and sumptuous banquets. The unsuspecting Britons spoke of such novelties as "civilization," when in fact they were only a feature of their enslavement.

—Tacitus, *Agricola*, trans. H. Mattingly

(98–117) decides to concentrate Roman forces on expansion in the Middle East, leaving Britain to stagnate. During his reign what remains of the Roman presence in Scotland is lost.

c.103 The Romans suffer significant losses in the north. A number of their forward fortifications are damaged or destroyed by fire.

107–8 The famous **9th Legion**'s last posting at York is recorded. Possibly it is wiped out by a local rebellion, although there is some evidence that it may simply have been withdrawn to the Continent.

118 A revolt among the **Brigantes** is put down.

122 Visiting Britain, the Emperor **Hadrian** (117–138) encourages the construction of a clear barrier between "Roman" Britain and the "barbarian" north. Work on **Hadrian's Wall** commences, reflecting a wider policy of defensive rationalization across the Roman Empire undertaken by Hadrian.

131 The distinguished general **Sextus Julius Severus** is appointed governor of Britain.

139 Work begins on the **Antonine Wall**, commissioned by the emperor Antoninus Pius, some 160km to the north of Hadrian's Wall, reflecting a renewed will to extend the Roman frontier in Britain.

155–8 There is a revolt in the north against the Romans.

163 The Antonine Wall is **abandoned**, though a number of forts north of Hadrian's Wall continue to be manned.

175 Rome's British garrison is re-enforced with the arrival of 5500 Sarmatian cavalrymen.

180 The "barbarian" **Picts** north of the Roman frontier and other British tribes revolt and break through Hadrian's Wall, killing a garrison.

c.185 The Antonine Wall is put back into operation.

197 Governor Lupus begins the reconstruction of forts along the **Pennines**, bribing the northern tribes to return beyond Hadrian's Wall.

205–7 Hadrian's Wall is **refurbished** by Governor Alfenius Senecio.

c.207 The Antonine Wall is **abandoned once more**.

208–9 Emperor Septimius Severus visits Britain. In a bid to reconquer the far north, he advances his forces as far as Aberdeen.

210 Yet again the northern British rise in rebellion against the Romans.

211 Emperor Septimius dies at York.

Campaigning against the Picts and other northern peoples beyond Hadrian's Wall is **abandoned**.

c.211 Britain is divided into two provinces: **Britannia Superior** (administered from London) and **Britannia Inferior** (from York).

212 Caracalla, formerly joint "Augustus" with Septimius Severus, extends Roman citizenship to almost the entire Empire, including Britain. He builds the first coastal fort at **Reculver**, designed to repel the raids being mounted by the Picts and Saxon pirates.

269–73 As the Roman empire experiences civil war, Britain forms a short-lived **independent empire** based on France.

287 Coastal defenses, designed to repel the increasingly frequent attacks of Saxon pirates and known as the "Saxon Shore," are started.

ROMAN BRITAIN

*B*etween Julius Caesar's initial reconnaissance of 55 BC and the Claudian campaigns of the AD 40s nearly a century elapsed—and still the conquest of Britain was never satisfactorily completed. Rome's legions were reluctant to venture across the English Channel to an island full of warring tribes, and once they did make the journey they struggled to impose the emperor's authority uniformly. The territory that would one day become Scotland remained intractable, and not very much could be done about the Welsh interior either.

Yet once the limitations of Roman rule in Britain were given concrete expression by **Hadrian's Wall**, all the trappings of a Roman colony were swiftly imported: fortified townships, temples, villas, public baths, straight roads to expedite the movement of troops in times of crisis. As the archeological record demonstrates, in England and southern Wales at least the Roman presence was both widespread and intended to last. The development of cities including **Londinium**, **Verulamium** and **Eboracum** created new urban communities, and in time many Britons seemed to adopt Roman

The Channel commander, **Carausius**, is accused of colluding with the Saxons in order to share their booty. To avoid trial he declares himself "Augustus" and establishes a **separatist empire** in Britain and northern Gaul.

293 Carausius is assassinated and replaced as Augustus in Britain by his chief financial officer, **Allectus**. In Rome, Emperor **Diocletian** reorganizes the Roman Empire, dividing it into twelve dioceses. Britain becomes one of the twelve and is divided into four provinces.

values. From Rome's point of view, the province became an important source not only of auxiliaries and front-line troops for its armies but also of grain and other products for its endless wars against the German tribes of central Europe. In the longer term, the Roman occupation underlined Britain's relationship with Europe, not least through the medium of **Latin**—which endured in its written form as the language of the Catholic Church.

However, the culture of the people conquered by the Romans did undergo a radical transformation. The Romans brought first their own religion, then **Mithraism** and **Christianity**. While social organization largely revolved around existing tribal units, some tribes adopted Roman military strategies—which persisted even as late as the 5th century and the defense of **Ambrosius Aurelianus** against the Saxons. And during the 4th century the province was used as a stepping stone for several ambitious generals aiming for the imperial crown. Britain's island position may have made it geographically detached from the mainstream of empire, but it was a crucial political component nonetheless.

296 The emperor **Constantius I** defeats Allectus and reunites the province of Britain with the Roman Empire. The northern frontier, however, is subjected to attacks from Ireland and the Continent.

306 Constantius I dies at **Eboracum** (York). The Roman army in Britain, perhaps encouraged by the Germanic chieftain Crocus, proclaims Constantius's son **Constantine** the new Augustus.

312 Having marched on Rome and established his imperial authority, Constantine **converts to Christianity**, which becomes recognized and promoted throughout the Roman Empire. Three British bishops,

HADRIAN'S WALL

*H*adrian's Wall expresses an early attempt to define the limits of "England" within the island of Britain. As such, the 140-km Tyne–Solway line chosen by Hadrian and his planners has lasted well, although today it is more a psychological than a physical barrier. The present border between England and Scotland has crept further north, but frontier towns like Carlisle remained focal points for English expansion and were much fought over during the Middle Ages. Impressive as it is, though, Hadrian's Wall is scarcely unique. The much longer Great Wall of China, originally constructed at the end of the 3rd century BC, is the obvious example of a similar attempt to demarcate the "civilized" and "barbarian" worlds. And before either, the Greeks built walls and fortifications to keep Dorian invaders at bay.

Of the Roman walls, though, Hadrian's is the most impressive. Intended as a division between two rebellious tribes, the Selgovae to the north and the Brigantes to the south, it was constructed using two million tons of

including the Bishop of London, will attend the **Council of Arles** in 314, convened by Constantine to settle the "Donatist heresy."

343 The Emperor Constans visits Britain and creates the position of **Count of the Saxon Shore** to oversee the defense of the southern and southeastern coasts, which are increasingly threatened by Saxon raids.

360 Emperor Julian dispatches one of his senior commanders, **Lupicinus**, to contain escalating attacks by Picts and Scots.

Britain is influenced by Julian's "apostasy" as he renounces Christianity; many areas return to paganism.

rock and soil. A ditch ten meters wide and three meters deep was dug to the north of the wall, providing material for the five-meter-high and two-meter-thick southern ramparts. Every mile was marked by the construction of a small fort, and in between each of these mile-castles were two further watch-turrets. In addition to these there were sixteen larger forts spaced along the length of the wall, providing accommodation both for troops and some civilian trading populations. Everything was constructed by some nine thousand legionaries, commemorated in a number of transcriptions along the wall's length.

The sheer scale of the project represents the seriousness of Roman investment in the province, but the development of Roman Britain was by no means settled by Hadrian's policy: under Antoninus Pius (138–161) expansion once more became the order of the day, and Roman forces again tried their luck in Scotland. After their failure, though, the frontier reverted to Hadrian's Wall—a rationalization which signaled the limitations of a wider imperial project.

367 An alliance of **Saxons**, **Picts** and **Scots** assault Roman Britain's coastal defenses, killing the Count of the Saxon Shore. The northern frontier is again breached.

369 A fifth Roman province, **Valentia** (possibly in the northwest of England), is created in honor of the emperors **Valentinian** and **Valens**.

383 Following a period of domestic upheaval in Rome, **Magnus Maximus** is proclaimed the new Roman emperor in Britain.

395 The ***Notitia Dignitarum*** ("Roll of Dignitaries"), recording the officials of the Roman Empire, cites three commands in Britain: the

Hadrian's Wall, Northumberland

Dux Britanniarum (duke of Britain); the **Comes Litoris Saxonici** (count of the Saxon Shore); and the **Comes Britanniarum** (count of Britain).

400 Hadrian's Wall is abandoned as the northern frontier disintegrates under the weight of persistent Pict attacks.

After the enemy's depredations had ceased, there was so great an abundance of corn in the island as had never before been known. With this affluence came an increase of luxury, followed by every kind of foul crime ... Not only were laymen guilty of these offences but even the Lord's own flock and their pastors. They cast off Christ's easy yoke and thrust their necks under the burden of drunkenness, hatred, quarrelling, strife, and envy and other similar crimes. In the meantime a virulent plague suddenly fell upon these corrupt people which quickly laid low so large a number that there were not enough people alive to bury the dead. Yet those who survived could not be awakened from the spiritual death of their kinsmen or by fear of their own death. For this reason a still more terrible retribution soon afterwards overtook this sinful people for their fearful crimes. They consulted as to what they should do and where they should seek help to prevent or repel the fierce and very frequent attacks of the northern nations; all, including their king Vortigern, agreed that they should call the Saxons to their aid from across the seas. As events plainly showed, this was ordained by the will of God so that evil might fall upon these miscreants.

—**Bede,** *The Ecclesiastical History of the English People,*
trans. Bertram Colgrave

401 Rome's remaining legions and other troops are withdrawn from Britain in order to protect Italy from **Alaric** and the **Visigoths**.

406 The **Romano–Britons** unilaterally elect **Marcus**, and—following Marcus's murder—**Gratian** as emperor.

407 Gratian's successor, **Constantine III**, abandons Britain when he takes his small forces to Gaul.

Burgundians beyond the control of the empire advance into **France** and **Spain**, further weakening Britain's links with the Empire.

408 The first substantial force of **Saxons** invade southern Britain.

409 The last Roman troops **leave** Britain.

THE COMING OF CHRISTIANITY

*A*ccording to legend the Christian Church in Britain was founded by Christ himself, traveling in the company of his uncle Joseph of Arimathea, who later returned to Britain with the Holy Grail and established a church at Glastonbury. What seems more likely is that merchants working the Cornish tin trade routes brought the new faith to Britain, assisted later by the Romans, who began to enlist Christians into the ranks of their armies. In around 200 the early Christian theologian Tertullian was commenting that areas of Britain had been Christianized, and Origen, a theologian of the early Greek church, confirmed this some forty years later. In 304 Britain acquired its first martyr, St Alban, and by 314 there were at least three British dioceses, at York, London and Colchester. Their bishops attended the Council of Arles, though they were absent from the Council of Nicaea in 325.

With Emperor Constantine's decree freeing Christians from persecution in 312, the church in Britain was able to grow: Christian iconography begins

410 Some British chieftains appeal to the emperor **Honorius** for help, but are told to fend for themselves.

c.417 A Roman presence may very briefly be re-established around this time (lasting until c.425).

426 After the Roman withdrawal, a number of local Romano-British **chieftains** emerge, including **Vortigern** in the west.

429 **St Germanus** is sent to Britain by the bishops of Gaul at the request of members of the British church to combat the **Pelagian heresy**.

432 **St Patrick** is at work in Ireland.

St Ninian, missionary to Scotland, dies.

to appear in villas and private chapels, demonstrating that it was permeating the upper levels of British society. Such too was the growing influence of British Christian thought that by the close of the 4th century Britain could boast its first renowned heretic. Casting doubt on St Augustine's doctrine of Original Sin, the British monk Pelagius (c.360–c.420) taught that man can attain salvation through his own efforts, irrespective of Divine Grace. To counter such unorthodoxy the Church of Gaul sent a stream of missionaries, among them the militant St Germanus of Auxerre (d.446), who demonstrated the validity of his case by leading the British to victory against the northern Picts and other wayward Pelagians. But the schism ultimately reinforced the separateness of Christianity in Britain and indirectly helped to bring about the formation of the so-called Celtic Church, at odds with mainstream continental Christianity. This division would last until the Synod of Whitby in 664, but on a deeper level it points to the course that later religious developments would take.

446 The Britons make a last appeal to the nominal emperor, **Aetius**, but are again refused assistance.

c.450 Vortigern, now a principal British chieftain, turns to the Angle mercenaries Hengist and Horsa from northern Germany to provide troops to help counter the Saxon and Pictish threats, offering them lands in the south and east as payment. But **Hengist** and **Horsa** take advantage of the British reluctance to fight by ousting them from their lands and expanding their own territories.

Further influxes of **Angles**, **Jutes** and **Saxons** add to the pressure on the British in the south, and they begin to carve out new kingdoms for themselves.

CHAPTER TWO

The Anglo-Saxons and the Vikings

{450-1066}

THE ROMAN WITHDRAWAL FROM BRITAIN left theRomano-British chieftains little chance to take stock before they were faced by the challenge of fresh invasions. Successive waves of Saxons, Angles and Jutes began to land on Britain's eastern shores, creating what became a significant and comprehensive settlement that eventually reached the Welsh and Scottish borders.

Retrospectively this colonization was given the collective name **Anglo-Saxon**, from which the term "England" itself is derived. Significantly, the Angles and Saxons (and perhaps the Jutes) shared a roughly common Germanic language which, once it had bedded down in its new domain, emerged as what we now call Old English. This provided the foundation for Middle English, developed after the Franco-Norman Conquest of 1066—which in turn evolved into Modern English.

In the two essentials of language and territory, then, the Anglo-Saxon settlement was integral to the emerging identity of England—and it is tempting to see the true history of the country as beginning now. As ever, though, the picture is blurred: although the political power of the Celtic British diminished under the Anglo-Saxons, not all Celtic people were forced to move. Substantial British enclaves remained, such as the kingdom of **Elmet** in Yorkshire and some areas of **East Anglia**, and here the Anglo-Saxons only gradually assumed control. The rarity of Anglo-Saxon graves in such places suggests, unsurprisingly, that England's new rulers eventually achieved pre-eminence by marrying into the existing hierarchy as much as through violent conquest.

Out of all this England derived an ethnically varied population, further enriched by Viking settlements from the 9th century onwards. The people eventually conquered by the Normans were of **Celtic-Romano-Anglo-Saxon-Jutish-Danish** descent, with perhaps a dash of pre-Celtic thrown in. For the historian trying to determine the precise proportions of these components the problem is an almost total lack of data—prior to the Domesday Book of 1087, there is practically no information regarding the numbers of settlers who crossed over from the Continent. In the future, **genetic sampling**—not just of today's British population, but of western Europeans in general—may provide some interesting clues. For now, our understanding of "early England" is necessarily restricted to the written and material records.

Thus it is not even clearly understood when the first Angles and Saxons arrived. The *Anglo-Saxon Chronicle*, begun in the 9th century to record the progress of the Anglo-Saxon people, is a valuable source in this respect, but it relies heavily on hearsay and myth to explain the earliest events of the English kingdoms. Even so, the Chronicle makes clear that settlement was piecemeal and drawn out over a period of at least a century-and-a-half. In all probability both Angles and Saxons had been employed as auxiliaries in Roman armies since the 4th century or before, so there may have been a handful of both living in England at the time of the Romans' departure. By then, coastal raids were common occurrences; equally, the newly assertive British chieftains, who sometimes invited Anglo-Saxon mercenaries to assist them in their wars—just as the Romans had done—surely encouraged Angles and Saxons to begin thinking of Britain as a permanent home.

The best-known instance of this was King Vortigern's appeal to **Hengist** and **Horsa** to help fend off attacks by Scots and Picts around 450. But this coincided with a much wider migration of people across the Eurasian landmass, possibly triggered by a volcanic eruption on the island of **Krakatoa** in the Indonesian archipelago which caused climate changes damaging livestock productivity in Central Asia. This movement of Huns, Vandals, Goths and Visigoths directly encouraged the break-up of the Roman empire; indirectly it caused demographic change in lands they never saw. And it was from this time that the "Anglo-Saxon Conquest" began in earnest.

The creation of Anglo-Saxon England
450-800

For the partly Romanized Britons left to fend for themselves, the Angle, Saxon and Jutish raiders were every bit as intimidating as the Vikings who terrorized later generations of settled Anglo-Saxons. While, as their name suggests, the Jutes arrived from an area of southern Scandinavia approximating to "Jutland," the Angles and Saxons came from northern Germany. Once in England, all three peoples established domains of varying size and effectiveness, usually described as the **Heptarchy** ("seven kingdoms"). Among these, **Wessex**, **Mercia** and **Northumbria** vied for supremacy. But as time went by the smaller kingdoms were swallowed up, meaning that eventually half of England was unified—albeit only in the face of Viking aggression—under the **royal house of Wessex**.

Even early on, though, there appears to have been some notion of overkingship, as evidenced by the term **Bretwalda**—the name generally adopted by the most powerful Anglo-Saxon king. While the actual authority exercised by a Mercian Bretwalda over, say, Kent or Northumbria is debatable, from the 8th century onwards the political will to establish a single kingdom strengthened. **Alfred "the Great"** could justifiably be described as "king of all the English" by his biographer Asser; and Alfred's successors **Edward the Elder** and

Athelstan certainly achieved greater cohesion among the now-blended English peoples than at any point before.

Anglo-Saxon England was always something of a mongrel state, though. As time went by, under-kings and their families became powerful local earls and ealdormen who frequently challenged their king and pursued their own territorial vendettas. Contrary to the nostalgic views of 18th-century historians such as **Viscount Bolingbroke**, England was not yet a democracy guided by a wise, paternalistic monarch—even though some administrative structures, as well as a feudal system of land ownership, fell into place under Saxon rule.

The Angle and Saxon invaders of the 5th and 6th centuries worshipped an array of gods, among them **Thor** (Donner), **Wodin** and **Loge** (Loki), and the Celtic church, such as it was, was steadily forced into small pockets in the north and west by those who they called the "fierce heathens." With the exception of Cornwall, by 550 Christianity was all but extinct in England. The British monk **Gildas**, writing around 547 in the unambiguously entitled *De Excidio Britanniae* ("the Ruin of Britain"), condemned his peers for their want of faith. Yet within a century the picture had once again been transformed. First from Ireland, then under the direction of the Roman papacy, a steady stream of missionaries strove to recover lost ground.

The most celebrated of these was **St Augustine**, who on Christmas Day 597 reputedly baptized some 10,000 souls at Canterbury. While such figures sound implausible, the mere fact of Augustine's and others' success points to continuing connections with continental Europe. The fact that Christianity reappeared most rapidly in the south suggests the cultural influence of merchants plying the Channel trade.

The Midlands and northern England proved more difficult to persuade. **Penda**, the ruler of Mercia, permitted four missionaries to preach in his kingdom in 653 but declined communion himself.

Only with the conversion of Penda's son Peada did the outcome of the Christian mission in England appear more certain. **Lindisfarne**, an island off the northeastern coast, became an important centre of Christian learning after a monastery was founded there in 635. Little by little the map of ecclesiastical England, with its Episcopal dioceses and small parishes, took shape. In terms of its influence on rural society, this was among the longest-lasting of all the developments that took place in Anglo-Saxon England.

England changed continually in the Anglo-Saxon period. The advent of the Vikings gave rise to two major power-bases in England: the Saxon lands dominated by the kingdom of **Wessex** and the Viking kingdom known as the **Danelaw**. Yet others too were significant players in "English" politics. The kings of Mercia sometimes made alliances with British princes in what came to be known as Wales, while the Northumbrians and Vikings of the Danelaw sometimes joined forces with the Scots and Britons of Strathclyde. The accession of **Edward the Confessor** as king of England further complicated matters. Edward's mother Emma was Norman, and with him came a number of Norman and Breton favorites—making Edward the first **Anglo-Norman** monarch. Yet while there was little sense of unity among the various factions vying for power, Anglo-Saxon rulers were expected to take regular advice from their council of wise men, the **Witan**, which was gathered from among the leading nobles and clerics of the day. The king was normally accompanied by a number of these advisers during his progress around the kingdom, but he would call larger council meetings—*witenagemots*—during major festivals such as Christmas and Easter, or to solve major disputes. It was also the Witan's responsibility to choose a new king. When they chose **Harold Godwinson** as Edward the Confessor's heir, in effect inviting Norman invasion, it was a decision which would have a larger impact than anyone could have realized.

c. 450 Vortigern, a British king, seeks help from the continent to contain incursions into his territories by Picts and Scots from the north. According to the *Anglo-Saxon Chronicle*, two brothers, **Hengist** and **Horsa**—leaders of three shiploads of Angles— respond to his invitation. After campaigning successfully on Vortigern's behalf, they decide to settle in Kent rather than return to their homelands.

455 Hengist and Horsa rebel against Vortigern, defeating his forces possibly at **Aylesford** in Kent. Horsa is killed in battle.

456 Hengist and his son Esc drive the British out of Kent and establish the **first kingdom** of Angles in Britain.

THE HEPTARCHY

Anglo-Saxon England developed slowly over a period of more than a century. During this time numerous bands of warriors and other settlers from Germany, Denmark and the Low Countries established settlements in southern Britain. These settlements gradually formed kingdoms, and out of these disparate realms grew what became known as the Heptarchy, the seven principal areas of early Anglo-Saxon England: **Northumbria, Mercia, Wessex, Sussex, Kent, East Anglia** and **Essex**. At times, though, there were more than that number. **Middlesex** and **Hwicce** were important settlements before being absorbed into Wessex, and Northumbria initially comprised three kingdoms: **Lindsey, Deira** and **Bernicia**. Alongside these, several British principalities also survived well into the 7th century. The last important British bastion in England was **Elmet** (near Leeds), but numerous British territories in **Wales, Dumnonia** (Cornwall) and **Rheged** (Strathclyde) also held out.

The fierce Saxons, of ever execrable memory, [were] admitted into the island, like so many wolves into a sheep fold, to defend [the British] from the northern Nations. A thing more destructive and pernicious than ever was done in this Kingdom. O the mist and grossness of this sense of apprehension! O the dullness and blockishness of these souls!

—Gildas, *De Excidio Britanniae*,
trans. L. and J. Laing

By the end of the 8th century there were effectively only four major Anglo-Saxon kingdoms: Mercia, Northumbria, Wessex and East Anglia. These vied with each other for ultimate supremacy, the ruler of the most powerful being accorded the title of overking or Bretwalda. This was in reality a fairly informal arrangement and for some leaders purely honorific, but for kings such as Offa of Mercia it represented a real determination to build political power outside his own borders. As tensions mounted between the Anglo-Saxon kingdoms and the remaining British enclaves (and later between Anglo-Saxons and Vikings), England became increasingly united. In the 7th century, King Penda of Mercia joined with the Christian Gwynedd of Wales against Wessex and Northumbria, and in the 8th century it was Mercia that had the upper hand. But it was Wessex that ultimately came to predominate, founding what became the first English royal house. By the time that the Danelaw began to unravel in the 10th century, Wessex held all the cards.

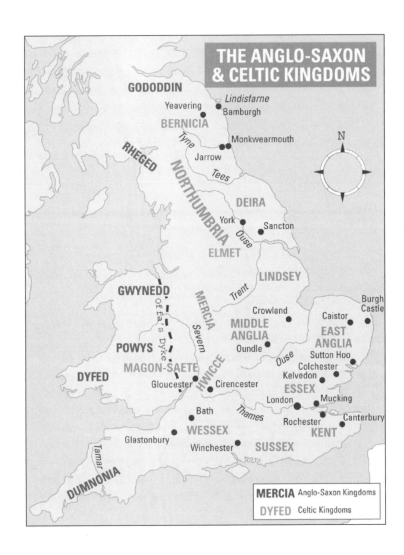

THE ANGLO-SAXON
& CELTIC KINGDOMS

GODODDIN

Lindisfarne
Yeavering ● Bamburgh
BERNICIA

Monkwearmouth ●●
Jarrow

RHEGED

Tyne

NORTHUMBRIA

Tees

N

DEIRA

York ● Sancton

Ouse

ELMET

GWYNEDD

LINDSEY

Trent

MERCIA

Crowland ●

Burgh
Castle

Caistor ●

MIDDLE
ANGLIA

EAST
ANGLIA

POWYS

Severn

HWICCE

Oundle

Ouse

Sutton Hoo

MAGON-SAETE

Colchester

DYFED

Gloucester ● Cirencester

Kelvedon

ESSEX

London ● Mucking

Bath ●

Thames

Rochester

Canterbury

WESSEX

KENT

Glastonbury

Winchester ●

SUSSEX

Tamar

DUMNONIA

| **MERCIA** | Anglo-Saxon Kingdoms |
| *DYFED* | Celtic Kingdoms |

Amid the wreckage of deserted cities destroyed by the enemy, the citizens who had survived the enemy now attacked each other. So long as the memory of past disaster remained fresh, kings and priests, nobles and commoners, kept their proper rank. But when those who remembered died, there grew up a generation who knew nothing of these things and had experienced only the present peaceful order. Then were the restraints of truth so utterly abandoned that no trace of them remained, and very few of the people recalled their existence.

—Bede, *Ecclesiastical History of the English People*,
trans. L. Sherley-Price and R. Latham

477 A Saxon community led by Elle settles in **Sussex**, displacing the British. According to Bede, Elle becomes the first **Bretwalda** or Anglo-Saxon overking.

488 Hengist is succeeded as king of Kent by his son **Esc**, who rules for 24 years.

493 According to Bede, a Saxon army is defeated by Britons led by the Romano-British nobleman **Ambrosius Aurelianus**, a figure identified by some historians with the mythical King Arthur.

495 Saxon settlers led by Cerdic and his son Cynric establish the kingdom of **Wessex**.

c. 500 As British resistance to Anglo-Saxon intrusion continues to stiffen, Saxons suffer another setback at **Mons Badonicus**, an unknown battle site possibly at or near Cadbury. According to tradition the British are led by **King Arthur**. In any event, the newcomers are temporarily restricted to the south and east.

501 Saxons led by **Port** establish a permanent camp at **Portsmouth**.

508 Cerdic and Cynric campaign westwards, defeating and killing a British king called **Natanleod**.

514 A Saxon band led by Stuf and Withgar establish a second kingdom in Wessex.

c. 539 According to legend, King Arthur is **killed** fighting his own followers, after his nephew (or illegitimate son) **Modred** rebels against him. In any event, it seems probable that renewed squabbling between Britons enables Angles and Saxons to **acquire more territory**.

c. 540 The British monk **Gildas** writes *De Excidio Britanniae* ("The Ruin of Britain"), a diatribe detailing what he considers the fall of his people.

As the British continue to fight among themselves, the Anglo-Saxons make **further inroads** westwards and northwards.

560 Ethelbert becomes king of Kent, and is later accorded the title **Bretwalda**.

577 By defeating the British at **Dyrham**, the West Saxons (Saxon settlers in Wessex) secure control of the townships of **Bath**, **Gloucester** and **Cirencester**.

597 Pope Gregory I ("the Great"), eyeing the vibrant new kingdoms of the Anglo-Saxons, dispatches the Benedictine monk **Augustine** to Britain. Augustine's mission of forty monks lands on the island of **Thanet** off the Kent coast, and is welcomed by King Ethelbert, perhaps through the intercession of his Christian queen Bertha. After converting both the court and its followers to the Catholic faith, Augustine founds Christ Church at **Canterbury** after he is consecrated "Bishop of the English" by St Virgilius of Arles. Canterbury consequently becomes the centre of Christianity in England and an important school for training later missionaries.

c. 598 Assembling at Edinburgh, northern British warriors march south to confront the Angles, but are comprehensively defeated at **Catreth** (Catterick). The northern Brythonic bard **Aneirin** witnesses the carnage, and composes the elegiac *Y Gododdin*, destined to become a cornerstone of early Welsh literature.

601 Augustine is accorded "metropolitan" jurisdiction over all the English by Pope Gregory as a new **archdiocese** is created.

604 Augustine establishes Episcopal dioceses at **London** and **Rochester**, their bishops being subordinate to Canterbury. As Christianity spreads among the Angles and Saxons, further bishoprics are created. Augustine fails, though, to bring members of the British Celtic church back into the Roman fold after meeting Welsh church leaders at **Malmesbury** in Wiltshire.

605 St Augustine dies.

616 **Edwin** becomes King of Northumbria. His authority is quickly undermined when in the same year the Bretwalda, **Redwald** of East Anglia, attacks his territory having led his forces through Mercia. Briefly Redwald imposes his rule over the whole of Anglo-Saxon Britain.

624 Redwald dies, and is perhaps buried at **Sutton Hoo**. Edwin of Northumbria is acknowledged Bretwalda.

625 **Paulinus**, bishop of Kent and one of St Augustine's original companions, accompanies **Ethelburga**, daughter of King Ethelbert, to Northumbria.

627 King **Edwin** of Northumbria marries Ethelburga and converts to Christianity. Paulinus becomes bishop of a new diocese founded at **York**.

632 Edwin dies fighting Cadwallon (Cedwalla), the British king of Gwynedd. Cadwallon successfully joins forces with the king of Mercia, Penda, against the kingdom of Northumbria and its new king Oswald. Paulinus is forced to flee south, where he becomes Bishop of Rochester.

633 Oswald of Northumbria regroups and defeats Cadwallon at **Heavenfield**, effectively bringing hopes of a British resurgence in

ANGLO-SAXON CRAFTSMANSHIP

*I*t was once thought that the Anglo-Saxons were culturally deficient, inhabitants of the "**Dark Ages**" between the fall of Rome and the revival of learning in the 11th and 12th centuries. In fact they designed fine buildings and produced highly refined and elaborate ornaments. An outstanding example of the latter is the ship-burial discovered at **Sutton Hoo** in 1939. The site contained a 7th-century body—a warrior of high rank—buried in a long boat beneath a mound, together with his weapons and other treasures. The artifacts, including a ceremonial scepter and an intricately engraved helmet, are among the finest of the period ever recovered. Also found was a well-constructed harp, symbolic of the importance attached to music and storytelling. Circumstantial evidence suggests that Sutton Hoo may well be the tomb of the Bretwalda **Redwald**.

A find of equal significance and beauty is the small pointer or estal known as the **Alfred Jewel**, discovered in 1693 in marshes near Athelney, Somerset, where King Alfred centered his resistance to the Vikings. A small golden oval with the figure of Christ (or perhaps Sight) in the centre picked out in precious stones, the Jewel is surrounded with rock crystal. Around the edge of the piece is the inscription *AELFED M/ED H/EH/T GEWYRCAN*—"Alfred had me made." Alfred's biographer Asser records that Alfred ordered several Bibles to be made for his bishops and abbots, and it is likely that a pointer like the Jewel would have accompanied each. While such discoveries are relatively few in number, they affirm literary descriptions of exquisitely crafted objects contained not only in the sagas of the time but also in the more prosaic *Anglo-Saxon Chronicle*.

the north to an end. The **alliance** between Gwynedd and Mercia, however, continues.

634 Paulinus is appointed **archbishop of Canterbury** by Pope Honorius I.

635 Influenced by King Oswald, King Cynegils of Wessex is **baptized** by the Roman missionary to Wessex, Birinus. He bases himself at Dorchester and enjoys modest success in converting Cynegils' Wessex men to Roman Christianity. **Aidan**, an Irish monk from Iona in the Inner Hebrides, founds a religious community on **Lindisfarne** (Holy Island), off the coast of Northumberland, at Oswald of Northumbria's invitation. Of the Anglo-Saxon kingdoms in England, only Mercia remains largely "unconverted."

642 King Oswald is killed fighting the British at **Oswestry**. He is succeeded by Oswy.

644 Death of St Paulinus.

653 **King Penda of Mercia** permits four missionaries to work among his people, although he does not himself convert to Christianity.

655 Penda **dies in battle** fighting Oswy of Northumbria. His son and successor, **King Peada**, who has already converted, encourages the spread of Christianity in his Mercian kingdom.

664 King Oswy convenes a **synod**, or council of churchmen, at **Whitby** to determine whether Northumbria should follow the Celtic or the Roman church. A Roman Catholic delegate, **Wilfrid**, persuades the synod to decide in favor of Rome; led by Colman, the Celtic Christians return to Ireland. But immediately after the synod, according to the *Anglo-Saxon Chronicle*, a "**pestilence**" sweeps across England, encouraging some Anglo-Saxon leaders to return to their previous beliefs. When the Archbishop of Canterbury **Deusdedit** dies, it is four years before the pope can find a willing replacement.

THE SYNOD OF WHITBY (664)

*T*he progress of Christianity in England was far from smooth. As St Augustine's mass conversion of "ten thousand" souls at Canterbury in 597 suggests, much depended on winning over the ruler of the day. If a king could be converted then so too were all his subjects, but such an outcome was easily reversed by political or even environmental events—natural disasters or unfavorable portents were taken very seriously, and all sides traded in superstition.

Nor did it help that two separate and increasingly antagonistic churches vied for power. As this division of loyalties—between the Celtic north and west and the Roman south and east—hardened, King Oswy of Northumbria summoned a council or moot of churchmen at Whitby in 664 to determine which version his kingdom should adhere to. Much of the acrimony centered on the dating of Easter. The Celtic Church set it slightly later than its Roman counterpart, giving rise to a curious situation in which the queen of Northumbria, a Roman Christian, celebrated Easter whilst her husband, a Celtic Christian, was still observing Lent.

Under the supervision of Hilda, Abbess of Whitby, spokesmen from both sides were invited to argue their case. On the Celtic team were SS Colman and Cedd; on the Roman, James the Deacon and St Wilfrid. Colman and his followers eventually lost the war of words and retreated first to Iona, a religious community in the Hebrides, then to Ireland: it was decided that Northumbria would be Roman Catholic.

In the annals of English history, though (written and manipulated in its early phases largely by Roman Catholic monks), Whitby became synonymous with something grander—the triumph not just of Roman Catholicism but of Christianity itself.

668 **Theodore**, originally from Asia Minor, is appointed Archbishop of Canterbury. Although he encounters some opposition from Wilfrid and other established figures, his reforming zeal strengthens the fabric of the Roman Anglo-Saxon church.

670 As the power of Mercia grows, Oswy of Northumberland is succeeded by his son **Ecgfrith**.

672 Theodore, Archbishop of Canterbury, convenes the **Council of Hereford** to resolve outstanding issues among Anglo-Saxon churchmen. It is agreed that Easter will be uniformly observed in all dioceses, and that bishops will meet annually at **Clofeshoh** (location now unknown). The bishops further agree to administer marriage laws and to establish rules governing the relations between themselves and monasteries and other religious foundations.

678 A Northumbrian army led by Ecgfrith is defeated by Mercia near the river Trent.

685 The Saxon **Cedwalla** becomes King of Wessex and immediately begins expanding his territory into the south-east of England.

According to the *Anglo-Saxon Chronicle* during the course of the year it **rains blood**; milk and butter turn to blood.

686 Continuing his expansionist policy, Cedwalla, together with his brother Mul, lays waste to **Kent**. A **plague** kills many members of a newly founded monastic community at Jarrow in Northumbria, but its abbot **Ceolfrid** and the young **Bede** survive.

687 **Mul** and twelve of his followers are **captured and killed** by a Kentish war party; exacting reprisals, Cedwalla again ravages the southeastern kingdom.

Cuthbert, one of the foremost patron saints of the English church, dies on the islet of Inner Farne, close to Lindisfarne (Holy Island).

688 Cedwalla journeys to Rome and, a week before his death, is **baptized** by Pope Sergius. He is succeeded as King of Wessex by **Ine**, founder of the first abbey at **Glastonbury**.

690 Archbishop (later Saint) Theodore dies.

693 Behrtwald, a native Englishman and formerly Abbot of Reculver, is appointed archbishop in succession to Theodore. From now, English archbishops are generally recruited by Rome from amongst the English.

694 King Ine of Wessex is paid substantial compensation by the people of Kent for the murder of Mul in 687.

698 Around this time the Lindisfarne Gospels, a sumptuously decorated Latin text (with later Anglo-Saxon glosses), are consecrated at the island's monastery—possibly to celebrate the elevation of the relics of St Cuthbert.

710 As border conflicts continue, ealdorman Beorhtfrith fights against the Picts in the north; Ine of Wessex and his kinsman Nunna fight against Geraint of Cornwall.

716 **Ethelbald** begins a 41-year reign as king of Mercia, which, under his rule, establishes itself as the pre-eminent Anglo-Saxon kingdom.

731 Bede completes his *History of the English Church and People* (also known as the *Ecclesiastical History*).

735 Bede dies.

757 Ethelbald of Mercia is succeeded by his son **Offa**. As well as extending Mercian authority over other Anglo-Saxon kingdoms, Offa either commissions or collaborates in the construction of extended defensive earthworks (known as **Offa's Dyke**) marking the boundary between Mercia and westerly Britons inhabiting modern Wales.

786 The first **papal legates** to arrive in England since St Augustine are welcomed at Offa's court.

787 Offa's son **Egfrith** is crowned king of the Mercians.

793 According to the *Anglo-Saxon Chronicle*, terrible **portents** appear in the skies over Northumbria. Heavy lightning and fiery dragons

ST CUTHBERT (634–687)

*O*ne feature of Anglo-Saxon history is its roll-call of local saints, including two of royal pedigree, **Edmund of East Anglia** (c.841–869) and **Edward the Confessor** (c.1002–1066)—who were regarded as the patron saints of England until they were displaced by the Turkish hero St George.

But perhaps the best-loved of all was **Cuthbert**, probably a native of Northumberland. Raised as a shepherd, he experienced visions in early adolescence and entered the Celtic Northumbrian monastery of Melrose when he was sixteen. In 660, when **Melrose** was struck by plague, he became its prior and, aided by a reputation for bringing relief to plague victims, worked to spread the Christian message among the Northumbrian people. He attended the Synod of Whitby, and thereafter promoted Roman rather than Celtic practice. In 664 he was appointed prior of **Lindisfarne** under Bishop Eata, and was mainly responsible for instituting the monastery's exacting Benedictine disciplines. At the same time he continued his missionary work, and is traditionally credited with founding the Christian community at **Durham**, which became an important centre of the Roman Church in the northeast.

But for all his energetic proselytizing Cuthbert was by nature a recluse, and in 676 he retired to the island of **Inner Farne** to pursue a contemplative hermit life. In 684, however, Ecgfrith of Northumbria persuaded Cuthbert to become **Bishop of Hexham** and the following year Cuthbert returned to Lindisfarne as its **bishop-abbot**, dying two years later during another retreat to Inner Farne. His body, first buried on Lindisfarne, was exhumed in 875 to guard against Viking desecration and eventually came to rest in the cathedral at Durham, where the treasures of his richly carved coffin remain preserved.

accompany the beginning of **Viking raids** on the monastic communities of **Lindisfarne** and **Iona**.

794 Offa asserts his authority over the East Anglians by beheading their king, **Ethelbehrt**.

796 Shortly before his death Offa is sent a **letter**—the only surviving missive from a European to an Anglo-Saxon ruler, and held to mark the high-point of Mercian ascendancy in England—from **Charlemagne** of the Franks praising his rule and describing him as "a brother."

ST BEDE (673–735)

*T*he "Venerable" Bede was a figure of European as well as national stature, and through his scholarly work he transcended a distinctly provincial background.

Born at **Monkton** in Jarrow, he began his schooling at the monastery of St Peter at **Wearmouth** in 679. He quickly fell under the influence of its cosmopolitan-minded Abbot, **Benedict Biscop**, who encouraged Bede to devote his life to learning and contemplation. In 685 he transferred to the sister monastery of St Paul at **Jarrow**, where he remained until his death, taking holy orders in 703.

From his pen flowed a steady stream of treatises, Biblical commentaries and historical writings. An early interest in the intricacies of dating events inspired Bede to devise the **AD** (*anno domini*) system for fixing a universal chronology from the birth of Christ. In this field his masterwork was *De temporam ratione* ("On the reckoning of time"), completed in 725, in which he endeavored to solve the contentious issue of Easter's placement

Offa is succeeded by his son **Egfrith**, but soon afterwards Egfrith also dies—a double death interpreted by the monk **Alcuin** as a divine judgment.

798 King **Coelwulf** (Coenwulf) of Mercia attacks Kent. The Kentish king, **Edbert Praen**, is captured. After being taken to Mercia, he is blinded and his hands removed. Despite this, though, Mercian power is increasingly challenged by the growing prestige of Wessex and by the Viking attacks.

in the calendar. But although Bede also delved into grammar and orthography, in England at least he is best remembered for his *Historia ecclesiastica gentis Anglorum* ("Ecclesiastical history of the English peoples"), which detailed the progress of Christianity in what became the Anglo-Saxon kingdoms from Roman times onwards. Although Bede restricts his historical enquiry to religious developments and is fond of hagiography when recounting the lives of missionary saints, his scrupulous attention to chronology makes his an invaluable guide to the early Anglo-Saxon settlement, one which stands alongside the *Anglo-Saxon Chronicle*. But if Bede (and his mentor Biscop) seems to epitomize the growth of a more literate culture in late 7th- and early 8th-century England, his wider reputation was only gained after his death. That it developed at all is due to one of his own pupils, Alcuin, who traveled to the continent with copies of Bede's texts, where they were gradually disseminated through monasteries.

The Viking invasions and the expansion of Wessex
800–1066

Although the Anglo-Saxons continued to fight among themselves—and although Britons and Picts continued to challenge their borders—from about 600 Britain had enjoyed two centuries of respite from large-scale continental immigration. It was this period of relative stability that enabled England to become Christianized. But from the end of the 8th century a new and violent threat appeared: the Vikings. Their appearance was, as it happened, just the first stage in a gradual Scandinavian encroachment which would finish three centuries later with the arrival of the Normans—who were, as their name suggests, of Nordic origin. It was this that would bring an end to the unified Anglo-Saxon state finally achieved by the Wessex kings.

The Viking attacks on England have long been represented as indiscriminate assaults perpetrated by brutal pagans intent only on violence and destruction. Such at any rate was the view shared by Bede's disciple Alcuin, the compilers of the *Anglo-Saxon Chronicle* and other monastic witnesses of the time—hardly surprising given that monasteries were among the Vikings' first targets. But their testimony is only part of the truth: the Vikings, just like their Saxon and Angle predecessors, were also interested in acquiring territory and establishing peaceful permanent settlements.

The vengeance for the blood shed by the father has now reached the son; for you know very well how much blood his father has shed to secure the kingdom on his son.

—Alcuin,
describing the deaths of Offa and Egfrith

In fact the Viking peoples went to extraordinary lengths to set up new settlements. **Harald Hardrada**, before he was killed at Stamford Bridge in 1066, had ventured as far as Russia and Byzantium in the search for land. The emperor Charlemagne's later years were regularly plagued by Viking raids, and Normandy itself was the price the western Franks had eventually to pay for peace. The Vikings also established colonies in Ireland, and—most famously of all—**Leif Ericson** explored what became America centuries before Christopher Columbus and other European settlers.

In England in particular the Vikings left a lasting impression. A Viking kingdom, the **Danelaw**, extended from the borders of Scotland to East Anglia, and other pockets of Viking influence are still to be found in northwest England. The Cumbrian dialect closely resembles some aspects of Norwegian, suggesting that it wasn't just Danish Vikings who traveled to mainland Britain. It was, though, a Dane— King Svein—who in the 11th century took control of the whole of England; and the accession of King Cnut (Canute) to the throne in 1016 might well have led to England's permanent attachment to Scandinavia—an outcome only prevented by the failure of his sons Harold Harefoot and Harthacnut to continue the family line.

Still, intermarriage and wrangling between the contending courts meant that Viking interests still played an integral part in the unfolding political drama. Edward the Confessor relied on a Viking Earl, **Siward**, to control Northumbria, and his successor, **Harold Godwinson**, owed his position as much to his Nordic as his Anglo-Saxon ancestry.

What is striking is the extent to which dynastic politics had, by the middle of the 11th century, become hugely important. Battles between different ethnic groups were as common now as they had been in the fifth and sixth centuries, but mass migration was no longer the principle instigator of conflict; rather it was the aims and objectives of individual power-brokers that began to shape events. If there is a single reason for the collapse of the Anglo-Danish state, it can be traced back to Edward the Confessor's penchant for preferring Norman favorites such as his nephew **Earl Ralph** and the Breton **Robert FitzWimarc**—which in turn enabled Duke William of Normandy to seize power.

This development could not have happened without the emergence of a single polity under the Saxon House of Wessex. Under Alfred ("the Great") and Athelstan in particular the court of **Wessex**

THE ROYAL HOUSE OF WESSEX

Egbert 802–39
Ethelwulf 839–855
Ethelbald 855–60
Ethelbert 860–866
Ethelred I 866–71
Alfred ("the Great") 871–899
Edward the Elder 899–924
Athelstan 924–939
Edmund I 939–946
Eadred 946–955
Eadwig 955–959
Edgar 959–975
Edward the Martyr 975–979
Ethelred II ("the Unready") 979–1016
Edmund II ("Ironside") 1016
(Edmund b.1016)
(Edward the Exile d.1057)
Edward the Confessor 1042–1066
(Edgar the Atheling d.1125)

became the centre of Anglo-Saxon life. And although the same Viking assistance that helped the Wessex monarchs secure their expanded kingdom also led to their eventual undoing, by 1016 there was a sense in which "England" existed as a unit—and a prize well worth having.

802 **Egbert** becomes king of Wessex. The Hwicce and the people of Wiltshire **meet in battle**. The Wiltshiremen win, putting an end to Hwicce as an independent kingdom.

815 Egbert campaigns in **Cornwall**, expanding the boundaries of the kingdom of Wessex and attacking the last outpost of the Celts in England.

825 Egbert turns his attention toward Mercia and defeats its king, **Beornwulf**, at **Ellandun**. The East Angles accept Egbert's overlordship and rebel against Mercian domination, killing Beornwulf.

Egbert's son **Ethelwulf** conquers Kent, Surrey, Sussex and Essex.

829 Egbert subdues Mercia and the lands south of the Humber, and becomes the **eighth Bretwalda**.

830 Egbert campaigns against the Celtic Britons of **Wales**.

835 Vikings, in their largest raid to date, lay waste to the island of **Sheppey** off Kent.

836 A Viking war-band defeats Egbert at **Carhampton** in Somerset.

838 A Viking war-band joins forces with the Cornish Britons but is defeated by Egbert at **Hingston Down**.

839 Egbert is succeeded by **Ethelwulf**.

851 The *Anglo-Saxon Chronicle* records that for the first time Vikings stay in England during the winter months.

853 **Ethelwulf of Wessex** and **Burghred of Mercia** band together against the Welsh Britons.

Invasion of the Danes, c.1130

855 Setting out on a pilgrimage to Rome with his youngest son **Alfred**, Ethelwulf divides his kingdom between his eldest sons **Ethelbald** and **Ethelbert**. En route father and son stay at the court of **Charles the Bald** of France. Ethelwulf marries Charles's daughter **Judith**.

In Wessex, **Ethelbald** attempts a coup to prevent his father's return. Although this fails, he is permitted to remain in power.

858 Upon Ethelwulf's death, **Ethelbald** succeeds to the throne of Wessex but creates unpopularity by immediately marrying his stepmother **Judith**.

865 A **Viking army** lands in England and over the next four years carves out a northern kingdom—the **Danelaw**—from territories previously belonging to Mercia and Northumbria.

In Wessex, Ethelbert **dies** and is succeeded by his brother **Ethelred**.

869–70 Edmund, king of East Anglia, is brutally killed at **Hoxne** in Suffolk, shot to death with arrows—perhaps in parody of the martyrdom of St Sebastian. Subsequently Edmund is **canonized** and becomes one of the principal English saints. Having established the Danelaw, the Vikings take over **East Anglia** and what remains of **Mercia**.

871 The Vikings begin attacking **Wessex**. King Ethelred and his brother Alfred resist, but their forces are worn down. Ethelred **dies** in April, and **Alfred** becomes king of Wessex.

875 Viking pressure compels the **monks of Lindisfarne** to evacuate. Fleeing inland with the remains of **St Cuthbert** they eventually settle at Durham, where a new community is founded.

878 A Viking war-band takes the Saxons of Wessex by surprise at the royal manor of **Chippenham**. King Alfred, accompanied by a handful of followers, is forced into hiding at **Athelney** in Somerset while the Vikings, led by Guthrum, ravage his kingdom. In May, however, Alfred rallies his forces and defeats Guthrum at **Ethandun** (Edington).

THE DANELAW

*W*hat began toward the end of the 8th century as little more than piratical raids had by the middle of the 9th developed into a more systematic process of colonization by the Vikings. The result was a relatively stable kingdom known as the Danelaw which grew to dominate Northumbria, East Anglia and Mercia from its capital at Jorvik (York) following the town's seizure in 919. This was just one part of a Viking expansion which covered parts of Scotland, Ireland, the Isle of Man and Normandy in northern France. Their presence also connected England with the wider limits of Viking exploration, which extended east into Russia and west as far as Vinland (America).

Alfred the Great's victory over Guthrum at Edington in 878 held on to Wessex, however, and his successors continued to expand their territory at Viking expense, Alfred's great-great-grandson Eadred finally expelling Eric Bloodaxe from York in 954. But by the 10th century the Vikings were once more gaining the upper hand, their control cemented in 1013 by the accession of the Danish Svein I Haraldsson as king of England. By then the Danes were accepted as part of the united kingdom created by Alfred's heirs: they were among Athelstan's forces at Brunanburgh, and leading Danish warlords such as Siward ruled the north on behalf of Saxon kings.

And it was not until William the Conqueror's defeat of the rebellion against him in 1071 that he could be reasonably safe from Viking incursions (not to mention secure against the Saxon people he had conquered). But of course the Normans, as Viking descendants, also represented a tradition of Norse expansion which stretched all the way back to the 790s.

Guthrum is coerced into converting to Christianity, and pledges not to stray outside the Danelaw. Effectively England is divided between two main kingdoms: the **Danelaw** and **Wessex**.

891 Alfred orders the composition in "English" (Anglo-Saxon) of an annal of principal events which will develop into the *Anglo-Saxon Chronicle.*

899 King Alfred dies and is succeeded by his son **Edward the Elder**. With his sister **Ethelfled**, "Lady of the Mercians," Edward begins challenging the Danelaw.

920 After twenty years of campaigning Edward completes the "**reconquest**" of England. He accepts the submission of Regnald of York, Ealdred of Bamburgh, the Strathclyde British and Constantine, king of the Scots at Bakewell.

925 Edward is succeeded by his son **Athelstan**, known as "**King of All England**."

927 The Scots and Strathclyde Britons take advantage of Edward's death to reassert their independence; Athelstan invades **Northumbria** and secures their submission.

934 Athelstan advances as far as **Kincardine** in Fife, but his success unites the northern peoples against him and he is forced to **abandon** the conquest of Scotland.

937 After his enemies form an alliance, Athelstan defeats a joint Danish, Scottish and Strathclyde army in the battle of **Brunanburgh**—events recounted in the Anglo-Saxon poem of that name.

937 Athelstan is succeeded as king of England by **Edmund I**.

946 Edmund is succeeded by **Eadred**.

954 Eadred expels the Viking king **Eric Bloodaxe** from York.

955 Upon Eadred's death his kingdom is divided between his sons **Eadwig** (who gets Wessex) and **Edgar** (Mercia).

959 The English kingdoms are **reunited** when Eadwig dies and Edgar takes his brother's dominions.

975 Edgar dies, leaving behind two sons, Edward and **Ethelred**. Because there are doubts about Edward's legitimacy there is dispute about which should succeed. Having secured the Church's backing, **Edward** becomes king but his short reign is politically turbulent.

978 Edward, who becomes nicknamed "the Martyr," is **murdered** at Corfe Castle, probably by a supporter of Edward's brother Ethelred and perhaps with the connivance of Edward's family. Ethelred, known as "the Unready," accedes to the throne.

991 Ealdorman **Byrhtnoth** and his followers are defeated, with heavy Saxon losses, by Viking raiders at the **Battle of Maldon** in Essex. In

ANGLO-SAXON LITERATURE

*T*he three most significant British pre-medieval literatures—in Welsh, Gaelic and Anglo-Saxon—share some important similarities. They all have roots in ancient traditions of oral poetry; they were practiced by bards and minstrels who worked at the courts of kings and other political leaders; and examples of their work were set down by monks schooled in Latin composition—and thus preserved in monastic libraries.

The chief poetic glory of Anglo-Saxon poetry (but one which makes no mention of Britain) is the 3000-line epic *Beowulf*, which recounts the exploits of the eponymous hero as he struggles against first the monstrous Grendel and then Grendel's equally monstrous mother. Probably composed in the early 8th century but almost certainly based on an earlier matrix, the version that has survived was transcribed around 1000. Other extant poems include *The Battle of Maldon* and *The Seafarer* and the more overtly religious work *The Dream of the Rood*. That the tradition of Anglo-Saxon

the same year, the Saxons offer to pay the Vikings money (**Danegeld**) in exchange for promises not to launch further attacks. This arrangement only encourages Viking raiders to extort greater sums, and so their raids continue.

993 The northeast of England is subjected to a series of particularly ferocious Viking attacks.

995 **Halley's Comet** crosses the skies above Britain, portending—in the minds of its interpreters at least—great adversity.

997 Viking raiders penetrate the west of England.

poetry persisted until at least the end of the 10th century is proved by the *Battle of Brunanburgh*, which is inspired by the conflict of that name in 937 but imbued with the values of earlier epics. Typically such pieces combine heroic pagan values with a sense of Christian humility— the latter sometimes interpolated by monastic scholars. The constant adaptation of existing poems to suit altered circumstances and new audiences means that most Anglo-Saxon poets are anonymous. One of the few whose names we do know, Cynewulf, left no clear indication of when he was writing.

The authors of the most significant prose work in the vernacular, the *Anglo-Saxon Chronicle*, are likewise obscure. Its initial composition is usually associated with King Alfred, who ordered the creation of an annal in 891. Thereafter the *Chronicle* was regularly maintained until well after the Norman Conquest. Its earliest entries refer to the 5th century, and its span of almost 700 years is unique in Europe.

In this year king Edmund, lord of the English,
Guardian of kinsmen, loved doer of deeds, conquered Mercia.
As far as Dore and Whitwell Gap the boundary form
And Humber River, that broad ocean-stream;
The Boroughs Five he won, Leicester and Lincoln,
Nottingham, Derby and Stamford too.
Long had the Danes under the Norsemen
Been subjected by force to heathen bondage,
Until finally liberated by the valour of Edward's son,
King Edmund, protector of warriors.

—The Anglo-Saxon Chronicle,
year entry for 942, trans. G.N. Garmonsway

998 Establishing bases in Sussex and on the Isle of Wight, Viking war parties terrorize **Dorset**.

999 The **Kentish** *fyrd* is defeated in battle by a Viking army advancing on Rochester.

1001 Viking warriors wreak havoc in many parts of England. The **Hampshire** *fyrd* attempts resistance, but is badly mauled.

1002 In desperation Ethelred agrees to pay substantial amounts of **Danegeld** to Viking leaders. In the same year he marries **Emma**, daughter of **Duke Richard of Normandy**—the beginning of an association that will result in Richard's descendant **William of Normandy** successfully laying claim to the English throne.

1004 King Svein of Denmark, at the head of a large Viking army, harries East Anglia and sacks Norwich. Breaking a **truce** with local ealdormen, he kills many English noblemen in savage fighting.

1005 England's troubles are compounded by a sizeable **famine**. The Vikings, however, temporarily **withdraw** to Denmark.

1007 Ethelred pays out more Danegeld.

1008 As it becomes apparent that Danegeld is unlikely to be anything other than a stop-gap measure, Ethelred orders a large **fleet** to be built so that the Vikings can be repulsed at sea.

ETHELRED (AETHELRAED) "THE UNREADY" (968–1016)

*I*t's somewhat ironic that one of the least successful Anglo-Saxon kings enjoyed one of the longest reigns in English history—nearly forty years on the throne. The "unready" nickname is deceptive, though: it is derived from the Anglo-Saxon for "badly advised," so that "Aethelraed Unraed" literally translates as "Good Advice, Badly Counseled."

To his credit it is true that he inherited a difficult situation that would have taxed someone far more able. From its beginning his rule was troubled by renewed Viking attacks, but in 991 he negotiated a treaty with Richard, Duke of Normandy which denied the raiders shelter across the Channel. But this success was effectively overturned a year later with the defeat of Byrhtnoth at **Maldon**. The huge implications of this catastrophe became apparent when Ethelred decided to renew the payment of **Danegeld**, a form of protection money that did little to temper the Vikings' appetite for adventure. Their raids escalated until finally, in 1013, Ethelred was forced into exile by **King Svein** of Denmark. Ethelred attempted a comeback in 1015, but was quickly undermined by Svein's successor **Cnut** and died in London a year later.

1009 Ethelred's navy is all but **destroyed** during a dispute between two of his ealdormen, **Beorhtric** and **Wulfnoth**.

1010 The Vikings resume their attacks against East Anglia. Among many English nobles killed is Ethelred's son-in-law **Athelstan**.

1011 Ethelred again offers Danegeld to the Danish Vikings. He has little choice: they now control a large swathe of southern England from Essex and Kent all the way to Hampshire.

1012 Again the Danish Vikings are bought off with Danegeld.

1013 No longer content to raid and extort Danegeld, King Svein of Denmark mounts a full-scale **invasion**. Ethelred **flees** to his wife's homeland in Normandy and Svein is acknowledged **king of England**.

1014 Svein is succeeded by his son **Cnut** (Canute). Ethelred returns to England and for a while fights successfully against the Vikings. Cnut returns to Denmark to raise a larger army.

1015 Cnut **re-invades** England, defeats Ethelred and secures his claim to the throne.

1016 Ethelred dies in London and is succeeded by **Edmund "Ironside"** as the English claim to the throne. Edmund is defeated in battle by Cnut at Abingdon and dies shortly after, probably murdered. Cnut's authority is acknowledged by what remains of

---

All these misfortunes befell us by reason of bad policy in that tribute was not offered them in time; but when they had done their worst, then it was that peace was made with them. And notwithstanding all this truce and peace and tribute, they went about everywhere in bands, and robbed and slew our unhappy people.

—*Anglo-Saxon Chronicle*, year-entry for 1011, trans. G.N. Garmonsway

THE ENGLISH SHIRES
AND THE *FYRD* SYSTEM

*T*he division of England into shires (counties) was completed relatively late in the Anglo-Saxon period. The first shires developed in Wessex, growing out of former kingdoms in the southeast such as Hampshire and Wiltshire and each presided over by a royal official, originally an ealdorman but later a Shire Reeve (Sheriff). The shires themselves were subdivided into hundreds or *wapentakes*. Like the shires, hundreds were far from uniform, their size and function depending largely on whether they were new administrative units—as was the case in the northern Danelaw—or rationalizations of previously existing units such as the Sussex "rapes" and the Kentish "lathes."

By the 11th century each hundred had some common features. A court presided over by a Reeve was responsible for policing, tax collection and local defense. Landowners were also required to assist in creating a *fyrd* (army) when called upon, providing a quota of soldiers based on the size of their estates. The speed with which such militias were formed demonstrates the effectiveness of the system—Harold Godwinson's ability to counter the invading forces of Harold Hardrada and Tostig at Stamford Bridge in 1066 being a case in point. But the system's flaws were dramatically displayed in 999 and 1001 when the Vikings attacked Kent and Hampshire respectively, wiping out the local armies—and of course when William, Duke of Normandy triumphed over Harold's *fyrd* at Hastings, a policy of rigid central control would come to predominate.

the English nobility, and England is added to Denmark's Scandinavian empire.

1017 Cnut marries Ethelred's widow, Emma of Normandy.

1018 Cnut is proclaimed **king of Denmark**.

1028 Cnut adds Norway to his domains by ousting **King Olaf**.

1031 Cnut accepts the submission of the **king of Scots**.

1035 Cnut dies at **Shaftesbury**. The succession is disputed between his designated heir **Harthacnut** and the illegitimate **Harold Harefoot**. Seizing the initiative, **Harold** is proclaimed king of England.

1036 Ethelred's second son Alfred is imprisoned by Godwin, the Earl of Wessex. Alfred is blinded and soon dies of his injuries.

1040 Harold Harefoot dies and is succeeded by **Harthacnut**, who immediately has his half-brother's body exhumed and flung into a marsh.

1041 Harthacnut adopts Ethelred's son **Edward** (known as "the Confessor" on account of his piety, and later regarded as one of England's patron saints) as his heir in England.

1042 Harthacnut **dies** during a drinking bout at the wedding of one of his nobles. The throne passes smoothly to Edward the Confessor, an **Anglo-Norman** by virtue of his father's marriage to Emma of Normandy. To the chagrin of his English and Viking lords, however, Edward rapidly begins promoting Normans at his court. Led by the House of Godwin, the "native" aristocracy will be driven to rebellion.

1043 Edward is crowned king of England at Winchester.

In a bid to defuse the stand-off between his Norman retainers and the Anglo-Danish faction, Edward marries **Eadgyth**, daughter of the Earl of Godwin.

1046 Edward exiles Earl Godwin's son **Svein** for seducing the abbess of Leominster.

1048 England suffers an unusual series of earthquakes.

1049 Godwin's son Earl Svein causes further outrage by murdering his cousin **Earl Beorn** after returning from exile. He is declared *nithing* ("without honor") and re-exiled. Edward declares his lands forfeit, and awards some of them to his mainly Norman followers.

1050 Aided and abetted by his father, Svein returns to England and is restored to his earldom.

1051 Political tensions come to a head when some followers of Edward's brother-in-law, **Eustace of Boulogne**, intending to visit Edward, brawl with Godwin's supporters at the port of Dover. Earl Godwin and his sons Svein and Harold (known as **Harold Godwinson**) gather their forces and demand that Edward hand over Eustace. Edward in turn summons the earls **Siward of Northumbria** and **Leofric** of Mercia to his aid, and Godwin is forced to back down. Edward then orders Godwin to appear before a *witangemot* (council of elders) to answer charges of murder and treason. Rather than attend, Godwin and Svein flee to **Bruges**; Earl Harold escapes to **Ireland**. Edward strips the Godwins of their lands, and again redistributes them among his Norman favorites. Godwin's daughter and Edward's wife, **Queen Eadgyth**, is sent to a nunnery. At about the same time it is possible that Edward is visited by **William, Duke of Normandy**, and that Edward offers to make him his heir.

1052 Determined to regain their inheritance, Earl Godwin and his sons **return to England** at the head of an army of invasion. Siward and Leofric fail to intervene on Edward's behalf, and Edward is forced to **capitulate**. Lands and titles are restored to the Godwin family, and Queen Eadgyth returns to the court.

1053 Earl Godwin dies in April and is succeeded as earl of Wessex by **Harold Godwinson**. In order to balance the power of the two principal non-royal families, Edward arranges for Leofric's son **Elfgar** to replace Harold as earl of East Anglia.

1054 Earl Siward campaigns successfully against **King Macbeth** of the Scots. Macbeth is killed and replaced by **Malcolm III**. Siward's eldest son Osbeorn is killed fighting.

1055 Earl Siward dies and is succeeded as earl of Northumbria by Godwin's third son **Tostig**. Earl Elfgar is exiled for treason, but quickly returns with a Viking war party reinforced by the army of the Welsh prince **Gruffydd** (Griffith). They defeat **Earl Ralf** of Herefordshire, but are confronted by the stronger forces of Harold Godwinson and sue for peace. Elfgar is restored to his earldom and Gruffydd permitted to keep some territory.

1056 Harold Godwinson travels to Flanders to negotiate the return to England of Edmund Ironside's son Edward Atheling.

1057 Edward Atheling dies soon after his return to England. Earl Leofric of Mercia and Ralf also die. Edward endeavors to fill the ensuing power vacuum by making further gifts to the House of Godwin: Harold's brothers Gyrth and Leofwine are given East Anglia and the southern shires. In effect, this leaves the Earl of Mercia surrounded by the Godwins, and so is driven to seek help from amongst the Welsh princes.

1058 Earl Elfgar is **re-exiled**, and again returns with a Viking force under the military command of Harold Hardrada's son **Magnus**. Helped by Prince Gruffydd, Elfgar regains the earldom of **East Anglia** at the Godwins' expense, and Gruffydd marries Elfgar's daughter **Ealdgyth**.

1062 Elfgar is succeeded by his son **Edwin** as earl of Mercia.

1063 Harold Godwinson attacks Gryffydd's north Wales principality from the sea while his brother Tostig mounts a coordinated offensive on land. Gruffydd's forces are reduced by guerilla warfare; Gruffydd himself is betrayed by his followers and **murdered**. His head is sent to King Edward, but his lands are divided amongst other Welsh princes, restoring peace to the Welsh borders.

1064 Harold Godwinson visits **Normandy**, perhaps as an ambassador from King Edward to William. At any rate William compels Harold to swear an oath of fealty, later used by William to strengthen his claim to the English throne.

1065 In Northumbria there is a **rebellion** against the rule of Earl Tostig. To restore order King Edward exiles Tostig, replacing him with Earl Edwin's brother Morkere. In London, a new minster is completed at Westminster, and a *witangemot* summoned for its consecration on December 28. King Edward, though, is too ill to attend.

1066 King Edward dies in January, and **Harold Godwinson** is chosen by the *witangemot* to succeed him. Almost immediately Harold is challenged by **Tostig**, who begins raiding the English coast. Tostig's forays are repelled by Earl Edwin of Mercia and Earl Morkere of Northumbria. In September Tostig joins an invasion force led by **King Harald Hardrada** of Norway. Together they defeat Edwin and Morkere at **Fulford** outside York. Rallying his army in the south, King Harold of England marches swiftly north and inflicts a decisive defeat on the Vikings at **Stamford Bridge** on September 25; both Tostig and Harald Hardrada are killed. But King Harold has little time to celebrate: determined to assert his claim to the English throne, **William, Duke of Normandy** has raised his own army of invasion. On September 27 he crosses the Channel and lands at Pevensea.

CHAPTER THREE

The Normans

{1066–1154}

ON SEPTEMBER 27, 1066, WILLIAM, DUKE OF NORMANDY landed on the shores of England. Two weeks later he was William I, the country's king. This event had a number of far-reaching geopolitical consequences—not least of which was that England became directly embroiled in the affairs of continental Europe for the first time since the Roman era. For centuries English armies would regularly cross the Channel to campaign on the continent to defend or extend the Crown's territorial interests not just in Normandy but elsewhere in France. Somewhat less regularly, traffic flowed the other way, as French armies laid claim to the English Crown itself. The succession of **Henry II Plantagenet** in 1154 was the outcome of one such counter-campaign—belying the myth that 1066 was the last time England was invaded successfully.

The Normans, originally from Scandinavia, had been established in France for little over a century when they landed at Pevensea. But they had adopted the French language and brought it with them as the language of the court (and those who aspired to it) and thus the language of government—in fact it persisted in the form of "law French," spoken in lawcourts, right up to the late 16th century. Although Anglo-Saxon survived, the vernacular was inevitably influenced by French, as well as by the continued survival of Cornish, Danish and of course ecclesiastical Latin. From this enriched hybrid form developed **Middle English**, which in turn laid the foundations for Modern English.

William's victory had other consequences, too. Although England was already extensively Christianized, his reign was decisive in drawing English ecclesiastical institutions much closer to their French counterparts, and through those to Rome and the authority of the pope—a shift signaled by the imposing continental styles of architecture employed for building cathedrals, monasteries and churches such as those at **Durham**, **St Albans** and **Ely**. Equally imposing is the **Tower of London**, commissioned by William I: perhaps the most famous edifice of the Norman period, and a symbol of his dramatic sense of power.

The Normans also brought with them an exacting administrative genius, best expressed by the **Domesday Book** of 1087—an example of royal record-keeping unrivalled in its scope and thoroughness. And it has been argued that the **feudal system** received systematic legal expression for the first time under Norman rule. The king took possession of all land, which he divided up amongst his leading followers and a handful of surviving Anglo-Saxon grandees. They in turn became feudal overlords, subdividing their estates among lesser barons and knights whose reeves oversaw villages and hamlets, in which narrow strips of land were allotted to villeins (serfs) and their families. Such land grants, whether hereditary or otherwise, were granted on carefully regulated terms—in return for military service, an amount of forced labor and other feudal duties. A significant exception to this top-down paradigm were the towns and cities, in part populated by freemen (later called 'yeomen')—although through the twin expedients of garrisons and charters the Norman regime also sought to bring these under its remit. Ecclesiastical lands, too, became increasingly anomalous. Although feudal dues were extracted from the serfs living on church lands, the fact that ecclesiastical estates were usually granted in perpetuity generated an inevitable source of tension between Church and Crown.

In the broader European context, the Norman conquest coincided with the emergence of two themes that dominate medieval politics and culture: the formation of well-defined **kingdoms** in which the arts of secular government were developed; and the consolidation of the **Roman Church**, not just as a spiritual authority but as a powerful organization with strong temporal interests. Even before the end of the 11th century the two had clashed head-on in England. The dispute was over the matter of who had the final say over church appointments, the king or the pope. Twice **Anselm**, the archbishop of Canterbury, was exiled by **William II**, sowing the seeds of a quarrel which would continue for many years to come and which would reach its climax in the schism of the **Reformation**.

But arguably the greater threat to political stability came from the apex of the royal structure itself, an edifice the Normans did their best to reinforce. Each time a ruler died there were a number of rival candidates for the succession: first among **William I**'s sons, then among **Henry I**'s self-proclaimed heirs. And this too, though scarcely new to England, was set to define the political tone of the Middle Ages.

1066 Learning that **William of Normandy** has landed on the south coast and constructed a stockade at **Hastings**, King Harold Godwinson hurries south following his victory at Stamford Bridge. Without allowing his men time to recover or waiting for reinforcements, he takes up a position against the Norman invasion force on **Senlac Ridge** (Sandlake Ridge), a short distance from Hastings at what is now **Battle, Sussex**. In the ensuing battle, fought on October 14, the Anglo-Saxons fight strongly for several hours, but towards the end of the day William's men gain ground. Harold is killed, as are his brothers **Gyrth** and **Leofwine** and many other English lords. The remaining English nobles elect **Edgar Atheling** king in Harold's stead, but their weakened armies swiftly submit to William after he ravages the southeast and seizes

London; Edgar and his court formally surrender at **Berkhamstead**. Although earls Edwin and Morkere continue to offer resistance in the north, William—who has shrewdly gathered the support of the pope and the Holy Roman Emperor—becomes **king of England**. Seizing the estates of those Anglo-Saxon nobles who opposed him, he begins rewarding his senior followers with grants of sizeable **overlordships**, as Norman garrisons are imposed on many English counties.

1067 Encouraged by Count Eustace of Boulogne, **Kent** revolts against the new Norman rule, but the uprising is put down.

In the summer William returns to Normandy, leaving his half-brother **Odo** (Bishop of Bayeux and newly created the earl of Kent) and **William Fitzosbern** to govern England as his regents. He returns in December.

William the Conqueror killing King Harold; detail from the Bayeux Tapestry

A strange manner of battle, where the one side works by constant motion and ceaseless charges, while the other can but endure passively as it stands fixed to the soil. The Norman arrow and sword worked on; in the English ranks the only movement was the dropping of the dead: the living stood motionless.

—**William of Poitiers,** *Chronicle*

1068 There is an **uprising** of William's English opponents, concentrated in the north of the country with **Edgar Atheling** as the nominal chief and supported by **Malcolm II of Scotland** and by a number of Welsh princes. Earls **Edwin** and **Morkere** soon surrender, however, and are restored by William to their existing lands and titles. Edgar Atheling and his remaining supporters flee to Scotland.

1069 In January there is a renewed revolt in the north. William's appointee **Robert de Comines, Earl of Northumberland**, is killed along with his garrison in Durham. Edgar Atheling returns from Scotland, and is joined by rebels from York.

Just as **Vikings** are threatening the coast, two of Harold Godwinson's sons attempt an invasion of **Devon** from their base in Ireland and **King Svein** of Denmark contributes a fleet of 240 vessels under the command of his brother Osbern. **York** is sacked. William responds brutally: the rebellion is crushed and much of the north laid to waste. He accepts the submission of **Earl Gospatric**, however, and also of Old Siward's son **Waltheof**—who is betrothed to William's niece **Judith**.

1070 Still warring against English rebels, William ravages **Cheshire** and **Shropshire**.

King Svein arrives to take personal command of his forces on the Humber, but after briefly allying with the English rebel **Hereward**

"the Wake" ("the watchful one"), the Danes concede defeat and return home.

The surviving English archbishop of Canterbury **Stigand** is deposed, and replaced by William's candidate **Lanfranc** (formerly the abbot of Bec), who begins reforming the English Church to bring it more closely in line with its French counterpart and thus with Rome.

1071 Hereward sacks **Peterborough Abbey**. In April earls **Edwin** and **Morkere** flee William's court. Edwin is murdered by his own followers as he heads for Scotland, while Morkere joins Hereward at his stronghold on the **Isle of Ely**. Ely falls after a prolonged siege, and **Hereward** escapes to the continent with a band of followers. He will

THE BATTLE OF HASTINGS

*F*rom the Anglo-Saxon perspective the Battle of Hastings was an unmitigated fiasco, its outcome less to do with William's military skill than the blunders of his opponent. Presumably exhausted by the hard-fought battle at Stamford Bridge and the march south again, Harold and his army would have been well-advised to wait for reinforcements before engaging William at what is now Battle in Sussex. Even so, on October 14, at the beginning of the day Harold enjoyed what should have been a decisive advantage. His footsoldiers occupied the high ground on Senlac Ridge, looking down on the 5000-odd Normans, Bretons and French assembled below.

After the two sides exchanged arrows and slingshot, the Normans attempted an uphill cavalry charge. Despite the fact that men and horses alike struggled on the slope, the English shield-wall failed to hold when a group of soldiers decided to attack the retreating horsemen, only to be cut down in the mud. Traditionally they have been assumed to be members of

enter English folklore as the last Anglo-Saxon to offer resistance to the Normans—even though some sources suggest that he is reconciled to William.

1075 About this time the **Bayeux Tapestry**, probably commissioned by **Odo of Bayeux** and depicting the Battle of Hastings with the events immediately surrounding it, is woven—possibly by a group of women in Canterbury.

1077 In the same year that a new cathedral is completed at **Canterbury** under the auspices of Archbishop Lanfranc, **William of Warenne** establishes the first **Cluniac monastery** in England. (Previously all monasteries have belonged to the Benedictine order.)

the *fyrd*, but the Bayeux Tapestry presents a different—though of course one-sided—view. It records that those killed included members of Harold's elite, including his brothers Gyrth and Leofwine, who fell in what may have been a Norman ruse. In any event, the Normans continued to charge and retreat, realizing that the English could be lured downhill. Despite rumors at one stage that William had been killed, as the day wore on this strategy began to pay off until the Norman cavalry reached Harold's close guard. As night approached, already severely wounded by an arrow in the eye—if the Tapestry is to be believed—the king was hacked to death. His leaders suffered the same fate: England's Anglo-Saxon warrior aristocracy was all but annihilated overnight. But had Harold risked an all-out assault on the Normans when they first seemed to be faltering, he would almost certainly have triumphed and Hastings would have gone down in history alongside Stamford Bridge as just another invasion averted.

THE DOMESDAY BOOK

*C*ompiled shortly before William I's death and demonstrating the Norman genius for administration, the Domesday Book was so thorough in its investigation of the land he had conquered that, according to the *Anglo-Saxon Chronicle*, not an ox, cow nor pig slipped through its net. Though the precise reasons behind its commission remain unclear, the book gave an exact picture of England's wealth—and therefore the likely scope and limits of taxation—at a time when the country was threatened with foreign invasion. It also provided William with useful information as to where his forces might most effectively be garrisoned.

The Anglo-Saxons had conducted similar investigations since the time of Alfred the Great, and perhaps it is a tribute to existing local administrative systems that most of Domesday was assembled within a year. That said, nothing on this scale had been attempted before. William's agents were instructed to demand of every official in charge of a hundred an array of detailed questions: how many people lived in the area? what sort of people were they? what sort of land lay in the hundred? how much was it worth? But this wasn't all. Information had to be compiled for three separate periods: when Edward the Confessor was alive, when King William granted the local lord the estate, and at the present time (1086).

The resulting survey was so complete that it became likened to the Day of Judgment, when everything, living and dead, would be judged. Domesday provides a uniquely detailed portrait of an early medieval kingdom—and thoroughly deserves its awe-inspiring title.

1078 Construction begins of the **White Tower**, the central keep of the **Tower of London**—a military and administrative complex designed to ensure Norman control over the country's largest city and its commercial capital.

1081 Anxious to extend Norman power westwards, William journeys through **southern Wales** and visits St Davids Cathedral. **Rhys ap Tewdwr** is acknowledged as ruler of the western principality of Deheubarth in return for paying William an annual tribute of £40. While the Normans have already begun erecting wooden castles in Wales, particularly along the border with England (known as **the Welsh Marches**), the Welsh are generally less amenable to the imposition of Norman rule and continue to resist in the mountainous interior.

1085 Threatened by an alliance between **Flanders** and **Denmark**, William imports the largest army ever seen in England. Partly to enable his administrators to raise sufficient taxes to maintain this force William orders the compilation of the **Domesday Book** at Gloucester, a hugely detailed survey of his English kingdom.

1087 William I dies campaigning in France against his rebellious eldest son **Robert Curthose** and King Philip I of France. Robert inherits Normandy while his second surviving son, **William Rufus** ("the red," so named because of his complexion), gets England. More cultivated than his father but capable of equal brutality, **William II** destabilized the close relationship William I had built up with the clergy and was not kindly viewed by contemporary chroniclers—who excoriated him for sexual depravity and accused him of homosexuality. A different perspective sees him as one of the early troubadours, a man open to the latest fashions and cultural developments on the continent.

1088 William II faces a rebellion orchestrated by his uncle **Odo of Bayeux** aimed at replacing William with Robert Curthose on the throne and reuniting England and Normandy. But when William gathers English support by promising to cut taxes and Robert fails to show up, the rebellion collapses.

1089 William begins a **seven-year campaign** against Robert Curthose to bring Normandy under England's control. Following **Lanfranc's death**, Canterbury remains without an archbishop for four years while a suitable candidate is sought.

1090 An attempted uprising against Robert in **Rouen** is foiled when William's youngest brother **Henry** sides with Robert and personally throws William's supporter **Conan** to his death from Rouen's battlements.

1091 Having led an army into Normandy, William makes a **temporary peace** with Robert. Each agrees that the other should become his heir, and that Henry should be barred from the succession.

Malcolm III of Scotland is compelled to acknowledge William II's overlordship, and the Norman presence in Wales is strengthened.

1092 William II again campaigns in northern England, stamping out rebellion in **Cumbria**.

1093 Malcolm III visits William II's court under safe conduct, but refuses to acknowledge Anglo-Norman jurisdiction in Scotland. Shortly afterwards Malcolm and his son Edward are ambushed and killed near **Alnwick** while mounting a raid against northern England; Malcolm is succeeded by his equally recalcitrant brother **Donald III** (known as "Donald Bane").

William nominates **Anselm** as archbishop of Canterbury to settle what is becoming an ecclesiastical scandal. Anselm accepts only on condition that William restores lands previously confiscated and acknowledges **Urban II** as the true pope against the claims of Clement III. He is consecrated in December, but almost immediately falls out with William when he asks to be allowed to travel to Rome to fetch the **pallium**, the symbol of his spiritual authority; William refuses permission. Out of these circumstances arises the **investiture controversy**—a dispute about whether Crown or Church has the final authority to appoint clerics.

Work begins on the cathedral at **Durham**.

1094 Now supported by his brother **Henry**, William Rufus again invades Normandy. As rumors of **rebellion** oblige the king to return to England, Henry assumes command in the war against Robert.

1095 Several of the rebels of 1088, dominated by barons from the Welsh marches, take up arms against William, intending to replace him with his cousin **Stephen of Aumerle**. The revolt is crushed, the rebels fined and mutilated.

As the investiture controversy intensifies, England's clergy side with the king against Anselm at the **Synod of Rockingham**. When a papal legate brings the pallium to England, Anselm refuses to accept it from William's hands. The king confiscates Anselm's lands, but gives him leave to travel to Rome—in effect sending him into exile.

Determined to bring about the recovery of the Holy Land from Islamic rule, **Pope Urban II** preaches the **First Crusade** at Clermont.

1096 To fund his participation in the First Crusade, Robert Curthose pawns the duchy of Normandy to his brother William II.

1097 William campaigns in Wales to defeat further rebellion.

1098 The **Council of Bari**, attended by Archbishop Anselm, confirms the papacy's view that only it has the right to invest prelates with the "ring and the crozier," symbolizing their spiritual authority.

1099 In July, Jerusalem is recaptured by Christian crusaders. 40,000 Muslims, an unknown number of Jews and Eastern Orthodox Christians are **massacred**. In London, the new **Palace of Westminster** is completed by the king's unpopular chief minister, **Ranulf Flambard**.

William II campaigns in **Normandy** to quash further outbreaks of rebellion.

1100 William Rufus is **killed** by an arrow while hunting in the New Forest. The marksman—thought to have been **Walter Tyrel, Count of Poix**—is believed by some to have acted on behalf of William's brother **Henry**, who does little to quell the rumors by rapidly seizing the **royal treasury** at Winchester and staking his

NORMAN CATHEDRAL ARCHITECTURE

*T*hough the motives behind William of Normandy's invasion of England are still hotly debated, it seems clear that his campaign was not simply a matter of personal aggrandizement backed up by a tenuous claim to the throne. For one thing, he had been careful to secure the backing of the pope for a "holy war" to save the English Church from the peril into which it had fallen and to restore its links with mainstream Christianity.

To this end England's early Norman rulers were visibly pious—endowing dioceses and monasteries with significant lands and setting aside considerable funds for the building of new cathedrals, abbeys and churches along the grandest continental lines. What is striking about these commissions is the sheer contrast in scale compared with previous buildings. Anglo-Saxon England was not entirely devoid of imposing architecture— Edward the Confessor had made the creation of **Westminster Abbey** his pet project—but nothing could compare with what was created by William and his successors. Of the several cathedrals that have survived, **Ely** (begun 1083) boasts a 76-meter-long nave, although its Norman tower collapsed in 1322 and was replaced by the now-famous Octagon. **Peterborough** (1118) also demonstrates many distinctive features of the Anglo-Norman style. But perhaps the purest example is found at **Durham** (1099), in which massive Romanesque decorated pillars and arches support a triforium and above that a rib-vaulted ceiling, the first of its kind in Europe. Every bit as significant is its site, perched high on a rocky promontory with a commanding view of the surrounding landscape and flanked on one side by the equally huge Bishop's Palace. This grandeur was not merely an imitation of fashionable architecture; it also revealed the Normans' determination to overawe their new subjects. Although relations between Crown and Church quickly soured, initially they were partners in the same enterprise.

claim to the throne. Three days after William's death Henry is accepted as king by the nobility, and crowned at Westminster by the bishop of London. As **Henry I**, he immediately recalls Archbishop Anselm from exile in a move clearly designed to win clerical support against Robert Curthose, whose claim to the English throne is stronger than his own. As a gesture to the nobility he issues a "Charter of Liberties," abolishing certain unpopular taxes.

In November Henry further consolidates his position by marrying **Edith** (known also as **Matilda**), the daughter of King Malcolm III of Scotland and Edgar Atheling's sister Margaret.

It is under Henry I that crown justices begin making regular tours, or circuits, of the English shires.

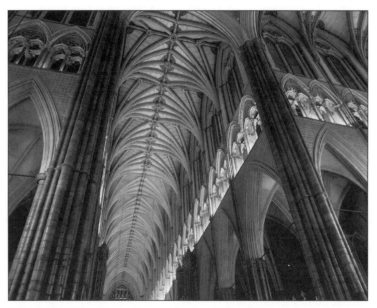

Westminster Abbey

1101 Having returned to France, Robert Curthose lands with an army at **Portsmouth**. Among his supporters are **Eustace III** of Boulogne and the earls of **Surrey** and **Buckingham**. Civil war is averted when Henry agrees to surrender his claims to disputed territories in Normandy and to pay Robert an annuity of £2000. Eustace of Boulogne is restored to his English estates.

1102 Queen Edith gives birth to a daughter, **Matilda**. At an ecclesiastical council held in London, Archbishop Anselm attempts to enforce clerical celibacy, but the majority of clergy resist this and other reforms.

1103 Queen Edith provides Henry I with a male heir, **Prince William**.

Archbishop Anselm begins a second period of **exile**, having refused to confirm several Episcopal appointments made by Henry I.

1104 Robert Curthose cedes territory to Henry in return for the king of England's help in crushing renewed rebellion.

1105 As relations between Henry I and Robert Curthose deteriorate, Henry invades **Normandy**.

1106 Henry defeats and captures Robert at Tinchebrai; among the estimated 400 knights and 10,000 soldiers taken prisoner is Edgar Atheling. But while Edgar is quickly pardoned and released, Robert remains in captivity as Henry seizes control of the whole of Normandy.

Archbishop Anselm returns from exile to Canterbury.

1107 **Louis VI** of France acknowledges Henry's claim to Normandy.

The investiture controversy is resolved—at least for the time being—when Church and king reach agreement at the **Synod of Westminster**. According to the agreement, the Crown renounces its right of investiture on condition that appointees render him feudal homage before being invested with the symbols of their office.

1109 Louis VI demands that Henry render homage for his "French" lands and abandon his castle at Gisors in the Vexin district of Normandy; Henry refuses.

Archbishop Anselm dies on **April 21**—later to become his Saint's Day. The king and Church are unable to agree his successor.

1110 Louis VI captures **Meulan**, a county on the Seine belonging to Henry's active supporter **Robert of Beaumont**.

1111 Backed by Henry, Robert of Beaumont attacks the French king's capital, **Paris**.

1112 Henry arrests and imprisons Louis VI's envoy, **Robert of Bellême**.

1113 Louis VI and **Fulk of Anjou** sue for peace; Henry's son Prince William is betrothed to Fulk's daughter Matilda.

1114 Archbishop Thomas II of York dies of overeating and is succeeded by **Thurstan**, another prelate from Bayeux.

Henry I's daughter **Matilda** is married to the Holy Roman Emperor, **Henry V**.

1115 Henry I's ally **Theobald of Blois** ambushes and imprisons Louis VI's ally **William of Nevers**.

1116 Largely because of their quarrelsome barons, Henry I and Louis VI again find themselves at **war**. Henry supports his nephews **Stephen** and **Theobald**; Louis supports **Fulk of Anjou** and **Baldwin of Flanders**.

1118 Henry and Louis come to terms after Henry's forces are defeated by Fulk at **Alençon**.

Henry's wife **Queen Edith** dies.

1119 Fulk's daughter marries **Prince William**. Louis VI invades Normandy, but is repulsed by Henry's forces at **Bremule**. At once Louis VI attempts a second invasion, but Pope **Calixtus II** persuades the two sides to call a truce. Henry remains in possession of Normandy.

1120 Henry's successes in Normandy are overshadowed by the deaths of his only sons **William** and **Richard** when the *White Ship* is wrecked crossing the Channel, possibly because the crew was drunk. A number of barons and royal officials are also drowned.

1121 Desperate for an heir to replace William, Henry I marries **Adelaide of Louvain**.

Returning from the Crusades, **Fulk of Anjou** demands that his widowed daughter Matilda and the country of Maine be returned to him.

1123 His demands unmet, Fulk **declares war** on Henry.

In Normandy several nobles rebel in favor of Robert Curthose's son **William Clito**.

ST ANSELM (1033–1109)

*B*itter disputes between Church and state were a defining feature of the early Middle Ages. At their heart was a debate about the nature of society itself—whether the advancing secular power of kings and princes or the spiritual authority of bishops, archbishops and ultimately the pope counted more. In reality, the best hope of survival for either side was compromise: in a superstitious age kings needed the moral sanctions offered by the Church quite as much as the Church needed the political and military support supplied by feudal courts.

In the post-Conquest period the first serious spat between Crown and Church in England centered on **Anselm**, William Rufus's unwilling appointee to the see of Canterbury. A pupil of the previous archbishop, **Lanfranc**, Anselm quickly began to agitate over the matter of **investiture**, insisting that only the Church had the right to select its own officials. William Rufus refused to make concessions, as at first did Henry I; as a result, Anselm was exiled twice. Henry I was the better strategist, however, and because he needed papal backing for his seizure of Normandy from his elder brother

1124 Henry I defeats the Normandy rebels at **Bourgtheroulde** and persuades **Emperor Henry V** to invade France. The emperor's campaign is swiftly curtailed, however, when rebellion breaks out at **Wurms** in his own domains.

1125 Henry I enacts a law sentencing **moneyers** (illegal minters of coin) to have their right hands severed and to be castrated.

Emperor Henry V **dies**, temporarily giving Henry I a free hand in his negotiations with the French crown.

Robert Curthose, willingly agreed to the compromise enshrined in the Westminster agreement of 1107 in which the Church came out marginally ahead—at least on paper.

Fittingly, Anselm's canonization later in the century was engineered by **Thomas Becket**, that most celebrated champion of ecclesiastical rights. But Anselm was the greater churchman: a formidable theologian, he is credited with fathering Scholasticism, the rationalistic movement which was the main theological foundation of the Catholic church until at least the Reformation. In his *Proslogium* he attempted to base belief in reason rather than in faith alone; his "ontological proof" of God's existence, arguing that even a fool must concede that God could not exist as an idea without a greater reality to sustain it, is influential even now. Of less appeal is Anselm's **satisfaction theory**, presented in *Cur Deus Homo*, where God is depicted as the ultimate feudal overlord: mankind's debts, accrued through sin, are such that only God's incarnation as Christ can balance the books.

1126 Henry I's daughter, **Empress Matilda**, returns to the Anglo-Norman court at Christmas and is presented to Henry's barons.

1127 The barons, led by **David, King of Scots** and by Henry's illegitimate son Robert of Gloucester, promise **allegiance** to Matilda in the event that Henry dies without a legitimate male heir.

1128 Empress Matilda (aged 26) marries **Geoffrey Plantagenet**, heir to Anjou (aged 15).

William Clito, the titular duke of Normandy, dies of wounds received at the siege of **Alost**.

1129 Empress Matilda returns to her father after her marriage to Geoffrey of Anjou breaks down.

1131 Empress Matilda again accepts an **oath of allegiance** from a gathering of Henry's "English" barons at **Northampton**.

1133 Having been reconciled to her husband Geoffrey, Matilda gives birth to a son who is called **Henry**.

1134 Robert Curthose **dies** in captivity in England. Matilda gives birth to a second son, named **Geoffrey**.

1135 Henry I **dies** at Lyons-la-Forêt in Normandy after quarrelling with his daughter Matilda and his son-in-law **Geoffrey of Anjou** on account of the latter's demands to be recognized as Henry's heir. The succession to Henry's crown is disputed between Matilda and Henry I's nephew **Stephen, Count of Blois**. While Geoffrey of Anjou has been specifically excluded from the throne by Henry I's will, it is probable that he intended Matilda to become queen. By invading southern Normandy, however, Matilda and Geoffrey alienate potential allies—who begin looking more favorably on Stephen's claims. Stephen crosses the Channel and is **accepted as king** by a significant proportion of England's nobility and London's merchants. Despite this, Stephen's reign will be marked by near-continuous civil war.

1136 Stephen confirms the Westminster Agreement of 1107, promising that the Church will be free from royal interference.

1137 David, King of Scots, seeking a restoration of his English earldoms, harasses the north.

1138 Stephen mounts a **counter-invasion** of Scotland. Discontented nobles in England, led by **Robert of Gloucester**, begin to rally to Empress Matilda's cause. Her husband, Geoffrey of Anjou, invades Normandy; as the year progresses, fighting between the two factions spreads in England. Stephen sends his queen, also called **Matilda**, to besiege Robert's stronghold at **Dover** while he campaigns against rebels in the West Country. An attempted invasion on August 22 by King David is halted by northern barons at the **Battle of the Standard**. But by the end of the year, Stephen has lost control of parts of both the north and the west. Geoffrey's attempted seizure of Normandy, however, fails.

1139 Stephen secures the Scottish border by the **Treaty of Durham**; David, King of Scots swears **fealty** to the English throne. In return David's son Henry is given the earldom of **Northumberland**. Empress Matilda, Geoffrey of Anjou and Robert of Gloucester remain at large, though, and now attempt to dispossess Stephen. Their supporter **Baldwin of Reviers** lands at Wareham and establishes a base at **Corfe**. Soon afterwards, Empress Matilda and Robert of Gloucester establish themselves at **Arundel**, where Stephen besieges them. When Robert escapes, the king unwisely allows Matilda to follow him. While the West Country remains in revolt, the Bishop of Ely adds to Stephen's difficulties by joining the rebellion.

1140 Stephen secures control over **Cornwall** and **Ely**. His opponents, angered by Stephen's Scottish policy and led now by the **Earl of Chester**, occupy **Lincoln**—which the king besieges toward the end of the year.

1141 As Stephen puts the pressure on Lincoln, a rebel relief force outnumbers and **captures** him. During the king's imprisonment, the Norman barons reluctantly acknowledge Geoffrey of Anjou's overlordship. But before the end of the year Stephen is **released** in exchange for Robert of Gloucester, captured by forces loyal to Stephen.

1142 Geoffrey of Anjou, still attempting to establish control over **Normandy**, declines to join his wife Empress Matilda in England. Instead he sends their son **Henry Plantagenet**, who joins forces with Robert of Gloucester.

1143 By attempting to curb the powers of the **earl of Essex**, the king merely encourages other barons to rebel.

1144 Unrest prevails in many parts of England and Normandy as the civil wars of Stephen's reign reach their fiercest stage yet. **Durham** falls to the Scots, and Robert of Gloucester ravages the **West Country**.

Towards the end of the year, though, Stephen **eliminates** several of his baronial opponents.

1145 Robert's son **Philip** abandons his father and pledges his loyalty to Stephen.

The **Second Crusade** is preached, offering many English knights and nobles an alternative to warfare at home.

1148 **Henry Plantagenet** fails to revive the flagging rebellion in England.

His mother Empress Matilda crosses the Channel to **France**, never to return.

1149 Henry Plantagenet engineers an **alliance** between David, King of Scots and the earl of Chester, but their forces are swiftly routed

---

England, once the seat of justice, the home of peace, the height of piety, the mirror of religion, became thereafter a place of perversity, a haunt of strife, a school of disorder, and the teacher of every kind of rebellion.

—*Gesta Stephani*, **trans. K.R. Potter and R.H.C. Davis**

STEPHEN AND MATILDA

*F*amously the reign of King Stephen has been called a time "when God and his angels slept." But this image of a period of unbridled anarchy following an era of peace and stability is hugely exaggerated: dynastic infighting among William I's heirs had continued intermittently since his death—even if the battles so far had taken place mainly in Normandy. Conversely, many senior Anglo-Norman barons, far from taking advantage of the Crown's difficulties, strove to resolve the outstanding issues.

In retrospect, it was the ambition of Geoffrey of Anjou—claiming the throne via his marriage to Henry I's daughter Matilda—that proved the flashpoint. Matilda was far from popular, but her husband was massively opposed by the barons in Normandy as well as those in England. As a consequence the Crown was offered first to Henry I's nephew Count Theobald of Blois, then to Theobald's younger brother Stephen. That this supposedly weak man accepted and held on to it lays to rest another myth—though no one could describe the events of his reign as anything but unfortunate.

But Stephen's accession also reflected the growing authority of the Church. Another candidate for the throne was Henry's illegitimate son Robert the Bastard of Gloucester. Though not in England, illegitimate children had achieved success elsewhere in claiming their fathers' titles, and Robert might well have expected to do the same had it not been for the unanimous opposition of the bishops. With no love lost between him and Stephen, he had little choice but to support his half-sister Matilda in the hope of some great reward to come. This in turn encouraged less scrupulous barons with their own territorial ambitions to enter the fray; that Stephen lost control of the situation was hardly surprising.

by Stephen; Henry himself is chased out of the country by Stephen's son **Eustace**.

1150 Henry Plantagenet becomes **Duke of Normandy**, temporarily lost to the English crown.

1151 On the death of his father Geoffrey, Henry Plantagenet becomes **Count of Anjou**.

1152 Henry Plantagenet marries **Eleanor of Aquitaine**, recently divorced from Louis VII of France. In due course Eleanor will bear Henry eight children. Four sons will survive infancy: **Henry**, **Richard**, **Geoffrey** and **John**.

1153 Following a four-year lull in hostilities, Henry Plantagenet returns with an army to England. Renewed civil war is averted, however, by the death of Stephen's son and heir **Eustace**. It is agreed that Stephen should remain on the throne, but that Henry should succeed him.

1154 King Stephen dies of natural causes. Henry Plantagenet, known as **Henry II**, becomes king of England. The territories under his control stretch from **Scotland** in the north to the **Pyrenees** in southwestern France.

CHAPTER FOUR

The Plantagenets

{1154–1399}

WHILE THEIR SURNAME SUGGESTS that the Planatagenets are a separate dynasty from the Normans, this isn't technically the case. The founding monarch, **Henry II**, was the grandson of Henry I, albeit via his mother rather than his father. Indeed, right up until 1485 and the final collapse of the houses of Lancaster and York, it can be said that England was ruled by a single dynasty whose line reaches directly back to William I.

Even considered as a discrete unit, the Plantagenets were still England's longest-serving monarchical house—outdistancing the Tudors, the Stuarts, the Hanoverians and, to date, the Windsors. The argument in favor of looking at them separately is that under their stewardship—intermittent though it was—England found an identity to call its own. The French wars and the dynastic infighting continued, as did tensions between Crown and Church, but amid the upheavals there is a sense in which the English community gained focus—demanding to be heard in its own language, exerting pressure over England's political institutions and finding expression in indigenous works of art and literature.

An important aspect of this evolution is that the Anglo-Norman barony became gradually more Anglocentric—less willing to be drawn into the Crown's costly continental escapades, more eager to exert power in their English estates. This was an inevitable source of tension: Henry II and his immediate successors **Richard I** and **John** were every bit as preoccupied with politics outside England as their Norman predecessors had been.

The early Plantagenets
1154–1272

Where the king went his courtiers followed—both literally and metaphorically. This situation didn't change until the very end of John's reign when, in the wake of the king's military humiliation at the hands of Philip II Augustus of France, his barons managed to impose a contract securing their rights, **Magna Carta** of 1215.

In the early days of Plantagenet rule this seemed worlds away. Through a combination of circumstances Henry II's inheritance was unprecedentedly large. From Stephen he gained England and Normandy; from his father Geoffrey he acquired Anjou; and through his wife Eleanor he exerted control over Aquitaine. His domains, sometimes called the **Angevin Empire**, constituted the greatest swathe of territory in western Europe; and Henry, who was nothing if not determined in everything he did, was determined to hold on to each and every bit of it—even extend it further. England in 1154 was more tightly involved in continental politics than it had been at any point during the preceding century. In France Henry II may have been—technically at least—subordinate to the French king, but his independent kingdom with its supply of arms and men meant that he became a potentially useful (and much-courted) ally of France's European rivals. Significantly, of his 34-year reign, over 20 years were spent in France.

Richard I, Henry's third son but his immediate successor, spent even less time on English soil. He ruled for ten years but was absent for all but six months—crusading in the Holy Land, languishing in a German prison, attempting to recover Normandy from the French king. Yet, paradoxically, the government of England benefited. Because Henry II often had to rule by proxy, he set up strong institutions headed by capable officials, and these continued under Richard. It was during Henry II's reign—and into the next—that something like a specifically English administration, supported by a reformed justice system, came into being.

Even so, it was a difficult inheritance for Henry's youngest son **John**, who came to the throne in 1199. John had to contend with the barons' growing disillusionment with the Crown's costly French campaigns and the warmongering of the French king, **Philip II Augustus**. Had John's forces triumphed against Philip domestic dissent would have been quelled, but losing Normandy permanently destabilized his power-base. He had little choice but to sign the Magna Carta.

John had also fallen out with the pope by refusing to accept the papal candidate for the archbishopric of Canterbury, **Stephen Langton**. In this too he was not unlike his father, who had notoriously provoked Rome by his handling of **Thomas Becket**. Both kings suffered the indignity of excommunication—a serious obstacle, not only because the spiritual status of rulers was a matter of public anxiety but also because the pope himself was a key player in European power politics, someone whose favor could make or break an alliance between princes.

There followed the long and fractious reign of John's son, **Henry III**. With Magna Carta and half a century of greater involvement in central government behind them, England's barons were in no mood to be dominated by a ruler who was sometimes as inconsistent in his policies as he was undiplomatic in their execution. If the focal point of English politics of the mid-13th century was the rudimentary emergence of **Parliament**—the initiative not of the English barons themselves but of another Frenchman, **Simon de Montfort IV**—this is revealing of the way things stood. De Montfort had two purposes in convening a consultative assembly made up of knights of the shire and burgesses as well as barons: to legitimize his usurpation of royal power, but also to provide a counterweight to the barons themselves.

In the short term his experiment failed. De Montfort's numerous opponents found in the heir to the throne, **Prince Edward**, a leader equipped to crush the "foreign" interloper, even if the price for this was the revived prestige and authority of the Crown. Yet in a longer view de Montfort's parliament was surprisingly influential, if only because it suited Edward to retain it as a mechanism of political control. Although it is difficult to claim that it represents the first flowerings of popular democracy—as nineteenth-century critics were fond of arguing—it proved to have more resilience than anyone can have thought at the time.

1154 The addition of England to his portmanteau of territories means that **Henry II Plantagenet** rules a huge body of land stretching all the way from the **Scottish border** to the **Pyrenees** in southwestern France. While this makes him a principal player in western Europe, it also necessitates long absences from his English kingdom, where he will spend only fourteen years out of a 34-year reign. Despite this, his reform of the **English legal system** will constitute a lasting legacy. Henry rapidly assembles a team of outstanding officials, basing them in the **Exchequer**—so called because of the use of a board divided into squares for accountancy purposes. Among these are **Richard de Lucy**, **Robert de Beaumont** and the archdeacon of Canterbury **Thomas Becket**, whom Henry raises to the office of chancellor. In the early months of his reign Henry is aided by Becket in razing the castles of several rebellious barons.

Nicholas Breakspear is elected pope as **Adrian IV**, the only Englishman ever to become pontiff.

1155 Henry II thwarts a rebellion by the **earl of York**, and secures the submission of the troublesome marcher lord, **Roger of Hereford**.

1156 Henry pays homage to King Louis VII of France in respect of his French fiefdoms. While on the continent, he dispossesses his younger brother **Geoffrey** of most of his territories.

1157 Henry receives homage from **Malcolm IV** of Scotland (to whom he awards the **earldom of Huntingdon**), and the northern territories of **Northumberland**, **Cumberland** and **Westmoreland** are returned to the English Crown.

Campaigning in **Wales**, Henry brings prince **Owain Gwynedd** to heel and receives homage from him. His intrusion into Wales falls short of complete conquest, however.

1158 Becket heads a diplomatic mission to the French court on behalf of Henry II; in **Paris**, the excessive splendor of the chancellor's retinue attracts disapproving attention. The way is smoothed for the betrothal of Henry's three-and-a-half-year-old heir **Prince Henry** to Louis VII's six-month-old daughter **Margaret**. This too incites scandal—particularly among those aware that such a marriage could eventually lead to the union of the French and English crowns.

Soon afterwards the king crosses to the continent, where he will spend five years away from the English court. The death of his brother **Geoffrey** enables Henry to lay claim to the remaining **Angevin lands**.

1159 Henry II quarrels with Louis VII, and the two kings' forces fight briefly and inconclusively until a **truce** is declared in November.

1160 A **papal schism** realigns European politics. While the Holy Roman Emperor supports the "anti-pope" **Victor IV**, Henry II gives his guarded support to the "official" pope, **Alexander III**—who in return allows Prince Henry to marry the French infant princess Margaret. Fighting between the English and French resumes when Henry seizes Margaret's **dowry** for himself.

1162 In May Thomas Becket, very much the king's candidate, is elected **archbishop of Canterbury** following the death of Archbishop Theobald in the previous year. Almost immediately Becket resigns as chancellor, and, in an apparently dramatic change of character, begins the defense of **ecclesiastical privileges** and rights that will occupy the rest of his life.

He traveled incessantly, and in stages intolerable, like a public carrier, and, in this matter, showed scant consideration for his retinue. In dogs and birds he was most expert, and exceedingly fond of hunting. He passed nights without sleep and was untiring in his activities. Whenever in his dreams passion mocked him with vain shapes, he used to curse his body, because neither toil nor fasting was able to break or weaken it. I, however, ascribe his activities not to his incontinence but to his fear of becoming too fat.

—Walter Map on Henry II,
in *De Nugis Curialium* (c.1190),
trans. F. Tupper and M.B. Ogle

1163 Returning to England in January, Henry II begins a series of acrimonious arguments with Archbishop Becket. These chiefly concern Becket's insistence that clerics should be tried for any misdemeanors in **ecclesiastical courts**; also Becket's readiness to **excommunicate** a number of leading barons for ungodly behavior also earns him royal displeasure.

1164 In January Henry II calls a council of senior ecclesiastics at **Clarendon** in Wiltshire to assert his "ancestral" rights over the English Church. The resulting **Constitutions of Clarendon** specify that the king has the powers of recommendation and veto over the appointment of bishops; that clerics suspected of misdemeanors (called "criminous clerks") are subject to trial in royal courts; that **vacant sees** should be held in custody by the Crown; that no royal official should be **excommunicated**; and that no appeal to **Rome** on any matter should be made without the king's consent. Archbishop Becket allegedly gives his verbal assent to these principles, but repudiates them soon afterwards. Matters are brought to a head in October, when Henry convenes a further council at

Northampton, having pressured Becket in the interim by ordering him to provide a full set of accounts for the period he was chancellor. Supported by the bishop of London, **Gilbert Foliot**, the king reaffirms the Constitutions of Clarendon. In November Becket flees in disguise to the court of Louis VII of France, intending to appeal directly to **Pope Alexander III**. But while the pope welcomes Becket's pro-Church stance, he is nervous about pushing Henry II into an alliance with Emperor Henry V, who supports the rival "anti-pope," and therefore keeps Becket at arm's length.

1165 Henry II fails to persuade Alexander III to repudiate Becket, despite threatening to give his allegiance to the new "anti-pope" **Paschal**.

1166 Alexander III at last throws his weight behind Becket, appointing him a **papal legate**. Becket uses his increased ecclesiastical powers to excommunicate the bishop of London and other senior English churchmen. In the same year major judicial reforms are promulgated by Henry II at the **Assize of Clarendon**. As a result of the king's determination to create a tiered system of **courts** capable of delivering swift and impartial justice, crime and disorder are significantly reduced in England.

1167 To limit the damage caused by Becket's exile, Henry II orders all English scholars living abroad to **return home**. Of those who obey, a number settle in **Oxford**, forming a community that will develop into England's first university.

Queen Eleanor gives birth to the youngest of Henry's surviving legitimate sons, the future king **John**.

1169 Eager to crusade, Henry II attempts a **reconciliation** with Becket at Montmirail, but the archbishop refuses to relent.

1170 In a move to clarify the succession—and in defiance of Becket—the king's heir **Prince Henry** is crowned as co-ruler by **Archbishop Roger of York**, who is promptly excommunicated by the exiled primate. In July, fearing that Pope Alexander III will issue a general interdict against England, the king meets Becket at **Fréteval**.

Although little is done to resolve their dispute, Becket is encouraged to return to England.

On December 2 the archbishop resumes residence at Canterbury but refuses to lift the **excommunications** of Roger of York and Bishop Foliot. On December 29, spurred into action by Henry's continuing frustration, four knights follow Becket into his cathedral and **murder** him—something that earns Henry papal excommunication and near-universal infamy as well as ensuring Becket's martyrdom.

Richard de Clare, the second earl of Pembroke, known as "**Strongbow**," initiates the English conquest of Ireland when he gains control of Leinster. Claiming that Pope Adrian IV had "given" him **Ireland**, Henry II approves of Strongbow's intervention on condition that Henry himself is recognized as Leinster's overlord. In due course Henry will add "**king of Ireland**" to his titles. The greater part of Ireland, however, remains autonomous.

1171 Henry II's continental territories are placed under an interdict by the **archbishop of Sens** as a punishment for Becket's murder; in Canterbury itself, stories grow from Easter onwards of **miracles** associated with Becket's tomb.

Henry attempts to call the Church's bluff by leading a **crusade** to Ireland, but fails to extend English rule beyond Leinster.

1172 Henry II's personal excommunication is lifted on condition that he maintains **two hundred knights** in the Holy Land and himself undertakes to crusade against Islam for three years.

1173 Just three years after his death, Becket is **canonized**.

Prince Henry falls out with his father when Henry II proposes giving territories to his youngest and favorite son **John** (known as **Lackland**) at the expense of Prince Geoffrey. As the family feud deepens, **Queen Eleanor** and **Prince Richard** side with the younger Henry and Geoffrey, who are also supported by **Louis VII of France** and **William "the Lion," King of Scots**. Such fighting as occurs is, however, mainly confined to the continent.

1174 On July 12, in order to restore his ailing European reputation and atone for his mistreatment of Thomas Becket, Henry II performs **public penance** at Canterbury Cathedral.

William, King of Scots is captured at **Alnwick** on July 13 and is only released after agreeing to pay England homage.

Towards the end of the year Henry succeeds in overcoming his rebellious family; his sons are pardoned, but **Queen Eleanor** is arrested and spends the next eleven years in custody. Henry II initiates **divorce proceedings**, but they are never finalized.

1177 Henry II has Prince John proclaimed "King of Ireland."

1180 Differences between Henry and the Vatican still outstanding from the 1164 Constitutions of Clarendon are **resolved** on the basis of compromise.

The theologian **John of Salisbury**—who continued Becket's impassioned defense of ecclesiastical rights—dies. A committed advocate of Church poverty and a forward-thinking educationalist, his work influences the development of humanism three centuries later.

1181 Feuding again breaks out in the royal family when the princes Henry and Richard dispute territory in **Aquitaine**.

In England, Henry II decrees that all freemen should possess and maintain such weapons as are appropriate to their wealth and social position—an instrument known as the **Assize of Arms**.

1183 The death of Henry II's eldest son, **Prince Henry**, intensifies the rivalries between his younger sons Richard, Geoffrey and John.

1184 King Henry stokes further dynastic conflict by encouraging Prince John to seize **Aquitaine** from his brother Richard.

Richard wars against John and his father.

1186 The death of Prince Geoffrey during a jousting tournament seemingly strengthens Prince Richard's claim to his father's throne; but as Henry II blatantly favors his youngest son John,

The murder of Thomas Beckett

THOMAS BECKET (C.1120–70)

*T*he relationship between Henry II and Thomas Becket—as well as the quarrel that led to the latter's death—has fascinated generations of historians. It wouldn't be nearly so interesting were it not for Becket's seemingly abrupt change of character mid-career.

The son of a Cheapside merchant, Becket completed his education in Paris before joining the household of Theobald, the archbishop of Canterbury. The exceptionally able archdeacon was talent-spotted by the new king, who made Becket his chancellor. In the years that followed, Becket proved himself useful and was invaluable in helping Henry restore the Crown's authority after the mid-century civil wars. When Theobald died, it was natural for Henry to assume that Becket—his friend and confidant—would take over and continue as before.

Instead the archbishop took a different path. Resigning the chancellorship, which the king had expected him to keep, Becket immediately began championing ecclesiastical autonomy—particularly with regard to the question of whether miscreant clerics should be tried before Church courts (where punishment was generally lenient) or before the king's judiciary. Becket was forced into exile, from where he launched an unrelenting campaign against his former master. This ignited the sequence of events leading to Becket's murder at Canterbury in 1170, by four knights who had been present when Henry raged that he wanted to be "rid of this turbulent priest."

Noting Becket's love of wealth and ostentation during his time as chancellor, some critics have explained his seemingly abrupt transformation as the behavior of a vain man unwilling to be outdone by his sovereign. More generous commentators have seen an individual who came to God in mid-life. Whatever the truth, in death he was even more influential than in life—his tomb become a focus of pilgrimage for nearly 400 years and his cult one of the most powerful of the European middle ages.

Richard forms an alliance with **King Philip II Augustus** of France against them. When Henry's forces are defeated, John joins Richard in rebellion.

1187 Saladin's recapture of **Jerusalem** from the Crusaders casts a blight over Christendom.

The late Prince Geoffrey's heir, **Arthur**, is born.

1188 Henry II and Philip Augustus meet and establish a **temporary peace**, but fighting between the English king and his sons in France continues.

THE MEDIEVAL UNIVERSITIES

*H*enry II's recall of English scholars studying in Paris had repercussions that lasted well beyond the immediate political crisis: it provided an incentive for the development of homegrown university education. A group of students from the continent formed an academic community at Oxford in 1185; everything went smoothly until 1209, when a group of disaffected clerks decamped for a fenland market town called Cambridge after brawling with local townspeople. Both universities were modeled on the Parisian schools, organized a curriculum based around study of the Seven Liberal Arts (Grammar, Rhetoric, Logic, Arithmetic, Geometry, Music and Astronomy) and offered degrees in Philosophy, Theology and Law.

Encouraged by the arrival of Dominicans and Franciscans—members of the new religious orders of mendicant friars—halls of residence, and eventually colleges, originally provided homes for poor students, enabling a limited social mobility otherwise hard to come by in early medieval England. At the outset it was the houses run by the friars that predominated:

1189 Henry II, grieved by his surviving sons' hostility toward him and still campaigning against them, dies at **Chinon** near Tours. Within a week Prince Richard succeeds to the English throne. As **Richard I**, known as *Coeur de Lion* ("Lionheart"), he grants his brother John substantial personal domains, but also exiles him from England for three years to prevent any seizure of his throne whilst he crusades in the Holy Land. Similarly Henry II's "loyal" son, Geoffrey the Bastard, is compelled into taking holy orders, made **archbishop of York**, but also exiled. Having thus disabled his likeliest rivals, Richard earnestly sets about raising funds for his participation in the **Third Crusade**.

it wasn't until the 14th century that non-monastic scholars and secular colleges challenged the supremacy of the older foundations. And even then, the first responsibility of Oxford and Cambridge remained to prepare young men for holy orders—little or no education was provided for laymen as such, and the vast majority of students were either priests or were heading there.

Yet slowly the universities became centers of learning in their own right, eventually rivaling their continental competitors. It is significant that of the two intellectual heavyweights produced by England during the Plantagenet period, the first, Roger Bacon, probably left Oxford for Paris, but the second, John Wyclif, studied wholly in Oxford. And that students had become an established feature of the medieval social landscape is confirmed by Chaucer's wry portrait in *The Canterbury Tales* of the gaunt, earnest "clerk of Oxenford," who spends so much money on his studies that he can't afford to keep himself—or his horse—properly fed.

RICHARD I (1157–99)

Richard I embodies the degree to which crusading came to dominate the minds—and the resources—of Europe's rulers during the 12th century. Partly it was a matter of chivalry, partly of faith, and partly of defending Christendom against the encroachments of Islam.

No sooner had Richard been crowned than he set about joining the Third Crusade, called in response to Saladin's capture of Jerusalem in 1187. Acre fell after a siege, but Jerusalem offered more resistance and the crusaders' objective remained beyond their grasp. When that happened, the Christian monarchs quickly began to squabble. In the aftermath Richard was seized by Leopold of Austria, and only released on the payment of a vast ransom. Even then, no sooner had Richard returned home than he left again to attend to his affairs in France.

Much as glamour and romance attached themselves to the king during his lifetime (the nickname *Coeur de Lion* appears as early as 1199), later historians have been quick to condemn Richard—not just for his mercilessness against Saladin's Muslims but for his apparent carelessness about the government of their own country. "Richard I was rather a knight-errant than a king," sniffed Sir James Mackintosh in his *History of England* (1830–32), continuing: "His history is more that of a crusade than of a reign." As usual, the truth lies somewhere in between. For a start, the French-speaking early Plantagenets had a wide view of their empire, of which England was just one part. Further, government did not collapse during Richard's absence. Thanks to the capable stewardship of the chief justiciar Hubert Walter, order was maintained, while the fact that Richard's ransom was easily raised indicates that his barons supported his activities abroad. Even so, his absence did provide England's earls and lords with a taste of power—as Richard's brother John discovered to his cost.

1190 Richard I leaves England for the **Holy Land**. He stops en route to lay claim to **Sicily**, the kingdom of his sister Joan's late husband, **King William II**. While traveling, he nominates **Arthur of Brittany** as his heir. On hearing this, John returns to England illegally and joins those opposed to Richard's chancellor **William Longchamp**.

1191 Richard marries **Berengaria of Navarre** and establishes his rule over the island of Cyprus. In the Holy Land he participates in the siege of Acre, which falls a month after the crusaders' arrival; its inhabitants, Jewish as well as Muslim, are massacred. Philip II Augustus of France abandons the crusade immediately afterwards, leaving Richard undisputed leader of the expedition. He marches towards Jerusalem, but although he defeats **Saladin** in open battle he is unable to close on his target.

In England, the monks of **Glastonbury** discover (or claim to discover) the graves of **King Arthur and Guinevere**.

1192 John succeeds in banishing the king's chancellor **William Longchamp** and briefly becomes effective ruler in Richard's absence, conspiring with Philip Augustus to take the throne for himself. Needing to return home, Richard initiates **peace talks** with Saladin, and recognizes first **Conrad of Montferrat**, then **Henry II of Champagne** as king of the Latin kingdom of **Outremer**. Saladin agrees to a truce lasting three years, three months and three days, and guarantees Christian pilgrims access to Jerusalem. On his way back, Richard is taken prisoner by his enemy **Leopold of Austria** after being shipwrecked off **Venice**.

1193 Emperor Henry VI persuades Leopold to transfer Richard to his own custody. Encouraged by his brother's misfortune, John continues to build an **alliance** with Philip Augustus, who begins seizing Richard's lands in **Normandy**. In England the government remains loyal to Richard, though, and John is forced to flee to the continent.

1194 John allows Philip Augustus to take possession of all **Normandy** north of the Seine.

In Germany, Richard is finally **released** after his supporters agree to humiliating terms: England is to become a fief of the emperor, to whom it must pay a **ransom** of 150,000 marks. Returning to England, Richard swiftly defeats John's followers and destroys their castles; John himself is deprived of all his lands and **banished**. In May, Richard leaves once more for the continent, never to set foot in England again. He is warmly greeted in Normandy, and in July defeats Philip Augustus at **Freteval**—a victory that enables him to reclaim nearly all his lost territories in France.

1196 Richard consolidates his position in Normandy by embarking on a massive program of castle-building, including the supposedly impregnable **Chateau Gaillard** on the Seine. The king and John are **reconciled**, the latter becoming heir to the English throne since Richard is childless.

1197 Hoping to secure the succession of his son Frederick, Emperor Henry VI releases Richard from vassalage.

1198 Henry VI dies and his brother **Philip of Swabia** is elected emperor. As factions within the empire begin feuding, Richard engineers the election of an alternative candidate—his nephew **Otto of Brunswick**. Richard's hand is strengthened by the election of **Innocent III**, a pope eager to prevent Sicily becoming part of the empire and to promote a new crusade.

1199 Richard I and Philip Augustus begin **peace talks** to end the fighting in Normandy, but before these can be concluded Richard is killed by a crossbow bolt at **Chalus** while attempting to subdue a rebellion led by **Audemar Taillefer of Angouleme** and his brother, the **viscount of Limoges**. The succession is disputed between his brother **John** and his nephew **Arthur of Brittany**. Reluctantly the barons of Normandy and England choose John, who is crowned at Westminster in May. Arthur is declared **count of Anjou**, and with the backing of Philip Augustus begins pressurizing John to make further territorial concessions in France. Forming an alliance with the counts of **Boulogne** and **Flanders**, John **declares war** against Arthur.

1200 Although John successfully defends England's northern counties against the **Scots**, he is unable to secure a meaningful victory in France and agrees instead to a peace concluded at **Le Goulet**. Although territorially the terms are favorable to Philip Augustus, Arthur of Anjou agrees to pay homage to the English Crown. The treaty is cemented by two marriages—between Philip's heir Louis and John's niece **Blanche of Castile**, and between John himself and **Isabella of Angouleme**. But while the latter extends John's influence in Aquitaine, it also provokes the **Lusignans** into rebellion, as Isabella has been previously promised to their count, **Hugh le Brun**. Crushed in battle by John, the Lusignans appeal to Philip Augustus to arbitrate.

1201 Philip II Augustus summons John as duke of Aquitaine to answer the Lusignan charge of mistreatment, and demands that he **surrender** several castles, including Chateau Gaillard. When John refuses to attend, King Philip declares him a "contumacious vassal" and **confiscates** all his French lands.

1202 Philip Augustus accepts the homage of **Aquitaine**, **Maine** and **Brittany** from Arthur. They then combine against John: Philip attacks Normandy and Arthur Touraine. Arthur is **captured**, along

[John] was the worst of all our kings: a man whom no oaths could bind, no pressure of conscience, no consideration of policy, restrain from evil; a faithless son, a treacherous brother, an ungrateful master; to his people a hated tyrant. Polluted with every crime that could disgrace a man, false to every obligation that could bind a king, he had lost his inheritance by sloth, and ruined and desolated the rest.

—Bishop **William Stubbs**,
The Constitutional History of England (1874–78)

with Geoffrey de Lusignan and Hugh le Brun, while besieging Eleanor of Aquitaine at **Mirebeau**.

1203 As the Anglo-French war continues, John has Arthur **murdered** at Rouen; his maltreatment of Arthur and other prisoners persuades a number of allies to **desert** him.

Philip Augustus continues his campaigns in Normandy, besieging **Chateau Gaillard**. Contemporary chroniclers criticize John for failing to defend Normandy adequately.

1205 The death of Hubert Walter, the archbishop of Canterbury and John's chancellor, inspires the king to take a more active interest in the administration of England. John prefers to promote members of his own household to high office instead of making appointments from among the nobility. Together with an excessively harsh—not to mention efficient—tax regime, this progressively undermines such baronial support as John has.

1206 John, continuing to defend his possessions in the south of France at the expense of those in the north, mounts an expedition to **Poitou**. To the dismay of some English he begins promoting Poitevins as government officials in England.

John quarrels with **Pope Innocent III** over the choice of a new archbishop to replace Hubert Walter. When the pope's choice **Stephen Langton** is elected at Canterbury in December, John refuses to recognize him.

1208 As John continues to refuse to recognize Stephen Langton, England is placed under a **general interdict** by Innocent III, effectively excommunicating the country's entire population.

Unfortunately for his reputation, John was not a great benefactor to monasteries which kept chronicles.

—**W.L. Warren**, *King John* (1978)

1209 John is **personally excommunicated** by Innocent III. Despite the ignominy of this, John profits by farming the revenues of vacant ecclesiastical appointments.

1212 In the summer John campaigns successfully in **Wales**, and foils a plot to murder him.

In November, anxious to form an alliance against Philip Augustus, he makes up with Innocent III by **acknowledging Langton** as archbishop.

1213 Relations with the papacy are fully restored when John "surrenders" England to a **papal nuncio at Ewell** near Dover in May. The king's excommunication is **revoked**, as is the general interdict against England the following year.

To finance further campaigns in France, John attempts to levy heavy taxes on English knights and other men-at-arms in the form of **scutage** (fees in lieu of military service), but some northern barons refuse to contribute to a war that has nothing to do with them.

1214 Although John enjoys initial successes against Philip Augustus at **Poitou**, his allies **Emperor Otto** and the **earl of Salisbury** are crushed at the climactic **Battle of Bouvines**, as a result of which Normandy is lost to the English Crown.

1215 Returning to England, John finds a majority of barons opposed to him. To buy time, he grants their demands by signing **Magna Carta** (the "Great Charter") at Runnymede on June 19. Almost immediately, however, the king appeals to the pope. Not wishing to be seen to support subjects against kings, Innocent III declares the charter **invalid**. As a result, **civil war** between king and barons breaks out.

1216 Encouraged by some of John's enemies, Philip Augustus's heir, the **dauphin Louis** (later Louis VIII), invades England. Securing a bridgehead in the east, he gains control of London and lays siege to Dover Castle. John wages war against his northern barons and terrorizes the northern counties. Journeying south to confront

Louis, however, he is either taken ill or poisoned, and dies at **Newark** on October 19, having beforehand suffered the indignity of losing the royal baggage train—including the crown jewels— while attempting to cross the Wash. He is buried at Worcester Cathedral, and is succeeded by his eldest son **Henry III**, who is hurriedly crowned at Gloucester Abbey. The 9-year-old king

MAGNA CARTA

auded by 18th-century historians and antiquarians as the cornerstone of the English constitution and a guarantee against monarchical oppression, Magna Carta was in fact a far more limited document.

Much of the charter deals with specific baronial grievances, among them such oddities as who held fishing rights on the River Thames. Mixed in with the ephemera, however, are more inspiring principles— notably the right to trial by jury and that of habeas corpus, whereby imprisonment without charge is deemed unlawful. Such clauses were sufficiently radical to prompt Pope Innocent III, a ruler himself, to declare the charter void. Yet in its intent Magna Carta was restricted to clarifying relations between monarch and lords alone, and only the imprecisions of its drafting allowed it to acquire the semblance of a contract between a king and all his subjects.

Even so, given that England's barons increasingly demonstrated an ability to act collectively (often in opposition to the throne), and that England's kings were frequently required to reaffirm Magna Carta, its libertarian reputation isn't too wide of the mark. While historically its beneficiaries were England's landowning elite, it articulated the bold statement that a king should be subject to the laws he made, and not—as many felt that John had attempted to rule—above them.

immediately sets his seal to **Magna Carta**, as the much-respected **William Marshal**, Earl of Pembroke takes on the responsibilities of regent. Baronial discontent is further defused by the support for Henry III of a papal legate.

1217 Louis is forced to return to France after his supporters are defeated on land at **Lincoln** and at sea off **Dover**.

1218 Judicial circuits ("justices in eyre") are re-established to combat the lawlessness that has increasingly affected the English countryside during King John's reign.

1219 William Marshal dies, commending England to the care of a papal legate and complaining that "there are no people in any land like those of England, where each person has his own opinion."

As Henry III's minority continues, government is delivered by a **royal council** dominated by **Hubert de Burgh**.

1220 Henry III is **re-crowned** at Westminster by the archbishop of Canterbury, signaling a resolution of differences between Crown and Church.

1221 The first Dominican and Franciscan friars arrive in England.

1223 Pope Honorius III declares that Henry III, now aged 16, has **come of age**. But Hubert de Burgh continues as England's effective ruler.

1224 The Crown's previously loyal commander **Fawkes de Breauté** mounts an unsuccessful rebellion.

1225 Magna Carta is again affirmed by Henry III.

1226 A **general eyre** (tour of royal justices), lasting three years, is initiated to investigate unlawful confiscations of land and to attend the clearing of gaols.

1229 The French nobleman **Simon de Montfort** comes to England to make good his claim to the earldom of Leicester.

1231 De Montfort establishes himself as a royal favorite.

1232 Henry III, endeavoring to assert personal rule, replaces Hubert de Burgh with **Peter des Roches** and **Peter of Rievaux**, two ambitious Frenchmen whose promotion irritates England's barons.

1234 Under pressure from his barons, Henry III **dismisses** Peter des Roches and Peter of Rievaux. It is from this year that Henry's **personal rule**, lasting until 1258, is usually dated. Henry III will be remembered as one of England's weaker monarchs, a man eager to play up the symbolic mystery of (pre-Magna Carta) kingship despite—or because of—the political realities. His costly rebuilding of **Westminster Abbey** despite the worsening financial situation is unpopular, and his persistent favoring of officials recruited from France becomes so offensive to England's "native barons" that they will endeavor to impose a form of **constitutional monarchy** in which royal appointments are taken out of the king's hands.

1236 Henry III marries **Eleanor of Provence**.

1237 Baronial disquiet is heightened by Henry III's appointment of his Savoyard relatives to high positions within his administration.

1238 Despite Henry III's sister, **Eleanor Plantagenet**, having taken an oath of chastity (and in the face of baronial opposition), the king arranges for her marriage to Simon de Montfort on January 7.

1239 Protest against de Montfort's elevation continues, now led by Henry III's younger brother, **Richard of Cornwall**. Faced by the threat of revolt, Henry exiles de Montfort and Eleanor.

1240 Richard of Cornwall and Simon de Montfort find themselves fighting side-by-side during a crusade and are reconciled.

1242 Through his Lusignan relatives, Henry III is drawn into a humiliating and costly regional **war** in France in which he displays his lack of military skill; heavily defeated at **Saintes**, the king only escapes capture through de Montfort's intervention. De Montfort is allowed to return to England, where he re-establishes himself at **Kenilworth**, and where he forms friendships with **Robert Grosseteste** (the Bishop of Lincoln) and other progressive figures.

1244 Although de Montfort's loyalty to the Crown is still apparently intact, he is made a member of a "**committee of twelve**" in an attempt to resolve outstanding differences between Henry and his barons.

1248 When rebellion flares in **Gascony** (Henry's last remaining significant possession in France), de Montfort agrees to restore order there in return for being created **regent** for a term of seven years. But so brutally successful is de Montfort in crushing the Gascon revolt that leading Gascons petition Henry III for his removal; as a result, de Montfort is recalled to England to **stand trial**.

1252 De Montfort is **acquitted** by the barons. Almost immediately renewed rebellion in Gascony leads to his **reappointment** as commander of the king's forces in France.

1253 De Montfort returns to England when Henry III terminates his command.

1254 Henry III agrees a pact with **Pope Innocent IV**, offering to finance a papal war in **Sicily** to the tune of 150,000 marks, in return for the Crown of Sicily being bestowed upon Henry's infant younger son **Edmund**.

Henry's eldest son and heir, the 15-year-old **Prince Edward**, is married to **Eleanor of Castile**, the half-sister of **Alfonso X**, and is granted a portmanteau of titles by his father that includes **Gascony**, **Ireland** and the "**Four Cantrefs**" in north Wales.

1255 Prince Edward endeavours to impose his authority on **Wales**, but is swiftly defeated by **Llywelyn ap Gruffydd**.

1258 Pope Alexander IV threatens to **excommunicate** Henry III for failing to provide the Sicilian funds promised in 1254. In desperation Henry turns to his already discontented barons. In May the barons capitalize on this and impose upon the king a 24-member "**parliament**" made up of twelve of his own supporters and twelve of themselves—sometimes called "**the commune**"—led by Simon de Montfort.

In June, in return for the promise of necessary taxes, the king is obliged to accept the radical **Provisions of Oxford**, which greatly limit his powers. England is to be ruled by a 15-member **Privy Council**, part-elected by the "commune" of barons but still led by de Montfort. The Provisions further determine that appointed officials should be made fully **accountable** to the Council, and that henceforward **"parliaments"** (in effect consultative assemblies composed of the great and good) should be held three times a year. Many of Henry III's appointees are dismissed from office and replaced by baronial candidates. As early as November, however, the king's position begins to recover when the Pope's Sicilian project is **abandoned**, releasing him from the need to raise further funds.

SIMON DE MONTFORT (1208–1265)

$\mathcal{S}$imon de Montfort was a charismatic French nobleman who was swift to stamp his seal on English politics in the 1250s. His father, also Simon de Montfort, had achieved fame throughout Christendom as the principal organizer of the Albigensian Crusade that, earlier in the century, had destroyed the Cathars and their Manichean "heresy" in Provence. Through the usual complexities of advantageous marriage contracts, the de Montforts had a legitimate claim to the earldom of Leicester, and it was this that brought the younger Simon to England in 1229. Despite being regarded at first by Henry III's barons as yet another foreign interloper, de Montfort gradually emerged as the leader of their opposition. In 1258 he organized the so-called "commune" of barons that, in the same year, succeeded in imposing the Provisions of Oxford on Henry, formalizing an alternative to autocratic royal rule that for its time was revolutionary. Six years later, following his victory at Lewes, de Montfort established his

1259 Henry's hand is strengthened when a comprehensive treaty with France is concluded at **Paris**. Although **Gascony** is confirmed as the English Crown's only substantial French holding, the treaty reduces the likelihood of Henry having to make further financial requisitions on his English subjects.

At home, divisions appear within the ranks of the barons opposing him. In October the *communitas bacheleriae* (knights bachelor) petition the king and his barons, voicing grievances about the exactions made upon them by their feudal overlords. To placate the knights, the **Provisions of Westminster**—sometimes regarded as cementing the place of the lesser aristocracy within the medieval English system—are issued.

own rule over England. Yet this was never likely to last long. Other barons resented his power, and enough of them supported the campaign of Prince Edward to ensure his downfall, and his death, in 1265.

In his years at the center, well aware that many of the barons were suspicious of his continental background, de Montfort had sought to consolidate his power by appealing to a larger cross-section of English society. Accordingly he invited knights of the shire, then burghers, to attend two "parliaments" convened by him—the earliest template for the modern British parliamentary system. De Montfort's motives, though, were anything but democratic. What he wanted was merely a broad-based consultative body to rubber-stamp policies he had already determined. It was primarily as an instrument of central control that Parliament gradually became a fixture in later medieval England—in much the same way that the Cortes became a fixture in Castile, or the Etats-Generaux in France.

1261 In April the pope declares the Provisions of Oxford **invalid**. As his barons quarrel amongst themselves, Henry III renounces the Provisions and dismisses those officials imposed on him.

1262 Full-scale civil war between king and barons is averted by de Montfort's decision to withdraw from England.

1263 De Montfort returns to England towards the end of the year to lead those barons still determined to get their way with Henry III.

1264 In January Henry III appeals to **Louis IX of France** to resolve his baronial dispute. Louis obliges by issuing the **Mise of Amiens**, affirming Henry's right to appoint his own ministers.

In April de Montfort raises a rebellion, sometimes called the **barons' war**. In May Henry III and Prince Edward are captured at the **Battle of Lewes**, and imprisoned. De Montfort assumes dictatorial powers. In June he convenes an **expanded parliament**, which now includes four knights from each shire—ostensibly to set up a new form of government, but also to broaden his power-base within the realm.

1265 A **second parliament** convened by de Montfort is further expanded to allow wealthy representatives from England's towns and cities to attend. Among the barons, opposition to de Montfort spreads, led by **Gilbert de Clare, Earl of Gloucester.** In May, abetted by these dissidents, Prince Edward escapes captivity in Hereford and at once begins raising a royal army. The greater part of de Montfort's forces are besieged at **Kenilworth**. On August 4 de Montfort himself is defeated and killed at the **Battle of Evesham** by Prince Edward, who becomes *de facto* ruler on behalf of his ailing father.

1266 Prince Edward campaigns successfully against the remaining rebels and **re-establishes** Plantagenet rule. His excessively harsh policies against **London**, provoked by the city's previous alliance with the rebels, are moderated by the **Dictum of Kenilworth**, issued by Henry III.

ROBIN HOOD

*I*n the aftermath of Evesham, a handful of de Montfort's supporters took to the fens and forests of England to continue a guerilla-type resistance to the king. Out of this grew the legend of Robin Hood, an amalgam of medieval outlaw and folk hero who also bears the imprint of other rebel exiles such as Hereward the Wake.

Tales of Sherwood Forest and of Robin's intimates—Maid Marian, Little John, Friar Tuck and the Merry Men—appeared from the 14th century onwards. His first literary reference occurs in a version of William Langland's *Piers Plowman*, while the earliest extant manuscript featuring him, *Robin Hood and the Monk*, dates from around 1450. Some of the orally transmitted ballads in which Robin Hood features go back further, however, and an attempt was made by the 18th-century antiquarian William Stukeley to establish a genealogy identifying Robin with the fictitious 13th-century rebel, Robert, Earl of Huntingdon.

Like all the best folk heroes, Robin has been flexible enough to champion a multiplicity of causes. Sometimes he appears as a loyalist defending "Good King Richard"; elsewhere he stands up for Anglo-Saxon rights against Norman barbarism; by the 16th century he had become incorporated into the Mayday Rite as a personification of fertility. Overall, though, his profile has been relatively consistent—that of an all-purpose thorn in the side of corrupt and dastardly government, usually with the interests of the common man at heart. And, unlike King Arthur, Robin seems to owe little to outside influence—the oak tree reputed to have been the center of his Sherwood camp symbolizes the enduring glamour of "English" justice and fair play.

1267 The Statute of Marlborough, issued by Edward and adopted by a parliament consisting of barons and commoners, confirms the Provisions of Westminster, but not the Provisions of Oxford. The same parliament also confirms the "peace terms" that conclude the War of the Barons, but baulks at some of the taxes requested by Edward so that he can crusade in the Holy Land.

The **Treaty of Shrewsbury** is concluded with Llywelyn ap Gruffydd, effectively acknowledging that the Welsh prince has succeeded in creating an autonomous Welsh principality.

1270 Having raised sufficient funds to crusade, Edward entrusts England's government to four dependable ministers (among them **Robert Burnell**) and his Welsh territories to his brother Edmund.

1272 Henry III, having devoted his final years to rebuilding **Westminster Abbey**, dies on November 16. Although Prince Edward is in Sicily at the time, on November 20 the barons swear **fealty** to him in his absence.

The later Plantagenets
1272–1399

The Plantagenets dramatically demonstrate the advantages and pitfalls of medieval kingship. A militarily capable monarch with a gift for administration could make the system work. But an overweening, militarily unlucky and tactless ruler could provoke civil discord—even civil war. Among the early Plantagenets Henry II proved himself strong; but John and Henry III, albeit in very different ways, demonstrated weakness. Among the later Plantagenets the story has been seen as much the same: two efficient monarchs, Edward I and Edward III; and two disasters, Edward II and Richard II.

Edward I had demonstrated his prowess before he came to the throne by containing Simon de Montfort and ending the **barons' war**. As king he fulfilled his promise, at least for the first twenty years of his reign. Accepting Parliament as a valuable means of generating (and enforcing) consent, he pushed through a far-reaching program of administrative reform bolstering royal power, while at the same time acknowledging that England's merchant community now constituted an important component of his realm. And by defeating **Llywelyn** and successfully subjugating Wales, he reinvigorated the Crown's reputation. Edward I's latter years were less positive, however. An attempt to subjugate Scotland along the same lines was unsuccessful and, if anything, fed Scottish nationalism; while the cost of his campaigns—coupled with the crippling expense of erecting vast castles in Wales—bankrupted the Exchequer and made him hugely unpopular.

It would have taken an astute successor to repair the damage, but his son, the hapless **Edward II**, only added to it. By flaunting his attachment to Piers Gaveston and then adopting the Despensers as replacement favorites, he antagonized his barons to the point of rebellion. Nor, in pursuing his father's policy toward Scotland, was he able to make up for lost ground. A tide of patriotic fervor overran the northern kingdom, and Edward II's inadequacies in battle heralded a dismal failure for the English.

Edward III ascended the throne under the iron control of his mother **Queen Isabella** and her lover **Roger Mortimer**. Within three years, though, the young king had shaken off their influence and assumed power in his own right. Whereas his grandfather had limited his ambition to dominating Britain, the new king—on the pretext of a claim to the French throne via his mother—resumed the family's continental aspirations. Once again English armies crossed the English Channel, at first with astonishing success: in the opening phase of the so-called **Hundred Years War**, Edward III and his son (another Edward, known as the Black Prince) scored devastating victories at **Sluys**, **Crécy** and **Poitiers**.

Almost the whole of France was theirs for the taking. But the French fought back, plague undermined England's economy, and by the end of Edward III's reign there was nothing to show for his campaigns other than the possession of four French towns. Once again the Crown was bankrupt and the country uneasy. At its zenith, Edward III's court—festooned with rituals partly derived from the myth of King Arthur—may have been the envy of Europe, but pomp and pageantry cost money.

Nor did things get easier. **Richard II**, besotted with unrealistic ideas about the grandeur of the Crown, lacked the realism or the political insight to retrench. Although 1381 saw him face down an uprising known as the **Peasants' Revolt** with a courage that won him support at the time, he was unable to deal with the complaints of his nobility. It was a failing that eventually cost him the throne—and which ignited a dynastic dispute that would plunge the country into civil war and last the best part of a century.

1272 At the time of his accession **Edward I** is virtually stranded abroad, and is able to return home only with the aid of a substantial loan advanced by the Italian bankers, the **Ricciardi of Lucca**. During his absence, **rebellion** flares in the northern counties. During his reign, however, Edward will provide the kind of military leadership—evidenced particularly by his subjugation of **Wales**—needed to maintain the authoritarian style of kingship favored by the Plantagenets.

1274 Edward lands in England, and is **crowned** at Westminster on August 19. Clearing the kingdom of rebels, he orders an investigation into the state of government locally, with a view to reclaiming royal lands usurped during his father's reign.

1275 Edward I begins issuing a series of **statutes** that over the coming fifteen years will counterbalance England's **common law**, usually to the advantage of the throne.

Edward's queen, **Eleanor of Castile**, ejects **Jews** from her English estates.

1277 Determined to avenge himself on **Llywelyn ap Gruffydd** for his youthful humiliation, and supported by his marcher lords, Edward stages a major invasion of **Wales** by land and sea. Llywelyn, holed up in the mountains of Snowdonia, is forced to concede the **Treaty of Conway**, which confiscates territorial gains made since 1247, and makes him a vassal of the English Crown. In the wake of his victory, Edward begins imposing an English **administration** on Wales, now divided up into shires and counties for the first time. He also embarks on a program of **castle-building** in north Wales to contain any further rebellion.

1278 Edward issues the **Statutes of Gloucester**, establishing the principle of *quo warranto*, by which royal feudal tenants are asked "by what warrant" they hold their franchises. Those unable to prove their entitlement are dispossessed or obliged to pay compensation to the Crown.

1279 The **Statute of Mortmain** prohibits future gifts of land to the Church without royal approval.

1282 Llywelyn ap Gruffydd, having refused to pay Edward homage, joins a **revolt** against English rule led by his brother **Dafydd**. Known

But the chief advantage which the people of England reaped, and still continue to reap, from the reign of this great prince, was the correction, extension, amendment, and establishment of the laws, which Edward maintained in great vigour, and left much improved to posterity; for the acts of a wise legislator commonly remain, while the acquisitions of a conqueror often perish with him. This merit has justly gained to Edward the appellation of the English Justinian.

—David Hume on Edward I,
in the *History of Great Britain* (1761)

CASTLE-BUILDING

*T*he years of unrest under King Stephen had seen a prolif-
eration of baronial castles in England, but by the beginning of the 13th century the increasing sophistication of
siege warfare meant that only the king and a handful of magnates
could afford the sort of massive structures now required for defense.
Simon de Montfort invested huge sums in his modifications to
Kenilworth Castle, enabling his supporters to hold out within its
walls for a year after the Battle of Evesham. And Henry III dedicated
equally vast resources to the development of Dover Castle following
its lengthy—though abortive—siege by the dauphin Louis between
1216 and 1217.

Much of the new castle technology derived from the Holy Land,
where the crusaders had experienced sustained assault by Islamic
armies; aptly, it was on the way back from Palestine that Edward I met
the Savoyard engineer known as Master James of St George whom he
entrusted with his castle-building program in Wales. Their partner-
ship enabled a number of imposing fortresses that dominate the
Welsh landscape to this day. At Caernarfon, the walls of
Constantinople were deliberately evoked by the construction of
polygonal towers surmounted by imperial eagles—a fitting assertion
of Edward's desire for conquest. Technically, though, the most impressive of his castles is Beaumaris on the island of Anglesey, innovatively designed as a series of interlocking concentric circles with hardly a
straight line in sight. But Beaumaris was the last of the Edwardine
constructions, and it remained unfinished. Edward's lavish building
spree had long since emptied the royal coffers.

as the "last prince of Wales," he is killed in an ambush at **Irfon Bridge**. His head is sent to London as proof of his death.

1283 The Edwardine conquest of Wales is completed when Llywelyn's brother Dafydd is **hung, drawn and quartered** at **Shrewsbury**—a symbolically brutal punishment invented specifically for him. But the huge cost of Edward's Welsh wars is such that the Crown falls further into **debt** with its Italian bankers.

1284 The **Statute of Wales** formalizes the new administration installed by Edward in Wales. As a sop to Welsh pride, Edward I gives his newborn son and heir, **Edward**, the title **earl of Caernarvon**, claiming that the infant "speaks no other tongue" than Welsh. In future, male heirs to the English throne will be known as the **Prince of Wales**, although not all are ceremonially invested as such.

1285 The **Statute of Winchester** regulates England's law-enforcement system by declaring that counties will be held responsible for unsolved crimes and ordering highways to be widened and made safer.

1286 Edward I pays Philip IV of France homage for **Gascony** and other minor continental possessions, but Philip begins supporting local unrest that erodes some of the lands.

In **Scotland**, Alexander III dies, leaving **Margaret** (known as the "Maid of Norway") as his only direct heir.

1289 Advised by **Robert Burnell**, Edward purges his government of corrupt and inefficient officials.

1290 Eleanor of Castile dies, depriving Edward III not only of his queen but a trusted adviser. Distraught by her death, the king orders the construction of **stone crosses** at each resting place along the route of her cortege. Perhaps also in her honor, and to the satisfaction of his other subjects, he expels all **Jews** from England.

The death of **Margaret of Scotland** leaves the Scottish throne without an heir.

In **Gascony**, French interference intensifies.

1291 By invitation of the Bishop of St Andrews, Edward presides over a "Scottish parliament" convened at **Norham** to decide between thirteen candidates for the Scottish throne. Eventually Edward recognizes **John Balliol**, in preference to **Robert Bruce** (known as "the Competitor") as king on condition that Balliol toes the line and recognizes Edward's overlordship.

1292 **Robert Burnell**, Edward's long-serving chancellor, dies. The ministers who follow are of lesser caliber, and unable to dissuade Edward—already financially hard-pressed—from pursuing the fruitless and costly policies of his later reign.

In December, John Balliol is crowned **king of Scotland**.

1293 By clever negotiation Philip IV dupes Edward's brother **Edmund**, sent to France to conduct negotiations, into surrendering **Gascony**. Preoccupied with **Scotland**, where he is determined to implant an English administration similar to that imposed on Wales, the English king fails to respond immediately.

1294 An attempted uprising in Wales is ruthlessly put down by Edward's forces.

1295 Under increasing pressure to adopt English institutions and with the backing of France, John Balliol **renounces** his allegiance to Edward I.

The English king convenes the **Model Parliament**, so called because the writs of attendance offer a clear statement of "**representation**"—a term that will become a keyword of parliamentary democracy.

1296 Determined to assert his control, Edward I invades and conquers Scotland. **Berwick** is sacked, a Scottish army is defeated by Earl Warenne at **Dunbar**, and John Balliol is forced to undergo ritual humiliation. Edward thanks Warenne with the words: "A man who gets rid of a turd does a good job." The **Stone of Scone**, used during the Scottish coronation ceremony, is removed to Westminster—it will stay there until 1996.

1297 Edward I assembles a task force to recover **Gascony** from Philip IV, but his English barons refuse to support him. In part they are motivated by a renewed outbreak of tension between Crown and Church; to raise money for his wars Edward imposes taxes on the clergy, but the clergy are instructed by **Pope Boniface VIII** not to pay and consequently Edward outlaws them all. Notwithstanding these difficulties, Edward sails for **Flanders**. During his absence the barons collectively confirm existing "**charters**" upholding their rights, and add the proviso that "arbitrary taxation" should not be allowed.

Rebellions break out in Scotland led by **Robert Bruce** (later Robert I) and by two charismatic knights, **Andrew Moray** and **William Wallace**, who defeat Warenne at Stirling Bridge. Edward returns home swiftly to tackle the new threat.

1298 Although Edward scores a significant victory over Wallace's forces at **Falkirk** on July 22, resistance to English rule continues.

1299 Anglo-French differences are resolved by peace terms agreed between Edward and Philip IV. A diminished **Gascony** is returned to Edward, who agrees to marry Philip's sister **Margaret**. It is also proposed that **Edward of Caernarfon** marry Philip's daughter **Isabella**.

1304 In Scotland, Edward captures **Stirling Castle**. A majority of Scottish leaders come to terms with him.

1305 Edward's Scottish campaigns are seemingly crowned with success when **William Wallace** is captured, then hung, drawn and quartered.

1306 Pope Clement V, more favorably disposed toward Edward than his predecessor, allows the English king to exile **Robert Winchelsey**, the troublesome archbishop of Canterbury.

In Scotland Edward's victories fall apart when **Robert Bruce** is proclaimed king.

1307 On his way to another Scottish campaign, Edward I dies at **Burghly Sands** near Carlisle. Amid lingering tensions with the barons, he is succeeded by the Prince of Wales. But although **Edward II** attempts to placate his father's enemies by appointing some of them to high office, he earns their contempt by making his favorite, **Piers Gaveston**, earl of Cornwall. Nor is his position helped by severely depleted royal coffers.

1308 Edward II marries **Isabella**, daughter of Philip IV of France. Early fears about Edward's suitability are reflected in a new clause added to his coronation oath compelling him to uphold the "rightful

ROGER BACON (C.1214–92)

*N*icknamed "Doctor Mirabilis," teacher of wonders, **Roger Bacon** secured a reputation as the foremost scientific investigator of his day. Born in either Gloucestershire or Somerset, after studying at Oxford his formal education was completed in **Paris**. In 1247 he returned to England and, inspired by the natural philosophy of **Aristotle**, set about using his family's considerable wealth to establish a private research institute. His aim, largely achieved, was to acquire a complete knowledge of every aspect of "science," stressing the need for experimental procedures. Although his own experiments were relatively limited, he carried out work in optics that almost certainly led to the invention of spectacles, and it seems likely that he understood the principles of the telescope. He also outlined more ambitious goals—predicting both mechanized flight and submarine travel.

After he joined the Franciscans in 1257, however, he began to confront serious obstacles. While Bacon believed that studying physical phenomena could only enhance human understanding of the divine, his superiors took a

laws and customs which the community of the realm shall have chosen." Rumors soon begin to circulate that Edward is more fond of Gaveston than of his 12-year-old bride, and Edward is forced to send his favorite into exile.

1309 Edward dismays his barons by allowing Gaveston to return, where he is again showered with honors.

1310 Edward undertakes his first major campaign in **Scotland**. It is a disaster and he is forced to agree to the appointment of 24 **Ordainers** to look into the question of reform of government

different view. Back in Paris, he was imprisoned for ten years, but managed to appeal secretly to the sympathetic **Pope Clement IV**. Clement responded by asking Bacon for a summary of his researches, out of which came the three books that established his reputation: *Opus Majus*, *Opus Minus* and *Opus Tertium* (the "Greater," "Lesser" and "Third" Works). But no sooner were these completed than the pope died. Deprived of protection, Bacon—who was never reluctant to criticize his fellow scholars and religious authority—was again confined, and he remained imprisoned until shortly before his death. Although never condemned as a heretic, he was strongly suspected of necromancy and his name became something of a byword for magic.

In the larger view, he was a prodigious man whose passion for manuscripts helped the spread of scientific knowledge from Islamic countries (where Greek learning had been preserved) and, via those, from China—Bacon is credited with being the first European to give a precise recipe for **gunpowder**, a Chinese invention.

1311 Four years into his reign, Edward II is forced to give way to his barons. Edward concedes their terms, which severely limit his powers, and agrees to **exile Gaveston**. By the end of the year, though, Gaveston is back at Edward's court.

1312 Besieged in his castle at **Scarborough**, Gaveston surrenders to the earl of Pembroke. Despite being offered safe passage, he is recaptured by the earl of Warwick, who hands him over to the earls of Lancaster, Arundel and Hereford, by whom he is brutally murdered. While suspicion of foul play encourages some barons to remain loyal to the king, opposition to Edward centers on his cousin, **Thomas of Lancaster**. Crucially, Queen Isabella and the king of France side with Edward—for the while.

1314 In an attempt to demonstrate military prowess, Edward II personally leads an army to crush Robert Bruce, but on June 24 is humiliated at **Bannockburn**, a battle that secures Scotland's independence.

1315 Effective government passes into the hands of **Thomas of Lancaster**.

In the country at large, a two-year **famine** begins.

1318 Thomas of Lancaster having failed to provide good government, **Aymer de Valence**, **Earl of Pembroke**, brokers a "truce" between Edward II and some of the barons, enabling Edward to resume his rule.

The **Treaty of Leake** is agreed between Lancaster and Edward, allowing for a permanent council of seventeen members. The king swiftly regains unpopularity when he adopts a father and son, both called **Hugh Despenser**, as his favorites.

1321 Thomas of Lancaster, a great enemy of the Despensers, takes up arms against the king, plunging England into a fitful **civil war**.

1322 Edward II captures Thomas of Lancaster at **Boroughbridge** in Yorkshire and orders his beheading.

1324 The death of the **earl of Pembroke**, "murdered suddenly on a privy seat," enables Edward II to centralize power within his Despenser clique.

Edward sends **Queen Isabella** as an emissary to **Charles IV** of France with Prince Edward. It is a crucial mistake. Angered by her husband's continuing favoritism for the Despensers, Isabella begins plotting with the banished baron **Roger Mortimer**, and begins an affair with him. Custody of the young heir strengthens their hand.

1326 With the support of the French Crown, Queen Isabella and Mortimer **invade** England, rapidly winning the allegiance of Edward's disaffected barons. Hugh Despenser the elder is captured and executed; the younger Despenser, also captured, is emasculated before being killed.

1327 In January, as the king's position becomes untenable, Edward II is deposed in favor of **Edward III**, his 15-year- old son by Isabella. Imprisoned, the ex-king is put to death in September at **Berkeley Castle**. As the new king is a minor, effective rule is supplied by Isabella and Mortimer.

1328 On January 24 Edward III is married to **Philippa**, daughter of the count of Holland and Hainaut. In the same year the **Treaty of Northampton**, concluded between the two crowns, affirms Scotland's independence from England.

1329 Robert I the Bruce of Scotland is succeeded by the young **David II**; the English Crown conspires with dissident Scottish lords to replace him with **Edward Balliol**. David flees to **France** where his faction gains the support of the French Crown.

1330 Edward III assumes **personal rule** by overthrowing the government of his mother Isabella and Mortimer. While Isabella is "retired" to her estates, Mortimer is tried before the lords in Parliament and executed in November. Edward III's reign will be noted for a series of stunning but finally unproductive victories in **France** and also for the lavishness of his court, which for a while becomes the most glittering in Europe. He is routinely faced by bankruptcy as a consequence, and the end of his reign is marked by a steep decline. At **Woodstock**, Queen Philippa gives birth to Edward's eldest son and heir, also named Edward, but later known as the **Black Prince**—supposedly because of the color of the armor he would choose to wear.

1333 An English victory over a Scottish force at **Halidon Hill** seemingly ensures Edward Balliol's tenure of the Scottish throne.

1337 As relations between the English and French thrones deteriorate and Philip VI "confiscates" Gascony, Edward III leads an

TRADE AND FOREIGN COMMUNITIES

*D*uring the 12th and 13th centuries—and up until the Black Death of the late 1340s—Europe experienced sustained economic growth, marked by the development of great port cities such as **Venice, Genoa, Barcelona, Seville** and **Antwerp**. With their growth came sweeping social changes. Merchants, who had been on the fringes of society, gravitated toward its center. England benefited from a thriving wool trade with the Low Countries, and London in particular—comfortably straddling the navigable Thames—emerged as an important center, one populated by an assortment of foreign communities. French and Flemish merchants were joined by Jewish and Italian businessmen, the latter encouraged especially by Edward I's dependence on Italian bankers to finance his costly castle-building in Wales and campaigns in Scotland. First he relied on the **Ricciardi**, and then (after they had been forced out business by Philip IV of France in 1294) the **Frescobaldi** of Florence, accumulating debts that topped £200,000 by the time of his

expeditionary force across the Channel, initiating a century-long but intermittent conflict known as the **Hundred Years War**. Edward's pretext for going to war is his claim, through his mother, to the French Crown itself. Other points of contention include Edward's persistent unwillingness to pay homage to Philip VI of France for his French possessions; French support for rebellious elements in the same possessions; Philip VI's support for David II of Scotland; and French aggression toward the Flemings, England's partners in the well-developed cross-Channel wool trade. Edward's opening campaign is cut short, however, when the king runs out of money.

death. Edward I was also the first English king to provide a legal framework for merchants operating in London and other trade centers such as Bristol and Norwich. This, the **Statute of Acton Burnell**, established debtors' prisons for those with trade as well as other debts, while the *Carta Mercatoria* (Merchants' Charter) of 1303 granted foreign merchants the right to trade freely in England on condition they paid supplementary dues to the Crown. As a result of such measures London became increasingly cosmopolitan—as evidenced by names such as Lombard Street in the heart of today's City district.

Yet not all foreign communities profited from Edward's open-door policies. Jews were excluded from an early Statute of Merchants, and then in 1290 they were given three months to get out of England altogether; despite being guaranteed safe passage, many were attacked and robbed en route. Jewish communities were not permitted to return to the country until Cromwell's reign, some three hundred and fifty years later.

The first "English" **dukedom** is bestowed upon Prince Edward, now styled **duke of Gloucester**.

1339 A second invasion of France again falters as Edward runs out of money.

1340 Mounting his third campaign against France, Edward III annihilates the French fleet off the Flemish city of **Sluys** (Sluis). But he lacks the funds to follow up this victory.

1341 **David II**, now adult, is restored to the Scottish throne after Edward Balliol is deposed by Scottish barons resentful of his willingness to subordinate himself to Edward III.

THE HUNDRED YEARS WAR

*T*he Norman Conquest and Henry II's accession to the English throne brought with it large tracts of French land, but at a time when the French Crown was trying to stabilize its boundaries. The problems were obvious: should the kings of England pay homage to the French monarchy for these continental territories? could the kings of France tolerate such powerful neighbors in even closer proximity? The situation was further complicated by the fact that the two royal houses were closely linked by marriage: it was only a matter of time before one throne would attempt to resolve matters by laying claim to the other.

This happened initially at the beginning of Henry III's reign, when the dauphin Louis attempted an invasion of England. And it occurred again in 1337 when Edward III decided to retaliate against Philip IV's seizure of Gascony. The immediate pretext for Philip's action was that Edward had offered shelter to the exiled **Robert of Artois**; Robert reputedly taunted Edward into claiming his inheritance by placing a heron (symbolizing cowardice) in front of the king at a banquet. So began what became known as

As Edward requests money from his subjects, Parliament is able to win important **concessions**—including the right to approve royal appointments and audit royal accounts.

1342 Edward III begins rebuilding **Windsor Castle** and, to foster martial and chivalric pride among England's knights, creates the **Order of the Garter**.

1343 Prince Edward is proclaimed **prince of Wales**.

1346 After a six-year lull in hostilities, in July Edward III lands in **Normandy** with an army and marches on **Paris**. Yet again running

the Hundred Years War, a term which only became current in the 1860s but which has been almost universally accepted since.

In its initial phase the French were stunned by a series of improbable victories—Edward III at Crécy in 1346, his son the Black Prince at Poitiers ten years later—which gave the English a reputation for invincibility. Yet by the end of Edward's reign his possessions in France had shrunk to a handful of towns. After years of indecisive wrangling Henry V launched the war's second main phase, triumphing at Agincourt in 1415 and briefly ruling the whole of France. As before, though, the French fought back. Inspired by Jeanne d'Arc (who led the army that liberated Orléans in 1429), they finally drove the English across the Channel in 1453. And despite attempts by Henry VIII to rekindle the conflict—with little success—the two kingdoms have remained separate ever since. For all that, it took the English monarchy over five hundred years to admit defeat: English kings called themselves "king of France" until 1802.

short of funds, he withdraws toward the northeast. When Philip VI attempts to intercept his retreat, Edward comprehensively defeats the French army at **Crécy** in Ponthieu on August 26. Integral to Edward's shock victory is his deployment of infantry armed with the **longbow**, of greater range and penetration than the conventional crossbow. In the same battle the youthful **Black Prince** gains his spurs, and adopts the crest and motto—an ostrich plume (four white feathers) and *Ich dien* ("I serve")—of the king of Bohemia. Encouraged by his success, in September Edward III lays siege to **Calais**, a main port on France's northern coast opposite Dover. In October David II, attempting to defend his Scottish throne, is defeated by an English army at **Neville's Cross**.

1347 Calais surrenders to Edward III in August, and will remain in English hands until 1558. Intending to make it a base for future campaigns, Edward expels its French inhabitants.

In September, however, insolvency forces him to come to terms with Philip VI. Nevertheless, on his return to England the king celebrates his victories in style.

In this season the king of Englande toke pleasure to newe reedefy the castell of Wyndsore, the which was begonne by King Arthure. And there first beganne the table rounde, whereby sprange the fame of so many noble knyghtes throughout all the worlde. Then Kynge Edwarde determyned to make an order and a brotherhood of a certayne nombre of knyghtes, and to be called knyghtes of the blue garter: and a feest to be kept yerely at Wynsore on saynt Georges day.

—Jean Froissart, *Chroniques*,
trans. John Bourchier (1525)

c.1348 Edward III, to foster martial and chivalric pride among England's knights, creates the **Order of the Garter**.

1348 Edward III is offered the **Holy Roman Empire**, but declines.

Bubonic plague, known as the **Black Death**, reaches the British Isles having already ravaged much of Europe; over the coming year between a quarter and a third of England's population will die. The plague discourages any immediate resumption of the war against France, and creates an economic downturn the effects of which last a century and beyond.

1349 **William of Occam** (b. 1285), the leading thinker of the **nominalist** school of philosophy opposed to the "realist" orthodoxy of Scholasticism, dies, perhaps of the plague. While his determined advocacy of logic and logical procedures at the expense of metaphysical speculation will earn the respect of 20th-century linguistic philosophers in particular, he is best known for **Occam's Razor**, a general injunction to avoid unnecessary complexity in philosophical argument.

1351 The **Statute of Laborers** attempts to fix wages and prices in the wake of the plague, but—in common with the rest of western Europe—market forces prevail. The **Statute of Provisors** restricts the access of foreign clergy to English clerical appointments.

1353 The **Statute of Praemunire** offers further protection for the English Church against papal interference in the matter of appointments.

1355 Edward III resumes his **campaigns** against the French, but with little immediate success. In France, the Black Prince is given an **independent command** for the first time.

1356 In January and February Edward III harries southern Scotland in a campaign known as the **Burned Candlemas**. Edward Balliol, having been persuaded by his followers to renounce Edward's overlordship, is forced to **surrender** Scotland to the English Crown.

THE BLACK DEATH (1348–49)

*A*n epidemic of the bubonic form of plague (*pasteurella pestis*) annihilated a huge portion of England's population in the space of just a few months between 1348 and 1349. The disease is thought to have originated in the Mongolian steppes, before being brought to Europe by transcontinental traders and spread by flea-infested rats. The "Great Mortality," as the Black Death was also known, first appeared at Melcombe Regis (now Weymouth in Dorset) in July 1348 and crept northeast across the country at a rate of about one-and-a-half miles per day. It devastated huge swathes of land, creating ghost villages with hardly anyone left alive. Newcastle, already weakened by continual attack from Scotland, faced financial ruin; other towns had so few working men that they were unable to pay taxes; the village of Ashwell in Hertfordshire has a moving year-entry scrawled onto the church wall which describes 1350 as "Miserable, wild, distracted. The dregs of the people alone survive to witness."

While prices fell steeply in the immediate aftermath, a shortage of labor meant that working men could demand higher wages, so in the long term the Black Death arguably contributed to England's prosperity. Those who did survive were able to take advantage of changed circumstances and so improve their social standing. Relations between lord and tenant also became more sophisticated, with cash becoming more widely offered instead of feudal services. Such arrangements, known as bastard feudalism, had existed before the plague, but in its wake they became widespread, fuelling the 15th-century Wars of the Roses. Though 1348 would never be forgotten, it would be remembered for a variety of reasons—a century later, the country was a place where "Everyman" could create his own chances.

The **Black Prince** campaigns in France, meanwhile, and on September 19 triumphs at **Poitiers**, where the longbow again proves decisive. In the company of many leading French nobles, **John II of France** is captured and sent to London.

1359 Having been royally entertained in captivity, John II concedes the **Treaty of London**, granting considerable French territories to Edward III. John is released on payment of a ransom of 1,500,000 gold crowns. In October Edward lands in France to enforce the terms of the treaty, but fails in his siege of **Reims**.

1360 Unable to make military headway, Edward III agrees by the **Treaty of Calais** to renounce his claim to the French throne in exchange for title to the whole of **Aquitaine**. Calais is also retained as an English possession.

1361 A fresh outbreak of **plague** ravages England.

In October the **Black Prince** marries **Joan**, the widowed countess of Kent—a union uncharacteristically based on love, not dynastic policy.

Jean Froissart joins the court of Edward III. Froissart, a cultivated Flanders scholar, will gain celebrity for his *Chroniques*, a stupendously detailed series of chronicles depicting contemporary events, most notably those of the Hundred Years War (though with a bias towards chivalry and courtly behavior which is rather unrepresentative).

1362 Edward the Black Prince is granted the title of **prince of Aquitaine** by his father, and becomes ruler of the French territory for ten years.

A self-generated act of parliament, widely ignored by lawyers, decrees that **English**, not French, should be the language used in law courts. Parliamentary statutes and increasingly other official documents begin to be written in the native tongue.

1363 The Black Prince establishes his own court at **Bordeaux**. Like his father's it quickly earns a reputation for extravagance and the practice of chivalric manners. As a ruler, however, the Black Prince is less popular—an often-absent landlord who is notoriously oppressive of his French subjects.

1366 Edward III formally repudiates the papacy's **feudal overlordship** of England, originally proclaimed during the reign of King John.

1368 The Black Prince's subjects in **Aquitaine** are unhappy with his harsh rule and appeal to John II's successor, **Charles V of France**, who summons Prince Edward to Paris. The Black Prince ripostes that he will indeed come, but only with 60,000 men at his back. Charles repudiates the **Treaty of Calais** and dispatches troops to Aquitaine.

KING ARTHUR

*K*ing Arthur owes far more to the so-called "Age of Chivalry" than he does to the "Dark Ages"; in fact, it's during the early Middle Ages that he can really be said to arrive on the cultural scene. Historically he may have been one of several British chieftains who took advantage of Rome's withdrawal in the 5th and 6th centuries, but other than a few nebulous references in early Welsh writings there is no hard evidence of his existence. But following the discovery of his alleged remains by the monks of Glastonbury in 1191 he quickly became an icon whose fairytale court mirrored the ideals of royal government—not just in England but on the continent too.

In his verse romances, the French poet Chrétien de Troyes (fl. 1160–1191) knitted Arthur into a world of *gentilesse* (noble behavior) and introduced French elements into the legend, among them Sir Lancelot and the quest for the Holy Grail. Sir Thomas Malory (d.1471), whose *Le Morte Darthur* is a glorious example of late medieval English prose, lends the Arthurian material fresh intrigue by introducing his

Edward III's third son, **John of Gaunt**, the **duke of Lancaster**, campaigns in France.

The king's second son, **Lionel, Duke of Clarence**, dies.

1369 Supported by Charles V, Aquitaine **revolts** against the Black Prince. Relying upon mercenaries he can barely afford, the prince appals the French by the brutality of his assault upon **Limoges** in October.

Following the death of **Queen Philippa**, Edward III takes a mistress, the commoner **Alice Perrers**.

own tempestuous career into the tale—claiming to write while in Newgate prison.

Inevitably, given the excitement aroused among the readers of such retellings (and the evidence suggests that Arthurian legends were hugely popular at court), Arthur emerged as a significant **political symbol**. England's Norman-French rulers, anxious to legitimize their kingship, were keen to adapt pre-Conquest legends to their own ends, encouraging stories that reworked the material within a continental tradition—and in the process changing them profoundly.

With Arthur, the Plantagenets certainly did both. While Glastonbury became a symbol of his revival, it suited the English throne that Wales's sometime (and theoretically future) king should be demonstrably dead. Meanwhile the mystical rituals and accoutrements of Arthur's court, including the Round Table, were incorporated into the living court—most notably by **Edward III** at **Windsor**. Yet the Celtic Arthur has the last laugh. The final royal house to invoke King Arthur were the **Tudors**, the "Welsh" usurpers who finally ended the long line of Anglo-Norman monarchs.

Plague again ravishes England; although it recurs at regular intervals, each epidemic is less severe than its predecessor.

c.1370 The poet **William Langland** completes the first of three versions of *Piers Plowman*, a visionary religious allegory and a masterpiece of Middle English.

1371 Having lost Aquitaine and other possessions, the Black Prince **returns** to England, perhaps suffering from dropsy.

John of Gaunt marries **Constance of Castile**, his second wife.

JOHN WYCLIF (C.1330–84)

*J*ohn Wyclif—reformer, theologian and philosopher—was educated at Oxford, and became rector of Lutterworth, a parish just outside the city, in 1374. He cultivated a reputation as an outspoken troublemaker, arguing that the Church had fallen into sin by accumulating excessive wealth, and that only by returning to poverty could it recover moral authority. John of Gaunt was quick to spot the political potential of Wyclif's criticisms, encouraging his attacks on papal authority and providing protection when the pope condemned him in 1377. But Wyclif had different ambitions too: he resolved to translate the Bible into English, founded an order of Poor Preachers to preach the Gospel in a way ordinary people could understand, and his adherents, the Lollards, continued to agitate for reform after his death. Wyclif was no paragon, though—it was only in his last years that he spent time in his parish, and as a practical reformer he was too heavy-handed to bring about real change.

1372 Claiming he no longer has the funds to continue fighting, the Black Prince "**surrenders**" Aquitaine back to his father. In reality Aquitaine is already lost to the French.

1374 At loggerheads with his brother Prince Edward, **John of Gaunt** uses Alice Perrers to ingratiate himself with Edward III. As the king's faculties decline, Gaunt becomes England's *de facto* ruler. His harsh government inspires dissent among lords and commoners alike.

It was as a theologian that he made the greatest impact. His major work, the *Summa de Ente*, contains a sustained critique of transubstantiation the doctrine that the bread and wine of holy communion actually become the body and blood of Christ. Wyclif never denied the "Real Presence" (the idea that Christ is present at the Eucharist) but he did reject the Church's teaching that the host was literally transformed. Such tenets were deeply heretical, and seen as undermining a society in which priests operated as intermediaries between humans and God. Wyclif grew too radical for many, and was eventually dropped by Oxford and the court after he glaringly failed to condemn the 1381 Peasants' Revolt.

Yet Lollardism never quite died, despite its suppression under Henry IV, and its tenacity in certain areas of the country has led some to argue that it contributed to the ease with which the Reformation was accepted in England in the 16th century. As for Wyclif himself, he was fortunate to die before the full impact of his theology became widely understood. Once it was, he was immediately condemned, and his remains exhumed and burnt in 1428.

1375 Anglo-French fighting temporarily ceases when a **truce** is agreed between Edward III and Charles V. Only **Calais**, **Bordeaux**, **Bayonne** and **Brest** are left in English hands.

About this time *Sir Gawain and the Green Knight* is composed, a highly stylized Arthurian fantasy written by an unknown author in a northwestern dialect.

1376 Early in the year the **Good Parliament** seeks to redress various grievances against Edward III and John of Gaunt. In the Commons, opposition to the Crown is led by **Peter de la Mare**. Alice Perrers is **removed** from court, and **impeachment proceedings** are instigated against Gaunt's followers and corrupt officials. In a new departure, the Commons acts as prosecution, presenting their indictments to the Lords as judges. The death of the **Black Prince** on June 8 spares Gaunt further embarrassment, however, as it is acknowledged that of Edward III's surviving sons he is best suited to govern.

1377 In return for Gaunt agreeing to acknowledge the Black Prince's son **Richard of Bordeaux** heir to the throne, Parliament **rescinds** its legislation of the previous year. **Edward III** dies at Richmond, and Richard is proclaimed king. Ten-year-old **Richard II** inherits a difficult situation: continuing tensions with France; a self-assertive, even subversive nobility; a depleted treasury; and general economic stagnation, stimulating unrest across the country. The early years of his government effectively stay in the hands of his bullying but experienced uncle John of Gaunt.

1380 The rector of Lutterworth, **John Wyclif** already in the public eye on account of his criticisms of ecclesiastical corruption and the Church's temporal ambitions—begins translating the **Bible** into a robust English designed to appeal to those with little education. He founds an order of **Poor Preachers** to disseminate his radical understanding of the scriptures, but it is a group of his followers, known as the **Lollards**, who will be better remembered for propagating his ideas.

Geoffrey Chaucer

1381 Against a background of economic hardship, Gaunt's attempts to apply the **Statute of Laborers** (1351) and to introduce a **poll tax** (levied on each head of the population) leads to a popular uprising known as the **Peasants' Revolt**. Peasants, members of the urban poor and artisans join forces to threaten the existing social order, primarily in the southeast but also in other areas of the country. The revolt is also colored by an **anti–clericalism** derived from the teachings of John Wyclif, and captured in the uprising's celebrated slogan: "When Adam delved and Eve span,/Who was then the gentleman?." The revolt begins in May in Essex. In June, led by **Wat Tyler**, the

GEOFFREY CHAUCER (C.1343–1400)

*H*ad he never written a single one of *The Canterbury Tales*' 17,000 lines, Geoffrey Chaucer would still enjoy a reputation as the most celebrated poet of his time. Partly this is to do with the accessibility of his language, which is relatively close to modern English—certainly closer than that used in a poem such as *Sir Gawain and the Green Knight*, whose gritty northwestern dialect is much harder to crack. Partly, too, it is a matter of national pride: generations of critics (beginning with poets such as Thomas Hoccleve and John Lydgate, a generation younger than Chaucer) have lauded him as the founder of a distinctively English poetic tradition.

But it is impossible to deny the range of his work, or the energy it must have taken to write so much while maintaining a successful career as a courtier and official. Chaucer was a busy man: as well as composing numerous poems including the *Book of the Duchess* (c.1370) and *Troilus and Criseyde* (c.1385), he translated the 6th-century philosopher Boethius and even found time to write a treatise on the astrolabe. Life was certainly

men of Essex and Kent march toward London. On June 13 the Kentishmen enter **London**, massacre Flemish merchants and destroy John of Gaunt's **Savoy Palace**. A day later, Richard II "courageously" meets the Essexmen at **Mile End** outside London, and persuades them to disband by promising reforms—including an end to enforced feudal labor, the provision of affordable land and a free market as regards wages and fees. On the same day the Kentishmen seize the **Tower of London** and murder the perceived architects of the poll tax—the chancellor and archbishop of Canterbury Simon of Sudbury, and the treasurer Sir Robert Hales. The following day

made easier by John of Gaunt's patronage (he was married to one of the duke's sisters-in-law), and Chaucer was fortunate—or well-connected—enough to have been the recipient of a number of prestigious appointments, including being MP for Kent and clerk of the king's works to Richard II.

He is most well-remembered, though, for the huge verse-cycle, *The Canterbury Tales*, which he started in around 1372 and left unfinished at his death. If its premise is simple—29 pilgrims heading to the shrine of St Thomas Becket at Canterbury meet at the Tabard Inn in Southwark and agree to tell each other tales on the way—its execution is virtuosic. Chaucer's various pilgrims and their varied stories permit the poet to show off an extraordinary range of subject matter and verse style. He mingles tragedy, comedy, tragicomedy, allegory, fable, philosophy, satire and classical learning, all brought together by an earthy sense of reality and a sharp eye for human detail. Though his status as "the father of English poetry" is currently rather unfashionable, this poem continues to demonstrate his enduring appeal.

THE WILTON DIPTYCH

*A*n exquisite example of late 14th-century art now housed in the National Gallery, the **Wilton Diptych**—named after Wilton House, where it was kept from the 18th century until 1929—is a portable altarpiece. It depicts the young Richard II, supported by St Edward the Confessor and St Edmund, being presented by John the Baptist to the Virgin and Child, who are attended by eleven angels. The kneeling boy-king is being blessed by Christ, and is either about to receive—or has just offered as a gift—a banner of St George surmounted with an orb depicting England set in a silver sea.

The allegorical statement is unambiguous. King Richard is Christ's servant, England his realm, and his right to rule is divinely sanctioned. But the diptych also carries more subtle messages. Richard's kneeling posture recalls that of the Magi adoring Christ at the feast of Epiphany, which falls on January 6 (Richard's birthday). It is significant, too, that the host of angels all wear the king's badge of the white hart: an echo perhaps of Pope Gregory the Great's punning description of Saxon slaves as "non Angli, sed Angeli"—angels, not Englishmen.

Why the diptych was commissioned, and by whom, remains uncertain. Possibly Richard instigated it himself, perhaps a wedding gift celebrating his second marriage to Isabelle of France—it was hoped the alliance might promote an Anglo-French crusade (for which a portable altar would have been essential). More probably, though, it was commissioned in 1397 to mark the twentieth anniversary of Richard's accession to the throne. Either way, the fact that within a few years of the diptych's crafting Richard was deposed and dead adds poignancy to its beauty.

Richard II appears before the Kentishmen at Smithfield. When the enraged Mayor of London has Wat Tyler pulled from his horse and killed, the assembly threatens to get out of hand, but the king again persuades the crowd to disperse. The revolt rumbles on outside London during the early summer, but is finally crushed when the men of **East Anglia**, under the leadership of **John Lister**, are crushed by the **bishop of Norwich** (another Hugh le Despenser) in June. In its aftermath the king's assurances of redress are forgotten; but no further attempts to levy the poll tax are made.

1382 Richard II marries Princess **Anne of Bohemia**. Simon of Sudbury's successor as archbishop of Canterbury, **Thomas Courtenay**, orchestrates a campaign against Wyclif and the Lollards.

1384 In May Archbishop Courtenay convenes a synod at **Blackfriars**, which condemns many of Wyclif's writings. **Oxford University** follows suit by banning all Wyclif's works. Wyclif is left alone, however, and dies of a stroke at Lutterworth on December 31.

1385 The barons' disquiet hardens as the king surrounds himself with courtiers who they regard as "frivolous," among them **Richard de Vere**, **Earl of Oxford**. Opposition to Richard II is led by the earls of **Gloucester** (his uncle Thomas of Woodstock), **Arundel** (Richard Fitzalan) and **Warwick** (Thomas de Beauchamp).

1386 Richard II's position is further weakened by the departure of John of Gaunt for **Spain** to pursue a claim to the throne of **Castile**. Isolated at his own court, the king surrenders government to an eleven-man committee of barons who use Parliament to impeach and execute the chancellor, **Michael de la Pole**, **Earl of Suffolk**. Later in the year, Richard declares that the barons' actions constitute treason.

1387 Geoffrey Chaucer begins work on his great verse cycle, *The Canterbury Tales*.

1388 The king's baronial opponents, again using Parliament as their front, succeed in executing or outlawing many of Richard's closest associates. Richard himself is forced to give way to five

appellant lords, including Gloucester, Arundel and Warwick, who assume the reins of government. The English are defeated by the Scots at **Otterburn**.

1389 In May Richard II, obsessed with what he considers the **divine right** supporting the throne, repudiates the appellants and proclaims himself **sole ruler**. Civil war between Crown and barons is averted by John of Gaunt's **return** to England, and the duke of Lancaster persuades Richard and his barons to work together. But while the king submits to Gaunt's compromise, in secret he begins building up his own support.

1394 Richard II is devastated by the death of his queen, **Anne of Bohemia**.

1396 Partly as a means of extending the truce that prevails between England and France, Richard II marries **Isabelle of Valois**.

1397 After eight years' apparent quiescence, Richard II moves against his baronial opposition by having **Arundel** arrested, convicted of treason and executed. **Gloucester** is imprisoned and killed, **Warwick** exiled. Perhaps in celebration of his successful coup as well as to commemorate the anniversary of his coronation, the king commissions the **Wilton Diptych**.

1398 In September a quarrel between the two remaining lords appellant, **Henry Bolingbroke** (John of Gaunt's heir) and **Thomas Mowbray** (earl of Norfolk), encourages Richard II to banish both from England.

1399 John of Gaunt **dies** in February. When Richard II seizes Gaunt's sizeable **Lancastrian estates**, Henry Bolingbroke is deprived of his inheritance. Unwisely, the king leaves England to campaign in **Ireland** in May; during his absence Bolingbroke returns and rapidly secures the loyalty of many of the barons. In August Richard surrenders to Bolingbroke in Wales, and on September 30 **abdicates** in his favor.

CHAPTER FIVE

Lancaster, York and the Wars of the Roses

{1399–1485}

ALTHOUGH THE REMOVAL OF RICHARD II FROM THE THRONE left Henry Bolingbroke in a controlling position, the abdication of the last Plantagenet monarch was to introduce a prolonged period of political friction. The spectacular but brief reign of **Henry V** (1413–22) would provide some respite, but the country would not gain stability until some time after the 1485 accession of **Henry VII**, the first of the Tudors.

England's 15th century was dominated by infighting among Edward III's many male descendants and their various factions. Edward's grandson Bolingbroke was crowned **Henry IV**, the first of the House of Lancaster, but had to rely on the support of powerful nobles including **Henry Percy, Earl of Northumberland** in order to get there. When Percy became disenchanted with the new regime and convinced that he had not received sufficient credit, he quickly rebelled.

This set the pattern for much of what followed. During the lengthy reign of Henry IV's mentally unstable grandson **Henry VI**, several relations tried their luck, including Humphrey of Gloucester and Henry Beaufort, Bishop of Winchester. The greatest challenge to Henry, though, came from **Richard of York**. Although Richard narrowly failed to secure the crown for himself, his son **Edward IV** twice succeeded in supplanting the Lancastrian king—first following his dramatic victories at **Mortimer's Cross** and **Towton** and again after Henry was murdered, almost certainly on Edward's orders. But just as

Henry's death removed one part of the problem, the kingdom was again jeopardized by rivalry between Edward's brothers, the **dukes of Clarence** and of **Gloucester**, and the family of his wife, **Elizabeth Woodville**.

In 1455 these internal squabbles boiled over into outright civil war, a conflict known as the **Wars of the Roses** after the red rose of Lancaster and the white rose of York—a picturesque description rooted in the Tudor propaganda of Henry VII, who proclaimed to unite the warring factions. As before, this brutal series of plots, rebellions and battles was perpetuated by dynasties from outside immediate royal circles. Private feuds merged with supposedly national causes to bring families such as the **Nevilles**, **Percies** and **Beauforts** into the political limelight.

The best-known of these "over-mighty subjects" was **Richard Neville, Earl of Warwick**, nicknamed "the Kingmaker" because he was the man to whom Edward IV owed both his crown and many of the difficulties he experienced holding on to it. This acute royal insecurity had a number of causes, among them what has been called **bastard feudalism**—a convenient term which describes the increasingly intricate relationships between lords and their retainers that developed after the Black Death and through the Hundred Years War. In such systems financial rewards and personal loyalties replaced the rigid hierarchical structures imposed by William I, meaning that magnates like Warwick could recruit large private armies with which they could threaten the monarchy itself.

Henry V's solution to all of this was simple: to revive the war against **France**. Risking his political credibility, he gambled on a foreign campaign and won—amazing not only his own subjects but also much of Europe by his victory at **Agincourt** in 1415. But like Crécy and Poitiers in the 14th century, the payout proved elusive. Henry V's early death, and the breakdown of England's alliance with Burgundy, destroyed the foundations of the "dual monarchy" Henry had envisaged. Instead, France and Burgundy—and also Scotland—served to compound England's domestic troubles.

This crisis across the Channel encouraged the Wars of the Roses to worsen. Royal control in the country broke down, and a series of battles between the competing houses added to the upheaval. When **Richard of Gloucester** maneuvered himself into the protectorship during **Edward V**'s minority, and from there to the throne, he created enough enemies for **Henry Tudor** to gain power relatively easily in 1485. It is largely because of Henry VII's propagandistic interventions—shoring up his somewhat distant claim to the throne—that Richard III has been so effectively demonized by historians, but there is little doubt that his two-year reign was controversial, then as now. Whether he was personally responsible for the deaths of the "princes in the tower" (the uncrowned Edward and his brother Richard), as was widely suspected at the time, is a mystery that is unlikely to be solved—but the perception that he was a murderer of innocents did little to help him retain support.

After his triumph at Bosworth in 1485, **Henry VII** sought to draw a line under the political turmoil of the previous century—visibly seeking to build prosperity and develop his government rather than toying with military fireworks. To an extent this was happening already: the Tudors inherited an England which had already witnessed profound social and economic change. Although a majority of English people continued to live off the land, increasing numbers of them were doing so as tenants, paying rent to their overlords instead of rendering service. Equally as significant was the fact that England had ceased selling raw wool to Bruges and other continental markets, and instead began to produce woven cloths. As a result, some parts of the country became slowly richer—a new wealth evidenced by the building of many parish churches in the costly

English perpendicular style, especially in East Anglia, the Cotswolds and Somerset, and the foundation of several large colleges at Oxford and Cambridge.

Technological developments continued, and at its close the period had witnessed the advent of printing in England. **William Caxton** simply used presses already available on the continent, but as a businessman-translator-publisher he heralded the emergence of a standard written language as well as laying the foundations for printed literature in the vernacular. Regional dialects persisted and varied spelling flourished, but on the printed page at least a truly common language had started to emerge.

1399 In September Henry Bolingbroke ascends the throne as **Henry IV**, the first monarch of the **House of Lancaster**. Although determined to reassert the authority of the throne, the earliest years of his reign are marked by near-continuous crisis and he will do little to overcome the Crown's chronic lack of money. His eldest son, also called **Henry** (sometimes known as "Prince Hal") is created **earl of Chester**, and subsequently **prince of Wales** as well as titular **duke of Aquitaine**. In October the usurped king, Richard, is imprisoned at **Pontefract Castle** in Yorkshire.

1400 In January Henry IV defeats a **rebellion** by Richard's supporters. Richard himself dies at **Pontefract** shortly afterwards, probably murdered on Henry's orders.

In August a previously loyal Welsh courtier, **Owain Glyndwr**, leads Wales into its last major revolt against English rule. Over the next three years Henry campaigns against Glyndwr but fails to capture him. Seizing **Harlech Castle** and holding assemblies there, at **Machynlleth** and **Pennal**, Glyndwr forms alliances with English nobles opposed to Henry IV, among them **Henry Percy**— the **Earl of Northumberland** and formerly a close supporter of the king—and the French Crown.

1401 To suppress the **Lollards**—adherents of the ideas of John Wyclif— the first Parliamentary statute ordering the **burning of heretics** is enacted. Although an example is made of **William Sawtrey** even before the bill is passed, Lollardism continues as a focus of dissent.

1403 Northumberland and his son Henry Percy (nicknamed **Hotspur**), having openly rebelled against Henry IV, are defeated by the king and Prince Henry at **Shrewsbury** in July. Hotspur is killed in battle. Prince Henry is given command of the campaign against **Glyndwr** in Wales.

1405 **Thomas Mowbray**, **Duke of Norfolk** and **Richard Scrope, Archbishop of York**, having plotted further rebellion on Northumberland's behalf, are executed for treason. Northern England is also troubled by **Scottish incursions**, loosely coordinated with the activities of Glyndwr.

Henry IV shows the first signs of **ill health**; around this time he suffers a stroke.

1406 **James I of Scotland** is captured and imprisoned until 1424, giving Henry IV reasonable security on the Scottish border.

1407 The **Merchant Adventurers**, a company of English traders specializing in the export of cloths to markets in the Low Countries, is granted a royal charter. Although its turnover is slow to begin with, towards the end of the century it will contribute significantly to England's accumulating wealth.

1408 Northumberland again rebels, but is defeated and killed at **Bramham Moor** in Yorkshire.

Although **Glyndwr** remains at large, Prince Henry deprives him of support through a combination of military action and diplomacy, and brings the Welsh campaign to a successful conclusion. Returning to his ailing father's court, the prince demands a place on the king's council. When this is refused he begins forming a faction with the **Beauforts**—Henry IV's half-brothers—against the king's chancellor **Thomas Arundel**, the archbishop of Canterbury.

1410 Prince Henry's faction ousts Arundel and the prince becomes co-ruler with his father, now incapacitated by illness. But the king resists his son's proposal to renew the war in **France**, which in any case the exchequer cannot afford.

1411 Intending to exploit increasingly volatile relations between the French throne and the emergent principality of **Burgundy**, Prince Henry takes a small army across the Channel but achieves little.

1412 Taking advantage of his son's French failure, Henry IV wrests power back from the prince of Wales.

1413 In March, **Henry IV** falls gravely ill; a prediction that the former crusader would "die in Jerusalem" is fulfilled in one sense when the king is carried into the "Jerusalem Chamber" at the Palace of Westminster, where he soon dies. The prince of Wales is immediately proclaimed king; but despite his general popularity among the nobility, it is not a peaceable kingdom that **Henry V** inherits. As well as renewed friction on the Scottish border, there are rumors of rebellion among those supporting **Edmund Mortimer**, the earl of March's claim to the throne, and also among the Lollards, now led by the king's former companion **Sir John Oldcastle**.

1414 An attempt by **Oldcastle** to raise rebellion is swiftly crushed by **Henry V**; harsh reprisals against the Lollards follow.

The king, determined to campaign in France, begins negotiating with the French Crown for the return of "English possessions" including **Aquitaine**, **Normandy** and **Maine**. At the same time he tries to convince Parliament to grant the necessary taxes.

1415 Following the "collapse" of negotiations with France in June, Henry assembles his forces at **Southampton**. As he is preparing to embark, news reaches him of a plot to usurp his throne in favor of **Mortimer**. The principal conspirators—**Henry, Lord Scrope of Masham, Sir Thomas Grey** and Henry V's cousin, **Richard,   Earl of Cambridge**—are seized and summarily executed. Other "traitors" are rounded up and dealt with harshly, although Mortimer, having revealed the plot to Henry V, is spared. The king crosses to France and, assured of the neutrality of **John the Fearless of Burgundy**, captures the port town of **Harfleur** in September. Thus resumes the **Hundred Years War**. As the campaigning season draws to a close, Henry turns back toward England but is forced to engage the French at **Agincourt** on October 15. Against huge odds (he has a depleted army of only five or six thousand against the French contingent of perhaps 20,000), Henry V turns a rearguard action into a comprehensive victory. Despite his **massacre** of French prisoners—against chivalric rules—this wins him domestic support and enables the king to borrow more funds from the banking community to fill his war chest.

Glyndwr disappears from view.

1416 An English fleet secures control of the Channel by destroying the main French fleet in the **Battle of the Seine**.

1417 Henry V campaigns in France to subjugate **Normandy**. In league with the Holy Roman Emperor **Sigismund**, he secures the unopposed election of **Pope Martin V**, ending the papal schism that has lasted since 1378.

1419 In January Henry V captures **Rouen**, which becomes another English garrison. In September the murder of **John of Burgundy** by partisans of the French throne ends Burgundy's neutrality—to Henry's advantage.

In the year of our lord 1415, Henry V King of England called together the prelates and lords of his kingdom, and asked their advice, on peril of their souls, whether he had a better grievance against the kingdom of Scotland or against the kingdom of France, to go to war about.

—From *The Book of Pluscarden*, **late 15th century**

The Battle of Agincourt, 1415

1420 Outmaneuvered militarily and politically, France concedes defeat. By the terms of the **Treaty of Troyes**, signed in May, Henry V is proclaimed heir to the French throne. The dauphin **Charles** is disinherited, and the king of France, **Charles VI**, acknowledges Henry as his regent—effectively giving the English king command of all of France.

To cement his position, in June Henry marries **Catherine of Valois**, Charles VI's daughter.

1421 As resistance to English rule in France begins, Henry V's brother **Thomas of Clarence** is ambushed and killed. Henry V resumes campaigning in France, laying siege to **Melun** and **Meaux**.

1422 Debilitated by constant warfare, **Henry V** dies aged 35 at **Bois de Vincennes** in September, and is succeeded by his infant son, **Henry VI**. In October Henry is also proclaimed **king of France**, following the death of his maternal grandfather **Charles VI** and according to the terms of the **Treaty of Troyes**. The government of England and those parts of France that remain loyal to the English Crown pass to the new king's uncles—**Humphrey, Duke of Gloucester, John, Duke of Bedford** and **Henry Beaufort, Bishop of Winchester**. The widowed **Catherine of Valois** soon marries **Owen Tudor**, a Welsh-born courtier.

1424 The **dauphin**, having repudiated the Treaty of Troyes, is heavily defeated by English forces at **Verneuil**.

1425 The erstwhile pretender to the throne, **Edmund Mortimer**, dies of plague in **Ireland**, making the House of Lancaster's controversial claim to the English throne somewhat easier. Further victories in France enable the English Crown to consolidate its territories in **Anjou** and **Maine**.

In England tensions between two of Henry VI's regents, **Gloucester** and **Henry Beaufort**, develop into a pitched battle between their followers on **London Bridge**.

1426 John of Bedford, responsible for England's continuing success in France, returns home to resolve the differences between his fellow regents.

1428 English fortunes in France prosper as **Normandy** is given its own Parliament; this means it is able to raise sufficient taxes in order to make the continuing English occupation financially workable. Against Bedford's advice, the ambitious **Earl of Salisbury** undertakes to campaign against the dauphin's power base in the south. In an attempt to secure a bridgehead over the river Loire he lays siege to **Orléans**.

1429 The dauphin's fortunes revive when a peasant girl, **Jeanne d'Arc** (Joan of Arc) convinces him that she has been sent from God to restore France and destroy the English. With her help the siege of

Orléans is lifted, and an English army is defeated at **Patay**. The dauphin is crowned at **Reims** as **Charles VII**.

1430 Henry VI is taken to **Paris** to be crowned **king of France**; but since **Reims** is the traditional venue for a French coronation this move only heightens awareness of the House of Valois' revival.

1431 Jeanne d'Arc is captured by Burgundian forces, then handed over to the English. Charged with being a witch, a heretic and a transvestite, she is burned at the stake in **Rouen** marketplace in May.

HENRY V (C.1386–1422)

*H*enry V owes much of his popular image to Shakespeare, who, in his two *Henry IV* plays, represents him as a quick-witted but dissolute youth who metamorphoses into a paragon of princely virtue on the death of his father.

The reality was somewhat different. Henry shouldered many of the responsibilities that came his way as a young prince, notably against Glyndwr in Wales. Taken under Richard II's wing while his father was out of favor, his education was directed by his uncle Henry Beaufort, and he was the first English king to read and write in the vernacular with fluency; in government he would encourage the official use of English rather than French. As prince of Wales, however, he did make trouble for Henry IV, forming an alliance against Thomas Arundel and stage-managing a coup that temporarily made him England's co-ruler. Indeed, Shakespeare has difficulty squaring this ambitious young man with his depiction of the fast-living Hal.

The figure depicted in *Henry V*, though, is far more conventionally charismatic, and touches on important aspects of the real king while omitting less palatable truths. Deeply religious and a merciless persecutor of

With Henry VI and Beaufort both out of England, Gloucester accuses Beaufort of Praemunire, infringing royal rights by dealing with secular matters in an ecclesiastical court.

1433 Again Bedford is obliged to return to England to resolve the Gloucester–Beaufort dispute. The king's council implores Bedford to remain in England, thus depriving its forces in France of their most effective commander.

heretics, Henry V embarked on his French campaigns with an absolute conviction in the justice of his cause. Yet his slaughter of those taken prisoner at Agincourt, many of them nobles, tarnished his reputation. Equally, Shakespeare's portrayal of the king wandering from tent to tent on the eve of battle, raising his men's spirits and offering those without stomach for the fight free passage home, is far removed from the brutal disciplinarian who promised to amputate the right ear of any would-be deserter. But the fact that he invaded France with a deliberate and effective strategy of reducing key towns and leaving English garrisons in them demonstrates his military skill. It was this practicality as much as his dazzling victory at Agincourt that, within seven years of his accession, won him the French Crown.

What he did not foresee was his own early demise. Although his brother John of Bedford for a while successfully continued his strategy, the accession of Henry VI while still a minor only encouraged England's other princes and barons to squabble among themselves. Henry V's victories—just like Edward III's—finally counted for little.

1434 Gloucester physically removes **Henry VI** to **Cirencester**, where the Council reconvenes in order to re-assert its authority.

1435 In France, the tide turns decisively against England when, following the breakdown of peace negotiations at **Arras**, the Anglo–Burgundian alliance collapses and, later in the year, **John of Bedford** dies.

1436 After Charles VII captures **Paris**, England is left with few French possessions outside Normandy.

1437 Aged sixteen, **Henry VI** assumes the reins of government as his minority ends. Studious and retiring by nature, as well as mentally unstable later in life, he will be remembered as one of England's weakest kings, held responsible for losing his father's French conquests and for allowing his own country to become embroiled in three decades of civil war.

1440 The 18-year-old Henry has the opportunity to fight in **Normandy**, but instead sends the **duke of York** as his lieutenant and busies himself with the founding of **Eton College** instead—one day to become the most famous of England's "public" (ie, private) schools.

This King Henry was chaste and pure from the beginning of his days... It happened once, that at Christmas time a certain great lord brought before him a dance or show of young ladies with bared bosoms who were to dance in that guise before the king ... but the king was not blind to it, nor unaware of the devilish wile, and spurned the delusion, and very angrily averted his eyes, turned his back upon them, and went out to his chamber, saying: "Fy, Fy, for shame, forsother ye be to blame."

—**John Blacman on Henry VI,**
in the *Memoir* **(c.1485)**

1443 Henry (now Cardinal) Beaufort's nephew **John, Duke of Somerset**, is dispatched to France at the head of a force intended to recapture lost territories. But his appointment leads to a bitter feud with **Richard, Duke of York**, commander of the English in France and another descendant of Edward III.

1444 Henry VI, swayed by those seeking peace with Charles VII, concludes a truce at **Tours**. It is agreed he should marry Charles's distant and impoverished—but strong-willed cousin—**Margaret of Anjou**.

1445 Recalled to England, **Richard of York** is fobbed off with worthless promises when he claims campaign expenses, while his adversary **Edmund, Duke of Somerset** (brother of the late duke John) is rewarded with money and lands. York's resentment deepens when he discovers that Henry VI has secretly conceded **Maine** to Charles VII, apparently at the instigation of Queen Margaret.

1447 As divisions between the factions at Henry VI's court harden and Somerset gains ascendancy, **Humphrey of Gloucester** is arrested and imprisoned, then possibly murdered. While popular opinion holds Queen Margaret and Cardinal Beaufort responsible for the "good duke's" death, Richard of York succeeds Gloucester as heir presumptive to the throne, and as such becomes leader of the main "opposition" party within the Council.

In Cambridge, **King's College** is founded at Henry VI's behest, its chapel (finished under Henry VIII) a masterpiece of the **English perpendicular** style that now dominates ecclesiastical architecture in England.

1448 Under threat of French attack, English garrisons are **withdrawn** from Maine. In England, Richard of York turns against **William de la Pole, Duke of Suffolk**, Henry VI's chief adviser and a leader of the "peace" faction. In Parliament there is mounting criticism of the king and his ministers.

1449 Henry VI is persuaded by Suffolk to resume hostilities against **Charles VII of France**.

1450 French forces defeat the English at **Formigny** in April, and complete the reconquest of Normandy in August. Suffolk is **attainted** by Parliament (condemned by parliamentary bill without trial) but, instead of agreeing to his execution, Henry VI exiles him. Suffolk's ship, however, is overtaken by "pirates" and he is beheaded.

In Kent, a popular uprising led by an Irish mercenary, **Jack Cade**, erupts. Styling himself "John Mortimer," Cade issues a manifesto against the king's "evil advisers," calling for the restoration of such "true" nobles as Richard of York. The rebels capture **London**, but disperse when Queen Margaret offers pardons to those agreeing to lay down their weapons. Cade himself is killed at **Rochester** while evading arrest.

1452 Richard of York openly rebels against Henry VI and the Beaufort faction, but lays down his arms on the understanding that the king will punish Somerset's excesses. Somerset remains in power, however.

1453 Somerset's position is seemingly strengthened when Henry VI lapses into a first bout of **insanity**, but a majority of councilors—distrustful of both Somerset and Margaret of Anjou—offer the **protectorship** to Richard of York. Shortly afterwards Queen Margaret gives birth to a royal heir, **Prince Edward**, rumored to be Somerset's child.

John Talbot, Earl of Shrewsbury, is killed while charging enemy cannon at **Chatillon**. His death crushes any hopes of the English re-establishing their position in France and, as all remaining strongholds except Calais fall, the **Hundred Years War** effectively comes to an end.

1454 Recovering in December, Henry VI dismisses **Richard of York**. As Somerset is restored to favor, York gains important new allies among the influential and seemingly loyal **Neville** family.

1455 Richard of York, supported by the **Nevilles**, rebels against Henry VI and Somerset. The two sides clash at **St Albans**, generally

THE WARS OF THE ROSES (1455–87)

*V*icious though they were, the domestic conflicts that came to be known as the **Wars of the Roses** were more intermittent and localized than that title suggests. Most people in England would have had little clear idea of what was going on within the ruling elite, and only those who had the misfortune to be the tenants or retainers of the more enthusiastic participants would have experienced violence first-hand. Even most of the nobility steered clear of the fighting, and lawcourts continued to be the preferred means of resolving disputes.

Over the years the immediate causes of warfare also changed to match whichever political arguments were fiercest. The first round, between 1455 and 1460, surrounded the grievances of **Richard of York**. Once he was dead, the next episode of fighting (between 1460 and 1464) stemmed from the peculiarity of there being two crowned kings, **Henry VI** and **Edward IV**. The wars' brief—but bloody—resurgence between 1469 and 1471 was inspired by the **earl of Warwick's** chagrin at his declining influence over **Edward IV**. And the culminating eruption of 1485 actually saw an alliance, led by Henry Tudor, of old Lancastrians and old Yorkists against the unpopular **Richard III**. Lesser conflicts continued until the mid-1490s—and Henry VIII was still executing Yorkist rivals in the 1530s—but his father's triumphs at **Bosworth** and **Stoke** marked the effective closure of three decades' tangled conflict.

Overall, the monarchy itself was the net beneficiary, if only because the more dangerous nobility had been culled. But as the Civil Wars of the mid-17th century were to demonstrate, the Crown could still be challenged by those of lesser pedigree—and in the process come seriously unstuck.

considered the start of the **Wars of the Roses**. Somerset and other of the king's favorites are engaged in violent street fighting. Henry VI is wounded in the shoulder by an arrow. York re-establishes his **protectorate** as Henry once more descends into madness.

1456 As Henry VI again **recovers**, York is eased out of the protectorate for a second time. In the vacuum that ensues **Queen Margaret** assumes real power, but her attempts to punish York and his followers are resisted by a great council of the nobility convened at Coventry.

York's supporter **Richard Neville**—the **earl of Warwick** and known to history as "**the Kingmaker**"—becomes captain of **Calais**, later a pivotal Yorkist base.

1458 To reconcile the different factions of his court, Henry VI proposes a "**Loveday.**" But although York and Queen Margaret walk arm-in-arm through London to a service of reconciliation at **St Paul's Cathedral**, their mutual antipathy survives.

1459 Deprived of any say in government, Richard of York launches a fresh **rebellion**. After a stand-off with royalist forces at **Ludford**, York flees to **Ireland** with his second son, the **earl of Rutland**. His eldest son, **Edward, Earl of March**, is taken by Warwick to Calais. Queen Margaret summons the "**Parliament of Devils**" at **Coventry**. York and his followers are attainted in their absence, and their lands and titles confiscated in perpetuity. But these measures succeed only in drawing more support to the Yorkist cause.

1460 Warwick and Edward of March return to England from Calais and defeat a royalist force at **Northampton**. Warwick seizes London, and then in May captures the king himself. A fresh Parliament is summoned, and the attainders of the **Parliament of Devils** overturned.

In October Richard of York returns to England and astonishes his supporters by claiming the throne. Henry VI agrees to an **Act of**

EDWARD IV (1442–83)

*T*he glamorous and handsome **Edward IV** came to the throne in 1461 on the back of his father Richard of York's persistent opposition to the House of Lancaster, but also thanks to the interventions of **Warwick the Kingmaker**. Unwisely, Edward elected to displace Warwick at court in favor of his wife's family, the **Woodvilles**, and in 1471 paid the price when Warwick combined with the Lancastrians to briefly restore Henry VI.

Like Henry VI, Edward got a second shot at the throne when he defeated his enemies the following year, but, unlike his predecessor, he learned from his mistakes. The second period of Edward's rule saw a restitution in the authority of royal government, even though it was marred toward its end by acrimonious rivalry between his brothers **Clarence** and **Gloucester**. Edward strengthened the judiciary and repaired the throne's finances; he also did much to advance the cause of English traders, repaying London for its staunch support for the House of York. But perhaps his greatest coup was to threaten **France** with a renewal of war in 1475, only to allow himself to be bought off with a handsome pension.

After 1475, due to the burgeoning success of the cloth trade in particular, prosperity returned to England, and increasingly historians have credited Edward IV with laying the foundations of the Tudor state, especially since 19th-century disapproval of his personal morals has been cast aside. But the popular rumor that he ordered his brother Clarence to be drowned in a butt of wine suggests his reputation for ruthlessness—and, like his reliance on a small circle of knightly intimates, points to something much more medieval in his outlook.

Accord, whereby the succession will pass to the House of York after his death. Queen Margaret dissents, however, and attacks York at **Sandal**, his stronghold near Wakefield. Badly prepared for a siege, York decides to leave his walls and fight, but is killed along with his second son Rutland and other supporters. His head, adorned with a paper crown, is impaled on Micklegate at **York**.

1461 Avenging his father, **Edward of March** defeats a Lancastrian army led by Henry VI's half-brother **Jasper Tudor** at **Mortimer's Cross** in February. Among those executed is **Owen Tudor**, the king's stepfather. Edward's ally Warwick is defeated at the **Second Battle of St Albans** and forced to flee. Queen Margaret attempts to enter London, but is refused entry. As she retreats to the north, the Yorkists gain the capital, and Edward of March is proclaimed king on March 4. As **Edward IV**, the first ruler of the **House of York**, he defeats the main Lancastrian force at Towton on March 29. In a particularly bloody engagement, many of his opponents are slaughtered. Henry VI, Queen Margaret and Prince Edward **flee** to Scotland. While some of England's aristocracy, notably the **Percies** of Northumberland, declare their support for Henry, the queen's request for French assistance enables Edward to project himself as the patriotic choice. Warwick meanwhile takes the Lancastrian strongholds of **Alnwick**, **Bamburgh** and **Dunstanburgh**.

1462 The Lancastrian cause remains strong in **northern England**, where Warwick is obliged to continue siege warfare against its strongholds.

1463 Although Lancastrians revolt again in **Northumberland**— led by Somerset and Sir Ralph Percy—at the end of the year Edward IV isolates his opponents by concluding treaties with **France** and **Scotland**.

1464 In April, Percy is killed at **Hedgeley Moor** fighting a Yorkist force led by Warwick's brother **Lord Montagu**. In May Montagu caps his success by defeating a larger Lancastrian force at **Hexham**, for which he is created **earl of Northumberland**. Among those captured is the **duke of Somerset**, who is swiftly executed. As the Lancastrian movement in the north collapses, Warwick crosses to **France** to arrange a marriage between Edward IV and a French princess. During his absence Edward secretly marries **Elizabeth Woodville**, widow of the Lancastrian **Sir John Grey**. Her two sons, five brothers and seven sisters are advanced by Edward to provide counterbalance to the influence of the Nevilles at court. Despite losing face in Paris, for the moment Warwick remains loyal.

1465 The fugitive **Henry VI** is captured by Yorkists in **Lancashire** and subsequently imprisoned in the **Tower of London**.

1467 To Warwick's dismay, in November Edward IV offers his sister **Margaret**'s hand in marriage to **Charles the Bold** of Burgundy, as well as agreeing a new commercial treaty between the two countries.

1468 Warwick begins plotting with Edward IV's brother **George, Duke of Clarence**, possibly offering him (as well as his own daughter's hand) the Crown itself.

1469 Edward is confronted by two fresh rebellions, led by "**Robin of Redesdale**" (probably Warwick's relative **Sir John Conyers**) and "**Robin of Holderness**." While both are crushed by Warwick's brother **Montagu**, Edward's failure to take a firm grip on events strengthens Warwick's hand. The earl crosses to **Calais** with Clarence, who is duly married to **Isabel Neville**. Issuing a manifesto against Edward's "evil advisers," Warwick and Clarence return to England. In July they defeat and kill **Lord Herbert**, a royal favorite, then capture Edward IV himself at **Olney**. But they fail to win any significant support from their fellow nobles, and in October agree to release Edward in return for a royal pardon.

1470 In March, Warwick and Clarence resume rebellion in Lincolnshire, but their forces are routed at the battle of "**Lose–coat field**" near **Stamford**. Fleeing, the rebels seek refuge at the court of **Louis XI of France**, who quickly brokers an alliance between Warwick and his relative, Queen Margaret. The compact is cemented when Warwick's younger daughter **Anne Neville** is betrothed to Henry VI's heir **Prince Edward**.

In September the rebels return to England, landing in **Devon** and wrongfooting King Edward, who is distracted by a secondary rebellion raised by Warwick's brother-in-law **Lord Fitzhugh**. Deserted by Warwick's hitherto loyal brother Montagu, Edward IV flees to **Burgundy** with his younger brother **Richard, Duke of Gloucester**. **Henry VI** is released from the Tower and nominally restored to the throne, though actual power stays in the hands of Warwick and Clarence. Their relationship is soon strained, however, when Lancastrians begin demanding the return of lands previously seized by Yorkists, and London's merchants resist Warwick's alliance with France at the expense of Burgundy.

Sir Thomas Malory completes his English prose romance *Le Morte Darthur*, possibly in prison, a year before his death; it will be printed by **William Caxton** in 1485.

1471 Supported by **Charles the Bold of Burgundy, Edward IV** and his followers return to England in March. Marching first to York, and unopposed by either Lord Montagu or the earl of Northumberland, he turns south again and besieges Warwick at **Coventry**.

In April **Clarence** defects to his brother's side, **Henry VI** is taken prisoner once more, and **London** opens its gates to Edward. On April 14 Warwick and his brother Montagu are killed in battle at **Barnet**.

On May 4 a second rebel army, headed by Queen Margaret, is crushed at **Tewkesbury**. As Margaret is captured, her son, Prince Edward, is killed attempting to flee. On May 21 King Edward returns to London; Henry VI dies on the same night, almost certainly murdered on his rival's orders. In the aftermath, Edward IV rewards both his brothers, Clarence and Gloucester, for their support—inadvertently sowing the seeds of contention between his siblings as each seeks greater power than the other.

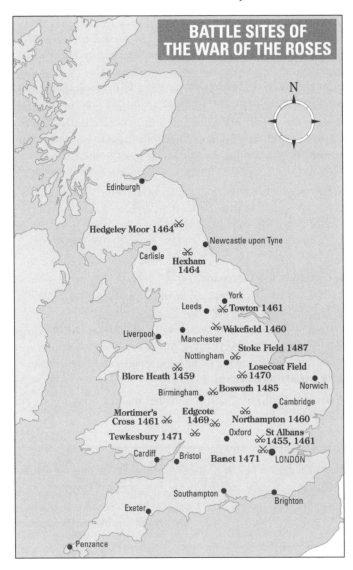

BATTLE SITES OF THE WAR OF THE ROSES

N

Edinburgh

Hedgeley Moor 1464

Newcastle upon Tyne

Carlisle

Hexham
1464

York

Leeds   Towton 1461

Wakefield 1460

Liverpool

Manchester

Stoke Field 1487

Nottingham

Losecoat Field
1470

Blore Heath 1459

Birmingham   Boswoth 1485   Norwich

Cambridge

Mortimer's
Cross 1461

Edgcote
1469

Northampton 1460

Tewkesbury 1471

Oxford   St Albans
1455, 1461

Cardiff   Bristol   Banet 1471   LONDON

Southampton

Brighton

Exeter

Penzance

1472 Clarence, married to Warwick's eldest daughter, attempts to prevent Gloucester marrying the younger daughter, **Anne Neville** (Prince Edward's widow). Gloucester strengthens his position by **imprisoning** his future mother-in-law under the pretence of protecting her from his brother. At the heart of the feud is the future of the substantial Warwick inheritance, which includes the lucrative estates of the **Beauchamp** family.

1473 Under pressure from the king, Parliament passes an **Act of Resumption**, returning alienated royal lands to the Crown.

1474 A further act of Parliament confirms a division of the **Neville estates** between Clarence and Gloucester in right of their wives; Warwick's widow is **disinherited**. In collaboration with Burgundy, Edward IV prepares to invade **France**.

A trading treaty is concluded with the powerful **Hanseatic League**, giving English cloth merchants access to new markets in the **Netherlands** and **Germany**.

1475 Edward IV lands in **France** with an impressive force, but Charles of Burgundy fails to give him promised support. The thrones of England and France instead conclude the **Treaty of Picquigny**, which promises Edward IV an annual pension of 50,000 gold crowns in return for withdrawing to England. France and England also conclude a **trade agreement**.

In **Bruges**, **William Caxton** publishes the first book to be printed in English.

Lord Wenlocke not having advanced to the support of the first line, but remaining stationary, contrary to the expectations of Somerset, the latter, in a rage, rode up to him, and beat his brains out with an axe.

—**Richard Brooke on Tewksbury,**
in *Visits to Fields of Battle in the Fifteenth Century* (1857).

1476 **Isabel Neville**, the duchess of Clarence, dies.

1477 Following the death of **Charles of Burgundy** in January, Clarence, seeking to lay claim to Burgundy itself, proposes marrying Charles's daughter **Mary**. As Mary is also Clarence's niece, **Edward IV** forbids the marriage to proceed—fearing that his brother will wreck his recently contrived peace with France. Clarence retaliates by seizing and executing two of his retainers, **Ankarette Twynyho** and **John Thursby**, having accused them of murdering Isabel and his young son. A summer rebellion in **Cambridgeshire** is also probably Clarence's inspiration. The king has Clarence arrested and imprisoned.

1478 In January Clarence is brought before Parliament and charged with **treason**. During his trial, eagerly promoted by the Woodvilles, the prosecution is masterminded by his brother **Gloucester**. Clarence is found guilty and dispatched to the Tower of London. There, on the king's orders, he is murdered—rumor has it, by being drowned in a butt of Malmesey wine.

1479 As the Woodvilles' influence grows, Edward grants one of the family the **earldom of Pembroke**, forcing the existing holder **William Herbert** to accept the inferior title of **Huntingdon** in compensation. Other families, including the Berkeleys and the **Howards**, are also eclipsed by the Woodvilles, and the young **duke of Buckingham** is forced to marry a Woodville against his will.

1480 As border clashes with **Scotland** escalate, Gloucester is appointed **lieutenant-general** in the north.

1482 A plan to place the rebellious **duke of Albany** on the Scottish throne appears. Gloucester invades Scotland in the summer, and succeeds in capturing both **Edinburgh** and **King James III**; but when Albany changes side, the English duke is forced to retreat, taking **Berwick** on his way back south.

WILLIAM CAXTON (1422–91)

*A*lthough printing with movable type was introduced into Europe by Johann Gutenberg in 1458, it was seventeen years before the first printed book in English appeared. The man behind it was **William Caxton**, a London merchant who had spent nearly all his adult life on the continent. Arriving in **Bruges** in 1441, he rose to become governor of the Merchant Adventurers. After a spell attached to the household of the duchess of Burgundy, he traveled to **Cologne** in 1470, where it seems likely that he gained firsthand knowledge of the new technology for mass-producing the written word.

A true entrepreneur with an abiding interest in literature, he invested his own money to acquire a press, which he used initially to publish his own vivid translation of the *Recueil des histories des Troyes*. This and two other books were printed in Bruges before Caxton resettled in **England** in 1476, from where he went on to produce around a hundred titles. In the best traditions of London publishing—his press was housed near Westminster Abbey—his list contained a mixed bag of subject matter: as well as further translations, there were books about gaming and chivalric etiquette, and popular romances including **Malory**'s *Le Morte Darthur*. Caxton also published devotional titles and—significantly for the poet's reputation—an edition of **Chaucer**'s *Canterbury Tales*. His object was to entertain, but also educate the affluent elite who could afford his products (his patrons included Edward IV). Not until well into the following century, when Protestant tracts began to circulate, would the subversive and radical potential of the printed word become fully apparent.

1483 Gloucester is rewarded by his brother Edward IV for his Scottish services with a **palatinate** (area of special control) encompassing **Cumberland**, **Westmoreland** and any areas of **Scotland** he is able to conquer.

On April 9 **Edward** dies after catching a chill boating on the Thames. At once the **Woodvilles**, determined to see the king's adolescent elder son take the throne as **Edward V**, seize the royal treasury; **Richard of Gloucester** hurries swiftly south from York to assert his role as his nephew's protector. The uncrowned boy king, leaving Ludlow, is met by Gloucester at **Stony Stratford**; Gloucester arrests such members of the Woodville family as he can. Told of Gloucester's actions, the king's mother **Elizabeth Woodville** seeks sanctuary in **Westminster Abbey** with her other son Richard and her daughters. With Edward V in his custody, on May 4 Gloucester enters **London**, where the royal council confirms him as protector. Over the following weeks, as he arrests and sometimes executes opponents—and postpones Edward's coronation—it becomes apparent that Gloucester seeks the Crown for himself. Notwithstanding, he persuades Elizabeth Woodville to surrender **Prince Richard** into his safekeeping. Richard joins his brother the king apparent in a royal apartment in the **Tower of London**. The two boys quickly disappear from view, and are probably murdered.

On June 26, following the execution of leading members of the Woodville faction at **Pontefract**, Gloucester proclaims himself king as **Richard III**—the second and last Yorkist monarch. In October dissent spreads among the nobility, and there is rebellion in **Kent**. Among those who desert the king is the **duke of Buckingham**, quickly captured and executed by Richard. And when the Kentish rebellion is also defeated, Richard's opponents transfer their allegiance to **Henry Tudor**, an obscure Lancastrian claimant living in exile in Brittany.

1484 The only **Parliament** convened during Richard III's reign attaints 104 members of the October rebellion. In April Richard's son and heir, another Edward, **dies**, raising doubts about the security of the succession.

1485 Rumors about Richard III intensify when his consort, **Queen Anne**, dies suddenly in March and the king expresses a desire to marry his niece, **Elizabeth of York**.

On August 7 **Henry Tudor** lands at **Milford Haven** in southwest Wales, then marches into England and northwards with his force. The king heads toward **Leicester** to confront him. On August 22 the two armies meet near Market Bosworth, at a battle site known as **Bosworth Field**. Initially Henry Tudor is outnumbered, but several of Richard's allies desert the king, among them **Lord Stanley**, Tudor's stepfather, while the **earl of Northumberland** refuses to

RICHARD III AND THE PRINCES IN THE TOWER

*U*sually portrayed as a murderous, scheming monster, **Richard III** has not been kindly treated by posterity. The malevolent Richard that Shakespeare depicted evolved from Thomas More's *History of King Richard the Third*, an account which is predictably hostile to the "croke backed" king because it was written for **Cardinal Morton**, Henry VII's archbishop of Canterbury—and, naturally, the Tudor regime had an interest in rubbishing Richard's reputation.

But Richard III deserves to be understood as a man of his time, someone who had to embrace whatever means it took to protect his own position. To his brother **Edward IV** he proved a loyal lieutenant, fighting for him in the north of England and campaigning in Scotland. Once Edward was dead, however, Richard's situation changed dramatically. The succession of a minor, **Edward V**, threatened a return to the sort of anarchy that had plagued the reign of Henry VI, and as the boy's uncle it was natural that Richard should become protector in order to defend against it. Yet his competitors at court, notably the **Woodvilles**, now wanted him out of the way.

Richard, who was slender and not tall, had one shoulder a little higher than the other: a defect, by the magnifying glasses of party, by distance of time, and by the amplification of tradition, easily swelled to shocking deformity; for falsehood itself generally pays so much respect to truth as to make it the basis of its superstructure.

—Horace Walpole,
Historic Doubts on Richard the Third (1768)

In these circumstances, striking first was the only means of survival. It's unlikely that Richard intended to seize the throne all along, but as the summer of 1483 unfolded that became his best hope. Having made that decision, elimination of Edward V and his brother became a necessity. So murky are the circumstances surrounding their deaths, however, that even now we cannot be sure that Richard was directly responsible.

But many at the time thought he was. Soon a rumor surfaced that Richard had also poisoned his queen, Anne, and, despite Richard's public rebuttal of the charges, the mood against him hardened. Even so, when Henry Tudor challenged the king it was by no means a done deal; Bosworth was a battle Richard stood a good chance of winning until Thomas, Lord Stanley and his brother, Sir William Stanley, defected. Faced with an impossible situation, Richard was presented with a stark choice: flight or death. It is a testament to his courage that he chose to embrace the latter.

engage his forces. **Sir William Stanley** goes one step further by switching sides midway through the engagement. Richard III himself is killed leading a desperate cavalry charge, and Henry Tudor is symbolically crowned by Stanley using the coronet from Richard's helmet. In October **Henry VII**, the founder of the **Tudor dynasty**, is formally crowned king of England at Westminster Abbey.

CHAPTER SIX

The Tudor Dynasty

{1485-1603}

HENRY TUDOR'S VICTORY AT BOSWORTH gained him the throne, but there was little reason to suppose that his reign would be any longer than his predecessor's. Within two years, in fact, **Henry VII** faced rebellion when the first of many pretenders to his crown, **Lambert Simnel**, landed in England. When they faced each other at Stoke Henry's luck held, though, and the new dynasty began to look as though it might survive.

It was fortunate for the Tudors that they held power during an era of both national and European economic acceleration. As the disastrous consequences of the Black Death finally receded, England's population grew, replenishing old cities, towns and villages. Trade with the Low Countries and elsewhere boomed, and this had knock-on effects that were felt throughout society. But perhaps the greater beneficiaries of the new order were the **landed gentry**. In 1485 England was still dominated by a baronial elite; as time passed this aristocracy survived, adapted and held on to many of its privileges—but the class of gentry immediately below steadily enlarged and prospered.

One reason they did so was precisely because of the growth in population, assisted by a greater supply of money. After a century of depression, **rents** began to rise in line with increased demand. Those who had assets had learned to manage them skillfully and profitably. A visible sign of this was the change in England's countryside. The **enclosure** of common land for private agricultural purposes was a process that continued well into the 18th and even 19th centuries, often with dire consequences for the rural poor—who could be deprived overnight of traditional grazing for their few animals. But from the mid-16th century the hedgerows, fences and narrow lanes that are still a familiar feature of rural England were beginning to make their mark.

Nor did government attempt to resist these changes. On the contrary, it was Tudor policy to encourage the gentry's ambition as a counterweight to the interference of dukes, earls and lords. Again, it was during the 16th century that the system of provincial justice administered by **justices of the peace** drawn from the "squirearchy" came fully into its own. And increasingly members of the gentry were expected to play a role in central government. For **Elizabeth I**, the last of the Tudors, the consequence was an increasingly ambitious House of Commons eager to flex its muscles. Yet this early emergence of institutionalized political dissent was scarcely her greatest concern. For much of her reign the most serious threats came from overseas, as they had done so often in the past.

In the wider picture, the most significant upheaval of the 16th century was the **Reformation**. Many thought that the Church had fallen into disrepute: prelates failed to control absentee priests; those near the top of the ecclesiastical edifice enriched themselves by acquiring multiple benefices (pluralism), and conferred appointments on often unqualified members of their own families (nepotism); clerics widely flaunted the rules of celibacy by keeping mistresses. The revolution against this began in Germany in 1517 when the Augustinian friar **Martin Luther** attacked the sale of **papal indulgences** (which enabled people to buy their way out of what the Church called sin), and then widened his assault to include key tenets of Roman Catholic doctrine. What emerged was a revolutionary theory that individuals should tend their own consciences and develop a more direct relationship with God, instead of depending on the intercession of the Church to attain salvation.

As reform gathered momentum, the political fallout was nothing short of spectacular. As old tensions and rivalries were realigned, the map of Europe was redrawn. In England, a number of scholars quickly joined the reformers by protesting against corruption and espousing their new ideas. Although the Roman Church rapidly regrouped—a backlash called the **Counter-Reformation**—every Christian ruler faced a stark choice between what soon amounted to opposing religions. The Reformation had scarcely begun to take root, however, when **Henry VIII** separated the English Church from Rome in what is usually interpreted as a purely political move. Thereafter England slowly entered the reformed fold, and increasingly found itself at odds with its former ally, **Spain**, a country that enthusiastically championed the revived Roman Catholicism and was determined to stamp out Lutheranism along with any other type of "heresy."

The showdown came in 1588, with the launch of the **Spanish Armada**. Its failure gave England breathing space, and enabled it to develop as a European power—all the more so as England's traditional enemy, **France**, was plagued by a series of civil wars fought in the name of opposing faiths. Though the Reformation would scarcely leave England untouched, that level of large-scale violence was largely avoided by Henry VIII's pre-emptive move.

The Tudor kings
1485-1553

The first of the Tudors, **Henry VII**, was a cautious realist, committed to reconciling England's warring factions with a hands-on approach to government and avoiding costly foreign wars. It's sometimes said that he owed his success to three women. His mother, **Margaret Beaufort**—fortunate not to have been executed for her role in Buckingham's rebellion of 1483—was instrumental in putting together the coalition of forces that secured his victory at Bosworth. Soon afterwards Edward IV's widow, **Elizabeth Woodville**, ensured both the survival of her own family and Henry's security as king by offering him the hand of her daughter, **Elizabeth of York**.

Since his advertised right to the throne was through his Lancastrian descent, Henry VII could claim to have united the two opposing houses. As a Tudor he also represented an advancement—albeit a symbolic one—for the people of Wales. Yet much of his reign was troubled by rebellion, most memorably in the shape of two impostors, **Lambert Simnel** and **Perkin Warbeck**, both supported by the Yorkist **Margaret of Burgundy**. It wasn't until the imprisonment of the earl of Suffolk in 1506, just three years before Henry's death, that the king could finally feel assured of no further threat. In the interim he worked enthusiastically to repair the machinery of government, and also sort out the royal finances. As a ruler he was far from innovative, but chose instead to resurrect policies and institutions that had worked well for Edward IV—and to that extent he was one of the more successful medieval kings.

The succession passed unchallenged to his more assertive and certainly more extravagant son, **Henry VIII**. Unlike his father, the younger Henry was prepared to delegate authority while seeking to cut a figure on the European stage. Emulating Henry V, and greatly assisted by his powerful lord chancellor **Cardinal Wolsey**, he endeavored to re-establish an English presence in France beyond the confines of Calais. When this failed, he allied himself with France against the Emperor Charles V. Nearer home, Henry VIII strengthened English rule in Wales, proclaimed himself king of Ireland, and toyed with subjugating Scotland. There was nothing especially new in these policies: England's kings had often looked beyond the Channel to fulfill their wider ambitions while seeking control of the British Isles.

But in the middle years of his reign an extraordinary combination of circumstances set England on an entirely new path. At his succession in 1509 Henry VIII had married his brother Arthur's widow, **Catherine of Aragon**, six years older than he was. By the late 1520s it was clear she would not provide him with a male heir, and in any case he had fallen in love with **Anne Boleyn**. In the normal course of events the king could have expected the papacy, after a little horse-trading, to grant an annulment. But the sitting pope, **Clement VII**, held back: Catherine was **Charles V**'s aunt, and Charles had Clement in his pocket. A drastic solution to this impasse was developed by Henry's new adviser, **Thomas Cromwell**. Relations with Rome were gradually severed and an independent English Church created—one amenable to Henry VIII's wishes, of course, and with him as its supreme head. Although its immediate ramifications were obvious, Cromwell's intervention had two unforeseen effects. First, although Henry VIII wasn't interested in reforming the Church, Cromwell had radical leanings, and the destruction of the monasteries undertaken at his behest only increased suspicions among other European nations that England was actually taking part in Luther's Reformation. Second, Cromwell used parliamentary means to get the king his way. Though it was initially merely used to rubber-stamp royal policies, the **House of Commons** (now established as a chamber in its own right) gained a new and lasting profile.

For all that, during Henry's lifetime the "**Henrican Reformation**" was primarily an institutional, not a doctrinal, revolution. Although the king took four more wives following Anne Boleyn's dramatic fall from favor, he continued in the Catholic faith and Catholic practice, promoting stern laws against Protestant "heresy." After his death in 1547, though, his young son **Edward VI**—the last of the Tudor kings—was entrusted to a council dominated by those sympathetic to the reformed religion. During Edward's reign England finally became what it was already assumed to be: a Protestant nation.

1485 Following his victory over Richard III at **Bosworth Field**, Henry Tudor is formally crowned **Henry VII** at Westminster on October 30. Significantly, he dates his accession from the day before the battle in order to **attaint** those who fought against him for treason; Yorkist estates are confiscated. Basing his claim to the throne on descent from his Lancastrian ancestor **John of Gaunt** as well as by the "judgment of God" shown in battle, in November Henry summons **Parliament** to legitimize his control still further. His anxiety to do so is perhaps symptomatic—much of his reign will be spent combating rebellion inside his kingdom, often in support of rival pretenders. Ruling through an **enlarged council** that includes lawyers and members of the gentry, Henry uses existing laws to curtail the powers of the barons.

1486 To strengthen his position among surviving Yorkists, Henry VII marries Edward IV's daughter, **Elizabeth of York**. During festivities held in York itself the **Tudor Rose**—an amalgam of the red and white roses of Lancaster and York—is displayed for the first time.

A rebellion mounted by **Francis, Lord Lovell**, formerly chamberlain to Richard III, is crushed.

1487 Henry VII's Yorkist opponents, led by Richard III's nephew the **earl of Lincoln** and his sister **Margaret**, the dowager **duchess of Burgundy**, encourage a rebellion by supporting the pretender **Lambert Simnel**. Simnel, an Oxfordshire apprentice who bears a striking resemblance to **Edward, Earl of Warwick** (the duke of Clarence's son) is proclaimed king in **Dublin**, with the connivance of the Irish nobility. In England the Yorkist forces, including 2000 mercenaries sent by Margaret of Burgundy, are routed at **East Stoke**, Nottinghamshire in June. Lincoln and the mercenary commander **Martin Schwartz** are killed, but Simnel is pardoned and offered a junior position in the royal kitchens.

A royal statute for the first time refers by name to the **Court of Star Chamber**, named after the decorated ceiling of the room in which

Henry's council meets as a judiciary to hear criminal cases. Under Henry's successors, Star Chamber develops a reputation as a formidable instrument of royal coercion.

1489 Henry VII signs the **Treaty of Medina del Campo** with Spain, beginning the Tudors' long association with Europe's emerging superpower.

Following the death of the **earl of Northumberland**—lynched while trying to collect taxes in York—Henry VII fills the power vacuum in the north by promoting the **Howard family**, gradually returning lands and titles confiscated after Bosworth.

The king contemplates war against France in order to recover **Brittany**, now absorbed into French domains, but is deterred by the likely expenditure.

1491 **Perkin Warbeck**, trained by Margaret of Burgundy to impersonate Edward IV's younger son **Richard**, emerges as a fresh and more threatening Yorkist pretender to Henry VII's throne. His first attempt to invade England fails, though.

1492 Henry VII concludes the **Treaty of Etaples** with France, securing an indemnity of £159,000—equivalent to twice the Crown's annual revenues at the time—in return for abandoning all his claims to French territories other than Calais. The treaty bolsters European recognition of Tudor rule in England.

1494 Henry VII's position in Ireland is strengthened by the passage of **Poyning's Law**, which requires all Irish legislation to gain the king of England's consent.

1495 **Perkin Warbeck** becomes the focus of renewed rebellion. Supported by the Holy Roman Emperor **Maximilian I**, James IV of Scotland and Margaret of Burgundy, Warbeck lands at **Deal**, but is soon forced to flee to Scotland.

1496 Although a Scottish army crosses the border in support of Warbeck, the pretender's cause is undermined when Henry VII joins

the **Holy League**—an alliance promoted by King Ferdinand of
Spain and Emperor Maximilian against French aggression in Italy—
and signs the **Magnus Intercursus**, a trading and defense treaty with
the Netherlands and Burgundy.

A royal charter is granted to an association of **Staplers**, responsible
for collecting and distributing England's raw wool.

1497 Warbeck invades **Cornwall**, but soon afterwards his forces are
defeated and Warbeck himself is captured at **Beaulieu** in Hampshire.

Henry VII concludes a **peace treaty** with James IV.

HENRY VII (1457–1509)

*H*enry Tudor's claim to the throne was genuine enough, but it
was remote. The founder of the Tudor dynasty was a curious, but not especially unusual, mix of Welsh, French and
English lineages. His mother, **Margaret Beaufort**, was a great granddaugh-
ter of John of Gaunt's mistress **Catherine Swynford**, whom Gaunt married
only after she had borne him children. Another source of royal blood was his
paternal grandmother, **Catherine of France**, who married Owen Tudor after
the death of her first husband, Henry V. Edmund, Owen's son and Henry's
father, rose to become earl of Richmond, but it was Henry's uncle,
Jasper Tudor, Earl of Pembroke, who raised the future king, removing him
to Brittany after the Lancastrian debacle at Tewkesbury in 1471.

As king, Henry's preoccupation was to secure the throne against the continuing Yorkist challenge. In this he succeeded, and he proved an outstand-
ingly successful monarch in other respects too. He ended up doubling royal
revenues by cannily enforcing royal rights to feudal dues and legal fees,

Armed with letters patent granted by Henry the previous year, and perhaps accompanied by his son Sebastian, the Italian navigator **Giovanni Caboto** (his name anglicized as **John Cabot**) sets out from **Bristol** with eighteen men on board the *Matthew* to cross the Atlantic in order to discover "new lands" for the English crown. He lands in **Newfoundland**, and begins charting the upper eastern American coastline. On his return he is granted a £20 royal pension.

1498 **Cabot** sets out on a **second expedition**, this time with 200 men aboard five ships. Although there is no certain record of Cabot's return and no attempt is yet made to create an English colony in the

and by levying fines instead of other forms of punishment. Internationally his greatest triumphs were agreeing the Treaty of Etaples with the French Crown and securing the hand of Catherine of Aragon for Arthur, his eldest son. He also brokered important commercial treaties, not only with Spain and the Netherlands but Florence and Denmark too. At home he tried—though with limited success—to limit the power and influence of the nobility.

But perhaps the main ingredient of Henry VII's success was his unrelenting dedication to the task of government: few English kings have worked harder. Perceived as an unglamorous, even parsimonious ruler, he has sometimes been seen as the country's first "modern" monarch. But it's more accurate to say that little was done to change or revolutionize the fabric of England: he left the country in a state of stability, albeit hard-won stability. His successor, Henry VIII, reaped the full rewards of that policy, in the process projecting himself as a "Renaissance prince" in a manner that would have been wholly alien to his father.

Americas, Cabot's voyages lay the foundation for England's later settlement in **Canada**.

1499 Warbeck and the **earl of Warwick**, Clarence's real son, are beheaded, but opposition to Henry VII continues under the leadership of **Edmund de la Pole**, the **earl of Suffolk** and eldest surviving son of Edward IV's sister **Elizabeth**.

1501 Henry VII's prestige is greatly enhanced when, to further Anglo-Spanish relations, his son and heir **Prince Arthur** is married to **Catherine of Aragon**, daughter of **Ferdinand** and **Isabella of Spain**.

1502 The peace with Scotland is consolidated by the marriage of Henry VII's daughter **Margaret** to **James IV**. But the English succession is jeopardized by the death of **Prince Arthur**, making his sickly brother **Prince Henry of York** the king's heir. Arthur's widow Catherine and her dowry, worth 200,000 crowns, remain in England.

1503 The death of Henry VII's queen, **Elizabeth**, encourages **Suffolk** to extend his plots against the Crown.

1506 Suffolk's imprisonment in the Tower of London effectively removes a major threat to Henry VII's throne.

1509 Henry VII dies, bequeathing his successor, the 18-year-old Prince Henry—now tall and renowned for his athletic ability—sound royal finances and a stable kingdom. **Henry VIII** reaffirms England's strategic alliance with an increasingly powerful Spain by marrying his brother's widow **Catherine of Aragon**, as his father had intended. Unlike his father, however, Henry VIII displays his taste for spectacle by mounting elaborate **entertainments** at his court.

1510 Henry VIII executes his father's unpopular ministers **Sir Richard Empson** and **Edmund Dudley**.

1513 In alliance with his father-in-law **Ferdinand of Spain**, Henry VIII crosses the Channel to fight against France. He succeeds in capturing **Tournai**, which is held until 1518, but his campaign is a pale imitation of Henry V's conquests of a century earlier.

The Scots, in league with **Francis I of France**, attempt an invasion of northern England, but are routed by **Thomas Howard**, the earl of Surrey, at **Flodden**. James IV and many of his nobles are killed in battle. As a reward Surrey is granted the lost Howard duchy of **Norfolk**.

1514 Peace terms are concluded with France.

Thomas Wolsey is appointed archbishop of York and then lord chancellor, and so becomes the dominant figure in English politics for fifteen years.

1515 Wolsey's power is further increased when he is appointed a cardinal by the pope.

1516 Queen Catherine gives birth to **Princess Mary**, the only one of her children to survive infancy.

Utopia, a brief tract by **Thomas More** that recommends a form of communist theocracy as the ideal society, is published at **Louvain** (now in Belgium).

1517 More is invited to join the king's council.

In **Wittenberg**, Martin Luther sparks the Reformation with the publication of his **95 theses**, denouncing the Roman Church for its abuses. The **Lutheran religion** that follows holds that man can achieve salvation by "faith alone," without recourse to the Church's intercession.

1518 Wolsey, now raised to legate *a latere* by the pope (resident ruler of the Church in England), scores a major but short-lived diplomatic triumph when he engineers the **Treaty of London**, a multilateral mutual security pact between Europe's leading powers.

1519 Following the death of Maximilian, **Charles V**, already king of Spain and duke of Burgundy—the latter giving him nominal control over the Netherlands—becomes **Holy Roman Emperor**, and so rules over a greater conglomeration of territories than has been seen in western Europe since the Roman Empire itself.

1520 As European politics realign to take account of Charles V's unprecedented empire, **Henry VIII** and **Francis I** stage a reconciliation of their diplomatic interests, organized by **Wolsey**, at the **Field of Cloth of Gold** outside Calais—a huge (and hugely expensive) three-week cultural spectacle of feasting, jousting and wrestling.

1521 As the **Reformation** spreads in northern Europe and the Roman Church comes increasingly under doctrinal as well as institutional attack, Henry VIII writes and publishes *Assertio*

CARDINAL WOLSEY (C.1472–1530)

*T*homas Wolsey was not the last churchman to play a leading role in English politics, but he was one of the more impressive. Reputedly the son of an Ipswich butcher, he became Henry VII's chaplain in 1507; noting his energy and appetite for work, the new king kept him on at court. It was after organizing the French campaign of 1513 that Wolsey rose to real prominence: by 1515 he was lord chancellor, in addition to being cardinal and archbishop of York. From then until the year before his death he was the most powerful man in the land after the king. Theirs was a close working relationship, and one Wolsey knew well how to manipulate: the Italian scholar **Polydore Vergil** observed that "every time he wished to obtain something from Henry, he introduced the matter casually into his conversation; then he brought out some small present or another, a beautifully fashioned dish, for example, or a jewel or ring or gifts of that sort, and while the king was admiring the gift intently, Wolsey would adroitly bring forward the project on which his mind was fixed."

Although Wolsey was appointed papal legate in 1518 to oversee reforms within the English Church, the cardinal concentrated his energies

Septum Sacramentorum Adversus Martinum Lutherum ("Defense of the seven sacraments against Martin Luther"). For this he is rewarded by the pope with the title **Fidei Defensor** ("Defender of the faith").

1522 Henry VIII and Wolsey attempt a further invasion of **France**, but this proves an expensive failure.

1523 Parliament is summoned to raise new taxes, but those granted are insufficient to the Crown's requirements.

on solidly secular matters. He deployed the Court of Star Chamber to bring unruly barons to justice, and he created the Court of Requests to hear cases brought by poorer subjects. With the Eltham Ordinances, Wolsey radically downsized the court by expelling Henry's controversial young companions, his "minions," from their sinecures. It was, however, in the international arena that Wolsey's star shone brightest—and where it finally fell. He endeavored to promote Henry VIII's European reputation by opportunistically exploiting differences between Francis I of France and Charles V of Spain. The Treaty of London (1518) and the Field of Cloth of Gold (1520) marked the high points of this policy, but thereafter it unravelled. At the same time Wolsey was becoming widely unpopular, being blamed for high levels of taxation and resented for his deliberately ostentatious household.

It was the king's displeasure that brought about his downfall. A treaty between Charles V and Francis I in 1528 isolated England diplomatically, and in the following year Wolsey failed to deliver the promised divorce from Catherine of Aragon. The more serious accusation of treason followed, but—ever the statesman—Wolsey died before his trial.

> Why come ye nat to court?
> To whyche court?
> To the kynges court,
> Or to Hampton Court?
> The kynges courte
> Shulde have the excellence;
> But Hampton Court
> Hath the preemynence.
>
> —John Skelton,
> *Why come ye nat to court?* (c.1522)

1524 Wolsey, appointed **papal legate** for life, declares **new taxes** without reference to Parliament, but is forced to rescind them.

1525 In Italy, **Francis I** is defeated and captured by Charles V's imperial army at **Pavia**. Wolsey, having supported France, is hard-pressed to defend his policies—the more so as England's trade with the Netherlands suffers as a consequence.

A combination of **economic depression**, **plague** and the growing impact of **Lutheranism** makes the country restless.

1527 Having fallen in love with **Anne Boleyn**, the sister of a former mistress, Henry VIII initiates **divorce proceedings** against Queen Catherine on the twin grounds of her failure to provide him with a male heir, and that as the widow of his deceased brother his marriage to her is biblically illegal. Wolsey, still wishing to pursue an alliance against Catherine's nephew Emperor Charles V, supports the king's wishes. Difficulties arise, however, when an annulment petition is forwarded to **Pope Clement VII**, effectively Charles's prisoner in Italy.

1529 After protracted negotiations with the papacy, the pope's legate, **Cardinal Lorenzo Campeggio**, arrives in England to hear Henry VIII's divorce case alongside Wolsey. But Campeggio pronounces that the case must be heard in **Rome**, where a ruling against Catherine is unthinkable. In August, Henry's position is further weakened when Charles V and Francis I resolve their differences by the **Peace of Cambrai**. Losing patience with his chancellor, Henry dismisses Wolsey in October, stripping him of all his secular titles and property. **Thomas More**, known to be held in high esteem by the pope but opposed to the divorce, is appointed chancellor instead.

In November, aware that Wolsey's harsh measures have made the Crown unpopular, Henry summons a parliament, known as the **Reformation Parliament**, in an endeavor to refurbish his image. The mood of the **House of Commons**, sitting separately from the Lords, is notably anti-clerical. Over seven years the same Parliament will enact 137 statutes, many of them designed to destroy the power of the medieval Church.

1530 In November Wolsey is arrested in York on charges of treason, but dies later on the journey to London to face trial.

1531 The English Church grants Henry VIII a gift of £119,000 after the king threatens legal proceedings against the church's "**infringements**" of royal rights.

1532 Still unable to secure a papal annulment of his marriage to Catherine, Henry VIII turns to his councilor **Thomas Cromwell**, a known Lutheran sympathizer, to further his divorce. Cromwell, who remains in power for the next eight years as Henry's principal minister, oversees the **Henrican Reformation**, relying heavily on Parliament to separate the Church in England from Rome. Cromwell also masterminds a comprehensive **reform of administrative departments**, leading to improved efficiency in government.

1533 In January Henry VIII secretly and bigamously marries **Anne Boleyn**, already pregnant with his child.

In April Parliament passes an **Act in Restraint of Appeals**. Forbidding appeals to be made to Rome in any matter whatsoever, this marks the beginning of England's formal repudiation of papal authority.

In May **Thomas Cranmer**, elected archbishop of Canterbury in March and sympathetic to Henry's plight, presides over ecclesiastical hearings that result in the **unilateral annulment** of the king's marriage to Catherine of Aragon.

THOMAS MORE (1477–1535)

*A*lthough the European Reformation had many root causes, it was nourished by a diffuse intellectual movement that became known as humanism, which was based on a revival of Greek learning that inspired a reappraisal of existing political, social and religious institutions. Although this "new learning" germinated in Italy, its leading light in northern Europe was the Dutch Desiderius Erasmus, and one of its most celebrated literary creations, Utopia, was written by an Englishman.

Thomas More was a Londoner who began his career as a lawyer, becoming an under-sheriff for the City in 1510. From 1499 he enjoyed a close friendship with Erasmus, who described him as "omnium horarum homo," a "man for all seasons," and encouraged him to develop his literary work in print. Deploying similar ironic strategies to Erasmus's own *Moriae encomium* ("the praise of folly"), which itself puns on More's surname, *Utopia* outlines a supposedly ideal society located on a mythical island off the Americas—its title, coined by More, means "no-place." While the author's earthly paradise is described with a perfectly straight face, it offers an

On June 1, Boleyn is **crowned** Queen of England. On September 7 she gives birth to a girl, **Elizabeth**. In the same month Henry is **excommunicated** by the pope.

1534 Parliament passes three key statutes in rapid succession: an **Act of Succession**, enforcing recognition of Henry's marriage to Boleyn and legitimizing any male offspring as heir to the throne; an **Act of Supremacy**, confirming Henry VIII's status as "supreme head of the English church" and abolishing papal jurisdiction in

oblique critique of contemporary values, advocating a communal lifestyle in which everything from labor to dining is shared—a mode of society which has been seen to foreshadow not only Marxist thinking but the communities some Puritans attempted to establish in the 17th century.

But as More's career advanced and Lutheranism gathered pace, more serious business began to occupy him. He became increasingly concerned with combating the "heresies" of the Reformists, publishing a steady stream of fierce attacks on the new religion. More entered royal service in 1517, and in October 1529 replaced Wolsey as lord chancellor. But his political usefulness to Henry VIII soon ended. In 1534 More refused to agree to the Act of Supremacy, and he refused to attend the king's wedding with Anne Boleyn; his resignation followed soon afterwards. After a swift show trial he was convicted of treason and sentenced to death. His last work, *A Dialogue of Comfort against Tribulation*, was composed while imprisoned in the Tower of London; the following July he was beheaded on Tower Hill. He was canonized in 1935.

England; and an **Act of Treason**, expanding the definition of treason to cover seditious writing and talk. The last, framed against "dissent," enables Cromwell to bring to trial and execute **Thomas More**, **John Fisher** (the bishop of Rochester) and other loyalists opposed to Henry's divorce.

1536 Catherine of Aragon dies in January. Shortly afterwards the king is **injured** whilst jousting, perhaps marking the beginning of the chronic ill-health that affects the remainder of his life.

Anne Boleyn **miscarries**; the allegedly deformed fetus encourages gossip that the eleven-fingered queen is a witch. But it is her failure to provide Henry (now in love with **Jane Seymour**) with a male heir that leads to her downfall. On May 19, following accusations of treason, adultery and incest with her brother **Lord Rochford**, Anne is **executed**. In August Henry VIII marries Seymour, already pregnant with his child.

Guided by **Cromwell**, Parliament begins enacting legislation that, over the coming four years, will bring about the **dissolution of the monasteries**. The argument against the monasteries is that as international Catholic bodies they undermine the king's position as supreme head of the English Church; needless to say, confiscation of monastic lands also brings with it a vast windfall for the royal treasury.

Parliament passes an **Act of Union**, giving the people of Wales legal equality with the king's English subjects, but prohibiting Welsh-only speakers from holding office.

> I pray you, Master Lieutenant, see me safe up, and my coming down let me shift for myself.
>
> **—Thomas More,**
> **mounting the scaffold, 1535**

Towards the end of the year, a major Catholic uprising, known as the **Pilgrimage of Grace**—comprising those dismayed by the separation from Rome, but which is also fuelled by economic hardship—begins in **Lincolnshire** and **Yorkshire**.

1537 To Henry VIII's joy, Jane Seymour gives birth to a male heir, **Prince Edward**. To his grief, she dies in childbirth.

The **Pilgrimage of Grace** is crushed and Henry stamps his authority on the north, executing scores of local nobility and gentry and the rebels' principal spokesman, **Robert Aske**.

In a concession to Protestant feeling, a translation of the **Bible** into English by **Miles Coverdale** is "authorized" by the king's government.

1539 To draw England closer to Germany's Lutheran princes, Thomas Cromwell "arranges" a marriage between Henry VIII and Anne of Cleves. To whet Henry's appetite, Cromwell commissions Hans Holbein the Younger of Augsburg, then resident in England, to paint a flattering portrait of the unseen bride.

1540 Anne of Cleves arrives in England. Meeting her for the first time, Henry VIII likens her to a "Flemish mare," but proceeds with the wedding. His disappointment, however, provides an opportunity for Cromwell's enemies: by June the king is persuaded that Cromwell is both a traitor and a heretic. On July 12 king and queen are **divorced**; sixteen days later Cromwell is **executed** without trial. On the same day Henry VIII marries his fifth wife, **Catherine Howard**.

Parliament enacts the **Six Articles**, which broadly define the English Church's doctrines in traditional, neo-Catholic terms; Protestantism remains illegal in England.

As the **dissolution of the monasteries** reaches completion, the Crown begins selling off some of the confiscated lands in order to meet its debts. This increases the land-share of England's gentry.

1541 Henry VIII assumes the title **king of Ireland**.

1542 Archbishop Cranmer, supportive of Protestant elements at court and opposed to the "conservative" Howards, writes in secret to Henry VIII accusing Catherine Howard of adultery. Catherine is executed after her supposed lovers "confess" under torture.

A Scottish army, in league with France, is crushed at **Solway Moss**. James V of Scotland dies shortly afterwards, and is succeeded by his infant daughter, **Mary, Queen of Scots**.

THOMAS CROMWELL (C.1485–1540)

Sometimes called England's first parliamentary statesman, Thomas Cromwell was Henry VIII's second great minister. He was born in Putney, the son of a cloth-worker, and while his early career remains shadowy—he appears to have spent time in Italy and the Netherlands—he entered Wolsey's service around 1520. Following the cardinal's disgrace, Cromwell extricated himself from the fallout and entered Parliament, where he gained Henry VIII's attention. He was admitted to the Privy Council in 1530, and in 1532 emerged as the most powerful of the king's officials.

His greatest coups occurred simultaneously: he realized Henry VIII's divorce from Catherine of Aragon and brought about the creation of an English Church wholly separated from Rome. To do this he relied upon his own skills as a parliamentary fixer to ensure the approval of several key statutes, culminating in the Act of Supremacy in 1534. Using the same means, and against considerable opposition, he oversaw the dissolution of the monasteries. As a result the Reformation in England was achieved with relatively little bloodshed, at least in its early stages. As importantly, the House of Commons became an integral aspect of the English polity. Nor was

To pay for his campaigns, Henry VIII fuels inflation by debasing the coinage.

A **Second Act of Union** provides for Welsh members to attend parliament, but also imposes full English administration throughout the principality.

1543 Anglo-Scottish hostilities are concluded by the **Treaty of Greenwich** which brokers the betrothal of Prince Edward and Mary,

Cromwell's strategy merely pragmatic: he nurtured constitutionalist ideas of a national sovereignty based on the king-in-parliament. During his ascendancy he also restructured the machinery of government, creating separate administrative departments outside of the king's household run by a more highly trained bureaucracy than had yet been seen in England.

Yet Henry's complex marital affairs proved, as for Wolsey, Cromwell's stumbling block. Fearing a hostile alliance between Charles V and Francis I, he pushed the king into a union with **Anne of Cleves** in 1540, attempting to promote a counter-alliance with the Protestant princes of Germany. Although he was created earl of Essex in the same year, seemingly assured of continuing royal favor, the increasingly unstable king had begun to listen to Cromwell's enemies. The Catholic-leaning dukes of Norfolk and Suffolk, suspecting that Cromwell wished to push reform of the Church further, seized their opportunity and arrested him. Cromwell's career was over, and he was beheaded in July. Yet Henry swiftly regretted the loss of his most able—and most faithful—servant. He never invested the same kind of power in a single minister again.

Queen of Scots. The treaty is quickly repudiated by the Scottish Parliament, however.

The English Parliament legislates an **Act for Abolishing Diversity of Opinion**, intended to discourage lingering loyalties to Rome.

Henry VIII marries his sixth and final wife, **Catherine Parr**.

1544 Charles V and Francis I, both loyal to Roman Catholicism, conclude a peace treaty without reference to Henry VIII, who launches a renewed attack on France. **Boulogne** is seized, and remains in English hands for eight years.

HENRY VIII (1491–1547)

*T*here were many Henry VIIIs. One was the sickly child who unexpectedly inherited his brother Arthur's position as heir to the English kingdom. Another was the glamorous Renaissance prince who ascended the throne in 1509. Another was the husband who executed two of his six wives. Yet another was the Henry of his last years—paranoid, vicious, so overweight that he had to be moved around with the aid of machines.

In one way, though, Henry remained constant. Although the young king seemed eager to stamp his personality on the new regime by reversing a number of his father's policies and launching into war with France (with little success), his interest in work soon waned. He never enjoyed the day-to-day grind of politics, preferring to hunt or dabble in music and philosophy while his ministers labored away. That his reign changed England so much is mainly due to the influence of two men, **Thomas Wolsey** and **Thomas Cromwell**, who alike realized that the king's personality allowed

The king also orders a fresh assault on Scotland by way of "rough wooing" on behalf of Prince Edward.

1546 Bereft of allies, Henry VIII finally abandons his French campaigns.

Anne Askew, burned at the stake for heresy, becomes England's first "Protestant" martyr. **Sir Thomas Wriothesley** (later earl of Southampton) and **Sir Richard Rich** attempt to implicate the Protestant-leaning Catherine Parr as a member of Askew's circle, but when Wriothesley "arrests" Catherine in front of the king, Henry intervenes.

1547 Henry VIII dies on January 28, and is succeeded by his 9-year-old son **Edward VI**. Loose ends are rapidly tied: the king's maternal

them unprecedented power to control and develop policy. Henry needed ministers who had the talent to realize his grand ambitions for the English throne: both Wolsey and Cromwell, in their different ways, provided that. But Henry's quixotic behavior—which grew ever more erratic as he aged—was also their undoing. The king was his own master, and could not tolerate failure.

He certainly found it hard to tolerate his own failure to provide a male heir. He had acted decisively in marrying his brother's widow, Catherine of Aragon, in 1509, but as their relationship deteriorated with no son in sight, it was a decision he came increasingly to regret. Genuinely fearful that God was punishing him for marrying illegally, he decided to have the union annulled—with spectacular consequences. But a lasting solution to Henry's problem proved elusive. Though he died believing his succession to be secure at last, his son would survive only another six years. In the end Henry's legacy was that of political division.

uncle **Edward Seymour** becomes Lord Protector, and is created **duke of Somerset**; Somerset's brother, **Thomas, Lord Seymour of Sudeley**, marries Catherine Parr and the younger of the king's two older half-sisters, **Princess Elizabeth**, lives with the couple.

Under Somerset's regency the regime is relaxed in some respects: a new **Treasons Act** significantly ameliorates the harsher measures introduced by Henry VIII to combat the spread of Protestantism. Allowed to speak and think more freely, English Protestants—beginning to be influenced by the more extreme views of **John Calvin** as well as those of Martin Luther—make use of print to disseminate their ideas more widely. But amidst the new climate of tolerance, other social and economic pressures create tensions in society and religion becomes a source of friction.

1548 Catherine Parr dies in childbirth. Thomas Seymour, seeking perhaps to oust his brother, endeavors but fails to marry **Princess Elizabeth**.

Somerset orders the removal of **religious images and statues** from churches and bans Catholic rituals such as the use of "holy water."

In the countryside, social unrest spreads as common land is **enclosed** by private landlords.

A group of twelve bishops and clergy, headed by **Archbishop Thomas Cramner**, is commissioned to draw up a uniform order of service for use throughout the English Church, which becomes known as the **Book of Common Prayer**.

The navigator **Sebastian Cabot**, son of John Cabot, having spent his career in Spanish and Imperial service, is given a naval command and becomes governor of the Merchant Adventurers. His attempt to establish a northeast passage to the Far East fails, but his expedition opens up a direct trade route between **England** and **Russia**.

1549 As religious dissent threatens to get out of hand, Somerset enforces an **Act of Uniformity** to impose the **Book of Common Prayer** on every church. **English** replaces Latin as the language of church services. Opposition to the Prayer Book, coupled with inflation and further land enclosure, sparks a **Catholic rebellion** in Cornwall, Devonshire and East Anglia.

Somerset also takes a more authoritarian line toward his brother **Thomas Seymour**, whom he executes for treason.

Somerset's troubles are compounded when war with **France** breaks out in the summer, following an unsuccessful intervention in Scotland. Blamed for the nation's troubles by fellow councilors, he is imprisoned in the Tower in October. In the ensuing power struggle, **John Dudley, Earl of Warwick** crushes **Kett's rebellion** in **East Anglia** and emerges victorious. Appointed lord president of the king's council, he swiftly terminates the war against Scotland.

1550 Warwick terminates the war against France by surrendering **Boulogne**. His decisive policies make him unpopular, though, when he presses for further reform of the Church. A dispute erupts when leading reformist **John Hooper** refuses to wear Episcopal vestments for his consecration as bishop of Gloucester. Several "conservative" bishops are imprisoned. In London, **Bishop Nicholas Ridley** orders altars to be replaced by simple tables. Although the young king becomes involved on the side of the reformists, his elder half-sister Mary refuses to use the Prayer Book.

1551 Warwick is created **duke of Northumberland**.

Somerset, released in 1550, is rearrested and returned to the Tower.

An exceptionally **bad harvest** adds to economic instability.

1552 To clarify "official" religious policy, a **second Prayer Book**, again written by Cranmer, is promoted. Bishop Ridley's London practices are adopted across the country, and the church is stripped of its surviving wealth.

Somerset is **executed**.

1553 As it becomes apparent that **Edward VI** is suffering from a wasting illness, Northumberland easily persuades him to draw up a will that excludes his half-sisters Mary and Elizabeth from the succession in favor of his cousin **Lady Jane Grey**, married shortly beforehand to Northumberland's own son, **Guildford Dudley**.

On July 6 Edward VI **dies**, and Northumberland proclaims Lady Jane queen. Uncrowned, her "reign" lasts barely nine days. Taking full advantage of Northumberland's unpopularity and banking on her Tudor pedigree, **Princess Mary** surrounds herself with followers at **Framlingham** (East Anglia), and marches on London. Northumberland is seized and executed; "Queen" Jane and her husband are imprisoned.

The Tudor queens
1553-1603

Before 1553 no woman had ruled England in her own right; in the half-century that followed two unmarried women acceded to the throne. The brief reign of Mary I coincided with a low-point in Tudor fortunes, exacerbated by her struggle to resuscitate Roman Catholicism in England. As a result of her subsequent marriage to Philip II of Spain, she helped draw the nation into a prolonged European contest between the two religions which all but resulted in a Spanish invasion thirty years after her death.

Elizabeth I was Protestant but, unlike her sister, she played her religion to political advantage. Her settlement of the English Church took a middle course: the Anglican service set out in 1559 incorporated a revised version of Cranmer's Book of Common Prayer, blended elements of Catholic and Lutheran practice, but retained an Episcopal structure. Archbishops and bishops continued to rule the roost, though now under the authority of the monarch. Elizabeth also displayed a degree of tolerance toward her Catholic subjects. The Mass was officially banned, but in reality she turned a blind eye to its continued celebration in many parts of the country—at least until the religion presented a more palpable threat.

That threat was epitomized by **Mary, Queen of Scots**: the grand-daughter of Henry VIII's sister Margaret and, until Elizabeth produced children of her own, heir presumptive to the throne. Indeed, in the eyes of some Catholics, Mary had an even stronger claim to the throne than Elizabeth. Because Elizabeth was the daughter of Anne Boleyn, who had "illegally" displaced Catherine of Aragon as Henry VIII's queen, she could be considered illegitimate. Inevitably Mary became the focus of plots to depose Elizabeth, both before and after her imprisonment in 1568. But even her execution in 1587 did not resolve the central conundrum. Who would succeed Elizabeth?

As an unmarried monarch Elizabeth attracted the attentions of many suitors, both domestic and foreign. Yet, perhaps recognizing that the potential for long-term disadvantage outweighed any short-term gain, Elizabeth opted to remain single. And this was the trump card of her widely acclaimed statecraft: whatever her personal motives, by not marrying she retained her independence and with it the independence of her people.

That said, it was not an easy reign. In addition to the Spanish threat, Elizabeth had to contend with the intermittent hostility of France and with rebellions at home and in Ireland. The well-documented Catholic plots against her life were tangible and dangerous, and increasingly a new breed of English Protestant, the **Puritans**, challenged not only her view of religion but also the aspirations of the Tudor dynasty: the monarch might be equal to the pope, but God was still above them both. Well before the century was out the Puritans had established a foothold in the House of Commons and began pressing for freedom of speech as well as further reform of the Church. Despite her careful-ly constructed image as the people's queen—"Gloriana"—Elizabeth faced more dissent at the end of her rule than she did at its beginning.

And the Crown faced further difficulty with the Commons. Courtesy of Thomas Cromwell, the House had become an integral part of English politics and, as the more vociferous of the two parliamentary chambers, it learned how to flex what muscle it had—especially with regard to the granting of taxes. Yet Elizabeth had the political skill to hold her own.

Although the Elizabethan "golden age" is more nostalgic gloss than fact (by the time of the queen's death she was deeply unpopular), it is undeniable that this era witnessed the belated flowering of Italianate Renaissance culture in England. Dazzling talents such as **William Shakespeare**, **Christopher Marlowe** and **Ben Jonson** filled London theaters with the latest dramatic spectacles; poets including **Edmund Spenser**, **Michael Drayton** and **Sir Philip Sidney**

MARY I (1516–58)

*B*y remaining loyal to both her religious faith and her husband, Philip of Burgundy, Mary I rapidly forfeited the popularity that swept her to the throne in the wake of her half-brother Edward VI's death. It is as "Bloody Mary" that she is often remembered, responsible for the deaths of up to three hundred Protestants at the stake.

Yet that reputation is not entirely fair. Heretics had regularly been beheaded or burned since the days of Henry V's persecution of the Lollards: her father Henry VIII had put dozens to death and so had the avidly Protestant duke of Northumberland, waging war against those Catholics who resisted Cranmer's Prayer Book. Such pogroms were a brutal part of the religious battles that dominated 16th-century Europe; in the Netherlands alone thousands went to their deaths. What singled Mary out for infamy was a combination of circumstances: a relatively high incidence of executions over a relatively short period; the brilliant propaganda of John Foxe's

gave English verse new eloquence; composers such as **Thomas Tallis**, **William Byrd** and **John Dowland** built a distinctively English musical tradition.

It was also during the reign of Elizabeth that the English began to look beyond Europe. Francis Drake's circumnavigation of the globe did much to enhance his country's reputation. And although Walter Raleigh and others still struggled to found a colony in the Americas, after what seemed like a miraculous deliverance from the Spanish Armada in 1588 England's maritime future looked bright.

1553 Shortly after Mary I accedes to the throne, aged 37, Parliament debates the question of her marriage. The queen is urged to marry an

Book of Martyrs (1563), describing those killings in gory detail; and the bald fact that, under Elizabeth, Catholicism was decisively displaced in England. In reality, the burnings were probably not masterminded by Mary herself—who was devout rather than fanatical—but by her zealous co-religionists, bishops Bonner and Gardiner, under the supervision of Cardinal Pole.

In fact Mary's devastatingly unhappy personal life leaves much to sympathize with. The political pawn of her father, stigmatized as a bastard and at one point reduced to a lady-in-waiting to her younger half-sister Elizabeth, Mary fervently believed that she was returning England to the true faith. After her long wait for marriage, the disappointment of her miscarriage in 1555 (if indeed she had ever been pregnant) was crushing; so too was Philip's swift departure for the Netherlands later that year. At the end she died largely unmourned, even by Philip—who wrote coldly that "I felt a reasonable regret at her death."

Englishman, perhaps her cousin **Edward Courtenay**, but Mary persists with her ambition to marry **Philip of Burgundy**, the staunchly Catholic son of **Emperor Charles V**.

1554 Rejecting Parliament's advice, Mary concludes a peace treaty with **Spain**, part of Charles V's empire. As her forthcoming marriage to Philip becomes a certainty, she faces rebellion. A revolt led by Jane Grey's father the **duke of Suffolk** miscarries, as a result of which Jane and her husband **Guildford Dudley** are executed; Princess Elizabeth, also implicated in the plot, only escapes because of a lack of evidence. Another rebellion breaks out in **Kent** under the leadership of **Sir Thomas Wyatt**, and reaches London.

Mary proceeds with her marriage to Philip, and the expatriate Cardinal Reginald Pole arrives from Rome specifically to oversee the restoration of the Catholic Church in England.

1555 Parliament passes an Act restoring **papal supremacy**. To discourage further rebellion, the titles of former Church and monastic lands

---

With thoughts intent upon a far higher object than the empty threats of man, he reached the spot dyed with the blood of Ridley and Latimer. There he knelt for a short time in earnest devotion, and then arose, that he might undress and prepare for the fire. Two friars who had been parties in prevailing upon him to abjure, now endeavoured to draw him off again from the truth, but he was steadfast and immovable in what he had just professed and publicly taught. A chain was provided to bind him to the stake, and after it had tightly encircled him, fire was put to the fuel and the flames began soon to ascend.

—**John Thomas describing Thomas Cranmer's execution in the *Book of Martyrs* (1563)**

are guaranteed to their new owners. **Heresy laws** are revived, though, and enthusiastically applied. During Mary's reign some three hundred Protestants are eliminated: the first, **John Rogers**, is executed in February; **Bishop Hooper** is burned in the same month, and bishops **Ridley** and **Latimer** are burned in October. Thomas Cranmer, now imprisoned, is replaced as archbishop of Canterbury by **Reginald Pole** and persuaded to sign papers accepting Catholic doctrines.

England's first joint-stock company, the Muscovy Company, is founded.

1556 Philip of Burgundy becomes **Philip II of Spain** following the abdication of his father.

In March, **Cranmer** recants his statement of faith and is burned at the stake in Oxford.

Plots develop to replace Mary with her sister **Elizabeth**.

1557 Philip II, intending to wage war against France, comes to England to raise troops; a French army is defeated by an Anglo–Spanish force at **St Quentin**.

As a result of a complex wrangle between the pope and Charles V, Archbishop Pole is deprived of his powers and investigated for heresy.

1558 The war in France turns against Philip, and England loses **Calais**, its last continental possession: "When I am dead and opened," Mary mourns, "you shall find Calais in my heart."

The queen dies on November 17, followed twelve hours later by **Archbishop Pole**. Immediately her sister is proclaimed queen as **Elizabeth I**. Among her first acts is to appoint **William Cecil** secretary of state.

1559 As Mary I's Catholic restoration is overturned, Parliament passes new **Acts of Supremacy and Uniformity**, making Elizabeth "**supreme governor**" of the Church of England. Public celebration of the Mass is outlawed, although Catholics are permitted to continue their rituals privately upon payment of a monthly fine. All but two of Mary's bishops refuse to accept the "**Elizabethan settlement**" and are removed from their sees. **Matthew Parker** becomes archbishop of Canterbury.

Philip II of Spain offers to marry Elizabeth, but is rejected.

In Scotland, Protestants revolt against the Queen Regent **Mary of Guise**.

In France, Mary Queen of Scots' husband **Francis II** succeeds to the throne. The **Treaty of Cateau–Cambresis** brings the war with France to an end.

1560 Robert Dudley, son of Northumberland and a favorite of the queen, is damaged politically by the mysterious death of his wife

ELIZABETH I (1533–1603)

*E*lizabeth I has sometimes been accused of reacting to events rather than shaping them. Although this criticism contains a grain of truth, it's difficult to see how things could have been much different. During her reign England was threatened not only by the upheavals of the Reformation, but by the very real prospect of a Spanish conquest. These difficulties called for a flexible response, but they also demanded a commanding personality in control. Elizabeth provided both.

The settlement of the English Church during the early years of her reign struck a lucky balance between the main religious elements of the day. In civil matters, too, Elizabeth presided over a government that helped England attain unprecedented prosperity—she had a gift for identifying able administrators, among them Burghley and Walsingham. But her most remarkable achievement was to show that a woman could rule as well as any man. She was not the first successful European queen—Isabella of Spain was that—but unlike Isabella she had no Ferdinand at her side.

Amy Robsart, leading to speculation that Dudley has murdered her in order to marry Elizabeth.

England gives **military assistance** to Scottish Protestants against Mary of Guise and her "French" court. The French withdraw, taking Mary, Queen of Scots with them. The **Mass** is outlawed in Scotland.

1561 Elizabeth refuses Mary, Queen of Scots permission to travel through England on her way back to Scotland following the death of her husband **Francis II**. Negotiations take place for a possible marriage between Elizabeth and **King Eric of Sweden**.

1562 Elizabeth narrowly survives **smallpox**.

Instead she manipulated her feminine allure, as well as her formidable intelligence, as an instrument of statecraft: her marital availability added an extra dimension to England's foreign relations.

She was fortunate, too, to have received an exceptional education: her tutor was the brilliant scholar and educationalist Roger Ascham, and she studied not only Latin and Greek but spoke French, Spanish and Italian. Her early life was far from uncomplicated, however. Her mother was beheaded when she was three, she was kept in seclusion at Hatfield House as a child and during Mary's reign she lived in constant fear for her life. The reasons behind her decision never to wed have been endlessly debated, but more certain than the gossip about her supposed lovers (Robert Dudley and Sir Christopher Hatton among them) is that, characteristically, she turned her marital status to political advantage. As "Gloriana," England's "virgin queen," she claimed to be married solely to her people.

Robert Dudley is restored to favor and admitted to the Privy Council.

England intervenes in the **French Wars of Religion** on the side of the Huguenot Protestants.

John Hawkins voyages for the first time to the **Caribbean**, carrying slaves from West Africa to the Spanish colonies.

1563 The **Thirty-Nine Articles**, expressing a middle way between the Catholic and extreme Protestant faiths, are approved by Convocation, and so become the bedrock of the **Anglican** faith of the Church of England. A dissenting minority in Convocation, the first **Puritans**, argue for a more simplified form of worship.

1564 Robert Dudley is created **earl of Leicester**, fuelling speculation that Elizabeth intends to marry him. Along with **Henry Stuart, Lord Darnley**, Leicester is also mentioned as a possible husband for Mary, Queen of Scots.

Peace with France is brokered by the **Treaty of Troyes**, which confirms French possession of Calais.

1565 Mary, Queen of Scots marries **Lord Darnley**.

In a crackdown on Catholic ritual, Elizabeth launches an inquiry into the use of **vestments** in the English Church.

1566 Relations between Elizabeth and Parliament deteriorate as Parliament continues to press her to marry.

1567 In Scotland, **Lord Darnley** is murdered, probably with the connivance of Mary, Queen of Scots, who aggravates matters by marrying the supposed assassin, **Lord Bothwell**. A rebellion amongst Scottish lords leads to her defeat and capture at **Carberry Hill**. Imprisoned, Mary is forced to abdicate in favor of her infant son **James VI**.

1568 Mary, Queen of Scots **escapes** captivity. After her followers are defeated at **Langside** by her son's regent, the earl of Moray, she flees to England, where she is **arrested** pending an investigation of her activities in Scotland.

Relations between England and Spain deteriorate after Elizabeth condones the seizure at sea of a cargo of **Genoese bullion** bound for the duke of Alba's army in the Netherlands.

1569 During a year of domestic disturbances, a plot is hatched to marry Mary, Queen of Scots to **Thomas Howard, Duke of Norfolk**, who joins forces with Leicester in an endeavor to oust Elisabeth's senior minister **William Cecil**. Norfolk is arrested and sent to the Tower.

In October, the earls of **Northumberland** and **Westmorland** initiate armed rebellion in the north, but their revolt is crushed within three months.

There is a rising in **Ireland**, led by **James Fitzmaurice**.

1570 A further northern rebellion, led by **Lord Dacre**, is crushed.

Negotiations open between England and France with a view to a marriage between Elizabeth and the **duc d'Anjou** (later Henry III of France).

To the discomfort of England's Catholics, **Pope Pius V** issues the bull *Regnans in Excelsis*, calling for Elizabeth's overthrow.

The Schoolmaster, or *Plain and Perfect Way of Teaching Children the Latin Tongue*, a short educational treatise that—among other things—warns Englishmen to beware of Italian licentiousness, is published two years after its author **Roger Ascham**, a former tutor of the queen, dies.

1571 Elizabeth demonstrates her continuing faith in Cecil by making him **lord treasurer** and creating him **Lord Burghley**; **Sir Francis Walsingham** becomes **secretary of state**.

The **Ridolfi Plot**, aimed at replacing Elizabeth with the **duke of Norfolk**, is uncovered and shown to be supported by the Spanish Crown. Norfolk, released the previous year, is returned to the Tower.

The queen and Parliament continue to disagree over the question of her **marriage** and succession, now complicated by the claim of **Mary, Queen of Scots**.

WILLIAM CECIL (1520–98)

*C*ecil was an outstanding example of how far a member of the gentry could rise during the Tudor period. He served Elizabeth for forty years, from the time of her accession until his death, having previously served in the administrations of her three predecessors. As a young man he had been drawn towards Protestant circles and later developed some sympathy for radical Puritans. But ultimately he balked at the prospect of dismantling the Church's Episcopalian structure, and is usually regarded as a contributing architect of the Elizabethan Settlement. As a court politician, he collided with the anti-Episcopalian **Robert Dudley, Earl of Leicester** and also with the Catholic-minded duke of Norfolk, and it was not until 1571, when he was created **Lord Burghley**, that his position as the queen's closest adviser was secure.

He remained her most loyal minister, prepared to share dissenting opinions with his sovereign but always ready to subordinate them to her interests and the national good; his motto was "to walk invisible." Burghley's greatest triumph was to forward the execution of Mary, Queen of Scots, ensuring England's continuance as a Protestant nation. While this inevitably incurred the wrath of Spain, Burghley endeavored to achieve a diplomatic outcome by negotiating with the **duke of Parma** in the Netherlands, at the same time prudently putting England's army and navy on a war footing. After the threat of the 1588 **Spanish Armada** had passed, Elizabeth's confidence in Burghley was unquestioned. When, later in the same year, in a rare emotional outburst she locked herself in her bedchamber after learning of her old favorite Leicester's death, it was Burghley who—knowing he was beyond rebuke—ordered the doors to be smashed open.

Harrow School is founded.

The **Royal Exchange**, built by Thomas Gresham, opens.

1572 Norfolk is executed.

Against a background of gathering Spanish strength, England and France conclude a treaty of mutual defence at **Blois**. Relations between the two countries are strained, however, following the massacre of thousands of **Huguenots** on **St Bartholomew's Day** in August. Even so, the duc d'Anjou's brother, the **duc d'Alençon**, is put forward as a suitor for Elizabeth.

Francis Drake, acting independently but never reprimanded by Elizabeth, sets off on a voyage to the Americas to plunder Spanish shipping.

The **Society of Antiquaries** is founded.

1573 Edinburgh Castle, held by supporters of Mary, Queen of Scots, surrenders to an Anglo-Scottish army.

1574 Charles IX of France is succeeded by **Henry III**, Elizabeth's former suitor.

The first secret **Catholic missionaries** sent by Rome to overthrow Protestantism arrive in England. From about this time **Catholic recusants** are targeted by Elizabeth's government as possible agents of sedition. Those who retain the Catholic faith—especially prevalent in the more rural parts of the country—are obliged to worship in secret. In some houses "**priest holes**" are constructed to hide Catholic clergy.

1575 Two Dutchmen, members of the extreme Protestant **Anabaptist** sect, are burned for heresy at **Smithfield**.

Edmund Grindal, sympathetic to Puritans, is elected to succeed Matthew Parker as archbishop of Canterbury.

William Byrd, perhaps the first English composer to gain a European reputation, is appointed organist to the Chapel Royal.

1576 Paul and **Peter Wentworth**, leaders of a growing faction of Puritans in the House of Commons, demand the right to discuss religious issues in Parliament, and are sent to the Tower after making disparaging comments about Elizabeth; the queen orders their release.

Martin Frobisher embarks on the first of three expeditions to discover a "northwest" sea-passage to **Japan** and **China**. Although he doesn't succeed, and also fails to establish a colony in North America, his explorations of the **Newfoundland** and **Nova Scotia** coastline contribute to England's eventual conquest of the North American continent.

ELIZABETHAN DRAMA

*T*he ancestors of Elizabethan theater stretch back into the early Middle Ages. Local pageants, aristocratic and university entertainments and the religious mystery and morality plays had entertained audiences (albeit socially segregated ones) for many years. But it took a surplus of educated university men, some curious restrictions and an architectural innovation to bring them all together into the distinctive form of professional Elizabethan drama.

Playhouses such as the **Theatre** (built 1576) and its descendants the **Rose** (1587), the **Swan** (1595) and the **Globe** (1599) offered all the world at least a view of the stage—galleried seating for the well-to-do, standing space for the groundlings. Although the earliest theaters were north of the Thames, **Bankside** in Southwark became the location of choice—timber from the dismantled Theatre even being carried across the river to construct the new Globe—perhaps because it had already become notorious for such nefarious pursuits as prostitution and bear-baiting. In any case the Puritan authorities would not license public stages within City limits, so players were forced into the "liberties" beyond.

In London, **James Burbage** begins building England's first purpose-built playhouse, the **Theatre**, in Shoreditch.

1578 As negotiations continue for a marriage between Elizabeth and d'Alençon, her favorite, Leicester, secretly marries her cousin **Lettice Knollys**.

1579 Continuing unrest in Ireland culminates in the **Desmond Rebellion**, which takes four years to suppress.

Expectations of a royal marriage are raised when d'Alençon visits England, but Elizabeth's privy council advises Elizabeth against the

The open-air playhouses encouraged drama to flourish in Elizabethan London, with professional companies including the **Admiral's Men** and the **Chamberlain's Men**, named after their aristocratic patrons, competing for audience loyalty. Because religious subjects were firmly off-limits, writers plundered a variety of sources to construct not only tragedies and comedies on the classical model but a brand-new genre, histories—these last particularly encouraged by the authorities because they were felt to reinforce national unity. That this was a rather optimistic assumption is demonstrated by the fact that a history play called *Richard II* by one **William Shakespeare** was revived by the earl of Essex on the eve of his abortive rebellion in 1601, the story of one corrupt monarch presumably intended to rouse support for the removal of another.

Most of the time the theater played safe, though—the main reason for its survival well into the next century. It launched the careers of **Christoper Marlowe** and **Thomas Kyd** (whose blockbusting *The Spanish Tragedy* was the most successful play of the 1590s) as well as later writers including **Francis Beaumont**, **John Fletcher**, **Ben Jonson**—and of course Shakespeare.

marriage. **John Stubbs** has his right hand amputated for writing *The Discoverie of a Gaping Gulf*, a virulently anti-d'Alençon tract.

The **Jesuits**, leaders of the Counter-Reformation against the spread of Protestantism, found an English college in Rome.

1580 Pope Gregory XIII declares that "it would not be a sin" to put Elizabeth "out of the world." Meanwhile two Jesuits, **Edmund Campion** and **Robert Parsons**, illegally enter England.

Francis Drake completes his **circumnavigation** of the globe.

1581 Fines against **recusants** are raised to £20 a month; **Edmund Campion** is arrested and executed.

Francis Drake is knighted by Elizabeth.

The **Levant Company** is founded to trade east of Constantinople.

1582 D'Alençon returns to France after a second visit to Elizabeth's court, his marriage proposals rejected.

1583 In September **John Whitgift**, commanded by Elizabeth to halt the spread of Puritanism, succeeds Grindal as archbishop of Canterbury. Greatly trusted by Elizabeth, Whitgift will defend and extend the values of the Anglican church during the latter stages of her reign.

In October the secretary of state, **Walsingham**, uncovers a further Catholic plot against Elizabeth. Its organizer, **Francis Throckmorton**, is arrested and later executed.

Humphrey Gilbert voyages to North America to colonize **Newfoundland**, but is drowned on the return journey.

As London's enthusiasm for theater-going grows, **Sir Edmund Tilney**, Master of the Revels, forms a new acting troupe called **The Queen's Players** to stage royal performances.

1584 The Spanish ambassador Bernardino Mendoza is expelled from England for complicity in the **Throckmorton Plot**. Relations with Spain deteriorate further when Elizabeth's Protestant ally in the Netherlands, **William I of Orange**, is assassinated.

A Franco-Spanish alliance forms aimed at preventing the Protestant **Henry of Navarre** succeeding to the French throne.

As threats against the queen multiply, representatives from every shire swear to avenge her in the event of an attempted assassination by Catholics in a **Bond of Association**.

Walter Raleigh sends an expedition to the Americas, leading in the following year to the first founding of **Virginia**, an English colony named in the queen's honor.

1585 Parliament passes an **Act for the Preservation of the Queen's Safety**, modeled on the Bond of Association.

As a **Catholic League** gains ascendancy in France, Elizabeth enters into the **Treaty of Nonsuch**, promising to assist Dutch resistance to Spanish rule in the Netherlands.

1586 A plot masterminded by **Anthony Babington** to replace Elizabeth with Mary, Queen of Scots is infiltrated by Walsingham's agents. In August Babington and his co-conspirators are arrested and executed. Both houses of parliament petition the queen to exercise her prerogative by executing Mary, Queen of Scots as well, to deter further attempts on her life. Elizabeth prevaricates, but agrees to the **Treaty of Berwick**, an Anglo-Scottish mutual defense pact.

In October Mary is arraigned by Parliament and found guilty of **treason**, but Elizabeth refuses to affirm her death warrant.

In the House of Commons the Puritan **Peter Wentworth** urges a bill to abolish the episcopacy. When ordered to desist, Wentworth speaks out in favor of free speech and is dispatched to the Tower for the second time.

In September, the adventurer **Sir Philip Sidney** dies three weeks after sustaining a musket-shot wound in the thigh while attacking a supply convoy on its way to the Spanish stronghold **Zutphen** in the Netherlands. In the years following his death Sidney's reputation as an outstanding courtier and poet is enhanced by biographical embellishments of his life and by the piratical publication of works such as *Arcadia* and *Astrophil and Stella*.

1587 Mary, Queen of Scots is executed on February 8 on the orders of the privy council. Elizabeth affects dismay when she is told, but is consoled when the bells of London's churches ring out for 24 hours. As the Queen had feared, however, news of Mary's execution incites Catholic Europe to redouble its efforts to remove her from the throne.

Drake is sent with a naval task force to **Spain**, where he "singes the King of Spain's beard" by destroying a battle fleet in the harbor of **Cadiz**.

THE BABINGTON PLOT

*I*n the wake of Pope Pius V's bull of 1570 excommunicating Elizabeth and ordering that she should be deposed, a number of plots were hatched against her. One was the conspiracy led in 1586 by the young Derbyshire gentleman **Anthony Babington**. Babington had been a page to Mary, Queen of Scots and, having fallen deeply under her spell, conspired with his accomplices **Chideock Tichborne** and **John Ballard** to set her free and assassinate Elizabeth.

Unfortunately their plans had been infiltrated by Walsingham's spies. Messages to the imprisoned Mary had been concealed in the bungs of beer-barrels delivered to her prison, but these were intercepted and doctored to persuade the conspirators to release further information. Having taken the optimistic step of sitting for a group portrait to commemorate their intended coup, the plotters and their associates divided into two groups—one to kill Elizabeth, the other to release Mary. By the time they realized that they had been discovered, it was too late.

1588 A rebuilt **armada**, numbering some 138 ships, sails toward England in April. But a combination of optimistic timing (a plan to meet with reinforcements at Calais goes badly wrong) and bad weather makes the fleet vulnerable to attack. The English commander, **Lord Howard of Effingham**, is not slow to realize this, and launches a fireship attack on August 7 with devastating results. The armada heads north, but is pursued and heavily attacked at **Gravelines**; in deteriorating weather the Spanish are forced around Scotland and Ireland, many ships being wrecked en route.

The **earl of Leicester** dies in September.

Babington attempted to switch sides, but was arrested anyway—though not before he had ordered an accomplice called **Savage** to go and kill the queen. This Savage might have done had he not lingered at a tailor's on the way, worried that without new clothes he would not gain entry to the palace. Tichborne, incapacitated by a bad leg, had no option but to sit at home and await arrest. Other associates fled to **Epping Forest** where they were soon rounded up and charged with treason.

When told all this, a furious Elizabeth asked Parliament whether, in the circumstances, the punishment of hanging, drawing and quartering could be made any more severe. Parliament replied that it had no authority to change the existing rules, but they were applied scrupulously. Babington, Tichborne, Ballard and Savage were dragged on a hurdle to the scaffold, hanged until they were unconscious, then revived, emasculated, disemboweled and finally cut up. When some spectators became distressed, Elizabeth decided to take pity on the remaining prisoners—they were hanged *before* being mutilated.

THE SPANISH ARMADA

*P*hilip II's decision to invade England was not simply based on a desire to depose his sister-in-law and reinstate Roman Catholicism. Spanish shipping on its way to the Americas was regularly attacked by English pirates, whose activities Elizabeth did nothing to prevent. England also intermittently supplied and supported Protestant rebels in the **Netherlands** fighting against Spanish rule there. The Armada wasn't simply a crusade: it was an instrument of revenge.

But from the beginning the expedition was bedeviled by setbacks. Philip's most experienced admiral, **Santa Cruz**, died before preparations were completed, and his replacement, the **duke of Alva**, was far less equipped to see the operation through. To achieve its purpose, the Armada had first to sail to the Netherlands, where the **duke of Parma**'s army was waiting to embark. But as soon as the Armada entered the English Channel units of Elizabeth's smaller navy—commanded by **Lord Howard of Effingham**, supported by **Sir Francis Drake** and **John Hawkins**—began to harry its flanks. Philip's ships were simply too large to manoeuvre effectively against the smaller and more agile English vessels. But the real damage was done by bad weather. A storm blew up, and Alva failed to rendezvous with Parma. Seeking to escape the confines of the Channel, Alva turned north, but the English continued to fight (inflicting substantial damage off **Gravelines**) and the weather only got worse. Alva's plan was to round the British Isles then sail home, but one by one his ships were wrecked off Britain's and Ireland's coastlines— though contrary to Elizabethan propaganda, some two-thirds of the fleet eventually made it home. Nevertheless Elizabeth was confirmed in her people's minds as a semi-divine figure protected by God Himself.

I know I have the body of a weak and feeble woman; but I have the heart and stomach of a king, and of a king of England too, and think foul scorn that Parma, or Spain, or any prince of Europe should dare to invade the borders of my realm; to which, rather than any dishonor shall grow by me, I myself will take up arms, I myself will be your general, judge, and rewarder of every one of your virtues in the field.

—Elizabeth I,
addressing her land forces at Tilbury
in anticipation of a Spanish invasion, 1588

1589 An English force is dispatched to **Portugal** to fight the Spanish, but achieves little.

England's immediate dangers are eased, however, when Henry III of France is assassinated, and is succeeded by the Protestant **Henry IV of Navarre**. As Henry's accession is resisted by the Catholic League, Elizabeth sends her co-religionist material support.

In Scotland, **James VI** marries the Protestant **Anne of Denmark**.

Archbishop Whitgift begins a campaign against **Presbyterianism**—an extreme, anti-Episcopalian form of Protestantism given voice in a series of anonymous tracts purporting to be written by "**Martin Marprelate**."

1590 Sir Francis Walsingham dies, and his office remains vacant.

Thomas Cartwright and other Puritan leaders are arrested for heresy, but Whitgift—anxious to deflect charges of bigotry away from the Anglican church—successfully urges them to be spared.

The American colony **Virginia** is found to be deserted by a relief and supply expedition.

The first three books of *The Faerie Queene* by **Edmund Spenser**, a chivalric epic celebrating Queen Elizabeth, are published.

1591 Lord Burghley's younger son **Robert Cecil** gains increasing prominence in government.

An army is dispatched to Brittany to assist **Henry IV** against the Catholic League.

1592 The text of *The Spanish Tragedy* by **Thomas Kyd** (a blockbusting drama of revenge and bloodshed), is published by its author during his lifetime—unusual for a play.

1593 **Robert Devereux, Earl of Essex**, the stepson of the earl of Leicester and Elizabeth's new favorite, joins the privy council.

In Ireland there is renewed unrest.

In May, **Christopher Marlowe**—author of *Tamburlaine*, *Dr Faustus*, *Edward II* and other outstanding stage-works, and possibly a government spy—is killed in a tavern brawl in **Deptford** in suspicious circumstances.

1594 Elizabeth's Spanish physician, **Dr Lopez**, is executed for attempting her assassination.

1595 The **earl of Tyrone** joins the burgeoning rebellion in Ireland.

Drake sets off on his last voyage to the **Caribbean**.

Sir Walter Raleigh sets out on his first voyage to **Guiana** in South America.

In the history of Essex, so perplexed in its issues, so desperate in its perturbations, so dreadful in its conclusion, the spectral agony of an abolished world is discernible through the tragic lineaments of a personal disaster.

—**Lytton Strachey,**
Elizabeth and Essex: A Tragic History **(1928)**

William Shakespeare

1596 A second **armada** sent from Spain to overthrow Elizabeth is dispersed by bad weather.

The ex-pirate and renowned explorer **Francis Drake** dies at sea off **Panama**. He is not mourned by the Spanish, who call him "the master-thief of the unknown world."

WILLIAM SHAKESPEARE (1564–1616)

*T*he plays of Shakespeare have been read and performed in more countries, and translated into more languages, than those of any other dramatist. One reason for this extraordinary celebrity is that nearly all the plays were collected seven years after his death by his colleagues John Heminges and Henry Condell, in a ground-breaking volume entitled *Mr. William Shakespeare's Comedies, Histories, & Tragedies* but now referred to as the **First Folio**. Folios were large, prestigious and expensive books, and that the editors employed the format for Shakespeare—the first time that plays alone had been published in this way—indicates not just the esteem in which he was held but the amount of money that readers were being asked to pay for his work.

Shakespeare's fame during his lifetime is revealed by the success of his poems, one of which, *Venus and Adonis* (1594), was so popular that it went through ten editions by the time of his death—only one copy of the first edition survives, the rest having presumably been read to destruction. But it was as a playwright, not a poet, that Shakespeare chose to build his career. He is recorded in 1595 as a member of the **Chamberlain's Men**, and it was with them that he remained as an actor and a shareholder in the company, an exceptionally stable working relationship that lasted nearly two

1597 Essex tries but fails to capture a Spanish treasure fleet; a third **armada** flounders off the French coast.

Pirated versions of **Shakespeare**'s plays *Romeo and Juliet*, *Richard II* and *Richard III* are published.

decades. During that time he wrote an average of two plays a year, a pattern which seems to have suited him well. An extraordinary burst of creativity around the turn of the 17th century saw him produce some of his finest works, including *As You Like It*, *Twelfth Night*, *Measure for Measure*, *Julius Caesar*, *Hamlet*, *Othello*, *King Lear*, *Macbeth* and *Antony and Cleopatra*. As the title of the First Folio testifies, he was called upon to write in a variety of genres, and by all accounts did very well out of it—the only surviving piece of correspondence addressed to Shakespeare requests a loan of £30 from him, a tidy sum in 1598.

His impact on the course of English history, like so much else, has been immeasurable. The series of "histories" he wrote in the late 1590s was hugely successful at the time and, despite the plays' unmistakably partisan view of history, they still shape popular perceptions of the past. His devilishly evil Richard III has been accused of obliterating the real king from the record, just as the dissolute but irresistible Prince Hal of the *Henry IV* plays possesses an enduring appeal for audiences and readers alike (perhaps more so than the canny careerist of reality). In his shaping of English history to form drama of remarkable power and depth, it's perhaps easy to agree with his fellow dramatist Ben Jonson that Shakespeare was "not of an age, but for all time."

The theologian **Richard Hooker** completes *Of the Laws of Ecclesiastical Polity*, an eloquent defence of the Elizabethan Church and the main source of subsequent Anglican theology.

1598 Tyrone defeats an English army at **Yellow Ford** in Ulster.

France and Spain conclude a peace treaty at **Vervins** shortly before Philip II is succeeded by **Philip III**.

Lord Burghley dies soon after his son **Robert** (later **earl of Salisbury**) is appointed secretary of state. **John Stowe** publishes the first edition of *A Survey of London*, which studies the city's history and antiquities.

1599 Against Robert Cecil's advice, Essex is appointed lord lieutenant in Ireland. He concludes a disadvantageous treaty with Tyrone and returns to London. Philip III begins planning a fourth *armada* against England. The **Globe** theater opens on **Bankside** in Southwark.

1600 Following his failure in Ireland, **Essex** is stripped of his offices and imprisoned in the Tower. Released in August, he determines to win back his position, if necessary by force.

Will Adams becomes the first Englishman to set foot in **Japan**.

The **East India Company**, a joint-stock venture destined to become the principal engine of Britain's eastern empire, is established by royal charter in London.

Richard Hakluyt publishes a second, enlarged edition of his *Principal Navigations, Voyages and Discoveries of the English Nation*, an enthusiastic account of English seafaring enterprises that encourages further expeditions.

The population of England and Wales is estimated at **four million**.

1601 Unable to win Elizabeth's favor, **Essex** half-heartedly attempts to stir **rebellion** in London but is quickly arrested. Tried for treason, he is **executed** in February.

When the House of Commons protests the grant of **monopolies** in important commodities to royal servants, Elizabeth agrees to abolish the most grievous of them and silences her critics by delivering her "**Golden Speech**" before parliament. In it she declares: "Though God hath raised me on high, yet this I count the glory of my crown: that I have reigned with your loves."

Spanish troops land in Ireland at **Kinsale**, but are besieged there by the new lord lieutenant, **Lord Mountjoy**. Tyrone, attempting to come to their rescue, is defeated, and the Spanish surrender the following year.

Ben Jonson's first solo play, *Every Man in his Humour*, is performed at the **Curtain** theatre.

1602 As Elizabeth, approaching her seventieth birthday, weakens, Robert Cecil enters into a secret correspondence with James VI of Scotland by way of preparing for the succession.

The first recorded performance of Shakespeare's ***Hamlet*** is given in July.

1603 Just hours before her death at **Richmond Palace** on March 23, Elizabeth I resolves the succession issue—begun 45 years before at her accession—by affirming **James VI of Scotland** her heir.

CHAPTER SEVEN

The Stuart Kings, the Republic, and the Restoration
{1603–1688}

THE PEACEFUL ACCESSION OF JAMES I in 1603 accomplished what Edward I and Henry VIII had attempted by force: a conjunction of the thrones of England and Scotland. The two kingdoms remained administratively separate, however. Despite the king's wishes, attempts at greater integration were resisted on both sides of the border, and it was not until the reign of James's great-grand-daughter **Queen Anne** in the early 18th century that a formal union was declared. And in England itself Elizabeth had bequeathed a complex situation. The country was financially weakened by its wars with Spain, the recent rebellion of the earl of Essex indicated a resurgence of aristocratic discontent and the Puritan movement was challenging the established Church, most vociferously in the House of Commons. These were the challenges that faced James when he crossed the border in the spring of 1603.

The new king did not cut an elegant figure: he was short (a full sixteen inches shorter than his queen), ruddy in complexion and some unflattering reports claim that he continually slavered because his tongue was too large for his mouth. He was, however, studious and intelligent and—perhaps most importantly—thoroughly Protestant. That said, he genuinely favored religious tolerance and prevented England from becoming embroiled in foreign wars until almost the last year of his reign. But, lazy in temperament and a firm proponent of the **divine right** of kings—which held that kings were the images of God upon earth—he was less adroit at handling domestic affairs.

It was widely believed that he was too dependent on a string of unpopular intimates, among them **Robert Carr** and **George Villiers**, and he was also contemptuous of the obstinate English Parliament. Despite a shortage of funds in the first years of his reign, he was reluctant to ask Parliament for money, and early in his reign authorized a sale of aristocratic titles that—whatever its short-term benefits—increased corruption and undermined the position of the Crown.

Charles I was certainly as cultured as his father—the collection of paintings he assembled was among the finest in Europe—but shared similar views about the divine status of the monarchy. And he could be equally stubborn, even autocratic, which made him many enemies over the course of his reign. When Charles attempted to initiate **personal rule** in 1629, dispensing with Parliament altogether, he failed to perceive that his enthusiasm for the **Arminians** was eroding his popular support. The Arminians, led by **Archbishop William Laud**, held high-church views and emphasized the importance of religious ritual—and as a consequence were treated with suspicion by many people, who regarded them as Catholics ("papists") in all but name. Despite his unpopularity Charles's personal rule lasted for eleven years, but he was eventually forced by lack of money to summon Parliament once more in 1640. The king's weakened position meant that he was also compelled to accept a number of humiliating restrictions on his power, among them the dismissal of Laud and his chief minister, the **earl of Strafford**, both of whom were later executed. When Parliament continued to make trouble, Charles took matters into his own hands and impeached his principal opponents for treason before marching into the House of Commons to arrest them. They had escaped beforehand, however, and as a consequence Charles decided to abandon London and set up base at the royalist stronghold of **Oxford**, in the process igniting what would become known as the **Civil Wars**.

The Civil Wars were vastly more complex than the simple image, often presented, of Royalist **Cavaliers** versus Puritan **Roundheads**. They were driven by social and economic as well as religious and political forces, and brought about domestic upheaval of unprecedented proportions. Ultimately, though, the overall political outcome began to seem inevitable: Charles only had enough money to fight a short war and, when it spiralled out of control after the 1645 defeat at **Naseby**, he was destined to lose his crown. After the army became convinced that peace was impossible while he was still alive, he also lost his head. A **Commonwealth**, controlled by a military junta headed by **Oliver Cromwell**, took his place.

As long as Cromwell survived, the Republic looked relatively secure. Despite a naval war against the Dutch, England allied itself with the other Protestant nations of northern Europe and trade continued to expand—as did colonization in **America**. But Cromwell's death in 1658 produced a vacuum at the centre of national politics which **General George Monck** exploited in 1660 when he made moves to restore **Charles II** to the throne. Yet the new king was faced by the same problems that had beset his father. Parliament failed to make adequate financial provisions for the Crown, and suspicions about Charles's involvement with Catholicism continued to dog the monarchy. Although addicted to the pleasures of life, among them a plethora of mistresses, Charles II dealt with the shifting sands of Restoration politics relatively successfully—and certainly more successfully than his brother and successor, **James II**. James's cataclysmic loss of support from all major factions in Parliament—and, crucially, the Anglican-dominated Army—led to his nervous breakdown and subsequent flight from England.

In retrospect the century was one of unusual commotion, private as much as public, but it was also a period of outstanding cultural achievement. It witnessed poets **Andrew Marvell**, **John Milton** and **John Dryden**; architects **Inigo Jones** and **Christopher Wren**; composers **Orlando Gibbons**, **William Lawes** and **John Blow**. In **Thomas Hobbes** the country could boast its first internationally significant—if somewhat idiosyncratic—political philosopher. And in the emerging sciences, too, **Isaac Newton**, **Francis Bacon**, **Robert Boyle** and **Robert Hooke** demonstrated that, in some respects at least, England was at the cutting-edge of intellectual progress.

1603 **James VI Stuart of Scotland** is warmly welcomed in England as he travels south to claim the throne—even if the risk of plague in London means that he is forced to avoid the elaborate public events celebrating his accession.

Sir Walter Raleigh is dismissed as captain of the guard and later imprisoned in the Tower on suspicion of conspiring to replace James with his Catholic cousin **Arabella Stuart**.

Father William Watson hatches the unsuccessful "**Bye Plot**" against the throne in response to the continuing collection of recusancy fines.

The war in **Ireland** ends in March following Tyrone's surrender.

1604 Parliament debates whether England, Wales and Scotland—now ruled by the same monarch—should be brought together in a single **union**, but although James I adopts the title **king of Great Britain** there is little enthusiasm for this move.

The **Treaty of London** formally ends hostilities with **Spain**, and James's heir by his wife Anne of Denmark, **Prince Henry**, is engaged to the Spanish infanta **Anna**, daughter of **Philip III**.

The **Hampton Court Conference** is convened by James to review the Church in England. The Elizabethan Settlement is retained, and existing anti-Catholic laws are kept in force. A new translation of the **Bible** is commissioned by royal authority.

The capture of Guy Fawkes, 1606

1605 Robert Cecil, kept by James as the government's chief minister, is created **earl of Salisbury**.

The second session of James I's first parliament is disrupted in November by the discovery of the **Gunpowder Plot**.

Francis Bacon publishes *The Advancement of Learning*, an attempt to classify existing scientific disciplines and promote experimentation.

1606 Following the trial and execution of the Gunpowder Plot's conspirators, tougher **recusancy laws** are introduced and a new **Oath of Allegiance** to the king is imposed on English Catholics.

THE GUNPOWDER PLOT

*W*hen he came to the throne in 1603, James was determined to extend his policy of religious tolerance by relaxing existing laws that penalized Catholics for practicing their religion. But the hard-line parliamentary response to his suggestion forced the king in the opposite direction: he had no option but to leave them as they were. One response to this decision would be infamous—the Gunpowder Plot.

The plan was simple enough: a group of Catholic gentlemen had decided to blow up the House of Lords during the state opening of Parliament on November 5, 1605, and with it the king and his entire government. The conspiracy was led by **Robert Catesby** and **Thomas Percy**, but the best-known conspirator was the explosives expert **Guy Fawkes**. Fawkes came from an established Yorkshire family, but had spent most of his adult life serving in the Spanish army after converting to Catholicism. He was recruited by Catesby in 1604, and was responsible for planting at least twenty barrels of gunpowder in a cellar that ran underneath the Parliament building.

Although James I orders the creation of a new **national flag** symbolizing England and Scotland, the House of Commons continues to resist formal union.

An expedition sets out across the Atlantic to re-establish the colony of **Virginia**.

Perhaps in order to honor the king, **Shakespeare** writes his Scottish play, *Macbeth*, around this time.

1607 The king's favorite, **Robert Carr**, is knighted, the first of several honors bestowed on him to the chagrin of the "Tudor" establishment.

The plot was derailed, however, by another conspirator, **Francis Tresham**, realized that a number of his friends and Catholic peers might die if not forewarned and wrote to persuade his brother-in-law **Lord Monteagle** not to attend the ceremony. The letter was passed to the Privy Council, and Fawkes was picked up on the day itself. Under torture he revealed the names of his co-conspirators, who were apprehended and charged with treason following a brief siege at Catesby's house. Following their trial in January 1606 all were condemned to execution—by the time-honored method of hanging, drawing and quartering.

The plot proved to be the last serious attempt by militant English Catholics to overturn the Anglican settlement, but its memory—commemorated annually in firework displays on **Guy Fawkes' Night** and more personally by the burning of the "guy"—demonstrated that there was continuing discord over questions of faith and toleration. When the Anglican settlement was suspended in the mid-century, it was not the Catholics but the Puritans who temporarily triumphed.

Raleigh, still imprisoned, is stripped of his estates.

Jamestown in Virginia becomes England's first permanent settlement in North America.

1609 To strengthen English rule in Ireland, commissioners are appointed to oversee the "**plantation**" of Ulster with English settlers.

1610 Salisbury endeavors to persuade Parliament to accept a "**Great Contract**" designed to ease the king's financial difficulties by the grant of regular subsidies, but the House of Commons rejects his initiative.

Prince Henry is created **prince of Wales**.

Arabella Stuart is imprisoned for marrying the **earl of Hertford**, another claimant to the throne.

1611 Parliament is **dissolved** in February. With a brief exception in 1614, James I rules without Parliament until 1621. To improve royal revenues, Salisbury devises the new title of **baronet**—a hereditary knighthood—which is widely sold for £1,095.

Arabella Stuart escapes captivity but is soon recaptured.

After four years' work by a team of 54 scholars, the so-called **"Authorized" Bible** is published (although it is never actually authorized as such). Drawing on unacknowledged previous translations made by **William Tyndale**, **John Wyclif** and others, the "King James" Bible rapidly achieves scriptural status among Anglicans and other English-speaking Protestants.

1612 Two "extreme" **Protestants** become the last heretics to be burned at the stake in England. The burning of "**witches**"—often distressed women ostracized by their immediate communities—continues, however.

Following the death of **Salisbury**, James I elects to become his own **secretary of state**.

In November, relations between king and aristocracy deteriorate when the popular **Prince Henry** dies; Henry's 12-year-old brother **Charles** becomes heir apparent.

1613 A scandal is created when the **countess of Essex** sues for divorce in order to marry **Sir Robert Carr** (created **earl of Somerset** later in the year) and the king intervenes in her favor.

James's daughter **Elizabeth** is married to the leading Calvinist prince in Germany, **Frederick the Elector Palatine of the Rhine**, dashing the hopes of "conservatives" anxious to see a Spanish match. Anglo-Spanish relations and the standing of the pro-Spanish **earl of Northampton** are improved, however, when James I strikes up a convivial friendship with the newly arrived Spanish ambassador, **Diego Sarmiento** (later **count of Gondomar**).

1614 James I summons a new Parliament in the hope of raising badly needed taxes, but the "**Addled Parliament**," as it becomes known, refuses his entreaties and is quickly dissolved.

Northampton dies, and is replaced as lord treasurer by his cousin, the **earl of Suffolk**; **Somerset** is appointed lord chamberlain. The future royal favorite, **George Villiers**, is presented at court and soon knighted.

Negotiations begin for a marriage between **Prince Charles** and a Spanish princess (infanta).

Sir William Cockayne persuades James to suspend the **Merchant Adventurers'** charter and prohibit the sale of unfinished cloth to the Netherlands. In the ensuing trade war with the Dutch, crisis is created in the English cloth industry when it fails to meet domestic demand.

1615 Somerset and his wife are arrested on suspicion of murdering **Sir Thomas Overbury**, an opponent of their marriage.

Villiers continues his rise to prominence by being appointed a **gentleman of the bedchamber**. The financier **Lionel Cranfield** is appointed surveyor-general.

A Spanish demand that any children born to Prince Charles and the infanta should be raised as **Catholics** creates widespread consternation, but James I persists with the marriage negotiations.

1616 Villiers is created a **viscount** and **knight of the garter**; Charles is made **prince of Wales**.

The Somersets are found guilty of Overbury's murder, but spared the death penalty.

Sir Walter Raleigh is released from the Tower to prepare an expedition to **Guiana**.

RALEIGH AND BACON

*T*he two figures most famously associated with Jacobean England were products of the Elizabethan age. Both trained as lawyers, turned their hands to writing history and were damaged by a penchant for intrigue. Both, too, have been accused of failing to make best use of their diverse talents.

Sir Walter Raleigh (1554–1618) was the son of a Devonshire squire who climbed to become Elizabeth's favorite. A pirate and adventurer who tried unsuccessfully to create new colonies in the Americas, his career was interrupted by imprisonment in the Tower of London in 1588, when the queen discovered his secret marriage to Elizabeth Throckmorton (one of her maids of honor). Released, he became obsessed with the myth of El Dorado, and in 1596 he sailed past Spanish guns up the Orinoco to claim Guiana. In 1603 he was accused of plotting against James I and was returned to the Tower. His second incarceration lasted thirteen years, during which he wrote the grandly titled *History of the World* and indulged a passion for chemistry. In 1616 he was again freed and revisited Guiana, but his attacks on Spanish shipping at a sensitive moment landed him in further trouble, and Raleigh was executed shortly afterwards.

Shakespeare dies, and is buried in his home town of **Stratford-upon-Avon**. His younger colleague, **Ben Jonson**, publishes *Works*, a collection of his plays and poems.

1617 Villiers is created **earl of Buckingham**.

As the **"Cockayne scheme"** flounders, the Merchant Adventurers' charter is restored and normal trading relations with the **Netherlands** resume.

Francis Bacon, Viscount of St Albans (1561–1626) pursued a more sedentary but finally more useful career. Although appointed a clerk to the court of Star Chamber in 1582, his early career soon ground to a halt—partly because he opposed the grant of royal subsidies in Parliament and partly because of his support for the earl of Essex. His burning ambition for high office, though, dampened continuing scruples: under James I Bacon openly advocated a fuller union between England and Scotland, and defended the royal prerogative. As a result he was rewarded with the posts of solicitor-general (1607), attorney-general (1613) and finally lord chancellor (1618). Preferment came at the expense of his rivals, however, and in 1621 Bacon's enemies had their revenge when charges of bribery were brought against him. His sojourn in the Tower was brief, but his career was finished. His last years were spent adding to the already voluminous list of his writings, including a third edition of his popular *Essays* (1626). But his more important legacy was his contribution to English science. Although he made no significant scientific discovery, his philosophical advancement of an experimental outlook, rooted in a belief that nature should be mastered for the benefit of man, helped establish an intellectual climate in which real breakthroughs could occur.

1618 **Raleigh** creates a crisis in Anglo-Spanish relations by attacking a Spanish settlement in **Guiana**. Returning to England, he is imprisoned and executed despite widespread rioting on his behalf.

The king's popularity, already weakened by the favoritism extended toward Buckingham, is further damaged when **tax reforms** instituted by **Cranfield** begin to bite.

The philosopher and scientist **Francis Bacon** is appointed **lord chancellor**.

In Europe, the **Thirty Years War** commences after Bohemians reject their king-elect **Emperor Ferdinand II** in favor of **Frederick of the Rhine**, James I's son-in-law. As pressure on James to assist Frederick mounts, negotiations with Spain are suspended.

1619 James's queen, **Anne of Denmark**, dies. The king's financial problems are so acute that her embalmed body lies in state for ten weeks before sufficient funds can be found to pay for the funeral—even though her death reduces royal household expenditures.

Inigo Jones begins work on the **Banqueting House** at Whitehall, architecturally the most significant new building of James's reign because of its introduction of the pure Classical style into England.

The painter **Nicholas Hilliard**, renowned for his miniature portraits, dies.

1620 James I enters into a covert treaty with **Spain** agreeing to the marriage of Prince Charles to the infanta.

Frederick of the Rhine is driven out of Bohemia following the **Battle of the White Mountain** (outside Prague), and later in the year even loses control of his own Palatinate.

Economic depression and continuing tensions between Anglicans and Puritans inspire the **Pilgrim Fathers** to set sail in the *Mayflower* and found an English colony in what they call **New England**.

1621 James I calls his third **Parliament**.

CHAPTER SEVEN } 1603-1688   239

Cranfield is appointed **lord treasurer**.

1623 **Prince Charles** travels to Spain incognito with **Buckingham** to arrange his marriage. The mission runs into severe difficulties when **Philip IV** insists on complete toleration of Catholics in England as part of the marriage settlement. Charles agrees to undertake instruction in Catholicism, but on returning to England in October he and Buckingham advocate that the marriage be broken off. His star now firmly in the ascendant, the earl is created **duke of Buckingham**, the first non-royal ducal creation since 1551.

1624 James I's **fourth Parliament** grants the king substantial subsidies in anticipation of war against Spain and the Holy Roman Emperor. But an army sent to restore **Frederick of the Rhine** is so badly equipped that most of its troops desert before even reaching the Netherlands.

A new marriage treaty for Prince Charles, this time with **Princess Henrietta** Maria of France, is swiftly negotiated.

As England's economy begins to recover, **Virginia** is made a royal colony.

1625 James I dies in March and is succeeded by **Charles I**, who marries **Henrietta Maria** in May.

Parliament grants the Crown **customs revenues** ("**tonnage and poundage**") for one year, but Charles will attempt to collect these for the rest of his reign without parliamentary approval.

As the **Thirty Years War** expands, England finds itself at war with Spain, but an expedition led by Buckingham to ransack **Cadiz** fails.

1626 Charles I summons a new **parliament**, but it refuses to grant fresh subsidies in protest at the king's continuing collection of tonnage and poundage, and instead attempts to impeach **Buckingham** for corruption. To finance the war against Spain, Charles orders a forced "loan" to be raised—in effect an arbitrary tax.

Francis Bacon dies of a chill contracted during an experiment to refrigerate a hen by stuffing it with snow.

1627 Five knights, arrested for refusing to pay Charles's enforced loan, are refused the writ of **habeas corpus**. When their case goes before the courts, judgment is given in the king's favor on the grounds that the king's special command is sufficient cause to warrant imprisonment.

Buckingham leads a disastrous expedition to France, to relieve **Huguenots** besieged at **La Rochelle**.

1628 Charles I calls his **third Parliament**. Among new members of the House of Commons is **Oliver Cromwell**, MP for Huntingdon. Before it will consider the king's requests for subsidies the House presents him with the **Petition of Right**, outlining grievances against the Crown—including the arbitrary arrest of its subjects.

In August, **Buckingham** is assassinated by **John Felton**, a Puritan. Since Buckingham is known to be sympathetic to **Arminianism**, a high-church doctrine espoused by some church leaders, his murder is indicative of increasing religious tensions. Shortly afterwards Bishop **William Laud of Bath and Wells**, the leader of the Arminians, is elevated to the see of London. **Thomas Wentworth**, previously a stern critic of Charles I, is made a baron, and later becomes **earl of Strafford**.

The fall of **La Rochelle** to **Louis XIII** delivers a body-blow to French Huguenots, many of whom seek resettlement in England.

William Harvey, a physician at St Bartholomew's Hospital in London, publishes *De Motu Cordis*, which outlines his theory of the circulation of the blood in animals and of the heart as a pump.

1629 The House of Commons passes resolutions against Arminianism and against the king's continued levy of customs dues without parliamentary consent. Angered, Charles dissolves Parliament and embarks on an eleven-year period of **personal rule**. Lack of funds makes him wary of further involvement in Europe's wars, however: hostilities with France are brought to an end by the **Treaty of Susa**.

1630 The war with Spain is ended by the **Treaty of Madrid**.

A bad harvest encourages more Puritans to emigrate to New England.

1631 The **earl of Castlehaven**, a well-known peer, is tried and convicted for sodomy and rape in a trial that causes a national sensation.

1632 Strafford is appointed lord deputy in **Ireland**.

The Flemish artist **Anthony Van Dyck** settles in England and is appointed court painter.

1633 William Laud becomes archbishop of Canterbury, an elevation that prompts some to speculate that the throne may be contemplating a return to Catholicism.

The Puritan **William Prynne** publishes *Histriomastix*, a huge tract attacking the "immorality" of the theater. The following year he is hauled before the Court of Star Chamber for his none-too-subtle description of female actors as "notorious whores," which is taken as an insult to the masque-loving queen. The fact that part of his ears are cut off as punishment does not deter him, though, and four years later he is sentenced to have the rest of his ears removed and his forehead branded.

The *Collected Works* of **John Donne**, erstwhile dean of St Paul's Cathedral, is published two years after his death—a volume containing, among much else, erotic lyrics that he was understandably eager not to see in print during his lifetime.

1634 Ship money, a royal tax aimed to supply the navy, is imposed on England's coastal counties.

1635 Ship money is extended to inland counties, causing widespread resentment and unrest.

1637 As **Arminianism** spreads, Puritan pamphleteers are increasingly sentenced to mutilation for speaking out against liturgical reforms introduced by Laud to promote the use of "Catholic" ritual. The Calvinist bishop of Lincoln, **John Williams**, is sent to the Tower for criticizing the archbishop. Severe restrictions imposed on the press by the **Court of Star Chamber** only add to the growing tide of dissent.

1638 Serious differences erupt between Charles I and his Scottish subjects over whether the **Scottish Church** should follow an Anglican or Presbyterian path. **Strafford**, having gained a reputation for brutality in Ireland, urges stern reprisals against the rebellious Scots.

1639 Charles I raises an **army** to bring the Scots to heel, but no campaign is mounted. Faced by a chronic lack of money, the king reluctantly decides to summon a parliament. Before it can convene, a "**taxpayer's strike**," aimed principally against ship money, spreads through England. Royal control over local government is seriously impaired.

PARLIAMENT AND PURITANS

Like its French and Spanish counterparts, the English Parliament grew out of an enlarged royal council, the purpose of which was to offer the throne advice and agree its policies. Initially nobles and others sat together in a single chamber, but as early as the 13th century Parliament began to divide into two houses. By Tudor times, the House of Lords and House of Commons were permanently separated. Those entitled to sit in the Lords by right were barons, viscounts, earls, marquesses and dukes, as well as bishops and—until the dissolution of the monasteries—some abbots. The "other house" was made up of knights of the shire and town burgesses. Since these far outnumbered aristocrats, however, some sort of selection process had to exist. Out of this emerged elective representation, which in turn meant that the throne gradually lost control of who sat in the Commons.

In the 1530s, Parliament's independence was further enhanced by Thomas Cromwell's deliberate strategy of using its power to realize the Henrician Reformation. The result, from the middle of Elizabeth's reign

1640 The "**short Parliament**" sits, but is dissolved within a month after it fails to agree new subsidies for the king.

Strafford is appointed the king's chief adviser and lord lieutenant in Ireland. In October, Charles I's deteriorating authority is further undermined when the Scots defeat an English force at **Newburn**. Charles is forced to concede the **Treaty of Ripon**, obliging him to pay the Scots £850 a day until a final agreement is reached—money he simply doesn't have. In desperation Charles summons a fresh parliament, known as the "**Long Parliament**," in November. Such is

onwards, was institutionalized opposition. This became further entrenched when a group known as the **Puritans**, who argued that the English Reformation had not gone nearly far enough, began to gain Parliamentary influence—and used it to demand "purer" forms of worship.

In retrospect the Puritans were perhaps the first parliamentary party, though in reality they were united as much by their high-church enemies—who insisted on calling all advocates of plain worship "Puritans"—as by common theological ground. When that enemy was weakened by the interregnum, the splits in the Puritan movement became wider than ever, with a number of different sects competing for freedom of expression. Some, such as the singularly named **William Fiennes, Lord Saye and Sele**, were sufficiently disgruntled with England to seek abandoning it altogether, and invested heavily in New England and the Bahamas in the hope of establishing godly aristocratic communities there. Even when these schemes failed they remained powerful—and it was out of these old, high-ranking Puritan families that the earliest manifestation of the **Whig Party** emerged to challenge another Stuart king, James II.

the weakness of his position he is unable to prevent the impeachment of either **Strafford** or **Archbishop Laud**. Sensing their hour has come, **Puritans** launch fresh attacks against Arminian reforms. A body of Londoners submit their **"Root and Branch" petition** to the Commons, calling for the abolition of bishops.

1641 Parliament forces Charles I to accept the **Triennial Act**, stipulating that a parliament be summoned at least once every three years. Another act legislates that no parliament should be dissolved without its own consent. **Strafford** is executed by an **Act of Attainder**, and the **Court of Star Chamber** is abolished.

In November, as confidence amongst Charles's opponents swells, a **Grand Remonstrance**, denouncing the king's misgovernment and the subversive influence of bishops, is passed in the Commons by 159 votes to 148. The king travels to **Scotland**, but fails to remedy the situation there. There is also renewed unrest in Ireland, where Catholics massacre Protestants in Ulster.

1642 Charles I attempts to arrest five of his principal critics in the Commons—**John Pym**, **John Hampden**, **Denzil Holle**s, **Sir Arthur Haslerigg** and **William Strode**—but they flee before his soldiers arrive. Relations between king and Parliament collapse and a broad coalition of opponents to Charles forms, including not just Puritans but merchants and members of the aristocracy too. As England slides into **Civil War**, Charles raises his standard at **Nottingham** on August 22. The first significant encounter between Royalists (sometimes called "**Cavaliers**") and the supporters of Parliament ("**Roundheads**") takes place at **Edgehill** on October 23, in an attempt to halt Charles's advance on London from his strongholds in the west. The king's nephew, **Prince Rupert of the Rhine**, commanding the Royalist cavalry, leads a devastating charge, but the effect of this is largely negated when Rupert's undisciplined soldiers begin looting the parliamentary baggage train. Led by the **Earl of Essex**, the parliamentary side counter-attacks, and although by the end of the day Charles narrowly holds the field, the battle is inconclusive. The weakened Royalists push on toward London, but are checked at **Turnham Green**, and the king is forced to set up his headquarters at **Oxford** while the capital remains in parliamentary hands.

1643 Minor skirmishes between Royalists and Parliamentarians are fought throughout the year, but neither side is able to secure a decisive advantage. At the **First Battle of Newbury**, fought on September 20, Charles is again prevented from seizing London. Parliament, hampered by a divided leadership and the reluctance of the earls of **Essex** and **Manchester** to fight too strenuously against the king, is weakened by the deaths of **John Hampden** in June and **John Pym** in December. Conversely the Scots, through a **Solemn League and Covenant**, agree to support Parliament. As a result the parliamentary position is consolidated, in the north especially.

1644 Charles I, unwilling to enter into negotiations with his enemies, summons a **royalist parliament** at Oxford. A Scottish army marches into England, and a major engagement is fought at **Marston Moor** on July 2. Despite the flight of the Scots commander the earl of Leven—who is convinced that Parliament has been defeated—the Parliamentary army led by **Oliver Cromwell**

Earl of Manchester: "If we beat the King ninety-nine times, yet he is King still and so will his posterity be after him; but if the King beat us once we shall be hanged, and our posterity be made slaves."

Cromwell: "My Lord, if this be so, why did we take up arms at first? This is against fighting ever hereafter. If so, let us make peace, be it never so base."

—**Calendar of State Papers, entry for November 10, 1644**

defeats Charles's forces under the command of **Prince Rupert** and the **earl of Newcastle**. Charles loses the last vestiges of authority in the north, while royalist hopes are further dashed by Rupert's decision to surrender **Bristol** and another defeat at the **Second Battle of Newbury** on October 27. Furious at his nephew's apparent cowardice in quitting his command, Charles orders Rupert into **exile**. It remains unclear at this stage, however, what the ultimate aims of the Parliamentarians are—whether to bring the king under control or remove him from the throne.

THE CIVIL WARS

*T*he so-called **English Civil War** (1642–51) was really nothing of the kind. It was a series of conflicts that spanned nine grim years, and it spilled over into Scotland, Ireland and Wales. Nor were its divisions clear-cut: there were Puritans amongst the royalists, traditionalists amongst the parliamentarians. And even the armies themselves had difficulty identifying one another in battle; although individual regiments may have worn liveries, there were no set uniforms. Even the abusive nicknames that became attached to the opposing sides don't tell us much: not all those who fought for the king were libertine "cavaliers" (from the Spanish caballero); nor were parliamentarians all "roundheads"—a term coined by Queen Henrietta Maria, remarking on the Puritan Samuel Barnardiston's short-cropped hair.

Perhaps it's not surprising that historians have argued over the nature of the wars. Some see them as an essentially medieval battle between king and over-mighty subject, while others have interpreted the conflict in Marxist terms as part of a revolution led by the middle orders of society. What seems certain is that it was the army and those in charge of it that

The poet **John Milton**, sympathetic to Parliament but opposed to its Presbyterian supporters, publishes *Areopagatica*—a sustained defense of freedom of expression.

1645 King and Parliament attempt to come to terms at **Uxbridge**, but negotiations quickly break down.

Archbishop Laud is beheaded by Parliament on January 10.

In response to criticisms of the poor quality and indiscipline of Parliament's troops, their commander **Sir Thomas Fairfax** creates

benefited. At the outbreak of the wars Oliver Cromwell was an obscure East Anglian landowner, but in the course of the conflict his genius as a cavalry commander came to the fore, and it was largely owing to his military success at Naseby and elsewhere that he ended up as leader of the Commonwealth and, later, Protector—king in all but name.

That Cromwell would end up in this position hardly seemed likely in the wars' immediate aftermath. The prospect of trying and executing the king was more than many on the parliamentarian side could stomach, and resolute old Puritans such as the earl of Manchester and Lord Saye and Sele retired to their homes rather than have anything to do with it. Nevertheless in January 1649 a court was established, and in spite of Charles's refusal to acknowledge it, he was tried and condemned to death. But the king went down fighting. In his final statement on the scaffold he declared: "[The people's] liberty and freedom consists in having government, those laws by which their lives and their goods may be most their own. It is not their having a share in the government, that is nothing appertaining to them. A subject and a sovereign are clean different things."

the **New Model Army**, and it is this force—together with Cromwell's mounted "**Ironsides**"—that wins a convincing victory at **Naseby** on June 14.

1646 Cromwell crushes a royalist army led by **Lord Ashley** at **Stowe-on-the-Wold** on March 26.

On May 5 **Charles I** surrenders to the Scots and is imprisoned at **Edinburgh**. As Oxford capitulates, the **First Civil War** is brought to a conclusion.

Parliament, now controlled by Puritans, orders a **Presbyterian Church** to be established in England, and the offices of archbishop and bishop are abolished. But the problem of what to do about the king persists, and there are widening divisions among Parliament's followers. In the army, **Agitators** and **Independents**, and also an extra-parliamentary group called the **Levellers**, begin pressing for political reforms. Hoping to take advantage of his enemy's disunity, **Charles** rejects terms proposed at **Newcastle**, which would give Parliament control of the militia for twenty years.

1647 **Charles I** is handed over by the Scots to Parliament, which orders its army to disband. Infuriated by Parliament's unwillingness to pay its wages, however, the **army revolts**, and on June 4 seizes the king from **Holmby House** in **Northamptonshire**. Joined by Cromwell and some other Parliamentarians, the army takes control of **London** in August. Supported by the Levellers, the army's Agitators form a deputation to meet with their commanders and representatives of Parliament. The ensuing **Putney Debates**, under Cromwell's chairmanship, open on October 28, but no conclusion is reached about the future government of England. While the Levellers recommend extending the parliamentary franchise to all adult males, "conservative" parliamentarians favor the retention of power among the landed elite. As a result, the Levellers inspire continued mutiny.

King Charles escapes custody on November 11 and flees to **Carisbrooke Castle** on the **Isle of Wight**, where, at the end of

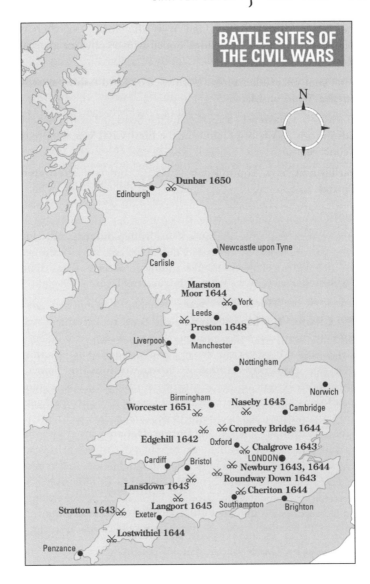

BATTLE SITES OF
THE CIVIL WARS

N

Dunbar 1650
Edinburgh

Newcastle upon Tyne

Carlisle

Marston
Moor 1644
York
Leeds
Preston 1648
Liverpool
Manchester

Nottingham

Norwich

Birmingham   Naseby 1645
Worcester 1651   Cambridge

Cropredy Bridge 1644
Edgehill 1642   Oxford   Chalgrove 1643
LONDON
Cardiff   Bristol   Newbury 1643, 1644
Lansdown 1643   Roundway Down 1643
Cheriton 1644
Stratton 1643   Langport 1645   Southampton   Brighton
Exeter
Lostwithiel 1644
Penzance

December, he signs an agreement with the **Scots**. In return for his agreement to abolish the episcopacy in Scotland, the Scots promise to restore Charles to his English throne by force.

George Fox forms the **Society of Friends** in **Leicestershire**, a puritanical sect dedicated to promoting "inward" spiritual experience and later known as the **Quakers**, possibly because of their bodily shaking when possessed by the holy spirit.

1648 As news of Charles's actions spreads, royalists resume arms, sparking the **Second Civil War**. But the conflict is short-lived: a Scottish army of invasion under the **duke of Hamilton** is defeated in a three-day battle at **Preston** beginning on August 17.

On 1 December the king is seized by the army, and a week later, with Cromwell's complicity, the Long Parliament is purged of the king's supporters by **Colonel Thomas Pride**. On December 13 the sixty-odd members who have not been purged—known as the **Rump Parliament**—vote that the king should stand trial.

In Europe, the **Thirty Years War** is brought to an end through the **Peace of Westphalia** (October 24).

1649 Charles I is tried by a specially convened court and sentenced to death by 59 signatories, known as **regicides**. Despite refusing to acknowledge the legitimacy of his accusers, the king is **beheaded** on an improvised scaffold outside the Banqueting House in Whitehall on January 30. England becomes a **republic** under the military dictatorship of **Oliver Cromwell**. In Scotland and parts of Ireland, however, Charles's son **Charles II** is proclaimed king.

In May, as theater, music and other forms of public entertainment are outlawed, England is declared a "**free commonwealth**."

In the same month there is further Leveller-inspired **mutiny** in the army as it becomes apparent that Cromwell has no intention of extending political rights.

In September, Cromwell campaigns in **Ireland**. Storming **Drogheda** and **Wexford**, he orders the massacre of Catholics in revenge for previous Catholic atrocities against Protestants.

At **Walton-on-Thames** in **Surrey**, a spin-off group of the Levellers known as the **Diggers** endeavor to institute a communist society based on shared ownership of land and dwellings.

1650 Cromwell returns from Ireland and is appointed **lord general** and **commander-in-chief** of all the Commonwealth's armies in succession to Thomas Fairfax.

Charles II arrives in Scotland, where, despite the defeat of a Scottish army at **Dunbar** by Cromwell on September 3 and the subsequent surrender of **Edinburgh Castle** to the English, he is crowned at **Scone**.

A group of extreme Protestants known as the **Ranters** becomes active in London and other English cities, but are suppressed by Parliament. By the end of the year the **Digger** movement has also collapsed.

1651 Having lost Perth to Cromwell, **Charles II** crosses the border into England, but his small army is decisively beaten at **Worcester** on September 3. He escapes to **France** in October.

Thomas Hobbes publishes *Leviathan*, perhaps the most brilliant work of political philosophy written in the English language.

1652 Cromwell continues with his brutal "pacification" of **Ireland**.

The **First Anglo-Dutch War** breaks out as a consequence of England's assertion of maritime sovereignty. Admiral Robert Blake defeats a Dutch fleet in the Battle of the Downs, but the English fleet is subsequently defeated by the Dutch at **Dungeness**.

England's growing number of colonies in **North America** agree to recognize parliamentary authority.

1653 Following further tensions with the army, Cromwell dissolves the **Rump Parliament** in April. He calls a fresh assembly, known as

THOMAS HOBBES (1588–1679)

*H*obbes was one of the most influential—and most contro-versial—thinkers in English political philosophy. His masterpiece, *Leviathan* (which means "monstrous beast," a metaphor for the state), famously declares that human life is, in its natural form, "solitary, poor, nasty, brutish and short." Given that this is so, Hobbes proposes a stark solution: it is in the subject's interests to embrace a strong government that will safeguard his secu-rity, even if it curtails his liberty. In other words, authoritarian rule is better than anarchy.

Hobbes's thesis was unmistakably engaged in the political debates of his time, particularly the ongoing civil wars, and it twice landed him in trouble: first in 1640 when he was forced to flee to France because he was believed to support royal absolutism; once again when he was sus-pected of atheism after *Leviathan* was published. At the Restoration he was criticized for his defense of the Cromwellian regime—a charge which has some basis in fact, but which undervalues his careful delin-eation of how "liberty" could be achieved and what it actually meant. He also argued that people must agree with each other to be ruled in this way (in effect, they must set up a form of social contract) and that it was in their interests to do so; thus his theory is in the truest sense inter-ested in the "common-wealth."

And while life was certainly solitary, poor, nasty and brutish for many of his contemporaries, Hobbes demonstrated that perhaps he was too cynical about the last component of his most-quoted statement—he lived to the grand old age of 91. Or, as his acquaintance John Aubrey put it in a collection of biographical snippets, *Brief Lives*, "he was against "too hasty concluding," which he did endeavor as much as he could to avoid."

Barebone's Parliament (named after an MP for London, **Praise-God Barebone**), which sits from July until December. It produces an **Instrument of Government**, outlining constitutional arrangements for an administration led by Cromwell under his newly proclaimed title of **Lord Protector**.

The English and Dutch navies fight inconclusively off **Portland** in February, but in July the Dutch are convincingly defeated in the **Battle of Texel**.

1654 In April, a formal union between England and Scotland is proclaimed. **George Monck**, previously a royalist, is appointed commander-in-chief in Scotland, and makes headway against the "**Glencairn**" rebellion.

The **Treaty of Westminster** brings to an end the Anglo–Dutch war and promotes a defensive alliance between England and the United Provinces, aimed partly at restraining **William II of Orange,** married to Charles I's daughter **Mary**. Further treaties are concluded with **Sweden**, **Denmark** and **Portugal**, to the benefit of the Commonwealth's international standing.

1655 Cromwell dismisses the first parliament to be convened under the Instrument of Government, and defeats a royalist uprising in **Wiltshire**.

Monck crushes the remaining Scottish rebels.

The government of Britain is modified so that each area is controlled by a **major general** given wide military and civil powers by Cromwell.

In the Americas, war breaks out with **Spain**. Cromwell dispatches a fleet to the **Caribbean** and **Jamaica** is seized.

A pact is concluded with **France** whereby the exiled Stuarts are excluded from French territory, forcing Charles II to seek refuge in the Netherlands.

Jews are admitted into England for the first time in three centuries.

1656 The second parliament of the Protectorate attempts to limit **religious toleration**. Discontent with the **major generals** grows.

1657 Cromwell abolishes the major generals after Parliament refuses to supply funds. Parliament offers him the Crown in May in its Humble Petition and Advice, but Cromwell declines, concerned that this will limit his power.

A military alliance with France against Spain is formed. Blake annihilates the Spanish Caribbean fleet off **Santa Cruz** in April, but dies in August.

The first of a succession of bad harvests induces **economic depression**.

1658 An Anglo-French army defeats the Spanish in the **Battle of the Dunes** on June 4, following which **Dunkirk** surrenders to the English.

On September 3 **Cromwell** dies, possibly of malaria; his son **Richard Cromwell** becomes Lord Protector.

Oliver Cromwell dissolves Parliament, 1653

1659 A new **parliament** convenes in January, but quickly falls foul of the army, which in April persuades Richard Cromwell to recall the **Rump Parliament** of 1648. In May he resigns. As political uncertainty continues, **John Lambert** suppresses a royalist uprising in Cheshire led by **George Booth** in August, but other rebellions proliferate, driven by fears among the well-to-do of a puritanical regime.

Abroad, tensions ease as **France** and **Spain** conclude the **Treaty of the Pyrenees**.

1660 Determined to restore order, **General Monck** marches south from Scotland, recruiting the Coldstream Guards along the way, and enters **London**. He recalls those members of the **Long Parliament** purged by Pride, but in March it is forced to dissolve; a "**Convention**" parliament is summoned by Monck a month later. The earl of Manchester and nine other peers take their seats in a reconstituted House of Lords. Although it has not been Monck's original intention to restore the monarchy, steadily this looks likely. Advised by **Edward Hyde**, Charles II issues the **Declaration of Breda**, promising as king of England he will promote liberty of conscience in religion, ensure that arrears in army pay are met and settle land disputes equitably. Following brief negotiations, on May 8 Charles is **proclaimed king**, and lands at **Dover** on May 25. Four days later he enters London. On August 29 he issues an **Act of Free and General Pardon, Indemnity and Oblivion**, pardoning all those who have rebelled against the monarchy (except surviving regicides). **Edward Hyde** becomes lord chancellor.

1661 **Thomas Venner**, a member of the **Fifth Monarchist** sect dedicated to establishing a theocratic state in England, leads an unsuccessful **rebellion** against the Restoration.

A newly elected parliament, the so-called **Cavalier Parliament** (not dissolved until 1679), enthusiastically endorses the restitution of the monarchy, and initiates legislation to re-establish the **Church of**

England. A **Corporation Act** enables boroughs to be purged of "dissident" (ie Puritan) officials, while a **Militia Act** allows the king to maintain a standing army. In addition **Charles II** is granted permanent annual subsidies with a nominal value of £1,200,000. Difficulties in collecting this money, however, coupled with the king's extravagance, mean that the throne continues to be threatened by insolvency. **Edward Hyde** emerges as the king's chief minister, and is created **earl of Clarendon**.

Robert Boyle publishes *The Sceptical Chemist*, in which he demonstrates the existence of many different chemical elements rather than the Aristotelian matrix of four basic elements (earth, air, fire and water).

OLIVER CROMWELL (1599–1658)

*O*liver Cromwell rode his luck during times of upheaval and emerged as the undisputed controller of events. Yet he was also a man of deep inward convictions, someone who genuinely believed that God was on his side and that the republican government he pioneered was in England's best interests.

Cromwell converted to Calvinism in his thirties and by 1640, when he was elected MP for Cambridge, had gained a reputation as "Lord of the Fens," attacking bishops in general and the bishop of Ely in particular. But Cromwell was not at the forefront of those opposed to the king in 1642, and at Edgehill in October he played only a minor role. In the immediate aftermath, though, he demonstrated his prowess as a military disciplinarian and organizer, and defeated a royalist army at Gainsborough the following January. Promotion rapidly followed, and by 1645 he had become second-in-command to Lord Fairfax. Crucially, when the army and Parliament fell out in June 1647, he sided with his troops. A signatory to the king's death warrant,

1662 Parliament passes further legislation in favor of the re-established **Church of England**, including the appointment of **archbishops** and **bishops**, and an **Act of Uniformity** that makes acceptance of a newly published **Book of Common Prayer** obligatory among England's school and university teachers.

Charles II's bride, the Portuguese infanta **Catherine of Braganza**, arrives in England. Astonished by her hair, arranged in wing-like ringlets, the king exclaims: "They have brought me a bat." But her dowry includes the port of **Tangier** in the Mediterranean and the island of **Bombay** in India, and the marriage goes ahead.

he was appointed chairman of the **Council of State**, and strengthened the new republic by campaigns in **Scotland** and **Ireland**—where his savage reprisals against Catholics bequeathed a legacy of sectarian hatred.

In England, however, his reputation was assured, and in 1653 he assumed the title of **Lord Protector**, which gave him all the authority of the deposed king. Cromwell advocated religious toleration, encouraged education, opposed trade monopolies and created a written constitution. But his unpopular appointment of **major generals** to supervise regional government and his kowtowing to Puritan sentiment (which included the abolition of public festivals such as Christmas) provoked discontent. When he died his legacy quickly unraveled: government came back into the hands of the monarch and little remained of the sweeping changes he had made. Following the Restoration, his body was disinterred, mutilated and hurled into the Thames. His severed head, impaled on a pole, was exhibited in Westminster Hall for 25 years.

Dunkirk is returned to France in exchange for £400,000.

A royal charter is granted to a body known as the **Royal Society**, dedicated to the advancement of science.

1663 Attempts by Charles II to extend religious tolerance to **Nonconformists** and **Catholics** alike, in line with the **Declaration of Breda**, are rebuffed by Parliament.

As the number of English colonies in **North America** grows, colonists are forbidden to trade directly with other nations.

1664 In North America, the township that will become the city of **New York** is captured by English forces from the Dutch.

Cromwell, our chief of men, who through a cloud,

Not of war only, but detractions rude,

Guided by faith and matchless fortitude,

To peace and truth thy glorious way has ploughed,

And on the neck of crowned Fortune proud

Has reared God's trophies, and his work pursued,

While Darwen stream with blood of Scots imbrued,

And Dunbar field resounds thy praises loud,

And Worcester's laureate wreath. Yet much remains

To conquer still; peace hath her victories

No less renowned than war: new foes arise,

Threatening to bind our souls with secular chains:

Help us to save free conscience from the paw

Of hireling wolves whose gospel is their maw.

—**John Milton,**
"To the Lord General Cromwell" (1652)

1665 The **Second Anglo-Dutch War** commences, much against Clarendon's wishes, as the two nations contest naval supremacy in northern waters.

In the autumn English cities are paralyzed by what will be the last great attack of **bubonic plague**, severely hampering economic activity. In London alone some 70,000 citizens die and the court withdraws to Oxford.

Robert Hooke, professor of geometry at Gresham College in London, publishes *Micrographia*, which contains illustrations of the structure of the snowflake and close-up views of the flea generated by Hooke's experiments with the microscope.

1666 **London** is dealt a second body-blow when the **Great Fire** breaks out on September 2. Starting in **Pudding Lane**, it spreads quickly through the capital's closely packed buildings. The lord mayor Sir Thomas Bloodworth, somewhat underestimating the severity of the fire, is heard to comment that "A woman might piss it out," but in all 13,200 houses, 87 churches and four bridges are destroyed and 100,000 people made homeless; some four-fifths of the City area is laid to waste. The architect **Sir Christopher Wren** puts forward a plan to rebuild London as a "model city," but he is commissioned only to rebuild a number of churches and, most significantly, a new **St Paul's Cathedral**, the first new Protestant cathedral in the world.

1667 England suffers an embarrassing defeat when Dutch war vessels penetrate the **River Medway** and reach the naval docks at **Chatham**. The war itself is ended by treaties drawn up in July. Despite his opposition to the war, the unpopular **Clarendon** is held responsible, and is dismissed as lord chancellor. In October the Commons, unsupported by the Lords, moves a motion for his impeachment. In November he flees to France, where he dies in 1674 after completing his monumental *History of the Rebellion*. In his wake government is placed in the hands of a group of five ministers known as the **Cabal** after the initials of their names: **Clifford**, **Arlington**, **Buckingham**, **Ashley** and **Lauderdale**.

Charles II, however, undermines their efficiency by exploiting their differences.

John Milton publishes *Paradise Lost*, a poem which proclaims to "justify the ways of God to men" and is often regarded as the finest verse epic in English.

1668 England enters into a Protestant **Triple Alliance** with **Sweden**

THE RESTORATION

*A*fter Cromwell's death in 1658 there was little debate about restoring the Stuarts, but his son and successor, **Richard Cromwell**, proved unable to resolve the underlying tensions between the military and Parliament. When he resigned the following year, only a limited set of options remained open. The public mood was turning against the political maneuvering of the army (particularly after its recall and rapid dismissal of the Rump Parliament), and **General George Monck** seized the initiative by opening negotiations which paved the way for Charles II's restoration to the throne.

Despite the widespread rejoicing that greeted the king's carefully staged return—not to mention his guarantee that those responsible for his father's death would be treated fairly—a number of people had good reason to be nervous. The prospect of royalists returning from exile and demanding their confiscated lands back held little appeal. Even less attractive was the possibility that old parliamentarians might be brought to book for rebelling in the first place. In the end, Charles kept his word that only the surviving regicides would suffer, and old opposition peers were bought off with government offices. Ironically, it was diehard royalists who felt short-changed.

And restoring the monarchy (and with it the Commons, the Lords and the bishops) didn't simply return England to where it had been eleven years

and the **Dutch United Provinces**, ostensibly to counter the growing power of **Louis XIV**'s France. Privately Charles II maintains contacts with the French court.

1669 An admiralty official, **Samuel Pepys**, is forced to give up writing his *Diary*, which he began on January 1, 1660, due to failing eyesight. It will remain in cipher and unpublished until the 19th century.

earlier. Rebellion and civil unrest were tangible threats, and there was more open political debate than ever before. Throughout major towns and cities a lively press had begun to circulate, providing up-to-date news on the major affairs of state, while numerous coffee-houses had become the focus for discussion—so many that in the 1670s the government contemplated shutting them all down. Perhaps the greatest change, though, was at court. Charles II created an entirely different—and far more factionalized—government to the one presided over by his father. Instead of allowing himself to rely on Parliament for funds, he accepted the largesse of **Louis XIV** of France and relied on the prospect of a Catholic succession to keep the politicians divided. Least attractively, he was thoroughly disloyal to those who supported him. Both **Clarendon** and **Danby** were thrown to the dogs, and even his favorite son, **James, Duke of Monmouth**, was snubbed. This cut-throat environment was mirrored by a permissive (and, some said, utterly amoral) atmosphere. The admiralty official and diarist Samuel Pepys was frequently scandalized by the goings-on at the Stuart court, but took great delight in noting down its gossip. He exclaimed, describing supper with some of the "merry gang" in 1688: "Lord! What loose, cursed company was this that I was in tonight, though full of wit and worth a man's being in for once, to know the nature of it and their manner of talk and lives..."

1670 Charles signs the **Secret Treaty of Dover** with **Louis XIV**, agreeing to join France in an attack on the Dutch and also to convert to Catholicism as and when the political climate permits.

1672 An invasion of the Dutch United Provinces by **Louis XIV** is supported by English naval actions. In desperation the Dutch turn to **William of Orange**, appointing him their *stadtholder*. As Charles's secret dealings with the French are exposed—though not his promise to become a Catholic—political opposition to the king grows in Parliament, coalescing into a faction that will become known as the **Whig Party**. Charles responds by entrusting his affairs to his minister **Thomas Osborne**, who begins organizing a "loyalist" faction, the beginnings of the **Tory Party**.

1673 Although Charles II has fathered many illegitimate sons and daughters with his numerous mistresses, **Queen Catherine** fails to provide him with a legitimate heir. It becomes, therefore, a matter of widespread political concern when his brother (and heir appar-

London in the aftermath of the Great Fire, 1666

So down, with my heart full of trouble, to the Lieutenant of the Tower, who tells me that it begun this morning in the King's bakers house in Pudding Lane, and that it hath burned down St Magnes Church and most part of Fishstreete already. So I down to the waterside and there got a boat and through bridge, and there saw a lamentable fire. Poor Michells house, as far as the Old Swan, already burned that way and the fire running further, that in a very little time it got as far as the Stillyard while I was there. Everybody endeavoring to remove their goods, and flinging into the river or bringing them into lighters that lay off. Poor people staying in their houses as long as till the very fire touched them, and then running into boats or clambering from one pair of stair by the waterside to another. And among other things, the poor pigeons I perceive were loath to leave their houses, but hovered about the windows and balconies till they were some of them burned, their wings, and fell down.

—Samuel Pepys, *Diary*
(part of the entry for September 2, 1666)

ent to the throne) **James, Duke of York**—a Catholic—marries the Catholic princess **Mary of Modena**. Parliament hurriedly adds the **Test Act** to the statute book, obliging all office-holders—and by implication the monarch—to take Anglican sacraments.

Osborne becomes Lord Treasurer.

1674 Osborne is created earl of Danby. As his hold over government tightens his policies prevail: cautious opposition toward France; strict adherence to Anglicanism; and the upholding of royal authority. Hostilities with the Dutch are ended.

The Puritan divine **John Baxter** speaks out against the shipment of black Africans to work as **slaves** on English plantations in the American colonies.

1675 The **Royal Observatory** at **Greenwich** is founded by royal charter to further astronomical observation and to investigate the problem of locating longitude at sea. **John Flamsteed** is appointed the first **astronomer-royal**.

THE SCIENTIFIC REVOLUTION IN ENGLAND

*T*he emergence of modern science was a Europe-wide movement spanning the 16th and 17th centuries, and was rooted in a number of developments: the thirst for new kinds of knowledge that accompanied the Renaissance, a revolution in mathematics and advances in technology. The declining authority of the Church probably played a leading role, too, though this has always been hard to quantify—despite the well-advertised face-off between Rome and **Galileo Galilei**.

England arrived on the scene later than Italy, France and the Netherlands, but during the Stuart period it saw a number of significant breakthroughs, culminating in the publication of **Isaac Newton**'s *Principia Mathematica* in 1687 with the assistance of the astronomer **Edmund Halley**—a work that provided the ground rules of physics until Einstein's work in relativity at the beginning of the 20th century. For his numerous achievements, which included his 1704 study *Optics* and the invention of **differential calculus**, Newton was knighted in 1705, the first scientist to be so honored.

But Newton's work was not isolated. His predecessor, **Robert Hooke**, claimed (not unreasonably) to have anticipated Newton's discovery of gravity.

1677 The marriage of Charles II's niece (and the duke of York's daughter by a previous marriage) **Mary** to **William III of Orange** goes some way to allaying fears about a Catholic succession. But Charles begins accepting secret "**subsidies**" from the French Crown to avoid becoming dependent on Parliament.

1678 Political tensions re-ignite when a London magistrate, **Sir Edmund Berry Godfrey**, is found murdered on London's Primrose

In the 1650s he had established the laws of **elasticity** and, taking full advantage of the **microscope**, went on to uncover cellular structures in natural materials. The Anglo-Irish **Robert Boyle** achieved even greater things. As well as suggesting the existence of chemical elements, Boyle experimented with gases, extrapolating the fundamentally important "**Boyle's Law**," which stated that the pressure of a given quantity of gas is in inverse proportion to its volume.

Both men were intimately involved with the **Royal Society**, established at the beginning of Charles II's reign to encourage scientific research (and rival similar European institutions). But although English science became famously empirical under the Society's influence, in the 17th century the quest to unlock the "laws of nature" was still closely tied to theology— those very laws, after all, were deemed to be devised by God. Newton himself spent much of his later life exploring prophecies contained in the biblical Book of Daniel, and Boyle's published works include lengthy attempts to define God's relationship with the physical universe. The stereotype of the scientist as an atheistical investigator belongs to a much later period.

Hill. **Titus Oates**, sometime Jesuit, testifies that Godfrey has been murdered by Catholic priests as part of a wider **Popish Plot** to assassinate Charles II, replace him with his brother James and restore Catholicism in England. In the ensuing panic five Catholic lords are imprisoned, many Catholics are executed and Parliament passes a **Disabling Act** barring "papists" from public office. The crisis is exacerbated when **Louis XIV**'s financial support for Charles is exposed. Danby is held responsible, impeached, and later sent to the Tower. Oates's evidence also implicates Queen Catherine, but the king dissolves Parliament before she can be investigated. Investigation of Oates, however, shows his testimony to have been a tissue of lies, and he is placed in the stocks for perjury.

John Bunyan publishes the first part of *Pilgrim's Progress*, a Christian allegory that becomes an instant bestseller.

1679 Despite Oates's perjury, anti-Catholic feelings continue to run high, underpinning the **Exclusion Crisis**—an effort to bar the duke of York or any other Catholic from the succession. Hoping to revive his fading popularity and increase his revenues, Charles II calls the first of three short-lived **parliaments**. Each is dissolved when it becomes clear no compromise is possible. To ease his position, however, the king orders his brother to leave the country.

1680 The poet and libertine **John Wilmot, Earl of Rochester**—upheld by some as an icon of contemporary wantonness—dies aged 33.

To apply himself with the most exact care and diligence to the rectifying the tables of the motions of the heavens, and the places of the fixed stars, so as to find out the so much-desired longitude of places for the perfecting the art of navigation.

—**Instructions to John Flamsteed,**
the first astronomer-royal, 1675

1681 Charles II dissolves his last **parliament**. Continuing French subsidies and a rigorous reform of the treasury enable the king and his privy council to govern England autonomously. Although Charles's popularity revives during his final years, political divisions remain. It is about this time that the terms "**Whig**" and "**Tory**" become common currency.

The poet and dramatist **John Dryden** writes *Absalom and Achitophel*, a verse satire that brilliantly captures the atmosphere of intrigue surrounding the king's court.

1683 Government ministers discover the details of the **Rye House Plot**—in fact two plots. One, supported by old Cromwellians, intends to assassinate the king at Rye House on his way back from the races at Newmarket. The second, the brainchild of **William, Lord Russell**, plans merely to capture the king and demand the formation of a government made up of MPs. Both plots are easily quashed, however, and Russell and his other conspirators are executed.

1684 Danby is released from the Tower.

1685 Charles II dies in London on February 6, after professing the Catholic faith and supposedly begging: "Let not poor Nelly starve" (referring to his favorite mistress, the actress **Nell Gwynn**). He is succeeded by his brother **James II** without immediate repercussions, at

---

There is no doubt that Rochester is the most witty man in the kingdom; but then he is likewise the most unprincipled, and devoid even of the least tincture of honor... He applauds your taste, submits to your sentiments, and whilst he himself does not believe a single word of what he is saying, he makes you believe it all.

—Miss Mary Hobart on John Wilmot,
Earl of Rochester, c.1667

least in England. In Scotland, though, there is an uprising led by the **duke of Argyll**. Although this is crushed in June, it inspires Charles II's illegitimate son, **James, Duke of Monmouth**, known as the "Protestant duke," to stage a second rebellion south of the border. Landing at **Lyme Regis**, Monmouth draws modest support in the West Country before his forces are defeated by Lord Feversham at **Sedgemoor** on July 6. A few days later Monmouth is discovered in a ditch disguised as a shepherd. Refusing him clemency, James II orders his execution. **Judge George Jeffreys** is appointed head of a commission to root out Monmouth's supporters. As a result of Jeffreys' "Bloody Assizes," hundreds are hanged in rows along the road connecting **Bridgewater** and **Chedzoy** in Somerset.

1686 Although James II honors his pledge not to forcibly impose Catholicism on England, suspicions are aroused when the Catholic **Lord Tyrconnell** is appointed lord lieutenant in **Ireland**. In response **Thomas, Lord Wharton** composes "**Lillibulero**," a satirical poem warning of the dangers of popery. Set to music by **Henry Purcell**, it is embraced as a popular anthem by the king's opponents. Wharton will later claim credit for having "sung King James out of three kingdoms."

The **East India Company**, having failed to gain its commercial ends in India by diplomacy, begins using force to secure trading priv-

---

Here lies a great and mighty king
Whose promise none relies on;
He never said a foolish thing,
Nor ever did a wise one.

—**John Wilmot, Earl of Rochester,**
"The King's Epitaph"
(on Charles II)

WHIGS AND TORIES

*T*oward the end of Charles II's reign it started to become fashionable to refer to the two main political factions in England as **Whigs** and **Tories**. Both were racist terms of abuse. The "Tories" were Irish bandits, while the "Whigs" (originally "Whiggamores") were Scottish cattle thieves.

In the political sense, Tories could be deemed loyalists. They stood for upholding the monarchy, and with it the Anglican Church. The Whigs, in contrast, were the opposition. They believed in a limited monarchy that respected the views of its subjects, and in the intertwined rights of liberty and property. Many Whigs were dissenters, or **Nonconformists**; and even those who were not extended sympathy toward dissent.

Inevitably, distinctions between Tories and Whigs tended to blur over specific issues, so that there were Tories with Whiggish leanings and vice versa. Where disagreement remained fundamental, however, was regarding the notion of protest. Tories, still haunted by the Civil Wars, could not countenance the idea of forcibly resisting the king—a tyrannical monarch was preferable to anarchy. Whigs, on the other hand, had no such qualms. Resistance in the name of liberty and property was not only right, it was necessary to maintain the rights of free Englishmen. And it was this cry of "Liberty and Property" that was, above all others, to resound in the politics of the following century.

ileges—a pattern that will be replicated by the English throughout the Far East and other parts of the world.

1687 Hoping to re-introduce Catholicism by the back door, James II develops a **Declaration of Indulgence**, allowing free worship throughout his kingdoms.

Isaac Newton publishes *Principia Mathematica*, which identifies gravity as the mechanism of planetary motion.

1688 Fears about James II's true intentions deepen when the king orders his **Declaration of Indulgence** to be read from every pulpit. The crisis comes to a head when **Queen Mary of Modena** gives birth to a son on June 10. The prospect of another Catholic succession, and James's arbitrary replacement of a number of key officials, leads **Danby** and six other leading noblemen—among them the earls of **Nottingham** and **Devonshire**—to invite **William of Orange** to England to secure the election of a free Parliament and their Protestant rights. Driven by the "Protestant wind," William lands with an army at **Torbay** on November 5. Deserted by his army, James II flees to **France** on December 11, throwing the Great Seal into the Thames as he goes.

CHAPTER EIGHT

The Age of Oligarchy

{1689-1820}

THE PERIOD BETWEEN THE JOINT ACCESSION OF **WILLIAM III** and **Mary II** in 1688 and the death of **George III** in 1820 has sometimes been dubbed the "long 18th century." During this time England increasingly found itself playing a role on not just the European but the world stage, and with this some historians have detected a growing sense of "English" or "British" identity. At best, though, nationalism remained an ambiguous concept. England and Wales had been formally united in 1536, union with Scotland was finally achieved in 1707 and union with Ireland in 1801 resulted in the formation of a Parliament of Great Britain. Yet the Parliament continued to sit at Westminster, and the members from Scotland, Ireland and Wales were never left in any doubt that England remained the dominant partner.

The story of England in this period is tied in, as ever, with events in France. One of the motivating factors behind the union with Scotland and Ireland, in fact, was to forestall a French invasion through the back door. But the reasons for warfare changed as the century passed, and were indicative of England's internal politics. William of Orange had been eager to secure English support for his ongoing conflict with **Louis XIV**, and he was keen to establish a balance of power within Europe that would curb Louis' despotic tendencies. William had been accepted in England as the protector of the nation's liberties and Protestantism against James II's francophile Catholic tendencies, and under **Queen Anne** the Whigs remained eager to see France humbled for the same reasons. A desire to curb the Jacobite threat posed by the exiled House of Stuart in part motivated the Hanoverians too to stand against France after 1714, but they were also heavily influenced by their interest in protecting their vulnerable German lands—which lay at the mercy of any passing army.

Increasingly colonial interests took on greater prominence, and it was these that came to the fore during the **Seven Years War** of 1756–63, which resulted in Britain driving the French out of Canada and adding India to its American and West Indian colonies. England and France clashed again during the **American War of Independence** (1775–83), which proved a costly embarrassment for Britain. But although colonial ambitions continued to motivate both sides, a new ideological flavor began to influence events too, first in the American War and later in the **French Revolution**. At its outset the Revolution seemed to promise England a more acceptable France stripped of its Bourbon absolutism—which for many conjured up images of torture and oppression—but as the country descended into bloodshed in the early 1790s many of the traditional hierarchies were torn down. They were replaced first by a republic, and then by the dictatorship of **Napoleon Bonaparte**, who was eager to dominate Europe. The **Napoleonic Wars** saw Britain ranged once more against France, in alliance from time to time with the other great European states: **Prussia**, **Austria** and **Russia**. These years were marked by the victories at **Trafalgar** (1805) and **Waterloo** (1815).

By the early years of the 19th century the British way of life had altered dramatically with developments in **industrialization**. People were moving to cities to find work in new industries, and the sweeping social changes that accompanied technological innovation would accelerate as the period drew to a close. **Colonialism**, at first driven by entrepreneurial private institutions as much as by government intervention, came to play a greater role in British finances with New World trades such as sugar, tobacco and slavery. This burgeoning global economy, based on overseas exploitation, created fresh domestic wealth and with it the support structure for continuing cultural development. **London** grew to be a world city (with a population to match) through the trade that passed through its ports, and the explosive growth of stately-home building at the latter end of the 18th century—employing the most fashionable architects, designers and painters—was in part financed by money made in colonies on the other side of the world.

Politically, for much of the period England was dominated by the **Whig Party**. It was they who took the credit for the "Glorious Revolution" of 1688–89, and who claimed to be the upholders of the ensuing settlement. Yet the monarch continued to exercise extensive power, as several politicians who earned royal displeasure—including the Whig **Thomas, Lord Wharton** and the **Tory Henry, Viscount Bolingbroke**—found to their cost. And, as the ideologies of the American and French revolutionaries began to take hold among some Whig factions, the Tory party, with its traditional ideals of upholding Church and monarch, came to be regarded as a safer pair of hands in dangerous times.

The Whig ascendancy: 1689–1759

Had James II not taken the decision to flee in 1688 he might well have remained in power, but it is likely that strong efforts would have been made to ensure that he was king in name only—and some form of regency would have wrested control from his hands. At any rate he had other reasons to quit: mass desertions from the army removed his military backing, and his political support within his own family was hemorrhaging. His effective "abdication" allowed Parliament, after much soul-searching, to find a way of offering the throne to William and Mary as joint monarchs, though William himself held executive power. It was not a particularly happy compromise, however, and the

"Bloodless Revolution" was neither bloodless (several died during a skirmish between the Gloucestershire militia and Lord Lovelace as he attempted to fight his way through to William's army) nor the touchstone of liberty it later came to symbolize. In the 17th century "revolution" meant "restoration," not the creation of something new, and it was in this sense that the Whigs attempted to portray William of Orange's coup. And indeed his accession reopened old wounds. Over the next five years a steady outpouring of Whig legislation—including an **Act of Toleration** and the 1694 **Triennial Act**, committing the monarch to a fresh parliament every three years—endeavored to limit the throne's room for maneuver, but the king remained a forceful presence and successfully made use of his new position to continue resisting Louis XIV.

Yet 1688–89 was an important watershed. It confirmed Parliament's role as the guarantor of the monarchy, and 25 years later, when William's successor **Queen Anne** died childless, it was Parliament that offered the throne to her German Protestant cousin, **George, Elector of Hanover**. The decision to adopt the House of Hanover over the heads of some fifty other candidates was perhaps the most significant outcome of the "Revolution." In William III's case it could be plausibly argued that his wife Mary was the legitimate heir to the English throne, but the accession of **George I** was the result of sheer expediency. Unable to speak more than a smattering of English and eager to keep in touch with his electorate at home (to which he often returned during the summer months), George surrounded himself with German favorites—among them his *kappelmeister*, **Georg Frederic Händel**.

The business of government came increasingly to be left to the king's ministers, which encouraged the office of **prime minister** to develop. There had been principal ministers before, but increasingly the "first lord of the treasury," as the position was known, came to be seen as the effective head of government under the king. This was partly because it became more difficult for the monarch to rule in defiance of whichever faction held sway in Parliament. But the office of prime minister was mutually beneficial: a party lacking the monarch's support found it difficult to dominate Parliament. It was in these conditions that **Sir Robert Walpole**, generally regarded as Britain's first prime minister, came to dominate affairs. As first lord of the treasury between 1721 and 1742, Walpole headed an administration comprised almost exclusively of Whigs. In the meantime the Tories were forced into the political wilderness by their association with the Stuart cause. Their ambitions were disappointed twice: first with the accession of **George II**, who soon came to appreciate Walpole's abilities, and once again with the early death of his son **Prince Frederick**. It was not until **George III** came to the throne, proclaiming an interest in the traditional ideologies espoused by "patriot"Tories, that the party's period in the wilderness appeared to be near its end.

In an age governed by the "rage of party," political office (or the expectation of it) became increasingly important, creating a climate in which the pursuit of patronage added to the power of the aristocratic elite. Authors, artists and satirists such as the poet **Alexander Pope** and the erstwhile dean of St Patrick's, Dublin, **Jonathan Swift**, employed their talents to win favor by engaging in the political and personal feuds of the moment. The artist and engraver **William Hogarth** threw in his lot with the earl of Bute in defense of his government, as did the Scottish novelist **Tobias Smollett**; while **Laurence Sterne**'s comic travelogue, *A Sentimental Journey through France and Italy*, boasted a host of the great and the good among its subscribers—including the earl of Abingdon and the dukes of Buccleuch, Richmond and Grafton. Under the influence of such powerful patrons, literature in England witnessed a new development: the novel. But the success of **Daniel Defoe**'s *Moll Flanders*, **Samuel Richardson**'s *Clarissa* and **Henry Fielding**'s *Tom Jones* demonstrates that it was not merely those at the top of the social ladder who were interested in consuming culture—people from many backgrounds were eager to experience the pleasures of polite leisure.

1689 Following the flight of **James II** and **William III of Orange**'s largely unopposed march on London, a hastily gathered **Convention Parliament** offers the throne jointly to William and his wife and cousin **Mary**, subject to their agreeing to a **Declaration of Rights**, which lists James's wrongs and asks them to take the throne. They accept in February, and in April they are crowned as **William III** and **Mary II**. Although many English people welcome the new monarchs, there is resistance by some Scots and among Ireland's Catholic majority. William brings with him a commitment to opposing the expansion of French power under **Louis XIV**. Instead he recommends a balance of powers between Europe's leading states—a recipe that, over the following decades, draws England into a series of continental wars.

Parliament passes an **Act of Toleration**, enshrining the principle of "liberty for tender consciences," but Catholics and dissenters (Nonconformists) remain barred from public office.

1690 Aided by Louis XIV, **James II** lands in Ireland in an attempt to recover his kingdoms, but is defeated by **William III** at the **Battle of the Boyne** in July and forced to return to France. As a result of William's victory, Ireland's Catholic majority continues to be ruled by a Protestant minority.

In England's Treasury (regarded as the most important department of state), the Whigs are displaced by three "**Tory**" ministers: the **marquess of Carmarthen** (later **duke of Leeds**), **Sidney Godolphin** and the **earl of Northampton**.

The philosopher **John Locke** publishes his *Essay Concerning Human Understanding*, an attempt to explain the relations between knowledge and perception.

1692 English and Dutch forces defeat a French navy at **La Hogue**, but on land William III suffers a reversal at the **Battle of Steenkirk**.

1693 The **earl of Sunderland** begins reorganizing the Court party to further William III's control of government.

1694 Parliament limits the monarchs' scope for political maneuver by imposing the **Triennial Act** on William and Mary, obliging them to summon a new parliament every three years. **Mary II** dies of **smallpox** in December.

Greenwich Hospital is founded, its architect **Sir Christopher Wren**.

The **Bank of England** is founded on the initiative of **Charles Montague** (later **Lord Halifax**).

1695 William Congreve establishes himself as England's leading dramatist with the first production of his polished comedy *Love for Love*, to be followed five years later with the equally successful *The Way of the World*.

The eminent composer **Henry Purcell**, whose works include the opera *Dido and Aeneas* and the funeral music for Mary II, dies—after being locked out in the rain by his wife, if legend is to be believed.

1696 A plot by supporters of James II—known as **Jacobites**—to assassinate **William III** is uncovered. When **Sir John Fenwick**, one of the conspirators, accuses **Godolphin**, the **duke of Shrewsbury** and **Admiral Edward Russell** of secretly corresponding with James's court-in-exile at St Germain, **Thomas, Lord Wharton** and **Sir John Somers** rally the Whig forces to defend their friends. This group—Wharton, Somers, Shrewsbury, Russell and **Charles Montague**—comes to be known collectively as the "**Whig Junto**" and it forms one of the most powerful and well-organized cliques in parliament. Through their efforts the three ministers are exonerated and Fenwick is executed.

1697 Anglo-French hostilities are brought to an end by the **Peace of Ryswick**, in which Louis XIV agrees to recognize William III as **king of England**.

1700 The succession is thrown in doubt when the son of William III's sister-in-law, **William, Duke of Gloucester**, dies. To prevent a Catholic Stuart return, the eventual succession is offered to **Sophia, Electress of Hanover**—a descendant of James I's daughter Elizabeth and 56th in line to the succession.

The poet, dramatist and critic **John Dryden** dies.

1701 Parliament passes an **Act of Settlement**, disallowing any future Hanoverian monarch from leaving England without parliamentaryapproval and banning the appointment of foreigners to government posts.

James II dies in exile. His son, **James Edward**, is recognized as **James III of England** by Louis XIV in contravention of the Treaty of Ryswick.

Europe is thrown into confusion when **Carlos II** of Spain dies childless, and **Louis XIV** of France supports his Bourbon grandson **Philip V** as Spain's new king. Following a French invasion of the Spanish Netherlands and the outbreak of the **War of Spanish Succession**, England enters into a **Grand Alliance** with the Dutch Republic and the Holy Roman Empire on September 5, determined to limit Catholic French influence. The war will last another twelve years.

Parliament passes a new **Act of Succession**, nominating the electress **Sophia** and her Hanoverian descendants as eventual heirs to the throne, and stipulating that any monarch must be a communicating member of the Church of England (in other words, one that accepts the Anglican Eucharist).

1702 William III dies from internal bleeding on March 8 after his horse stumbles on a molehill. Thereafter Jacobites drink toasts to "the gentleman in black velvet." The succession passes to William's cousin and sister-in-law **Queen Anne**. Despite seventeen pregnancies, Anne and her husband, **Prince George of Denmark**, are childless following the death of their son, **William, Duke of Gloucester** in 1700, so a crisis over the succession looms. Ill-disposed toward the Whigs, Anne makes **Godolphin** her chief minister; but Tory hopes that Anne will rescind the Act of Settlement and offer the throne to her half-brother **James Edward** are dampened when he refuses to become an Anglican. Jacobite ambitions are further damaged when the queen indicates her support for the war against **France**. A British army is dispatched to the Netherlands under the command of **John Churchill, Earl of Marlborough**, created duke after a successful first campaign.

1703 Portugal joins the Grand Alliance against Louis XIV and the Bourbons.

1704 In July the Allies capture **Gibraltar**, which passes into English hands. Louis XIV attempts to bring hostilities to an end by ordering a daring march on **Vienna**. His army is comprehensively beaten, however, by an allied army under Marlborough at **Blenheim** on August 2.

1705 In gratitude for his outstanding generalship, Parliament votes to reward Marlborough with the royal estate at **Woodstock** outside Oxford and the funds to build **Blenheim Palace**. Designed by **Sir John Vanbrugh** in the fashionable baroque style, the palace is considered one of England's architectural glories.

The Allies capture **Barcelona** in October.

1706 Marlborough again defeats a Bourbon army, this time on May 23 at **Ramillies**. In June the allies enter **Madrid**.

To strengthen British security, an **Act of Union** between England and Scotland is drawn up in July, and submitted to Scotland's Parliament in October.

1707 In January the Act of Union is approved by Scotland's Parliament.

1708 In Spain an allied army is defeated at **Almanza**, reviving Bourbon fortunes, but Marlborough delivers another crushing victory over the French at **Oudenaarde** in Flanders in July.

In March Louis XIV gathers an invasion fleet to carry the 19-year-old pretender, **James Edward**, to Scotland. After several delays the flotilla sails, but bad weather and the appearance of the English fleet under **Admiral Byng** force the Jacobites to head for home. One French ship, *The Salisbury* (previously taken by the French), is recaptured.

In May the **Act of Union** becomes law, creating a formal bond between England and Scotland. Some commentators, notably **Jonathan Swift**, protest Ireland's exclusion from the act.

Following elections to the House of Commons, the Whigs under **Lord Wharton** gain a massive parliamentary majority and assume control of government in an uneasy alliance with **Harley** and **Godolphin**.

1709 Marlborough inflicts another heavy defeat on France at **Malplaquet** on September 11.

On November 5 the Tory cleric **Dr Henry Sacheverell** causes outrage in the Whig ranks when he preaches against "occasional" conformists and "low" churchmen. The damaging thrust of his argument, though, is that by advocating the old "high" church doctrine of "nonresistance," he suggests that the 1688–89 settlement is unjustified. The Whigs call for his impeachment.

Richard Steele founds *The Tatler* magazine.

Construction of the main section of **Castle Howard** in Yorkshire, a grand new house built by Vanbrugh for the **3rd earl of Carlisle**, is completed.

1710 Sacheverell's trial opens on February 27, but is brought to a halt within a week following the outbreak of widespread rioting. The House of Lords is sharply divided along party lines—the Whigs voting for impeachment, the Tories for Sacheverell's acquittal.

In an October **general election** Tories gain from a swing against the Whigs, and secure a large majority in the House of Commons.

The **duke of Shrewsbury** and **Robert Harley** initiate secret negotiations with the French through the mediation of the English Jacobite **earl of Jersey**.

THE ACT OF UNION

The union of England and Scotland had eluded countless rulers since the days of Agricola, but in 1707 it was enshrined in the Act of Union. Even then, any enthusiasm on either side of the border was conspicuously absent. The main impetus behind it was the matter of English security. Above all the Whigs feared that when Queen Anne died, the Scots might reject the planned Hanoverian succession and instead offer their throne to James II's Catholic-leaning son James Edward. The Calvinist Scots saw a similar danger, and so a deal was struck.

Scotland lost its own parliament, but in return was allocated 45 seats in the English House of Commons; sixteen Scottish peers, elected from within their own existing ranks, were provided places in the House of Lords. For most Scots, who had looked to the duke of Hamilton to negotiate a more advantageous settlement, these were less than inspiring terms—but at any rate they were preferable to the possible alternative. For a few, particularly in the Tory highlands, the settlement was unacceptable, and so encouraged the very thing the Whigs had been anxious to avert: hopes for a Stuart succession in Scotland.

But away from these sensitive political fronts, union brought with it significant benefits for both nations, mainly because the whole of mainland Britain (including Wales) was now a single economic zone, supported by a common currency. The Scots, who had never possessed foreign colonies of their own, began to participate in an expanding British empire, and with it Scottish businessmen were able to reap the lucrative rewards.

1711 The anti-French alliance falters when **Archduke Charles** becomes **Holy Roman Emperor**, threatening the Bourbons with an even greater Habsburg power bloc.

Following the machinations of his domestic (mainly Whig) enemies, **Marlborough** is dismissed as captain general on December 9, accused of embezzling public funds.

Encouraged by Queen Anne's government, Tories set up the **South Sea Company**, intended to provide alternative investment opportunities to those offered by the Whig-dominated Bank of England.

Richard Steele founds a second magazine, *The Spectator*, with politician and writer **Joseph Addison**.

1712 A duel between the **duke of Hamilton** and **Lord Mohun**—in which both combatants are killed—shocks society by underlining the violent disagreements between Whigs and Tories.

The German composer **Georg Frederic Händel** (Handel) settles in London, and will remain in England until his death in 1759. In that time he will produce an astonishing volume of work—including operas, oratorios, sacred music, concertos and ceremonial music (some of it for royalty).

1713 The **Treaties of Utrecht** bring to an end the **War of Spanish Succession**. Although Philip V remains king in Spain, the treaties are favorable to British colonial expansion in the Americas and elsewhere.

1714 Following the death of **Queen Anne** on August 1, Parliament offers the throne to **George Lewis, Elector of Hanover**. Speaking little English, **George I** arrives in England accompanied by two mistresses—the tall and thin **Ehrengard Melusina von Schulenberg** (created the duchess of Kendal) and the short and stout Charlotte Sophia von Kielmannsegge (later countess of Darlington). Together they are known as the "Elephant and Castle." George's wife, convicted of adultery, is left behind in Hanover.

Marlborough is restored as commander-in-chief of the English army, but plays little further part in public affairs.

1715 George I's tenure of the throne is threatened by the first **Jacobite Rebellion** after James Edward lands in Scotland. But James is beaten at **Sheriffmuir** and forced to flee back to the continent.

1719 A second **Jacobite Rebellion** is led by the exiled (Irish) **duke of Ormonde** and **Earl Marischal**, but it fails to attract sufficient support in either Scotland or England.

The sometime Tory propagandist **Daniel Defoe** publishes *Robinson Crusoe*, a fictionalized autobiographical account of a man shipwrecked on a desert island, perhaps based on a true story.

1720 The **South Sea Company**, set up in 1711, collapses in spectacular style after an attempt to drive competitors to the wall creates panic among investors—resulting in the **South Sea Bubble**. As catastrophe threatens, George I is forced to restore the Whig **Robert Walpole** to government. Walpole resolves the crisis, restores confidence in the economy, and in so doing lays the foundations for his 21-year domination of English politics.

1722 In a March **general election**, the Tories are heavily defeated by their Whig rivals, whose majority in the House of Commons now extends to over two hundred seats.

A Jacobite conspiracy is unmasked when **Walpole** is informed of a plot surrounding **Francis Atterbury, Bishop of Rochester**. Habeas Corpus is suspended, Atterbury is forced into exile and another conspirator, **Christopher Layer**, is executed.

1725 Fearful of the trade consequences of the **Treaty of Vienna** between Spain and Austria, Britain, France and Prussia enter into the **Alliance of Hanover**.

1726 As the Walpole administration extends its influence, Lord Bolingbroke—in alliance with a Whig faction led by **William**

THE SOUTH SEA BUBBLE

*T*he South Sea Company was founded in 1711 with government backing to provide an alternative to the Whig-dominated Bank of England. Investors in the Bank had enjoyed good returns, and the Tories hoped to open up a little honest competition. At first the Company did well: an Anglo-Spanish Treaty of 1713 gave it a monopoly in the Spanish slave trade and a foothold in other European markets. But problems started with a 1719 scheme to redistribute the national debt—not a bad idea in itself, but one that came quickly unstuck as a result of unrealistic demands for profits from the Company's directors, investors, court interests and government ministers. As expectations rose, speculators piled in, creating an investment frenzy akin to that which preceded the Wall Street crash of 1929. As the bubble grew, more and more projects were devised, many of them fraudulently implausible.

And in 1720, after the Company spread bad rumors in the hope of destroying its competitors, confidence failed: the bubble had burst. Hundreds were bankrupted, including some who had sold their estates in the hope of multiplying their wealth. Parliament hurriedly pushed through emergency legislation regulating joint-stock ventures in the future, but for those who lost everything there was no compensation. Only the Whigs, swept back into power under Robert Walpole, could glean any immediate satisfaction. But while governmental integrity had suffered a severe blow, the long-term consequences of the South Sea Bubble, as it came to be known, weren't all bad. The introduction of tighter regulations and the recognition of a need for steady investment laid the foundations for sustained economic growth.

Pulteney (later **earl of Bath**)—launches a new Tory opposition journal, *The Craftsman*.

1727 In June **George I** dies while en route for Hanover. He is succeeded by his Tory-favoring son, **George II**. The new king attempts to replace Walpole with **Spencer Compton** but, backed by a Whig majority in Parliament, Walpole easily outmaneuvers them both.

A **general election** in August results in further humiliation for the Tories.

Sir Isaac Newton dies.

1728 George II's first parliament votes to appoint **Arthur Onslow** as speaker of the House of Commons, a post he holds for 33 years.

The king's son **Prince Frederick** arrives in England from Hanover and is created **prince of Wales**.

Alexander Pope publishes *The Dunciad*, a scathing satire on his fellow poets.

John Gay's *The Beggar's Opera*, a vaudeville piece comparing the politics of the so-called "Robinocracy" with the world of highwaymen and "thief-takers" (bounty-hunters), receives its first performance.

1729 John Wesley becomes leader of the small Oxford society of Nonconformists. Inspired by his teachings, **Methodism**—with its emphases on godliness and honest toil—grows to become one of Britain's principal religious denominations.

1731 Georgia is added to Britain's enlarging number of colonies in North America.

The *Gentleman's Magazine* is founded.

1732 The extent of **smuggling** around England's shores and attacks on customs officials is revealed in a report drawn up by a parliamentary committee and presented to the Treasury. The resulting **Excise Scheme** removes domestically consumed wine and tobacco—the main contraband goods—from the customs net, making them subject to **excise duties** (internal taxation) instead. Through *The Craftsman*, the Tories mount a vigorous attack against the perceived threat of all customs duties being replaced by excise.

1733 There are widespread **demonstrations** against the Excise Scheme.

Alexander Pope publishes his *Essay on Man*, a philosophical verse satire.

1734 The Whig administration suffers heavily at the polls during fresh **parliamentary elections**, largely as a result of the Excise controversy, but remains in power. **Walpole** continues to demonstrate his usefulness to George II by persuading Parliament to vote the Crown greater supplies for a larger army the following year.

1735 "**Hogarth's Act**," named after the artist and engraver **William Hogarth**, legislates in favor of copyright protection by making it illegal for pirated editions of engravings to be sold.

1736 Parliamentary tensions rise as the Whigs fail to achieve greater toleration for **Nonconformists**.

1737 George II's stormy relations with his son and heir **Prince Frederick** boil over into public view when the prince is expelled from **St James's Palace** in London. The prince establishes a rival "court" at **Leicester House**, where he is wooed by members of the opposition.

1738 The exiled Tory **Viscount Bolingbroke** writes the *Idea of a Patriot King*, a political testament that inspires some of Prince Frederick's followers and which later influences **George III**.

1739 Tensions with **Spain** over illegal trading by British merchantmen in Spain's American colonies spill over into outright war—the conflict is called the **War of Jenkins' Ear**, after an incident the previous year in which the Royal Navy captain **Robert Jenkins** was disfigured during a clash with Spanish coastal vessels.

1740 As the Spanish war continues, members of the House of Lords warn of the consequences should **France** enter the conflict on

Houses, churches, mixed together,
Streets unpleasant in all weather,
Prisons, palaces contiguous,
Gates, a bridge, the Thames irriguous.

Gaudy things enough to tempt ye,
Showy outsides, insides empty;
Bubbles, trades, mechanic arts,
Coaches, wheelbarrows and carts.

Warrants, bailiffs, bills unpaid,
Lords of laundresses afraid;
Rogues that nightly rob and shoot men,
Hangmen, aldermen, and footmen.

Lawyers, poets, priests, physicians,
Noble, simple, all conditions;
Worth beneath a threadbare cover,
Villainy bedaubed all over.

Women black, red, fair and grey,
Prudes and such as never pray,
Handsome, ugly, noisy, still,
Some that will not, some that will.

Many a beau without a shilling,
Many a widow not unwilling;
Many a bargain if you strike it:
This is London! How d'ye like it?

—**John Bancks, "A Description of London" (1738)**

Spain's side. Popular feeling against Spain rides high, however, and the patriotic chorus "**Rule Britannia**" from **Thomas Arne**'s new masque, *Alfred*, becomes a popular hit.

The **War of the Austrian Succession** begins in December as **Frederick the Great of Prussia** openly challenges the Habsburgs by invading **Silesia**.

1741 British naval assaults on the Spanish-held **Cuba** and **Carthagena** fail. The government's majority in Parliament falters, and Walpole begins to look insecure.

SIR ROBERT WALPOLE (1676–1745)

obert **Walpole** dominated politics during the reigns of the first two Georges, his enormous bulk an unmistakable presence in the House of Commons. In control of the nation's affairs between 1721 and 1741 almost without interruption, his supremacy was so complete that the age is often referred to as the "**Robinocracy.**"

Appointed to the council of Queen Anne's husband, George of Denmark, in 1705, he maintained a cautious balance between moderate Tories such as **Godolphin** and the **Whig Junto**, enabling him to climb the ladder of promotion with relative ease. The accession of **George I** ended Tory influence, and Walpole served in the ensuing Whig administration first as paymaster general and then, in 1715, as both first lord of the treasury and chancellor of the exchequer—a combination of offices that has led historians to call Walpole England's "first prime minister."

Party jealousies prompted his resignation in 1717, but he resumed office as paymaster general three years later, thanks in no small part to the influence of the King's mistress, the **duchess of Kendal**. The event that

1742 Outnumbered in the House of Commons, **Walpole** resigns on February 2. **Spencer Compton**, now **earl of Wilmington**, succeeds Walpole as First Lord of the Treasury.

Händel composes the first version of his oratorio *Messiah*.

1743 Following Wilmington's death in July, **Henry Pelham** becomes prime minister and forms a Whig administration.

Supporting the Austrian **Habsburg** cause, British contingents fight alongside Hanoverian and Hessian regiments against the French at the **Battle of Dettingen** in Bavaria on June 23.

truly secured his return to power, however, was the **South Sea Bubble**. Walpole was credited with being the only man capable of addressing the country's financial turmoil, and in 1721 he again became "prime minister." The accession of **George II** caused another brief hiatus in his career: the new monarch disliked Walpole, and replaced him with the ineffectual **Spencer Compton**. But Compton foolishly asked Walpole to assist him in arranging the civil list, giving the ousted leader a perfect opportunity to prove his value to the throne. Walpole guaranteed the monarch extensive subsidies, and, supported by **Queen Caroline**, he moved smoothly back into power.

Eventually, though, he fell foul of the Hanoverian habit of sons opposing their fathers. The Queen's death in 1737 left Walpole exposed to the machinations of Prince Frederick's circle, who orchestrated an increasingly unruly House of Commons. Defeated in Parliament over a relatively minor issue involving a disputed election case, Walpole resigned two days after being created the earl of Orford.

1744 As the European conflict widens, France enters the "Family Compact" with Spain and declares war on Austria and Britain.

John Wesley's **Methodist Society** holds its first national conference.

The poet **Alexander Pope** dies.

1745 Jacobite rebellion is renewed when James Edward's son **Charles Edward Stuart** (known as "Bonnie Prince Charlie") lands in Scotland and raises the clans against George II. A government force commanded by **Sir John Cope** is defeated by the pretender's highland army at **Prestonpans** on September 21. The rebels progress toward **Edinburgh**, capturing the city but not its castle. As winter sets in, Charles Edward marches into England, recruiting a small regiment in **Manchester** and reaching **Derby** on December 4. Unable to attract further followers, though, he is forced to retreat northwards two days later by his newly formed council of war.

1746 During a government crisis induced by the Jacobite rebellion, the Pelham administration resigns but is quickly reinstated after a replacement headed by the **earl of Bath** and the **earl of Granville** fails to attract public or political support. **William Pitt "the Elder"** is appointed joint- vice-treasurer of Ireland.

Pursued across the Scottish border by government forces, the Jacobites mount a successful rearguard action at **Falkirk** on January 17, but their main army is routed by George II's younger son, the **duke of Cumberland**, at **Culloden Moor** on April 16. **Charles Edward** spends five months in hiding before being spirited out of Britain.

1747 As the Whigs consolidate their hold on government, an increasing number of Tories turn toward **Prince Frederick**, who issues the **Carlton House Declaration** on June 4, outlining a "patriot" program of reform. **George II** responds by dissolving Parliament and calling fresh **elections**, during which the Tories are heavily defeated and the government hand is further strengthened. The government, however, is divided on whether and how to pur-

JACOBITISM

*T*he cause of the exiled Stuarts attracted widespread support in Britain and on the continent, but a second Stuart Restoration was never truly on the cards. James II's son James Edward's refusal to renounce Catholicism left him with insufficient parliamentary support for a peaceful return to be possible, and, despite French sympathies, no major European state was prepared to underwrite an armed invasion. Most English Jacobites were attached to the Stuarts only in an abstract way, their support seldom going beyond covert toasts raised to the "king across the water."

Even so, there were three Jacobite rebellions against the unpopular Hanoverians: in 1715, 1719 and, most famously, during 1745–46. Strictly speaking, the story of the last rebellion is a Scottish one: the majority of the action was fought on Scottish soil by Scottish participants. But it didn't always seem so—the last Stuart Pretender, Charles Edward, affectionately known as "Bonnie Prince Charlie," assumed his invasion would be enthusiastically greeted in England and marched south, reaching as far as Derby and recruiting some 250 down-and-outs in Manchester. But no one else flocked to his banner, and his homesick Scottish and Irish commanders soon urged retreat. Harried by English forces, Charles Edward made it back to Scotland, but was ignominiously defeated at Culloden. His hopes dashed, he ended life an alcoholic.

1745 was a disaster for highland society, but it reassured the Hanoverians that although the English might grumble, actual revolt was far from a reality. In any case, after Bonnie Prince Charlie there were no more pretenders. When his brother Henry Benedict entered the Church, Jacobitism lost its *raison d'être*. It survived only as lively subject matter for romantic novelists, among them Sir Walter Scott.

sue the war against **France** and **Spain**. Led by the dukes of **Cumberland** and **Newcastle** the war party wins the argument, and an army of 100,000 is raised. Cumberland is defeated at **Lauffeldt** by the **Marshal de Saxe**, but a French convoy setting out for the West Indies is destroyed by Admiral **Edward Hawke** off **La Rochelle**.

The first volumes of **Samuel Richardson**'s epistolary novel, *Clarissa*, are published.

FREDERICK, PRINCE OF WALES (1707–51)

*F*rederick, like his father, suffered from the traditional loathing Hanoverian fathers seemed to feel toward their eldest sons. George II and "Fritz," as he was known inside the family, could barely endure to be in the same room, yet the king perversely blocked any attempt by his son to establish an independent household until he was expelled from St James's Palace in 1737. When the prince finally did get his own establishment, **Leicester House**, he used it with a vengeance. He gathered a motley collection of politically disaffected men and wits around him, and from this gathering flowed the reinvention of the "patriot" cause in politics. Frederick's vision of a "Patriot King," who would do away with oligarchy and end Whig dominance, was eventually taken up by his own son, **George III**, in the years immediately following George II's death.

But there was a seamier side to the prince's activities. Quite how involved he was with the peculiarities of the **Hellfire Club** is uncertain, but he was associated with several of its leading intimates, and members of the fraternity such as **Bubb Doddington**, **Francis Dashwood** and **Lord Sandwich** all found places in the new "Patriot" ministry of their friend **Lord Bute** after

1748 The **War of the Austrian Succession** is brought to a close by **the Treaty of Aix-la-Chapelle**. **Prussia**'s possession of **Silesia** is confirmed, but in almost every other respect eight years' fighting has done little to resolve Europe's tensions, including those between Britain and the Bourbon nations of **France** and **Spain**. Even so, the peace is celebrated in London by the first performance of **Händel**'s *Music for the Royal Fireworks*. Prime minister **Henry Pelham** immediately begins reducing military

1762. Set against this, Frederick was a passionate patron of the arts as well as a musician of some talent, and did much to champion the concept of a paid **Loyal Opposition** in Parliament. But his positive qualities are rarely remembered now, buried beneath a famous mock epitaph:

> Here lies Fred,
> Who was alive and is dead:
> Had it been his father,
> I had much rather,
> Had it been his brother,
> Still better than another;
> Had it been his sister,
> No one would have missed her;
> Had it been the whole generation,
> Still better for the nation:
> But since 'tis only Fred –
> Who was alive and is dead –
> There's no more to be said.

expenditure, and wins popularity for his government and the king by **lowering taxes**.

1749 To counter the success of French colonists in Canada, a British fort, backed by the government, is established at **Halifax, Nova Scotia**.

Henry Fielding publishes his novel *Tom Jones*.

1750 A split develops in the ranks of the Whig government between the Pelhamite "**Old Corps**" and **John Russell, Duke of Bedford**'s "**Bloomsbury Gang**," but in effect little divides the various Whig factions—they all aim to uphold the Revolutionary Settlement.

1751 Hearing that **George II** is seriously ill and eager to assume power, **Prince Frederick** rushes to his father's bedside but catches a chill on the way and dies. As the Tory opposition is thrown into confusion by the loss of its figurehead, the king recovers his health. Frederick's own son, **Prince George**, created **prince of Wales**, becomes heir apparent.

An act to replace the Julian with the Gregorian calendar, already adopted by most of Europe, is passed in May to take effect the following September.

1752 With the introduction of the **Gregorian Calendar**, time in England jumps from September 2 to 14. A confused population takes to the streets, riotously clamoring for the government to "bring us back our eleven days."

1753 Parliament passes a **Jewish Naturalization Bill** (permitting Jews the right to full citizenship in England), greeted in the country at large with mounting hostility.

The last significant Jacobite plot ends with the execution of **Dr Archibald Cameron** in June.

The library of **Sir Hans Sloane** and the remains of the **Harley collection** (containing some 7660 manuscripts) are bought for the nation by the government and housed in what will become the **British Museum**.

EXCISE. A hateful tax levied upon commodities.

LEXICOGRAPHER. A writer of dictionaries, a harmless drudge.

NETWORK. Anything reticulated or dessucated at equal distances, with interstices between the intersections.

PATRON. Commonly a wretch who supports with insolence, and is paid with flattery.

—Some definitions in Samuel Johnson's
Dictionary of the English Language (1755)

1754 Following his death, **Henry Pelham** is succeeded as first lord of the treasury by his brother **Thomas Pelham-Holles**, the **duke of Newcastle**.

The government repeals the "**Jew Act**" of the previous year as parliamentary members fear its electoral consequences.

In **North America**, a critical situation develops after **Colonel George Washington** fails to capture **Fort Duquesne** from the French. A thousand British troops under **Edward Braddock** are dispatched to the colonies to bolster English interests.

1755 William Pitt (dismissed as paymaster later in the year) and **Prince Frederick**'s Leicester House grouping join forces in opposition to the **duke of Newcastle** and his government.

In **America**, Braddock's expeditionary force is annihilated by the French on the banks of the **Monongahela River** in July.

Lord Bute is appointed groom of the stole to **Augusta, Princess of Wales**, and **Henry Fox** becomes secretary of state for the Southern Department.

Dr Samuel Johnson sets new lexicographical standards with the publication of his *Dictionary of the English Language*, which uses citations from English authors to confirm the meanings of English words.

1756 As tensions between Europe's leading nations escalate—both as regards the balance of power in Europe itself and rivalry in the acquisition of overseas possessions and trading rights—Britain forms an alliance with **Prussia** by the **Convention of Westminster** on January 16. In May **France** and **Austria** conclude a similar treaty at **Versailles**. On May 18, its interests challenged in both America and India, Britain declares war on **France**, inaugurating the **Seven Years**

THE EAST INDIA COMPANY

Europe's first overseas empires, belonging to Spain and Portugal, developed through sponsorship provided by the monarchies and governments of those countries. The British Empire, however, followed a different course, in which private enterprise was the guiding force. The American colonies were initially settled by adventurers funded by **joint-stock companies**, although they were quickly converted into "Crown" colonies by the issue of royal charters. But in the eastern hemisphere the joint-stock principle held sway for almost two hundred years.

The East India Company was set up by royal charter in 1599, intended to create a monopoly among English traders plying the East Indies spice trade, but thereafter pursued a course very much its own. From around 1623 it focused on the Indian subcontinent, in time driving out all its European rivals. But the Company continued looking further afield, and periodically used brute force to open up the China market. By 1760, following Clive's victory at **Plassey**, the Company stood on the brink of assuming control over

War. But with previous spending cuts still in place, Britain is ill-prepared for hostilities, and experiences initial reverses.

In **India**, the **East India Company**'s trading settlement at **Calcutta** is overrun by **Siraj-ud-Daula**, the French-backed **nawab of Bengal**. There is a public outcry in Britain when it is learned that a number of Company officials have died following their incarceration in the guard room of **Fort Williams**—known as the **Black Hole of Calcutta**.

all of India, and was responsible for supplying England's growing thirst for Chinese tea.

Yet there were difficulties. China itself seemed uninterested in importing manufactured goods, and the cost of administering India threatened to get out of hand, even though these were supported by land revenues from the subcontinent. The solution to the first problem was to develop business between India and China, and from around 1770 Indian-grown opium—for which the Chinese did have an appetite—was traded for tea, silks and other goods. Then, when mills in England began processing American cotton, the Company began importing raw Indian cotton into Britain instead of finished fabrics. Both policies had catastrophic consequences: the Chinese became a nation of addicts, and India's garment-makers were dealt a body blow.

In 1784, in return for much-needed subsidies, an India Act brought the Company under governmental supervision, and by the mid-1830s it had lost its autonomy. The end eventually came after the Indian Uprising of 1857, when it was abolished for good.

In June, **Admiral John Byng** fails to prevent the seizure of **Minorca** by the French, and in August the French commander **Montcalm** captures a British fort at **Oswego** on Lake Ontario.

Newcastle and **Fox** resign in November, and are replaced by a ministry headed by **Pitt** and the **duke of Devonshire**.

Russia joins the Versailles alliance against Britain.

There are **food riots** in the **Midlands** and the **West Country** following a bad harvest.

1757 Pitt is ordered to resign from government on April 5, and in Europe Britain's army continues to fare badly under the command of **Cumberland**.

National fortunes revive sharply in **India**, when **Robert Clive** recaptures **Calcutta**, defeats **Siraj-ud-Daula** at **Plassey** on June 23 and overruns the French settlement at **Charndernagor**. As a consequence of these victories—secured in part by Clive blackmailing the nawab of Bengal's Indian allies—Clive becomes **governor of**

Out of the field of Plassey and the victors' 18 dead there spouted forth the power of the nineteenth century. Mammon now rode into supremacy to become the unchallenged god of the western world. Once in the lands of the rising sun western man had sought the Holy Sepulchre. That sun had long set, and now in those spiritually arid regions he found the almighty sovereign. What the Cross had failed to achieve, in a few blood-red-years the trinity of piston, sword and coin accomplished: the subjection of the East and for a span of nearly 200 years the economic serfdom of the Oriental world.

—J.F.C. Fuller,
The Decisive Battle of the Western World (1954–56)

Bengal, the French are effectively driven out of India and India itself is opened up to British control.

Admiral Byng is court-martialed and shot for his failures of the previous year—in the words of the French philosopher **Voltaire**, "pour encourager les autres."

In June, following the failure of a British amphibious assault on **Rochefort**, **Pitt** and the **earl of Holderness** rejoin the government, and **Newcastle** is reappointed first lord of the treasury at the end of the parliamentary session.

1758 Prince Ferdinand of Brunswick wins major victories for the Anglo-Prussian alliance over the French at **Krefeld** (June 23), pushing the French back westwards across the **Rhine**. The tide of war also turns against the Versailles alliance in North America, where British contingents under **James Wolfe** and **Jeffrey Amherst** capture a number of French forts, including **Frontenac** on August 27. Across the English Channel, British forces take **Cherbourg**, but are pushed back at **St Malo**.

Pitt breaks his ties with the **Leicester House group** and **Lord Bute**.

In line with a prediction made by the astronomer **Sir Edmund Halley** in 1705, a **comet** appears in the skies on Christmas Day.

1759 The "**Year of Victories**" begins with an English fleet repulsing a French attempt to seize **Madras** in southern India. In May the French surrender **Guadeloupe**, and on August 1 an Anglo-Prussian army led by **Frederick the Great** defeats a French army at **Minden**, although on August 12 Frederick himself is defeated by an Austro-Russian army at **Kunersdorf**. On September 13 **James Wolfe** comprehensively defeats the main French force under **Montcalm** on the **Plains of Abraham** outside **Quebec**, even though Wolfe himself is killed. British naval supremacy is assured by another victory in November, won by **Admiral Hawke**, over the **Brest** fleet in **Quiberon Bay**.

The first **Canal Act** is steered through Parliament by the **duke of Bridgewater**.

Josiah Wedgwood leases a pottery factory at Burslem.

The **British Museum** opens to the public.

1760 The French formally surrender their interest in **Canada** to the British at **Montreal** on September 8.

On October 9 a Russian army sacks **Berlin**.

On October 25 **George II** dies aged 77, and is succeeded by his 22-year-old grandson George III, who will reign for sixty years.

Laurence Sterne publishes the first volumes of his experimental novel, *The Life and Opinions of Tristram Shandy, Gentleman.*

The reign of George III
1760-1820

George III came to the throne claiming that he "gloried in the name of Briton." He saw himself as a "patriot king," embracing a creed espoused by his father **Prince Frederick** and drummed into him by his mother **Princess Augusta** and his tutor **John Mackenzie Stuart, Earl of Bute**. During his long reign, England underwent a radical transformation. It witnessed the humiliating loss of **America**, and found itself faced with a new ideological threat in the form of the **French Revolution**. Yet the bloodlettings across the Channel made the Tory party respectable again, while British prestige was restored with the final defeat of **Napoleon** at **Waterloo** in 1815.

Quite what George III hoped to achieve is hard to determine. His Whig opponents argued vociferously that he aimed to create a kind of continental-style absolutism, but the long tenure in office by both **Lord North** (1770–82) and **William Pitt the Younger** (1783–1801) demonstrate that, once satisfied with a ministry, George III wanted nothing better than to let it do its job. And even if he had intended to be an absolute monarch, his own mental instability rendered the ambition futile. In 1788, dejected at the loss of America, he suffered a mental breakdown caused by the hereditary disease **porphyria**; relapses followed until in 1810 he descended into permanent madness. When it became clear that he would not recover, Parliament transferred his authority to his son **George, Prince of Wales**, and thus the last ten years of George III's reign are known as the **Regency**.

In 1760, though, at his accession, hopes were high. George III seemed determined to do away with the oligarchical Whig groupings who dominated government and, like both William III and Anne before him, to attempt to create a non-party ministry. Crucially, too, George III wished to bring an end to the **Seven Years War**. A year after Britain's most significant wartime achievements, this policy attracted widespread criticism, and the king received still more by appointing his one-time tutor Bute prime minister. The appointment of a court favorite—and one, moreover, that bore the name of Stuart—gave rise to dire predictions of monarchical tyranny. Inexperienced and easily flustered, Bute was a poor choice and soon resigned, but not before the damage had been done.

Party in England was a diverse patchwork of factions and different interest groups and, although those calling themselves "Whig" mostly attempted to uphold the Revolution Settlement, they didn't by any means all operate in harmony. One result of George III's apparent meddling in the 1760s, though, was the growth of a clearer sense of party ideology, and among one of the more coherent groups—those attached to the leadership of the **marquess of Rockingham**—an "opposition manifesto" gradually developed. The outbreak of the **American War** gave greater impetus to the Rockinghams' concerns, and at their forefront was **Charles James Fox**, who became the King's especial *bête noire*. In 1783, Fox (in an unlikely alliance with George III's previous prime minister **Lord North**) forced the king to accept them as his government under the nominal leadership of the **duke of Portland**. Yet George was not finished, and at the close of the year engineered their defeat in

Parliament and the appointment of the 24-year-old **William Pitt the Younger** as the new premier.

Pitt's eighteen-year period of office puts the lie to the suggestion that George III wished to rule as a despot, though the king did make it plain that he would not support any extensive reform of the political system. Between 1783 and 1789 Pitt busied himself with balancing the books, but his hour came with the outbreak of the **French Revolution**. Although this cataclysm was at first greeted by the Foxites as a glorious re-enactment of 1688, the onset of the guillotine showed that they had been mistaken and that Pitt's cautious suspicion was the wiser reaction. As fear of revolution in England spread, Pitt turned from his reforms of the economy, and instead instituted a wide-reaching program of repressive legislation, restricting press freedom and the size of public gatherings. Pitt succeeded in keeping England safe from revolt at home, and free to pursue the continental war. He did not live to see the final triumph of **Waterloo**, but did return to power in time to reap the rewards of Nelson's victory at **Trafalgar** in 1805 before his own premature death the following year. And the Revolutionary War vindicated not only Pitt, but also served to restore the Tories' to respectability—from 1807 to 1832 Tory ministries dominated politics again, as the Whigs took their turn in the wilderness.

Yet despite the rejoicing Waterloo inspired, its aftermath proved a sour time for England. Unemployment, social unrest and economic stagnation affected much of society and calls for parliamentary reform became increasingly widespread. In the midst of the depression, the **Prince Regent**, addicted to the fine things in life and surrounded by an array of dandyish companions such as **George "Beau" Brummell**, attracted increasing criticism. The other royal dukes proved similarly disappointing, and as the mad, blind George III neared the end of his life, the future of the Hanoverian dynasty—and indeed of the monarchy itself—seemed in question.

1760 Influenced by his friend and ex-tutor the **earl of Bute**, the king endeavors to bring Britain's participation in the **Seven Years War** to an end. At the first meeting of his Privy Council, however, he is persuaded to modify his objections: a "bloody and expensive war" becomes a "just and necessary" one.

1761 The remains of the French army in India surrenders to the **East India Company** at **Pondicherry** in January.

Britain takes possession of the "neutral" West Indian island of **Dominica**.

Belle Isle off the coast of Brittany is captured in June.

Bute, still determined to bring about peace, replaces the earl of Holderness as secretary of state, and the **duke of Bedford** is appointed to negotiate peace terms with the French.

George III marries **Charlotte of Mecklenberg-Strelitz** on September 8, and is crowned king four days later.

On December 19 **Spain** declares war on Britain.

The **Bridgewater Canal**, built by **James Brindley**, is opened between **Worsley** and **Manchester**, initiating a network of canals that greatly improves trade and communications.

In an early manifestation of industrial unrest, 42 miners from **Northumberland** are killed by Yorkshire militiamen as they march toward **Hexham**, demonstrating against the **Militia Act** (in effect conscription).

1762 **Admiral George Rodney** and **General Robert Monckton** capture **Martinique** in the Caribbean. Later they occupy **St Lucia**, **St Vincent** and **Grenada**. Peace negotiations with **France** continue in secret as **Spain** invades Britain's ally **Portugal**.

The **duke of Newcastle** resigns as **first lord of the treasury**, a post now assumed by **Lord Bute**, who forms a ministry that includes members of the **Society of the Medenham Monks** (better known as the "Hellfire Club") as well as some from the Leicester House grouping.

On the continent, French armies are defeated at **Wilhemsthal** and **Luttenberg** in June and July. British forces seize **Havana** as Spain sustains setbacks in Portugal. **Bedford** travels to Paris to finalize peace terms which **Henry Fox** is appointed to present to the House of Commons. The preliminaries are signed at **Fontainebleau** on November 3, and approved by Bute's cabinet seven days later.

John Wilkes begins publishing the *North Briton*, a political newspaper set up to rival the pro-government *Briton* (edited by **Tobias Smollett** and backed by **William Hogarth**).

1763 As the "**King's Friends**" tighten their grip on power, the ousting of senior Whigs, masterminded by **Bute** and **Fox** and known as the "**Slaughter of the Pelhamite Innocents**," draws to a conclusion.

The **Seven Years War** is formally ended when the **Treaty of Paris** is signed on February 10. According to its terms, France cedes its **Canadian territories**, **Grenada** and **Senegal** to Britain, but retains **Guadeloupe**. Britain relinquishes **Cuba** in Spain's favor. The treaty is swiftly and strenuously attacked by **William Pitt the Elder**, who also campaigns against Bute's decision to tax **cider**. Bute suffers a nervous breakdown and, despite the king's annoyance, resigns as prime minister. **George Grenville** is appointed in his place, and attempts to deflect Pitt's attacks by mounting an attack on **John Wilkes**. Wilkes is arrested for seditious libel on the basis that he made defamatory remarks about Bute and George III in an edition of the *North Briton*. On the orders of **Chief Justice Charles Pratt**, Wilkes is released, then re-arrested after Parliament votes that parliamentary privilege does not extend to publishing seditious libel. But he is released again when Pratt declares the **General Warrant** against Wilkes to be unconstitutional. He fights a duel with **Samuel Martin MP**, one of Bute's supporters, then flees to France.

1764 Wilkes is formally expelled from the **House of Commons** for his presumed authorship of the pornographic "**Essay on Woman**."

Grenville puts forward plans to impose a **stamp duty** on such items as newspapers, pamphlets, legal documents and playing cards in the American colonies, but the scheme is delayed a year to give the colonists time to submit alternative proposals.

James Hargreaves invents the **spinning jenny**, the first step toward a fully mechanized loom, and the **Bolting Machine** is devised by John and Thomas Morris.

The painter and engraver **William Hogarth**, whose work depicted the foibles and vices of his age, dies.

1765 **George III**'s endeavors to control government collapse with his first descent into madness. A **Regency Bill**, designed to provide security for the throne, is heavily opposed in both houses of Parliament.

In July, the **Grenville administration** falls, and is replaced by a cabinet headed by the **dukes of Cumberland** and **Newcastle** and the **marquess of Rockingham**.

The Stamp Act is passed on March 22, but stamp duty is restricted in all thirteen of Britain's American colonies, led by **Virginia**; there are riots in **Boston** and assaults on officials trying to collect the tax. A "Stamp Act" Congress convenes in **New York** in October and votes a boycott of all British goods.

The death of **Cumberland** on October 31 means that Rockingham becomes *de facto* prime minister.

1766 Following the death of **James Edward Stuart**, known as the **"Old Pretender,"** the pope and other Catholic kings decline to recognize **Charles Edward Stuart** as **Charles III** of England.

Rockingham's government, supported by **Pitt**, endeavors to calm the situation in **America** by repealing the **Stamp Act**, but then makes the mistake of passing the **Declaratory Act**, which asserts Britain's right to impose direct taxes in the colonies. The **cider tax** is also repealed and **General Warrants** (by which people could be arrested without specific charges) are declared illegal.

WILKES, "HELLFIRE" AND LIBERTY

*I*n the middle years of the 18th century a group of politicians led by Sir Francis Dashwood formed a secret fraternity known as the Brothers of St Francis of Medmenham, taking their name from a ruined abbey at Medmenham in Berkshire where many of their meetings were held. Guided by their motto *Fay ce que vouldras* ("do as you will"), the brothers indulged in a variety of bizarre rituals, feasts and orgies, in the process shocking many in society. Among them were Thomas Potter MP, the rakish son of the archbishop of Canterbury, the earl of Sandwich and George Bubb Doddington. Hogarth too may have been a member, and possibly Frederick, Prince of Wales.

But the most notorious was John Wilkes, a strikingly ugly man and a brilliant conversationalist. For Wilkes, "Hellfire," as the club came to be known, was a means to political office, which he needed to pay off his gambling debts. When Bute became George III's principal minister in 1762 the Brothers naturally benefited through their links with him, but Wilkes was left out in the cold. He responded by savagely attacking Bute's policies—and by implication George III—in the *North Briton*. Bute quickly resigned, but his successor, Lord Grenville, retaliated on Bute's behalf by having Wilkes arrested.

But this put Wilkes in his element, and he began inciting popular unrest in the name of "liberty." After being released on the orders of the lord chief justice he fled to France, returning to London in 1768 to battle his way into Parliament. Denied his place at Westminster, Wilkes became first an alderman of London, then its mayor—positions he skillfully exploited to embarrass the establishment still further. But it was the petitioning movement launched to support him, in the name of "Wilkes and Liberty," that became his lasting legacy and which formed a direct antecedent of the dissident Chartist petitions of the 1830s and 1840s.

The **duke of Grafton** resigns from the government, triggering four months of ministerial instability. The Rockingham–Newcastle faction disintegrates, and Rockingham himself resigns in July. **William Pitt**, now the **earl of Chatham**, becomes prime minister.

Henry Cavendish discovers hydrogen.

1767 In January **Charles Townshend** announces the government's intention to impose indirect taxation on the American colonies in the form of **import duties** on tea, paper and other goods. **Grenville**, the **Rockinghamites** and followers of the **duke of Bedford** unite in opposition. Notwithstanding, Townshend's **Revenue Act** is passed on June 29, shortly before Parliament breaks for the summer. The legislation is greeted in **Boston**, **Philadelphia** and other American cities by renewed calls for a boycott of British goods. Bedford's followers are persuaded to join the government, thus isolating the "Rockingham Whigs."

As harvests fail and grain prices soar, there are further **food riots** in the **Midlands** and the **West Country**.

Joseph Priestley publishes *The History and Present State of Electricity*, an early attempt to explain **electromagnetic conductivity**.

1768 John Wilkes returns from France to stand for the **City of London** in parliamentary elections. Although he comes last in the poll, his name is also put forward for **Middlesex**, which he wins. Having regained membership of the Commons, he presents himself to answer the charges of blasphemy and pornography still outstanding. His outlawry (by which he is considered automatically a criminal and "outside of the law") is overturned but he is remanded in custody pending trial, causing celebrations among his supporters— which soon turn into rioting in London amid the familiar cry of "Wilkes and Liberty." The government brings in soldiers to disperse the rioters, but their heavy-handed treatment results in the **"St George's Fields Massacre"** of May 10 which leaves seven dead and fifteen injured. The scale of the violence shocks the

Wilkeites into quiescence, during which time Wilkes is convicted, fined £1000 and imprisoned for 22 months.

There is also rioting in **Boston**, after customs officials seize John Hancock's sloop *Liberty* on June 10. Throughout the American colonies resistance to Townshend's duties stiffens.

In October **Chatham** resigns after the sacking of the **earl of Shelburne** from his government. He is replaced as prime minster by the **duke of Grafton**.

A Royal Navy lieutenant, **James Cook**, embarks on a series of great voyages in the southern Pacific aboard *HMS Endeavour* that open the way to British colonization of **Australia**, **New Zealand** and other islands in the eastern hemisphere.

1769 Released from prison, **Wilkes** attempts to take his seat in the Commons, but is thrown out. When voters in Middlesex re-elect him three times, the House finally declares his election illegal and confer his seat on his defeated opponent, **Henry Lawes Luttrell**. The Rockingham Whigs come out in Wilkes's support, and organize an unsuccessful **national petition** calling for his reinstatement.

As the **American colonies** teeter on the brink of rebellion, the government repeals all the Townshend duties, with the exception of the **import tax** on **tea**. The few Chathamites who remain in government resign their posts. Grafton's ministry is further damaged by the publication of scathingly critical letters published in the *Public Advertiser* and signed "Junius." They warn that Grafton is playing a "foolish game" by taking on Wilkes, and one letter ominously ends: "He rose by Mr Wilkes's popularity, and it is not improbable that he may fall by it."

1770 Bowing to public pressure, **Grafton** resigns in January, and **Lord North** becomes prime minister. North, however, is unable to persuade Parliament to rescind the **import tax** on tea in America, and on March 1, during an incident known as the **Boston Massacre**, three colonials are shot by British troops during renewed rioting.

The Irish-born writer and parliamentarian **Edmund Burke**, sometimes perceived as the greatest advocate of English liberties, publishes *Thoughts on the Present Discontents*, arguing for economic reform and warning of the dangers inherent in arbitrary monarchical government.

Priestley discovers **sulphur dioxide**.

1771 Press freedom in Britain becomes an important political issue when a number of **London printers** are summoned to the House of Commons accused of publishing details of parliamentary debates. The **lord mayor** and **city aldermen**, among them **Wilkes**, protect the printers by arresting the Commons' messenger. In riposte, the Commons arrests the **mayor**. The situation is defused by North's disinclination to insist on the secrecy of debates, and from 1774 onwards approved transcripts will be published by **Luke Hansard**. Wilkes becomes **high sheriff** of London.

Tobias Smollett publishes *The Expedition of Humphry Clinker*, a novel that satirizes the decrepitude of English society, and dies later in the year.

1772 Against the wishes of Rockinghamites and Chathamites alike, Parliament passes an act making all future **royal marriages** subject to the monarch's approval.

In India, **Warren Hastings** begins a thirteen-year stint as the **governor of Bengal** that will see the East India Company's hold on the subcontinent greatly consolidated.

Continuing poor harvests provoke **food riots** in all parts of England.

Daniel Rutherford isolates **nitrogen**.

1773 North's ministry pushes through legislation that grants the **East India Company** a monopoly on tea sales to the American colonies, but which also increases government control over the Company itself. On December 16, in an event which becomes known as the **Boston "Tea Party,"** dissident colonials disguised as

"Mohawks" board the Company's ships and throw 342 chests of tea into the harbor.

1774 Charles James Fox, dismissed at the king's bidding from a post at the Treasury, joins the **Rockingham Whigs**. The crisis in America mounts as the **First Continental Congress** is convened in **Philadelphia** in September to consider ways of resisting British interference. North's government raises the stakes by closing **Boston Harbor** until the East India Company is compensated for its losses. The **Quebec Act**, extending religious toleration to Canadian Catholics, expands the frontiers of Quebec as far south as the **Mississippi** at the expense of **Massachusetts**, whose charter is revoked.

As a domestic crisis develops in **France**, English-speaking radicals on both sides of the Atlantic—including some Whigs—are vociferous in their condemnations of royal absolutism. Notwithstanding, the British government secures a substantial parliamentary majority following a general election.

You will doubtless soon after your return to England be a Member of one of the two Houses of Parliament; there you must take pains to distinguish yourself as a speaker. The task is not very hard if you have common sense, as I think you have, and a great deal more... The late Lord Bolingbroke had accustomed himself so much to a florid eloquence even in his common conversation (which anybody with care may do) that his real extempore speeches seemed to be studied. Lord Mansfield was, in my opinion, the next to him in undeviating eloquence, but Mr Pitt carried with him, unpremeditated, the strength of thunder, and the splendour of lightning...

—The earl of Chesterfield,
writing to his godson c.1773

Priestley isolates **oxygen** and discovers **ammonia**.

1775 In the House of Lords **Chatham** proposes resolving the American crisis by returning to the original status quo, but his motion is defeated by 68 votes to 18. In response, North's ministry declares **Massachusetts** to be in a state of rebellion. An attempted reconciliation put forward by **Edmund Burke** is also rejected. The government orders **General Thomas Gage** to arrest **John Hancock** and his fellow patriot **Samuel Adams** in America, but as news of this leaks, armed colonials intercept his force of seven hundred British "red coats" at **Lexington** and **Concord** on April 19—two minor skirmishes that mark the beginning of the **American War of Independence**. But in the opening months of hostilities, neither side is able to secure a clear advantage.

1776 **Chatham** and **Rockingham** combine forces to reverse North's American policy, but are unable to defeat the government. As a result the Rockinghamites withdraw from Parliament.

John Wilkes attempts to introduce a parliamentary reform bill, but is unable to find anyone in the Commons to support it.

On July 4 the **Continental Congress of Philadelphia** adopts on behalf of the American colonies a **Declaration of Independence**, inspired by the English Quaker and radical **Thomas Paine**'s pamphlet *Common Sense* and drafted by **Thomas Jefferson**. **William, Viscount Howe** captures **New York** for the Crown, but the Americans gain victories at **Trenton** and (in January 1777) at **Princeton**, enabling them to take control of **New Jersey**.

Edward Gibbon publishes the first two volumes of his epic history, *The Decline and Fall of the Roman Empire*.

1777 The **Rockinghamites** return to Parliament to oppose—unsuccessfully—a bill to pay off **George III**'s debts. **Grafton**, supported by **Chatham**, also fails to persuade the Lords to adopt an address calling for an immediate cessation of hostilities in America. As the **Chathamite–Rockinghamite** alliance grows, **Howe** defeats the

American general **George Washington** at the **Brandywine** and captures **Philadelphia**. General **John Burgoyne**'s army, however, is surrounded by the Americans at **Bemis Heights** and forced to surrender at **Saratoga** in October.

1778 As **France** enters the war on the Americans' side, Fox proposes to the Commons that no more troops be sent to the colonies, but is defeated by 259 votes to 165. Attacking the government's war policies in the House of Lords on May 11, **Chatham** collapses and dies. While leadership of the Chathamites is assumed by the

EDWARD GIBBON (1737–94)

*I*f Britain's outstanding contributions to the 18th-century European Enlightenment were made by two Scotsmen—the philosopher **David Hume** and the economist **Adam Smith**—the Englishman Edward Gibbon provided a literary monument that is as readable and challenging today as it was when it was written.

The History of the Decline and Fall of the Roman Empire, published in six volumes between 1776 and 1788, spans the thirteen centuries up to the fall of Constantinople in 1453. It is not simply the story of the dying Roman court, but deals more widely with Islam and offers sympathetic portraits of the Slavs and Mongols. It also provides fascinating intellectual history, Gibbon taking mischievous delight in drawing out the squabbles of the early Christian sects—which earned him the loathing of several contemporary churchmen. Yet if Gibbon's conception of the past is sweepingly vast, his brushstrokes are detailed and intimate. Human foibles and corruption are lovingly depicted, and famously *Decline and Fall* is accompanied by eight thousand footnotes. The book is all the more remarkable for having been

earl of Shelburne, Rockingham names his terms for joining the government, but is rejected by George III. The **earl of Carlisle** is dispatched to **America** to explore peace terms with the rebels, but returns empty-handed. As the war in America continues to seesaw, the French and English fight an inconclusive naval battle off **Ushant**.

1779 Admiral Augustus Keppel, a supporter of Rockingham, is unsuccessfully court-martialed for his "failure" at **Ushant**. On the day of his vindication **Fox** and other supporters travel to **Portsmouth** to

composed entirely while standing up: Gibbon constructed a writing lectern at one end of his London study with his library at the other end, and the tracks he made when pacing between them are still visible today.

The young Gibbon spent fourteen months at Oxford, but he was later to describe them as "the most idle and unprofitable of my whole life." He converted to Catholicism and left, whereupon his father sent him to Lausanne for corrective instruction. Much of the rest of his life was spent in Switzerland, although for a few years until the fall of North's ministry in 1782 he was MP for **Liskeard**. Gibbon also served as an officer in the Hampshire militia, at least according to his posthumously published *Memoirs* (1796). And although *Decline and Fall* guaranteed Gibbon personal celebrity, it was not received favorably by everyone. In words which are variously ascribed to the duke of Gloucester, the duke of Cumberland and even George III, the author was castigated for his labor: "Another damned, thick, square book! Always scribble, scribble, scribble! Eh! Mr Gibbon?"

encourage widespread rioting in celebration. Returning to London, Fox makes political capital by renewing his parliamentary attacks on the government's handling of the war.

Spain joins in on the American and French side, laying siege to **Gibraltar**. The **duke of Bedford**'s faction deserts the government in an attempt to force **North** to resign.

As the **national debt** grows, Burke introduces an **Economical Reform Bill**. His plan is to reduce the Crown's influence over Parliament by abolishing a number of sinecures that are a central part of government patronage, but he makes little progress as North's ministry succeeds in destroying it at the committee stage.

Samuel Crompton invents the "**spinning mule**," improving on Hargreaves's "spinning jenny," which enables the mass production of muslin cloth.

England's first **Iron Bridge**, a showcase construction that spans the Severn River at **Coalbrookdale**, is built by **Abraham Darby**. The area will become an epicenter for industry and a great iron manufacturing area.

Richard Brinsley Sheridan's tragedy *The Critic* receives its first performance in London's **Drury Lane**.

James Cook, now a captain, is killed while in **Hawaii**.

1780 As the Crown's forces fail to bring the rebels in **America** to heel, North's government finds itself under attack from all sides. The Rockingham Whigs too press for **Burke**'s economic reform program, while the **Yorkshire Association**, formed by **Christopher Wyvill**, urges **parliamentary reform**. The government defeats the Rockinghamites over the economy, but in turn is defeated over a motion bemoaning the apparently increased influence of the king. North attempts to resign, but George III refuses him permission.

On July 2 a mob of 50,000 rampages through **London** in protest at an **Act of Catholic Relief**, passed in 1778 to restrict some of the injustices suffered by English Catholics. The so-called **Gordon Riots**, named after their leader **Lord George Gordon**, founder of the hardline **Protestant Association**, cause widespread dismay. Even radicals like **Wilkes** take to the streets against the protesters. After six days the rioters are dispersed and order is restored, but Lord George Gordon is acquitted of treason.

James Watt constructs a steam-powered flour mill.

1781 As the war in **America** turns against the Crown and North's government, a peace motion in the Commons fails by only 34 votes. On October 19 **General Charles Cornwallis** is forced to surrender at **Yorktown** when **Admiral Thomas Graves** fails to relieve his besieged army.

1782 North's ministry survives a further Commons motion to end the American war by a single vote, and two motions of no confidence by margins of nine and ten votes. But the prime minister again tenders his resignation, which George III now accepts. A new administration is formed under **Charles Watson-Wentworth, 2nd Marquess of Rockingham**. George III insists on the inclusion of the Chathamite **Lord Shelburne**. When Rockingham dies in July, the King appoints Shelburne prime minister, prompting Fox and the **duke of Portland** to resign in protest.

Although **Admiral Rodney** reasserts British dominance in the Caribbean by defeating a **French** navy at the **Battle of the Saints** in July, **Spanish** forces recapture **Florida**, and also the island of **Minorca** in the Mediterranean.

British forces abandon **Savannah** in the same month, and in December the surrender of **Charleston** marks the effective end of the British campaign in America.

1783 The **American War of Independence** ends in comprehensive victory for the colonials, sealed by a multinational **Treaty of Versailles** signed on September 3, but not before further political turmoil in England. Earlier in the year, as preliminary talks are held

THE LOSS OF AMERICA

*D*espite its reputation, the American Revolution was a blown-up civil war rather than a grand anti-imperialist colonial uprising. And it was one that more or less excluded the original inhabitants of the American mainland: the native Americans had been conquered and displaced by the English, but they played little part in the unfolding drama, which was essentially a dispute between Britons on one side of the Atlantic and those on the other.

In England itself, political society was sharply divided over what should be done. The perceived despotism of George III—and the secretive Tory government that surrounded him—persuaded many in opposition that the colonists' grievances were entirely just. As the war developed, domestic opinion split three ways. First came the government line. Led by Lord North, and heavily influenced by King George, the government took the view that America was simply in a state of rebellion, and should be dealt with accordingly: the only solution was the reimposition of direct rule. A middle view, espoused by William Pitt the Elder, Lord Chatham, advocated that the Americans should be granted representation in the British Parliament, but that the colonies themselves should remain Crown territories. But a radical stance was taken by the Rockingham Whigs, who came to support the idea of full American independence. Various leading lights of this party (including Charles James Fox) took to wearing blue and bluff, the colors of George Washington's army, and openly taunted the government about its handling of the crisis.

In the event, the issue was decided militarily, not in the House of Commons. George III himself never quite recovered from the loss of a land he cherished but had never visited. It's not altogether fair that he has become known as "King Who Lost America," yet the fact remains that it was a government whose ministers he appointed that increased transatlantic tensions to the point where a fissure was inevitable.

with **France** and **Spain**, **Charles James Fox** and **Lord North** form an opportunistic alliance against prime minister **Shelburne** that stuns their friends, foes and society alike. Yet the alliance holds together, Shelburne is forced to resign, and a "**Fox–North**" ministry under the nominal leadership of the **duke of Portland** takes office in April. **George III**, determined to remove a government imposed upon him through Parliament, at once seeks to undermine it. The ministry comes under immediate fire from the king and his supporters when it attempts to secure funds to pay off the debts of the king's heir, **George, Prince of Wales**. Fox, a close associate of the Prince, is held responsible for his predicament.

In November the government introduces a bill to further regulate and provide subsidies for the **East India Company**, now in serious debt as a result of its administrative costs in India. The bill aims to establish a Commission to oversee the Company, but fears that it will be filled with Fox's own appointees lead to concerns that the bill will concentrate too much power in his hands, and so it is roundly defeated. George demands Fox's, North's and Portland's resignations. In their place he appoints as prime minister the precocious but untried 24-year-old son of Chatham, **William Pitt the Younger**.

1784 The Rockingham Whigs, now called **Foxites**, are annihilated in a **general election**. Fox himself comes under pressure in his Westminster seat, where the returns are submitted for scrutiny by a parliamentary committee. The **duchess of Devonshire** and other society ladies campaigning for Fox are lampooned in the press for attempting to woo the Westminster electorate by offering kisses for votes.

Pitt the Younger's substantial parliamentary majority enables him to introduce a series of **economic reforms** not dissimilar to those earlier proposed by Edmund Burke. In August, he introduces an **India Act** that adopts many of the measures proposed by Fox and North the previous year: in return for government subsidies to repay its debts, the **East India Company** is made answerable to a government-appointed **Board of Control**, effectively making India a British colony in all but name.

1785 Pitt introduces a bill proposing to **reform Parliament**, but its defeat permanently dissuades him from any further work in that direction, leading some to question his commitment to political innovation.

The Times newspaper is founded.

1786 Pitt continues his economic reforms by introducing the **Sinking Fund**; revenue placed in the Fund is earmarked to pay off the **national debt**.

A **commercial treaty** with **France** creates the most open trading relationship between the two countries in more than fifty years as tariffs are lowered on both sides of the Channel; but while French wine becomes cheaper in England, the export of inexpensive British manufactured goods quickly leads to protests in Paris.

1787 The **Foxites** attempt to damage Pitt's ministry by impeaching **Warren Hastings** for corruption and embezzlement during his time as **governor of Bengal**. But the (finally unsuccessful) eight-year hearings merely distract opposition energies, allowing Pitt to concentrate on his own agenda.

George, Prince of Wales begins building the **Brighton Pavilion**, an oriental pleasure dome that will become a centre for political dissent and dissolute elements in high society.

The **East India Company** establish a trading post on the island of **Penang**, the beginning of Britain's colonization of **Malaya**.

1788 Britain's diplomatic isolation in the wake of the American War of Independence is ended when the government concludes an alliance with the **Dutch** in April, joined by **Prussia** in August.

George III slides into a second episode of insanity.

1789 By the time the opposition is able to introduce a **Bill of Regency** into the Commons, the king exhibits signs of recovery.

From the spring onwards, England and the rest of Europe are increasingly preoccupied with the events unfolding in **France**. The storming of the **Bastille** on July 14 heralds the beginnings of the **French Revolution**, which will eventually lead to the overthrow of the monarchy. In London, responses are sharply divided. **Charles James Fox** salutes the revolution as a re-enactment by French Whigs of the "**Glorious Revolution**" of 1689. **Edmund Burke** divides from his Foxite companions, and in his *Reflections on the Revolution in France* (1790), paints a disturbing picture of events across the Channel—which he fears will soon replicate themselves in England.

In the south Pacific, the crew of *HMS Bounty* mutinies against the harsh regimen of its captain, **William Bligh**.

1790 **Charles James Fox** weeps in the House of Commons as it becomes apparent that his differences with his old ally **Burke** concerning the French Revolution are irreconcilable.

A **general election** in October–November confirms Pitt's political dominance, returning him with an overwhelming majority over the Foxites and other parties.

The Spanish agree to pay **compensation** to Britain following a series of attacks on British fishing boats at **Nootka Sound**, off the northwest coast of Canada.

1791 Although **Pitt** suffers a foreign policy reverse when **Russia** seizes the Turkish port of **Ochakov**, he successfully prevents England's immediate entanglement in the hostilities that threaten Europe in the wake of the French Revolution.

Responding to Burke's *Reflections*, **Thomas Paine** publishes the first part of his *The Rights of Man*, destined after its completion in 1792 to become a mainstay of Western radical liberalism.

The **Canada Act** creates a partition between English-speaking **Upper Canada** and mainly French-speaking **Lower Canada**, each awarded a representative assembly.

James Boswell publishes *The Life of Samuel Johnson*, an unprecedentedly intimate literary biography that establishes Johnson's reputation as his generation's leading man of letters.

The Observer newspaper is founded.

1792 Pressure for radical political reform in England grows with the founding of the **London Corresponding Society** and the **Whig Friends of the People**.

Mary Wollstonecraft, cattily (and unfairly) described by Horace Walpole as a "hyena in petticoats," publishes *A Vindication of the Rights of Women*, widely regarded as the first attempt in English to establish

CHARLES JAMES FOX (1749–1806)

*T*he darling of the Rockingham Whigs, and for many the finest prime minister England never had, Charles James Fox was an unmistakable and glamorous figure in Georgian society. An eager follower of every passing fashion, in the 1770s he was among the most prominent of the "Macaronis," so called because of their Italianate style, perched on high heels and sporting a tall blue-powdered periwig. In the 1780s he adopted a fashionable undress, abandoning wig and closely tailored outfits for blue and buff (the colors of the American rebels) and a healthy growth of stubble. And Fox was certainly well-connected: in appearance he was remarkably like his great-grandfather Charles II—his mother was a daughter of the duke of Richmond.

In politics he was an inveterate foe of George III, coming to see in the king all the woes that befell his own party, particularly the period in the 1760s when Whig ministries were destabilized in George III's quest for his "non-feminist principles and an immensely influential work.

Disillusionment with the French Revolution sets in toward the end of the year as the full horror of the **September Massacres** becomes known.

1793 The executions of **Louis XVI** and **Marie Antoinette** add to the English establishment's nervousness over the course of events in France. In February Britain enters the European war against the revolutionaries, but some English radicals persist in defending the Revolution's values, among them **William Godwin**, author of *Enquiry Concerning Human Justice* (and husband of Mary Wollstonecraft).

party" patriot government. And it was to combat what he regarded as autocracy that he sided with the Americans in the **War of Independence**, using his formidable powers of oratory on their behalf. He rallied to the cause of the **French Revolution**, at least in its initial phases, for similar reasons, but was devastated by the terrors into which France was plunged and was disappointed to find so little to admire in Napoleon Bonaparte.

But Fox's career, so much a part of the Whig cult, is a story of unfulfilled potential. Despite becoming foreign secretary twice, he was never prime minister. Partly this was down to personal weakness: although he could be brilliant at times, he was also cripplingly lazy and was frequently absent from Parliament. His gambling was legendary, and to the end he was unable to manage his own finances. He also caused widespread consternation by following an epic series of love affairs by settling down with his mistress **Elizabeth Armistead**. But when he died at the age of 57, he was widely mourned.

A trade and diplomatic mission to **China**, led by **Lord Macartney**, funded by the **East India Company** and directly supported by **George III**, is snubbed by the **Emperor Qianlong**. As a result the East India Company increases its supplies of opium to the Chinese market, and increasingly contemplates the use of force to overcome Chinese isolationism.

1794 Amid growing fears of a threat to national security, Pitt lays aside his own inclinations toward reform and suspends **Habeas Corpus**. In his defense of the English constitution, Pitt is supported by a majority of Whigs, leaving Fox and his reduced following politically isolated.

On June 1, **Admiral Richard Howe** defeats a French fleet outside **Ushant**.

A diplomatic breakthrough is achieved when differences with England's former American colonies, now called the **United States of America**, are resolved by the **Jay Treaty** on November 19.

1795 Though bankrupted by his legal costs, **Warren Hastings** is finally acquitted of wrongdoing by the House of Lords.

Pitt strengthens his increasingly authoritarian regime by securing a **Treasonable Practices and Seditious Meetings Act**, banning unlicensed public gatherings and fringe political parties.

Cape Colony (South Africa) and the Malayan port of **Melaka** (Malacca), both seized from the Dutch, are added to England's rapidly expanding portmanteau of overseas possessions.

Food shortages and high prices, induced by failing harvests and wartime expenditure, provoke widespread disturbance.

A new system of part-means-tested **poor relief** is introduced by magistrates in the Berkshire town of **Speenhamland**.

1796 Bourbon **Spain** joins **France** in the war against Britain after peace negotiations between London and Paris fail. **Ceylon** (Sri Lanka) is seized from the Dutch and becomes a British colony.

Edward Jenner invents and disseminates a vaccine against **smallpox**.

WILLIAM PITT THE YOUNGER (1759–1806)

*T*he younger son of the "Great Commoner," Pitt the Elder, William Pitt the Younger is often described as a Tory prime minister. But he always described himself as an Independent Whig, and it was as such, at the head of a small association of MPs, that he was chosen by George III to form a government after the fall of the Fox–North administration in 1782. Mockingly described by the Foxites as a "mince-pie administration" it was not expected to last beyond Christmas, but in fact survived eighteen years.

Pitt had entered the Commons as an avowed supporter of reform, but it was only in the financial sphere that he was able to muster sufficient support to make real changes. His plans for electoral reform—based on a widening of the franchise by abolishing rotten boroughs and redistributing seats to more populous areas—were shelved within two years of taking office, and Pitt dedicated his first decade in power to balancing the books. Like others, he initially welcomed the French Revolution, not least because he thought it would weaken France to England's benefit. But the Terror—and with it a French declaration of war—forced his hand, and the remainder of the 1790s found him grappling with the prohibitive costs of a conflict that undermined many of his earlier fiscal achievements. He believed deeply that the Irish should be given a better deal if their loyalty was to be assured, and it was over his plans for Catholic Emancipation that he clashed with George III—and then resigned in 1801.

Recalled as prime minister in 1804, he presided over England's great victory at Trafalgar in 1805. Worn out though by years of unrelenting hard work (not to mention unrelenting hard drinking), he died the following January, to be remembered, in George Canning's phrase of 1802, as "the Pilot that weathered the Storm."

1797 The war against **France**, until now broadly confined to naval operations, is placed under severe strain by naval mutinies at **Spithead** (May) and the **Nore** (June), eventually suppressed by force.

A small French force lands at **Fishguard** in **Wales**, but fails to establish a beachhead for an invasion of Britain.

Economic crisis induces the **Bank of Englan**d to suspend cash payments temporarily.

1798 To the dismay of **William Cobbet**t and other extra-parliamentary radicals, Pitt's government imposes a **stamp duty** on British newspapers.

As **Napoleon Bonaparte** campaigns in **Egypt**, a British fleet under the command of **Horatio Nelson** daringly destroys the French fleet anchored at **Aboukir** on August 1—an engagement known as the **Battle of the Nile**.

The poets **William Wordsworth** and **Samuel Taylor Coleridge** publish their joint anthology *Lyrical Ballads*, widely regarded as a watershed in the emergence of English Romanticism.

Thomas Malthus publishes *An Essay on the Principle of Population*, which will influence **Charles Darwin**'s theory of natural selection.

1799 Pitt's government introduces **Income Tax**, an entirely new revenue with variable rates affecting higher and lower earners. Intended as a stopgap to defray Britain's mounting war expenditure, Income Tax will eventually become the bedrock of the Treasury's fiscal policies.

While a number of radical organizations, among them the **London Corresponding Society**, are outlawed, the **Missionary Society** is founded with the specific purpose of spreading the gospel among Britain's "heathen" colonies.

1800 The **Combination Act** proscribes trade unions.

The social idealist **Robert Owen** founds a "model" factory at **New Lanark**, greatly improving the working and living conditions of his workforce.

Richard Trevithick designs a new **high-pressure steam engine**, used to power the first mechanical road vehicle.

Sir William Herschel discovers **infrared rays**, and the **Royal College of Surgeons** is founded.

1801 On January 1 the **United Kingdom** comes into being as a further **Act of Union** fully incorporates **Ireland** (subject to recent attempted French interference in its affairs). As Parliament is expanded to include Irish members, Ireland's own parliament is dissolved.

In March **William Pitt** dramatically resigns as prime minister after failing to win the king's support for Catholic Emancipation, and is replaced by **Henry Addington**.

Nelson's fleet defeats the French at the Battle of the Nile, 1798

On April 2 a Danish fleet is defeated at the **Battle of Copenhagen**, but only after **Vice Admiral Nelson** turns his blind eye on an order to retreat issued by **Admiral Sir Hyde Parker**. Faced with possibility of a court martial, Nelson is instead created a viscount and replaces Parker as **admiral of the fleet**.

The first **national census** confirms that **London**, with a population of just over a million, is Europe's largest city.

Legislation known as the **Horne Tooke Act** disqualifies Anglican clergymen from sitting in the House of Commons.

The **London Stock Exchange** is founded.

THE INDUSTRIAL REVOLUTION

*B*ritain in the latter stages of the 18th century experienced an unprecedentedly rapid acceleration in the development of technology that eventually transformed the face of the land. The country could boast, particularly in areas such as **south Wales** and Derbyshire, essential resources like coal, iron and water, and it had an established tradition of capital investment. But there was also a revolution in transport. A new network of roads run by "turnpike" trusts was followed by canals, and finally—in the 19th century—a sophisticated rail system, meaning that raw materials, finished goods and labor could be moved with increasing ease. At the same time a stream of new inventions came on line—not least steam power itself, enabling the mass production of textiles and other consumables.

In England alone the population shot from 7.1 to 13.1 million between 1780 and 1831, and many gravitated towards the newly productive towns and cities, which offered an alternative to agricultural labor or a life in

1802 In March the **Treaty of Amiens** buys Europe's warring nations temporary respite from the **Wars of the French Revolution**. Britain is ceded **Trinidad** by Spain.

Fox leads a delegation of Whigs to Paris to meet **Napoleon** himself, but is unimpressed both by the man and by conditions in France.

1803 The **Amiens** peace collapses and war with **France** resumes in May.

The Manchester scientist **John Dalton** devises a table of **atomic weights** and so founds the modern discipline of physical chemistry.

service. Urban conglomerates such as **Liverpool** and **Manchester** mushroomed, bringing with them a renewed sense of civic pride—embodied in impressive city halls, monuments and bridges—but also unprecedented problems of overcrowding and disease. And working conditions inside the factories were frequently brutal: hours were long and wages were low. This too brought positive change, though. If the industrial townships provided a natural opportunity for the positive social involvement of the Methodists and for charities dedicated to ministering the needy, the organization of trade unions contributed to the pressure for electoral reform and the institution of a fuller democracy.

Yet even so, until well into the 19th century the majority of English people still worked the land or served in the houses of the affluent. The Industrial Revolution altered England forever, but its progress was more gradual than some of its startling images suggest.

1804 **Addington**'s ministry collapses in May and **Pitt** returns as prime minister. In the same month **Napoleon** is proclaimed **emperor** in France.

An improved **steam engine** designed by **Trevithick** comes on line at the **Penydarran** ironworks in south Wales.

Around this time the artist, poet and engraver **William Blake** starts to compose a work later published as *Milton: A Poem in Two Books, To Justify the Ways of God to Men*, an epic visionary poem. Its preface ends with what will become some of the most famous lines in English poetry: "And did those feet in ancient time / Walk upon England's mountains green?," and attacks the rapidly developing industries by describing their "dark Satanic mills."

1805 The French admiral **Pierre Villeneuve** takes a fleet intended to ferry an army of invasion assembled by **Napoleon** at **Boulogne** to **Cadiz**, where he is blockaded by Admiral Lord Nelson. Attempting to break the blockade, his own and Spanish men-of-war are crushed at **Trafalgar** on October 21, a sea battle that confirms Britain's overwhelming naval supremacy. But Nelson is shot on board his flagship *HMS Victory* and dies in the heat of the action, whispering what might be either "kismet" (fate) or "kiss me" to his comrade **Captain Thomas Hardy**.

1806 **Pitt** dies in January, and is succeeded by a mainly Whig coalition "Ministry of all the Talents" led by **Lord Grenville**. **Charles James Fox** is made foreign secretary, ending 25 years out of office, but dies in September.

1807 The "**Talents**" ministry falls in March, and is replaced by a mainly Tory government led by the **duke of Portland**.

George III continues to resist **Catholic Emancipation**.

During a year in which relations with the **USA** deteriorate, Britain is threatened with isolation when **Napoleon** concludes the **Treaty of Tilsit** with **Russia** following a series of brilliant land victories. But **Portugal** refuses to join Napoleon's "**Continental System**."

1808 **Sir Arthur Wellesley**, having demonstrated his military acumen in **India**, is dispatched with an army to **Portugal** in August after **France** invades **Spain**. His campaign, known as the **Peninsular War**, marks the beginning of the end of Napoleon's ambition to rule all Europe. **Crabb Robinson** is sent by the *Times* to follow Wellesley and so becomes the world's first paid **war correspondent**.

1809 **Sir John Moore** is defeated and killed by French forces at **La Corunna** in January, but in July Wellesley defeats Napoleon's brother **Joseph Bonaparte** at **Talavera**—a victory that earns Wellesley the title of **viscount**.

At home, **Portland** resigns and **Spencer Perceval** becomes prime minister.

1810 **Trading relations** with the **USA** resume, but England is split by industrial unrest caused by the government's harsh policies, which are geared to furthering the war effort.

In September, the secretary of state **George Canning** retires in protest at the War Office's reluctance to give Wellesley (later made the **duke of Wellington**) the supplies he needs. The Secretary for War, **Viscount Castlereagh**, takes personal umbrage and wounds Canning in a duel.

George III, now blind, makes a final and permanent descent into insanity.

1811 In January **George, Prince of Wales** becomes **Regent**, taking over the throne from his incapacitated father.

Industrial unrest turns to violence as the machine-breaking **Luddites**, named after their mythical leader "General Ludd," attack cotton factories in **Nottingham**, claiming that mechanization is causing unemployment.

British forces twice defeat French forces in the **Peninsula** in May, at **Fuentes de Onoro** and **Albuera**.

The architect **John Nash** begins work on London's **Regent Street**.

1812 As food prices rise, **Luddite** attacks against factories become widespread.

In June Britain finds itself at war with the **USA** following a trade dispute.

Spencer Perceval becomes the only British prime minister to date to be assassinated when he is shot by a merchant called **John Bellingham** in the lobby of the House of Commons, mistaken for someone else. He is succeeded by **Lord Liverpool**.

Wellington again defeats the **French**, at Salamanca on July 22, and enters **Madrid** in August.

In the east, **Napoleon** faces further humiliation as his army is forced to retreat from **Moscow** in October.

Gas lighting is installed in some of **London**'s streets.

1813 Following a victory over **Marshal Jourdan** at **Vittoria** on June 21, which secures the independence of **Spain** and **Portugal**, Wellington pushes French forces out of the Iberian peninsula and pursues **Marshal Soult** into **France** itself. Simultaneously **Napoleon**'s armies suffer a series of setbacks in central Europe.

The **East India Company** is stripped of its monopoly in Britain's Indian trade.

Jane Austen publishes *Pride and Prejudice*, the first of several witty satires of rural gentry life.

1814 Napoleon abdicates as emperor in April and "retires" to the Mediterranean island of **Elba**.

In September the **Congress of Vienna** meets to restore order in Europe; Britain agrees to back the accession to the French throne of **Louis XVIII**.

The "**War of 1812**" between Britain and the USA is formally ended by the **Treaty of Ghent**, signed on December 24.

The world's first **steam rail locomotive**, adapted from an earlier design by **Trevithick** by **George Stephenson**, is unveiled at **Killingworth Colliery**.

The **Marylebone Cricket Club** (MCC) adopts the **Lord's Ground** in North London as its permanent home.

1815 Napoleon escapes confinement on Elba, rallies his supporters in France and launches his "**Hundred Days**." His forces defeat **Wellington** at **Quatre-Bras** and a Prussian army at nearby **Ligny**, both on June 16, but on June 18, close to the Belgian town of **Waterloo**, he is decisively defeated by Wellington and **Marshal von Blücher**, supported by Dutch and Belgian troops. The **Congress of Vienna** reconvenes, and Napoleon is exiled to the Atlantic island of **St Helena**.

The war's end—initiating the demobilizing of many regiments—induces **economic crisis** as prices tumble. Parliament enacts the first **Corn Law**, helping English farmers maintain their income by

Wellington at the Battle of Waterloo

regulating the import of foreign grain. **Income tax**, however, is abolished, and will remain so until 1842.

1816 As England's economic depression deepens, **Luddism** is rekindled.

Demobbed soldiers, failing to find employment, are encouraged to join **"Hampden" clubs**, seeking political reform through a broadening of the franchise. A reform meeting held at **Spa Fields** in Bermondsey, London, erupts into violence, though, and is broken up by the authorities.

THE BATTLE OF WATERLOO

aterloo was a watershed in European political history. It inspired generations of historians, poets and novelists. It was also the first battle to be commemorated with a medal for all those who participated, irrespective of rank.

It was triggered by Napoleon's return from exile in March 1815. Within a month of his arrival in France, the restored monarchy collapsed, and Napoleon calculated that it would be in the allies' best interests to leave him be. But he was wrong: a coordinated assault was planned between an Anglo-Belgian-Dutch force under **Wellington**, the Prussians under **Marshal Gebhardt von Blücher**, and the Austrians and Russians. Unable to withstand such a massive attack, Napoleon resolved to take on his nearest enemies—the British and Prussians—in the hope that this would deter the others. On June 16 he attacked the Prussians at **Ligny**, defeating both them and the British at **Quatre-Bras**. Believing Blücher to be finished, it only remained for Napoleon to defeat the main British army to have achieved his goal.

On June 18 Napoleon caught up with Wellington's forces, who were commanding a defensive position on high ground across the Brussels road. Concerned that remaining Prussians might attempt to link up with their allies, Napoleon opted for a risky frontal attack, hoping that a diversionary

1817 As social unrest continues, **Lord Liverpool** reintroduces some of **Pitt the Younger**'s repressive measures, including a revised **Seditious Meetings Act**.

In Ireland, where unrest is verging on rebellion, the English minister **Robert Peel** introduces a new **police force**, known as "Peelers" and later transferred to the mainland, where they will also be known as "Bobbies."

assault on the British lines at **Hougumont** would compel the enemy to spread its forces too thinly. As the day wore on, though, the foot guards at Hougumont held out, and the French were forced to pour in more troops. Next, the French infantry mounted an attack on the British centre, but although some defensive positions fell, a counter-attack under **General Thomas Picton** recovered the ground, and a charge by the heavy cavalry put the French to flight. The French then responded with their own cavalry assault, but were met with well-prepared troops, who withstood all that the French could throw at them.

As the situation began to look increasingly desperate, news began to filter through that the Prussians were appearing on the eastern flank. Under extreme pressure, the French undertook another huge infantry assault and managed to dislodge the soldiers of the King's German Legion from **La Haye Sainte**, but as the French mounted the ridge they were presented with Wellington's fresh reserve troops. With the Prussians now pressurizing him, Napoleon had no choice but to engage his elite reserve force, the **Imperial Guards**, but they too were forced back. As they retreated down the slope, Wellington at last—after withstanding eight hours of continual assault—ordered his men to advance.

1818 The Tories enjoy a comfortable majority in a **general election** and **Lord Liverpool** continues as prime minister.

The **Treaty of Aix-la-Chapelle** readmits France to the "concert" of nations.

Mary Shelley, who married the poet **Percy Bysshe Shelley** two years earlier, creates a sensation with the publication of *Frankenstein: or, The Modern Prometheus*, in which Frankenstein, a student from Geneva, creates a monster and brings it to life.

The first successful **blood transfusion** is carried out at Guy's Hospital, London.

1819 An illegal gathering on August 16 at **St Peter's Fields, Manchester**, breaks up in violence after an attempt is made to arrest the main speaker, the radical **Henry "Orator" Hunt**. In the ensuing "**Massacre of Peterloo**" eleven citizens are killed by a cavalry charge. In response, Liverpool's government pushes through the **Six Acts**, each designed to further suppress the expression and dissemination of radical ideas.

Stamford Raffles founds a colony on the Malayan island of **Singapore**.

The English engineer **Thomas Telford** begins construction of a suspension bridge across the **Menai Straits** between mainland Wales and Anglesey.

1820 George III dies aged 81 on January 29.

CHAPTER NINE

The Age of the Empire

{1820-1914}

THE ACCESSION OF **GEORGE IV** IN 1820 was a disappointment
to those who had once looked upon him as a figurehead for reform.
Now aged sixty, the former Prince Regent was portly in stature, politically conservative and the constant butt of satirists. Almost immediately a crisis developed when he attempted to divorce his wife, **Caroline
of Brunswick**. In the indecorous squabbling that ensued the monarchy itself came under serious threat. Actual government, however, continued in the hands of Lord Liverpool, and the 1820s proved a period
of steady economic and social improvement. Although the throne still
had an important part to play in English and British affairs, the political agenda was being increasingly determined by Parliament.

The point is made by the reign of **Queen Victoria** (1837–1901),
the longest in English history. Her husband, **Prince Albert of
Saxe-Coburg**, was publicly active, notably in promoting the
Great Exhibition of 1851 and encouraging entrepreneurs and inven-
tors. At his side Victoria willingly undertook the public duties expected of her. But after Albert's death in 1861 she retreated into a shell of
grief, rarely appearing in public and playing little part in political
developments. Only after cajoling from the Conservative prime minister **Benjamin Disraeli**, who was eager to improve his popularity
ratings, did she emerge in the late 1870s.

But in a way Disraeli's maneuverings proved that the royal family
were still an integral part of England's (and Britain's) make-up. While
previous prime ministers had managed to survive despite the queen's

absence, Disraeli saw that the nature of political life had yet again moved on. Even before Victoria's accession, the **Great Reform Act** of 1832 had taken a hesitant step toward greater democratization, widening the franchise to include a further 200,000 voters. A second reform act in 1867 tripled the number of men qualified to vote to around two million, and a third in 1884 extended the franchise still further, even though as late as 1911 no more than 60 percent of potential electors were registered—and of course women would be excluded until 1918. This new mass electorate meant that politicians had to take notice of middle- and working-class views, perhaps for the first time, spurring Disraeli to refashion the old Tory party into the modern Conservatives. By allying a new sense of patriotism with an idealized image of the monarchy (helped, of course, by the queen's re-emergence), he created a populist platform designed to appeal to a broad cross-section of the nation. Leadership styles also changed: both Disraeli and his Liberal adversary, **W.E. Gladstone**, developed the modern system of a prime minister backed by a cabinet and party machine—all aware that at regular intervals their policies must be vindicated at the polling booths.

But greater democratization was only one aspect of a wider program of reform, sponsored mainly by the Whigs (called the **Liberals** after 1859 following the amalgamation of the old Whig party and liberal radicals), which sought to deliver a fairer society. Religious freedom, labor relations, education, health, and social benefits—including unemployment support and pensions at the beginning of the 20th century—were areas in which successive governments made lasting changes. These changes were spurred on by increasingly vocal popular movements. At its beginning Victoria's reign was marked by the **Chartist** protests, which sought to reverse the limitations of the 1832 Act. And the 19th century ended with the birth of the **Labor Party**—dedicated to defending and advancing the interests of those who had been ignored by previous administrations.

And then of course there was the Empire. Though **India** under the Raj was the jewel in the imperial crown, British colonies and dependencies stretched across **Asia**, **Australasia**, **Africa**, the **Caribbean** and **Canada**. It has been estimated that, by 1905, something in excess of 345 million people were ruled by a United Kingdom with just 40 million domestic inhabitants. And although the colonies were maintained with Britain's maritime strength, it was commercial industry that held the Empire together—it was a profitable source of labor, a captive market for British goods and a lucrative area for investment. For all the talk of "free trade," a conspicuous theme in parliamentary debates, the Empire was run almost entirely as a closed shop.

British rulers, assured of their supremacy, saw themselves as exporting positive values—among them the efficacy of hard work, a strong sense of Christian endeavor and (far more nebulously) a sense of moral "fair play." That such ideas were frequently optimistic at best is evidenced by the genocidal outrages perpetrated by British colonists in the rush to acquire land, horrors which recent historians have painstakingly attempted to catalogue. In all corners of the empire, and throughout its history, various methods were used to remove indigenous peoples from their land. The native peoples of Tasmania were almost totally wiped out by colonizers in the first half of the 19th century; maize meal laced with arsenic was regularly used to decimate Australian aboriginal populations in the early 19th century; Canadian Indians, swamped by an immigrant population, saw their numbers halve between 1815 and 1911; when local communities in Rhodesia objected to their land being seized in 1896, dynamite was dropped into the caves in which they were hiding; even smallpox was pressed deliberately into service in the mid-18th century to reduce the population of Native Americans colonists had to deal with.

For all this, the British Empire was to prove short-lived. Within less than a century of its zenith it had all but disappeared—even if it left behind the widespread use of English as the language of business and a parliamentary model for democratic institutions in many former colonies. Partly it was facing mounting competition from other nations. By 1900 the American economy was stronger and more dynamic; in Central Asia, Russia was growing more powerful; in the East, Japan flexed new-found muscle; while in Europe, Germany, now unified under Prussian leadership and determined to enter the imperial game, expressly announced its intention to challenge Britain.

Rivalry between England and Germany led directly to the **Great War** of 1914–18, confirming an alliance between Britain and its traditional enemy, France. Yet before the onset of that cataclysm, England itself enjoyed a decade of curious tranquility, the "Edwardian Era," named after Victoria's son and immediate successor **Edward VII**. If you were rich enough, this was a time to look back on a century of rare cultural, technological and scientific achievement: to read through a library of gifted novelists and poets; to enjoy the prestige of swift travel by train, steamship and latterly the motorcar; to follow the fortunes of Scott and Shackleton in the Antarctic; to ponder the implications of Charles Darwin's new theory of evolution.

1820 The Prince of Wales succeeds his father as **George IV**. When his estranged wife, **Caroline of Brunswick**, presses to be acknowledged queen, the king reveals his plans for a divorce. When a **general election** affirms Lord Liverpool as prime minister, his Tory government introduces a bill of divorce into Parliament. During her trial Caroline—previously an unpopular figure—becomes a magnet for political opposition to both Liverpool and George IV.

In February, a plot to assassinate the cabinet known as the **Cato Street Conspiracy** is uncovered by an informer, Oliver "the Spy," and its ringleaders executed.

1821 Parliament refuses to pass a **divorce bill** for George IV and Caroline, instead voting Caroline a personal annuity. The king's **coro-**

nation descends into a farce when Caroline attempts to enter Westminster Abbey but is barred from entering its doors.

Following his discovery of **electromagnetic rotation**, **Michael Faraday** invents a simple electric motor.

John Constable paints *The Hay Wain*, which influences the modern school of landscape and Romantic painters.

Thomas de Quincey establishes his reputation by publishing *Confessions of an Opium Eater* in the *London Magazine*—a lurid account of his addiction to the drug.

The *Manchester Guardian* newspaper is founded.

The poet **John Keats** dies of tuberculosis in Rome, aged 25.

1822 Lord Castlereagh, embroiled in a scandal over a male prostitute he assumed was a woman and unable to face the onslaught of adverse publicity, commits suicide. He is succeeded as foreign secretary by his former rival **George Canning**. Against a background of economic revival, Liverpool uses Castlereagh's exit to promote younger ministers, among them **Robert Peel**.

The *Sunday Times* newspaper is founded.

Francis Place MP urges working-class men and women to adopt the **uterine sponge** as a form of contraception.

The poet **Percy Bysshe Shelley** drowns off Livorno, aged 29.

1823 As prosperity returns, the government abolishes the **death penalty** for over a hundred minor crimes, and Peel introduces the **Gaol Act**, alleviating conditions in England's crowded prisons. Some trade restrictions are also lifted, although the **Corn Laws** remain on the statute books.

William Wilberforce establishes the **Anti-Slavery Society** in London.

Lord Byron publishes *Don Juan*.

William Webb Ellis, a student at **Rugby College**, unwittingly creates the game of rugby when he attempts to score a goal using his hands during a game of football.

THE ENGLISH ROMANTIC POETS

*T*here is no simple formula for literary Romanticism. It was more a pan-European cultural watershed than a movement, and is more easily defined by what it reacted against rather than what it embodied—many of its adherents detested Classicism, organized religion, sexual inhibition, authoritarian politics and Enlightenment rationality. The Romantic idiom caught on early in England, and although it produced no one of the poet **Johann Wolfgang von Goethe**'s philosophical reach or the novelist **Walter Scott**'s continental reputation, it did create a cluster of gifted poets who flourished in the last decades of the 18th century and during the first half of the 19th.

The thinking of the French philosopher **Jean-Jacques Rousseau**, with its emphasis on humanity and utopian ideals, was one starting point for English Romanticism. Another was the 1765 publication of **Thomas Percy's** *Reliques of Ancient English Poetry*, which included traditional ballads and other "metrical romances." Yet another was the work of the brilliantly idiosyncratic engraver and poet, **William Blake**, who rejected rationalism and authority in favor of imaginative freedom and mysticism—wonderfully exemplified in his long poem, *Jerusalem* (1804–20), which proclaims that "Poetry Fettr'd Fetters the Human Race."

But it was the 1798 publication of *Lyrical Ballads*, a joint anthology by William Wordsworth and Samuel Taylor Coleridge, that gave English

1824 Canning begins to support selected independence movements against Spanish rule in South and Central America, including **Mexico** and **Colombia**.

The **National Gallery** and the **Royal Society for the Prevention of Cruelty to Animals** are both founded in London.

Romanticism its first manifesto. Wordsworth added a preface calling for apoetry that operated with simple language and themes, placed emotive subjectivity at its core and tried to establish a dialogue between consciousness and memory (which he termed "recollection in tranquillity")—ideas that he would exploit in various versions of his autobiographical *The Prelude*, which is subtitled "Growth of a Poet's Mind" and addressed to Coleridge.

Later Romantic poets—sometimes called the "second generation" Romantics by family-minded critics—included the sometime apothecary John Keats, the rebellious Percy Bysshe Shelley and the libertine and dashing George Gordon, Lord Byron. Keats's major works, including *The Fall of Hyperion*, "The Eve of St Agnes," "To Autumn" and six "Odes," were squeezed into a brilliantly productive twelve-month period between 1818 and 1819, but two years later he was dead of tuberculosis. Shelley argued that poets were the "unacknowledged legislators" of the world in his 1821 *Defence of Poetry*, and his great drama *Prometheus Unbound* (1820) is a bold exposition of the yearning for intellectual and physical liberty. Like Keats, though, his life was cut short by a boating accident. Byron's career was scarcely longer: he died of fever after rushing to fight for Greek independence, leaving behind a copious quantity of poems, drama, letters and journals—not to mention a fashionably amoral reputation only enhanced when his body was refused burial by both Westminster Abbey and St Paul's Cathedral.

Lord Byron dies at **Missolonghi** aged 36, fighting for Greek independence from the Ottoman Empire.

The ***Westminster Review***, a radical quarterly dedicated to opposing the Tory-leaning *Quarterly Review* and the Whig *Edinburgh Review*, is founded by **James Mill** and **Jeremy Bentham**. It will become one of the most influential journals of the 19th century and in its early years will publish work by **John Stuart Mill**, **Samuel Taylor Coleridge**, **Thomas Carlyle** and **Alfred Tennyson**, among others.

1825 A **Catholic emancipation bill** is defeated in Parliament, but laws against trade unions are partially relaxed, making it legal for workers to delegate representatives to discuss wages and other issues with employers.

The **Stockton and Darlington Railway Company** begins operating the world's first rail passenger service, its locomotive *Active* designed by **George Stephenson**.

John Nash begins rebuilding **Buckingham House**, known as Buckingham Palace from 1837 when it becomes the capital's principal royal residence.

1827 **Lord Liverpool**, incapacitated by a stroke, resigns as prime minister in February and is succeeded first by **George Canning** in April then, when Canning dies in August, by **Viscount Goderich**.

Peel continues his reforms of the **criminal code**.

1828 **Goderich** resigns in January when it becomes clear he lacks any following in Parliament. The **duke of Wellington** is appointed prime minister. He introduces a new **Corn Law** to protect domestic grain production, but is forced by public pressure to repeal the **Test and Corporation Acts**.

London University is founded.

Dr Thomas Arnold becomes headmaster of **Rugby School**. The reforms he introduces form the blueprint for public school education in the 19th century and well into the 20th—a liberal curriculum based on the classics, a particular brand of "muscular Christianity," harsh discipline and an emphasis on sporting prowess.

1829 **Wellington** effects the passage of the **Catholic Emancipation Act**, which allows Catholics the rights to vote, to stand for Parliament and to hold most public offices.

Peel creates a new **police force** for London, modeled on his previous experiments in Ireland.

Stephenson's **Rocket** wins the Liverpool and Manchester Railway Competition for the fastest locomotive.

The first **Boat Race** between **Oxford** and **Cambridge** universities is held.

1830 Britain joins with **France** and **Russia** in guaranteeing **Greece**'s freshly won independence.

George IV dies on June 26 aged 67 and is succeeded by his brother, the duke of Clarence, as **William IV** (aged 64).

Amidst growing agitation for political reform, a severely divided Tory party is badly beaten in an autumn **election**, and on November 22 the Whig **Earl Grey** replaces Wellington as prime minister.

The official opening of the **Manchester–Liverpool passenger railway line** in September is marred when a cabinet minister, **George Huskisson**, is killed after he falls in front of the train.

William Cobbett publishes *Rural Rides*, a documentary account of the Industrial Revolution's adverse impact on England's poorer classes.

The law does nothing for us. We must save ourselves. We have a little land which we need for ourselves and our families to live on, and they drove us out of it. To whom should we address ourselves? We ask for work at eightpence a day and we are refused. To whom should we address ourselves? Emancipation has done nothing for us. Mr O'Connell and the rich Catholics go to Parliament. We die of starvation just the same.

—**Alexis de Tocqueville,**
Journeys to England and Ireland (1835)

1831 As clamor for reform mounts, the radical Whig politician **Lord John Russell** (later **Earl Russell**) introduces his first **Reform Bill** into Parliament. It is defeated, but a **general election** returns a Commons even more committed to electoral change. A **second bill** passes through the Commons, but is defeated in the Lords. As a result there are **mass protests**, aimed also at the bishops, who have opposed reform.

The naturalist **Charles Darwin** sets out on a voyage aboard *HMS Beagle* to the **Galapagos Islands**, where his observations of previously unknown species of finch and turtle encourage him to formulate a theory of **natural selection**.

1832 A third **Reform Bill** passes in the Commons, but is again blocked in the Lords. **Earl Grey**, who supports the legislation, briefly resigns in May, but Wellington is unable to form a replacement administration. Grey resumes office, and the **First ("Great") Reform Act**, pertaining to English and Welsh constituencies, passes in the Lords on June 4. Separate bills for **Scotland** and **Ireland** are steered through Parliament in July and August.

Jeremy Bentham, founder of **utilitarianism**—a social philosophy that promotes the "greatest happiness of the greatest number"—dies aged 83.

1833 Following persistent pressure from the Anti-Slavery Society, **slavery** is finally abolished in all British territories and colonies, including those administered by the East India Company.

A **Factory Act** alleviates some of the more shocking working conditions in the worst of England's factories, including the employment of very young children.

Britain occupies the **Falkland Islands**.

The **East India Company** loses its monopoly in the China tea trade.

John Keble publishes *National Apostasy Considered*, a defense of "high church" values within the Anglican communion that inspires a group of like-minded clergymen and scholars to found the **Oxford Movement**.

1834 In the year of four prime ministers, **Lord Grey** resigns in July and is replaced by **Lord Melbourne**. In November Melbourne gives way to **Wellington**, and in December Wellington

THE "GREAT" REFORM ACT (1832)

*T*he Great Reform Act was less an exercise in democracy than a last-ditch attempt by England's landowners to shore up their own interests. It admitted the principle of change while giving most people little experience of it.

Its rationale was essentially to increase democracy by bumping up the size of the electorate (the "franchise") from 450,000 to 650,000 males—which of course left most of the adult population still without the vote. An arbitrary figure of £10 was set as the minimum amount of property one had to own in order to count, meaning that in some areas skilled craftsmen qualified, while in others clerks and other "minor" professionals were cut out. And this democratizing impetus was really a defensive measure: after the upheavals in France and elsewhere, the elite were paranoid that the same thing might happen on home soil. When disturbing symptoms of social unrest emerged, especially in the new industrial towns, they were galvanized into action.

The changes had a mixed effect. Although the Act brought about the end of "rotten boroughs," where MPs had been returned to Parliament on the basis of a handful of buyable votes, the bias was simply shifted, not removed—many newly organized constituencies were fixed by the Whig administration to the Tories' disadvantage. Yet for all its imperfections, the Act became an important milestone in that it created a precedent for further reform. Within a century full adult suffrage in England was a reality.

is superseded by **Sir Robert Peel**, who issues the **Tamworth Manifesto** to revive flagging Tory spirits. The rapid turnover of ministries points to the instability still rife in English politics following the Great Reform Act.

Parliament burns down on October 16.

At the beginning of the year, a **Grand National Consolidated Trades Union** is formed under the leadership of **Robert Owen** and **John Doherty** to press for an eight-hour working day in Britain's factories, if necessary by means of a general strike. In March six of its members, known as the **Tolpuddle Martyrs**, are arrested outside **Dorchester** and deported to Australia. Sporadic strikes occur, but the immediate crisis passes.

1835 Following a general election, Whigs join forces with Irish and radical politicians (known as the **Lichfield House Compact**).

Peel is removed from office, and **Melbourne** returns as Prime Minister.

The **Municipal Corporations Act** introduces long-overdue reforms in local government.

1836 The **Tithe Commutation Act** abolishes the practice—established in medieval times—of paying taxes in kind to the Church.

The **London Working Men's Association** is formed to promote further industrial and political reform.

1837 William IV dies and on June 20 his niece **Alexandrina Victoria**, daughter of Edward, Duke of Kent, becomes queen. In **Hanover**, where female succession is disallowed, the Crown passes to Victoria's uncle, the **duke of Cumberland**.

Lord Melbourne, an avuncular influence over the young monarch, remains in power, though a **general election** reduces the Whigs' parliamentary majority.

The **civil registration** of births, marriages and deaths begins.

The publication in book form of **Charles Dickens**' comic novel *Pickwick Papers* marks the arrival of an innovative writing talent.

Charles Wheatstone invents the **electric telegraph**, enabling the near-instant transmission of information over potentially unlimited distances.

1838 The politically radical **Chartist** movement, calling for far wider reforms than those enshrined in the 1832 Reform Act, is inaugurated with the publication in May of a **People's Charter** devised by **Richard Lovett**. The Chartists launch their own increasingly influential newspaper, the *Northern Star*, edited by **Feargus O'Connor**. At the same time a mainly middle-class organization, the **Anti-Corn Law League**, calling for the abolition of protectionist grain tariffs, is founded in **Man-chester** by **Richard Cobden**. While the Leaguers describe the land-owners who benefit from the Corn Laws as a "bread-taxing oligarchy," prime minister **Melbourne** vilifies the League as "the wildest, maddest scheme that has ever entered into the imagination of man to conceive."

A British army invades **Afghanistan** in an attempt to counter **Russian expansionism** in Central Asia.

The first **transatlantic crossings** achieved by steam power alone are made by two British vessels, the *Sirius* and **Isambard Kingdom Brunel**'s *Great Western*.

The **Public Record Office**, a government archive, is founded in Chancery Lane, London.

The **National Gallery** opens in London.

William Henry Fox Talbot, an inventor and scientist from Wiltshire, sets up an exhibition in London demonstrating his use of the negative—one of the defining moments in the development of **photography**.

1839 The first **Chartist National Convention** meets in February, but almost immediately descends into squabbling about aims and methods. In July Parliament rejects a **Chartist Petition**, prompting further infighting within the movement's leadership—some preferring persuasion as the proper means to success, others openly advocating violence.

In April the **Treaty of London** guarantees Belgian independence following the partition of the **Netherlands** in 1830—a pledge that, 75 years later, takes Britain into World War I.

In the Far East the **Opium War** is triggered when the Chinese government attempts to prevent English and other foreign merchants importing opium into **China**. To protect British interests, the foreign secretary, **Lord Palmerston**—instituting the "**gunboat diplomacy**" for which he will later become famous—orders a fleet of twenty warships into the South China Sea.

CHARTISM

*F*ollowing widespread dismay at the limitations of the 1832 Reform Act, it was clear to many that the changes it brought were not going to be enough. A radical movement sprang up to campaign for further reform, named "chartism" after the demands set out in the "Six Points" of its People's Charter of 1838: universal male suffrage; a secret ballot; equal size of constituencies; the abolition of any property qualification for MPs; a salary for MPs; and annual parliaments. Individually there was nothing new in any of these—they had each been proposed by radicals back in the 18th century—but as a package they presented a manifesto to which the working and lower middle classes could alike subscribe.

Despite the fact that the Chartists' demands had all been met by the end of the century (with the exception of annual parliaments), no less an authority than Karl Marx regarded Chartism as a failure. He argued that, while its ends were transparent, its means were contradictory. Two of the movement's leading lights, William Lovett and Francis Place, favored

J.M.W. Turner, one of the best-known English artists of the 19th century, paints *The Fighting Temeraire*—one of his most famous seascapes.

The first **Grand National steeplechase** is run at **Aintree**, Liverpool, and the **Henley Regatta** is founded.

1840 Queen Victoria marries **Prince Albert of Saxe-Coburg and Gotha**.

A British fleet commanded by **George Elliot** blockades the **Bai He** river in northern China, threatening the capital, **Beijing**.

Upper and Lower Canada are **reunited**, and Britain adds **New Zealand** to its Australian dominion.

---

peaceable persuasion, but a third, the flamboyant Irishman Feargus O'Connor, advocated force in the last resort—and it was the eruption of sporadic and uncoordinated episodes of violence (such as the Newport uprising in November 1839) that discouraged a greater following. Also, Chartism has been viewed by some as being too dependent on "bread-and-butter issues." At times of hardship it attracted widespread support, but the majority of workers were unprepared to campaign actively when the price of bread was low and employment was plentiful.

In the end, perhaps it was what Chartism led to that made it truly significant. The Chartist Convention showed that working people could organize an assembly and co-ordinate their efforts. Although it was short-lived (it was effectively dead by 1848), it paved the way for other collectivist bodies, notably the Trades Union Congress, the assembly of all the major unions in Britain. More broadly and profoundly, the movement bequeathed a legacy of hope for the disenfranchised.

Sir Rowland Hill introduces the **penny post** as the world's first adhesive postage stamp, the **Penny Black**, goes on sale.

The **Royal Botanical Gardens** at **Kew** are opened to the public.

The architect **Charles Barry**, assisted by the young **A.W. Pugin**, begins rebuilding the **Houses of Parliament** in the increasingly fashionable **Neo-Gothic** style.

1841 Sir Robert Peel displaces Melbourne as prime minister in August after Peel's Tory "**conservatives**" win a July General Election. Peel abolishes some **trade tariffs**, but is unable to gain enough support to repeal the **Corn Laws**. Nor is he able to avert a downturn in the economy, and **Chartist** activities revive.

In China, **George Elliot** comes to terms with the emperor's representatives. The opium trade is allowed to continue, and the island of **Hong Kong** is ceded to Britain. War resumes almost immediately, however, when **Palmerston** sacks Elliot for not having secured better terms. **Sir Henry Pottinger** again harasses China's coast with a British fleet.

The satirical magazine *Punch* is founded under the editorship of **Henry Mayhew** and **Mark Lemon**.

1842 Peel reintroduces **income tax**, abandoned in 1816. Parliament's rejection of a **Second Chartist Petition** sparks widespread riots and strikes, particularly in England's northern cities.

The war in **Afghanistan** ends when British troops concede defeat and withdraw from the territory.

In China, **Pottinger** secures the **Treaty of Nanjing**, ending the Opium War and securing unfettered trading rights for British merchants and the future opening-up of designated treaty ports.

Edwin Chadwick completes a government report on the "**sanitary conditions**" of the laboring classes, drawing attention to the much greater prevalence of disease among the poor.

An Act of Parliament prohibits **women and children** working underground in Britain's mines.

1843 The *Economist* magazine is founded to promote free trade.

Dickens writes *A Christmas Carol*, a novella described by fellow writer **William Makepeace Thackeray** as "a national benefit, and to every man or woman who reads it a personal kindness."

1844 A **Railways Act** requires rail companies to run at least one train per weekday at a maximum fare of one penny for adults and a half-penny for children.

The **YMCA** (Young Men's Christian Association) is founded, as is the first modern **co-operative society**, by a group of Rochdale weavers known as the "**Pioneers**."

1845 Peel alienates the support of many followers by increasing government aid to a Catholic seminary at **Maynooth** in Ireland.

Throughout the British Isles—but particularly in **Ireland**, where serious **famine** sets in—**potato crops** are blighted. Although many Irish people emigrate to the United States in the coming years, many also move to Liverpool, London and other English cities. As food shortages grow, the government comes under heavy pressure over the **Corn Laws**. Peel earnestly favors repeal, but is unable to persuade a majority in the Commons. He resigns, but **Lord John Russell** is unable to form a government and Peel continues in office.

Benjamin Disraeli publishes *Sybil*, a novel with Chartist sympathies that depicts England as being composed of "two nations," the haves and the have-nots.

1846 Relying on Whig support in Parliament, Peel is able to effect the **repeal of the Corn Laws**. Tory opposition is led by **Lord George Bentinck** and **Benjamin Disraeli**. The Tory party splits, Peel resigns as prime minister, and **Lord John Russell** forms a Whig administration on June 30. Although Peel is castigated for wrecking the Tory party, his followers, around a hundred in number and called the

"**Peelites**," continue as a separate parliamentary faction occupying the political ground between Tories and Whigs. Under Russell, the government expands its social role, creating a new teacher-training scheme.

Edward Lear publishes his first book of limericks, *A Book of Nonsense.*

1847 The reforming Lord John Russell continues in power after his Whig party, now known as the **Liberals**, win a **general election**.

THE COMING OF THE RAILWAYS

*N*othing epitomizes the Industrial Revolution and the changing face of England so much as the spectacular growth of the railways. By the end of the century there were 9000 stations in all, servicing a network of lines that connected every city and town, every port and a great number of country villages, cutting journey times across Britain to seldom more than a few hours. Some stations, notably London's St Pancras—fronted by **George Gilbert Scott's** fashionably Neo-Gothic Midland Grand Hotel—were nothing less than grandiose monuments to steam, whose splendor and scale were designed to rival England's ancient cathedrals.

The emphasis on speed and the need to create locomotives capable of pulling heavy payloads provided an enormous impetus to the engineering industry, and the export of engines and rolling stock to other countries became a significant money-spinner. Copious reserves of coal and iron ensured Britain's temporary pre-eminence in the new technology. And the domestic social consequences were equally far-reaching. Though the railways were initially developed as a means of transporting manufactured goods and raw materials, when fresh produce began to be carried by rail,

Responding to extra-parliamentary pressure, Russell's government passes the **Ten Hours Act**, restricting the working hours of women and children in textile factories.

The new **parliament buildings** are completed at last.

As the price of grain temporarily rises Britain experiences its last **food riots**.

the effects were revolutionary. Even remote fishing communities such as **Milford Haven** in west Wales found themselves rapidly connected to markets in London, Birmingham and elsewhere.

But it was passenger services that initiated the most telling social changes. Private companies such as the **GWR** (Great Western Railway) and the **LNER** (London North Eastern Railway) began offering third-class as well as first- and second-class carriages, putting rail travel within the reach of more people than ever before. Aristocratic watering holes like **Brighton** found themselves besieged by working-class day trippers, and brand-new seaside resorts like **Blackpool** catered specifically for budget holidaymakers. Nor was it just leisure activities that were transformed. The opening of London's **Victoria Station** in 1860 heralded commuterism, expanded further by the first metropolitan underground line between **Paddington** and **Farringdon Street**, which appeared three years later. The sheer growth in passenger numbers over the century demonstrates the scale of these changes: the number of journeys made by rail rose from 73 million in 1850 to a dizzying 2000 million by 1912. The railways were perceived as good for business, good for people and good for Britain.

Charlotte Brontë publishes *Jane Eyre* and her sister **Emily** publishes *Wuthering Heights*, both under male pseudonyms—but the identity of the authors is an open secret in London literary circles.

1848 While the rest of Europe is gripped by revolutionary fever (King Louis Philippe is displaced in France by Louis Napoleon, and other attempted uprisings spread across Germany and Italy), Britain escapes serious disruption.

The **Chartists** hold their last great meeting on **Kennington Common**, but a Chartist petition is exposed as a largely fictitious assemblage of names.

In **Ireland**, the continuing famine leads to widespread **rioting**.

A **Public Health Act** establishes a General Board of Health headed by **Edwin Chadwick** to monitor the outbreak and spread of epidemics.

Commissioned by London's **Communist League**, *The Communist Manifesto*, written by **Karl Marx** and **Friedrich Engels**, is published.

The **Pre-Raphaelite Brotherhood**, a school of artists and writers devoted to a highly mannered appreciation of late medieval values, is formed by **Holman Hunt**, **John Everett Millais** and **Dante Gabriel Rossetti**.

W.M. Thackeray publishes his masterpiece, *Vanity Fair*, a novel that caricatures the pretensions and hypocrisies of English society.

1849 Charles Kingsley and **Frederick Maurice** launch the **Christian Socialist** movement.

Women gain a foothold in higher education with the foundation of **Bedford College** in London.

The future department store **Harrods** begins as a grocery shop in Knightsbridge.

1850 Britain enters a period of sustained **prosperity**, during which wages rise but prices either fall or remain level.

Foreign secretary **Lord Palmerston** earns the distrust of the queen and many of his colleagues by resorting to gun-boat diplomacy on behalf of **Don Pacifico**, a Portuguese Jew with a British passport mistreated by anti-Semites in Athens.

Sir Robert Peel dies after a riding accident in July.

The **Vatican** begins funding new **Catholic bishoprics** in England, the first since the Reformation.

Alfred Tennyson (later Lord Tennyson) publishes *In Memoriam A.H.H.*, an elegy for his dead friend Arthur Henry Hallam—one of his most celebrated works.

1851 An **Ecclesiastical Titles Act** prohibits Catholic bishops from adopting the same titles as their Anglican counterparts.

The first religious census shows that support for the **Church of England** is in steep decline, fuelling arguments for its disestablishment.

Britain's worldwide commercial and colonial prestige is celebrated under the patronage of Albert, the prince consort, by the **Great Exhibition**. It is housed in the glass-walled **Crystal Palace** designed by **Joseph Paxton** and erected in London's **Hyde Park**. Opening in May, it attracts six million visitors over five months. When the exhibition closes, the Crystal Palace is removed to **Sydenham**, where it is destroyed by fire in 1936.

1852 Weakened by Palmerston's resignation the previous year, **Russell**'s Liberal government falls in February. **Lord Derby** forms a minority Tory government, with **Disraeli** as chancellor of the exchequer, but this too fails in December, after Derby's budget proposals are defeated in Parliament. **Lord Aberdeen** forms a new Whig administration with **W. E. Gladstone** as Chancellor.

1853 The **Northcote–Trevelyan Report** criticizes the way in which patronage rather than merit often determines promotion in the **Civil Service**.

THE ENGLISH NOVEL

*T*he name of **Samuel Richardson** is indelibly associated with the development of the novel in English. He perfected one of its earliest forms, that of the **epistolary novel** (in which characters communicate by letter), in *Pamela* (1740–41) and *Clarissa* (1747–48). The former was lampooned by **Henry Fielding** in *An Apology for the Life of Mrs Shamela Andrews* (1741), the success of which encouraged Fielding to write his comic masterpiece of eight years later, *Tom Jones*. A more extraordinary book still was the Irish-born **Laurence Sterne**'s *The Life and Opinions of Tristam Shandy, Gentleman* (1760–67), which has been called the first and greatest English experimental novel. Women writers also found themselves catering for large new audiences. **Ann Radcliffe** was a leading early exponent of the Gothic novel, and the hugely successful work of **Jane Austen**—including *Pride and Prejudice* (1813), *Mansfield Park* (1814) and *Emma* (1816)—fed an appetite among readers for her particular brand of social observation and subtle satire. Books like these established a new enthusiasm for English literature, and from the mid-18th century no educated household was without a few works of fiction.

Although novels in the next century engaged with a bewildering array of concerns and themes, practically all owed their popularity to the growth in middle-class book buying and reflected the preoccupations of that audience. **William Makepeace Thackeray** began his career as a journalist and ended it as one of the most popular novelists of his generation, drawing vivid tableaux of London society including *Vanity Fair* (1848) and *The History of Henry Esmond* (1852). **Anthony Trollope's** workmanlike "Barsetshire" series, set in the fictional town of Barchester, was just one section of a prolific output that totaled some 47 novels. **Charles Dickens** was even more successful, using serial publication—in which novels were published in monthly magazines such as the author's own *Household Words*—so astutely that by the time of his death he was one of the best-loved writers in English and the first international literary celebrity. Novels such as *Oliver Twist* (1837–38), *David Copperfield* (1850), *Bleak House* (1853), *Little Dorrit* (1857) and *Great Expectations* (1861), despite their London backdrops, won Dickens plaudits the world over.

Perhaps it is the writing of 19th-century female novelists that has had the most impact on the course of English literature. The books of **Elizabeth Gaskell**—including *Ruth* (1853) and *Wives and Daughters* (1866)—articulated the author's concern with social issues and focus closely on female characters. The work of the three **Brontë** sisters, Anne, Emily and Charlotte, pushed the novel in new directions—most famously in Charlotte's *Jane Eyre* and Emily's *Wuthering Heights* (both 1847), which drew directly upon experience of life in Yorkshire and passionately assert their female characters' need for independence. But Marian Evans, published as **George Eliot**, was perhaps the most cosmopolitan (and learned) novelistic talent of her time, drawing on topics as diverse as German philosophy and first-hand observation of small-town English life in an extraordinary range of works—among them *Adam Bede* (1859), *The Mill on the Floss* (1860), *Middlemarch* (1871–72) and *Daniel Deronda* (1874–76)—which guaranteed her reputation as the foremost English novelist then alive.

John Ruskin publishes *The Stones of Venice*, an architectural study that measures aesthetic ideals against social and moral values.

1854 Britain and **France** form a military alliance against **Russia** as Russia seeks to take territorial advantage of the crumbling Islamic **Ottoman Empire**, popularly known as the "Sick Man of Europe." British involvement in the **Crimean War**, fought on the Crimean peninsula of the **Black Sea**, lasts two years. The allies gain victories at **Balaklava** in October and **Inkerman** in November, but neither proves decisive.

1855 Lord Aberdeen resigns at the beginning of February amidst mounting criticisms that the Crimean War is being unnecessarily prolonged. A new Liberal government is formed by 70-year-old **Lord Palmerston**, who will continue as prime minister until his death in 1865.

Sebastopol, the main Russian stronghold in the **Crimea**, besieged by the French and British, falls in September, while **Florence Nightingale** wins public acclaim for her reforms of military nursing conditions.

Crystal Palace at the Great Exhibition, 1851

Stamp duty is abolished on British newspapers and the *Daily Telegraph* is founded.

In Africa, the Scottish evangelical explorer **David Livingstone** discovers what he christens the **Victoria Falls**. **Anthony Trollope** publishes *The Warden*, the first of his Barchester novels depicting English provincial life.

1856 Hostilities in the **Crimea** end in February.

In March a congress of European powers meets in **Paris** and resolves to uphold the independence of the **Ottoman Empire**.

Britain faces mounting tension in **India**, and in October a fresh **Anglo-Chinese war** breaks out.

Henry Bessemer discovers a new method of **processing steel** that is cheaper than any of its predecessors.

1857 In India, a major revolt erupts against East India Company rule, known in England as the **Indian Mutiny**. On February 15, over 200 English women and children are massacred at **Cawnpore**, fuelling anti-Indian sentiment at home. Palmerston's popularity is undiminished, though, and his Liberals win a convincing **general election** victory.

The **Science Museum** opens in London.

Thomas Hughes publishes *Tom Brown's Schooldays*, a novel based on the author's experiences at Rugby School during the headmastership of Thomas Arnold.

1858 Discontented Liberals and Tories form an **alliance** against **Palmerston**, whose government falls in February. **Lord Derby** forms a minority Tory government.

Largely with the help of "loyal" local troops, the revolt in **India** is finally crushed. The **East India Company** is sidelined, however, and in its place **direct colonial government** is imposed on the subcontinent.

1859 A Tory attempt to introduce further **electoral reform** is heavily defeated in Parliament, and in June **Palmerston** returns to power as Liberal prime minister.

Charles Darwin publishes *On the Origin of Species by Means of Natural Selection*, which argues the principle of **evolution**—an uncomfortable and unwelcome theory for many.

John Stuart Mill, a disciple of **Jeremy Bentham** and a keen advocate of Utilitarianism, publishes *On Liberty*, a seminal defense of England's emergent liberal democratic ideology.

THE CRIMEAN WAR (1853–56)

*A*s Russia sought to incorporate vast areas of central and western Asia into its expanding empire, it inevitably ran head-on into the Turkish Ottoman empire. The immediate pretext for war between the two countries was a Russian demand to be allowed to "protect" Orthodox Christians living in Ottoman domains around the Black Sea, but the conflict also involved an obscure dispute between Russia and France about the rights of Russian Orthodox and Roman Catholic monks living in Palestine.

Hostilities began in 1853 when Turkey defensively occupied the eastern part of present-day **Romania**. Anxious to contain Russian aggrandizement, Britain joined France in sending a fleet to the Black Sea in January 1854, and war was formally declared in March. For much of the conflict fighting centered on **Sebastopol**—a Russian stronghold on the Crimean peninsula besieged by Turkish, French and British troops—but there were tactical engagements at the Alma River, Balaklava, Inkerman and elsewhere. The war effectively ended in September 1855 when Russia withdrew from Sebastopol.

Samuel Smiles publishes *Self-help*, extolling the "Victorian" values of thrift, moderation and hard work.

1860 Chancellor **W.E. Gladstone** continues to lower tariffs and so promote free trade in his annual budget.

T.H. Huxley, championing Darwin's theory of evolution, vehemently clashes with the creationist **Bishop Samuel Wilberforce**.

The right of **Jews** to claim **full citizenship** in England is finally acknowledged by parliamentary legislation.

The **Open Golf Championship** is founded.

While one key significance of Crimea was that the English and French willingly fought together against a common enemy, it also became the first media war. The *Times* journalist **William Russell** used the newly invented telegraph to file his reports, so that for the first time a distant conflict landed fresh on English breakfast tables. Great public excitement was also generated by the **Charge of the Light Brigade**, famously commemorated in a specially penned poem by **Alfred Tennyson**, who described how a detachment of British cavalry rode futilely into Russian guns at Balaklava, watched by civilian spectators who had traveled to the Crimea in holiday mood. The hapless **earl of Cardigan** was publicly ridiculed for his role in the debacle, but it also demonstrated the shortcomings of wider military planning. Total casualties climbed to 250,000, many dying not from wounds but from cholera and other contagions. While the originality and success of the medical improvements initiated by the "Lady with the Lamp," **Florence Nightingale**, have been hotly debated since, no one could have made a better media icon.

1861 As the **American Civil War** erupts, Britain remains neutral, dependent upon both grain imports from the northern Union states and cotton imports from the slave-owning Confederacy of southern states.

The first entirely **iron warship**, *HMS Warrior*, is launched. Prince Albert contracts typhoid and dies in December. **Queen Victoria** will mourn the loss of her husband for the rest of her long life.

Mrs Isabella Beeton publishes her *Book of Household Management*, a comprehensive practical guide for middle-class housewives that quickly becomes a bestseller.

1862 Gladstone enhances his reputation as a popular reformer by undertaking the first of several tours of northern England.

As **cotton supplies** from the American slave states are interrupted, a British-built war vessel, the *Alabama*, inflicts damage on Union shipping.

At ten minutes past eleven our Light Cavalry advanced. The whole Brigade scarcely made one effective regiment, according to the numbers of continental armies, and yet it was more than we could spare. As they rushed toward the front, the Russians opened fire on them from the guns in the redoubt on the right, with volleys of musketry and rifles. They swept proudly past, glittering in the morning sun in all the pride and splendour of war. We could scarcely believe the evidence of our senses! Surely that handful of men were not going to charge an army in position? Alas, it was but too true—their desperate valour knew no bounds, and far indeed was it removed from its so-called better part—discretion.

—W.H. Russell,
The British Expedition to the Crimea (1858)

Gilbert Scott designs the **Albert Memorial** for London's Hyde Park, the first of several projects to commemorate the prince. Others will include the nearby **Albert Hall** and the **Albert Bridge** crossing the Thames.

A second great **trade fair** in the capital creates a vogue for Japonaiserie.

Notts F.C. (later Notts County) becomes England's first professional **football club**.

For the first time an **English cricket team** tours **Australia**.

1863 Although the recent "reunification" of Italy by its military leader **Giuseppe Garibaldi** has been warmly welcomed in England, the progressive unification of an industrialized **Germany** by the Prussian **Otto von Bismarck** is viewed with mounting apprehension because it threatens Britain's imperial and commercial interests.

The **London Metropolitan Railway** marks the beginning of the world's first underground railway system.

Charles Kingsley publishes *The Water Babies*—a children's book that practically caricatures the Victorian belief in the innocence of children.

1865 Lord Palmerston's continuing popularity ensures a handsome Liberal victory in a July **general election**, but in October he dies. **Lord Russell** becomes prime minister, and agrees to consider further changes to the electoral system under pressure from **Gladstone** and the **Manchester Reform Union**. The **Reform League** is founded, a nationwide association of political radicals.

William Booth establishes his **Christian Mission**—later the **Salvation Army**—to alleviate the suffering of Britain's increasing number of urban destitutes.

The Reverend **Charles Dodgson**, an Oxford mathematician writing under the pseudonym **Lewis Carroll**, publishes *Alice's Adventures in Wonderland*, a children's fantasy constructed out of logical absurdities.

1866 Following almost two decades of steady economic growth there is a sudden panic amongst Britain's financial institutions, leading to a run on the banks on May 11, known as "**Black Friday**." **Lord Russell**, already faced by a split among his ranks over the matter of reform, is unable to manage the crisis, and resigns in June. **Lord Derby** becomes prime minister for a third time at the head of a minority government.

DARWINISM

*F*ew books have had as profound an impact on modern culture as *On the Origin of Species*. By apparently establishing the principle of biological evolution, its author **Charles Darwin** (1809–82) not only provided a framework for work in the "life" sciences worldwide, but challenged Christian and other scriptural accounts of creation.

That it did so was partly due to the thoroughness with which Darwin presented his thesis: namely, that all existing species in the plant and animal kingdoms are relatively complex adaptations of earlier, less complex life forms, and that those adaptations are brought about by mutation and inheritance. To prove his case Darwin left no stone unturned. The first-hand observations he made while voyaging on the *HMS Beagle*—including descriptions of new species of turtle and finch in the Galapagos Islands—were central to his research, but Darwin's argument was also sustained by findings from fields such as embryology and morphology. He cast his net outside biology, too: **Thomas Malthus**'s *Essay on the Principle of Population* (1798) gave Darwin the idea of the "struggle for existence," from which came the notion that adaptive advantage and evolutionary success are directly related; and **Sir Charles Lyell**'s ground-breaking *Principles of*

Following decades of unrest in **Ireland**, the **Irish Republican Brotherhood** (also known as the **Fenians**), a new militant grouping seeking the end of English rule, begin to campaign.

Dr Thomas John Barnardo opens a home for orphans in **London**.

The **Amateur Athletics Association** is founded.

The **Marquis of Queensbury** sets out a code of rules for **boxing**.

Geology (1830–32) described a huge swathe of prehistoric time in which the gradual processes of biological evolution were able to take place. Evolution was not exactly a new idea, though. The French biologist Jean-Baptiste Lamarck had proposed the inheritance of acquired characteristics as an evolutionary mechanism back in the 1790s, and Darwin himself was only persuaded to publish his findings because another Englishman, Alfred Wallace, had arrived at a similar theory independently.

Within hours of its publication the *Origin* had sold out, and it immediately created a furor—not least because Darwin's examination of the fossil record indicated evolutionary dead ends that undermined the idea of a divinely purposed creationist program. Darwin was reluctant to engage in theological controversy, however, leaving it to his champion T.H. Huxley (1826–95) to publicly fight the evolutionist corner. It also befell an obscure Austrian monk, Gregor Mendel (1822–84), who studied pea plants at a monastery in Brno, to discover genetics—the "chance" biological mechanism that has underpinned the scientific validity of Darwinian evolution in the 20th century and beyond. Ironically, a paper by Mendel found its way into Darwin's library at Down House in Kent, but at Darwin's death its pages remained uncut.

1867 In February the **Fenians** begin campaigning on the mainland, attacking a police barracks in **Chester**, followed by an assault on **Clerkenwell Prison** in **London** during which twelve people are killed.

LORD PALMERSTON
(1784–1865)

*H*enry John Temple, 3rd Viscount Palmerston, was a curiously modern politician, and one often accused of being of no fixed political abode. During a long career he served in Tory, Canningite, Whig and Liberal governments. He was war secretary once, foreign secretary three times, home secretary once and prime minister twice. Most innovatively, he actively wooed popular success, writing articles and leaking information to the *Morning Post*.

Palmerston ruthlessly promoted Britain's imperial ambitions, advocating and frequently employing his patented "gunboat diplomacy" as a way of cajoling other nations to respect and abide by his concept of a "Pax Britannica." Both Queen Victoria and Prince Albert found his high-handedness in dealing with foreign monarchs (not to mention his reluctance to brief them properly) outrageous, and were always looking for excuses to fire him. In an earlier age enemies such as these would have ruined Palmerston, but in the circumstances of the mid-19th century he could demonstrate to the full his skills as a political survivor. When he died, the *Times* obituary column cattily remarked: "constant only in the retention of office ... his one principle was that of the Vicar of Bray," drawing a parallel between Palmerston's political principles and that of the famous 17th-century cleric who made self-preservation his sole policy.

On August 15 Parliament passes the **Second Reform Act**, which extends the franchise to 36 percent of adult males aged 21 and over. A companion bill to give **women** the vote fails.

Joseph Lister pioneers the use of **antiseptics** in surgery.

1868 Amidst fierce political infighting, **Benjamin Disraeli** scrambles to the top of what he calls the "greasy pole" and replaces Derby as prime minister on February 27. But his minority Conservative government collapses after the Liberals convincingly win a November election, and on December 3 **W.E. Gladstone** becomes prime minister.

The first **Trades Union Congress** is held.

The **Royal Historical Society** is founded.

1869 The opening of the **Suez Canal**, linking the Mediterranean to the Red Sea, dramatically reduces the journey time of goods and people between Britain and its eastern possessions.

A **Contagious Diseases Act** gives police the power to arrest prostitutes but not their clients, and therefore does little to halt the spread of syphilis and other venereal infections in England.

1870 William Forster's **Elementary Education Act** provides for state-funded elementary schools to be established wherever church schools do not already furnish an equivalent facility.

Entry into the **British Civil Service** by competitive examination is introduced, based on an already successful similar system in India.

A **Married Women's Property Act** for the first time gives married women significant legal rights over their own possessions.

Disraeli sets out to rebuild the **Conservative Party**, which opens a **Central Office** to co-ordinate the party's activities across the country.

In July, the **Franco-Prussian War** erupts and a German army invades France, but Britain stands aloof.

The novelist **Charles Dickens** dies.

1871 **Gladstone**'s Liberal government passes the **Trade Union Act**, for the first time giving unions legal status.

1872 Swayed by a vociferous temperance movement, the government passes a **Licensing Act** that regulates and restricts the sale and consumption of alcohol.

The **Ballot Act** introduces the secret ballot into British elections.

BENJAMIN DISRAELI (1804–81)

*D*israeli did more than any other 19th-century politician to adjust his party to the needs of an electorate that was larger than ever before, transforming the declining Tories to the rebranded "Conservatives," who went on to dominate Britain well beyond his death. Put simply, he realized the way to win votes was to offer populist policies—or at least policies that could, with adequate spin, be made to look populist. Looked at one way, this was a triumph for democracy. Looked at another, it was blatant opportunism, a charge from which Disraeli has never been wholly exonerated.

Perhaps his background had something to do with this chameleonic instinct. His father, Isaac, was of Italian–Jewish descent and, but for an altercation with the local synagogue, Benjamin would never have been baptized a Christian—which would have automatically barred him from any kind of political career. Having tried and failed to become the Whig member for Wycombe in 1832, he drifted towards the Tories, and was elected MP for Maidstone in 1837. His maiden Commons speech was judged a failure, but he made his mark by demonstrating that he had a head for figures and

Marian (or Mary Anne) Evans, a well-known editor and translator, completes what many regard as her masterpiece, the novel *Middlemarch*, which she publishes under the pseudonym **George Eliot**.

Thomas Hardy publishes *Under the Greenwood Tree*, the first of his "Wessex" novels, exploring rural and town life in the West Country.

1873 A "**New Domesday**" survey of England reveals that 80 percent of the land is owned by only seven thousand people.

adopting an independent line on specific issues. Marriage to the widowed Anne Wyndham Lewis gave him status and financial security, though these were insufficient to obtain office in Peel's 1841 government—a setback Disraeli met by reviving an earlier interest in fiction, publishing a trilogy of books (*Coningsby*, *Sybil and Tancred*) between 1844 and 1847 that have sometimes been considered the first political novels in English.

Peel's death in 1850 revived Disraeli's parliamentary fortunes. Determined to reunite the Tories, he emerged as their natural leader in the Commons, and in 1852 briefly became chancellor under **Lord Derby**. Disraeli made his mark overseeing the **Second Reform Bill** in 1867, and a year later became prime minister for a few months. After six years in opposition, during which time he greatly strengthened the Conservatives' party organization, he returned to power in 1874, and remained there another six years— much to the satisfaction of Queen Victoria. Gladstone, she found, always addressed her "as though I were a public meeting," but "Dizzie" knew how to lay on the charm. In 1876 he saw to it that she was proclaimed empress of India, and so the Tories became the party of Crown and Empire.

The first season of the cricket **County Championship** is dominated by the tall, heavily bearded figure of **Dr W.G. Grace**, unrivalled as both batsman and bowler.

1874 Disraeli becomes prime minister for a second time in February.

1875 On Disraeli's initiative Britain acquires a controlling interest in the **Suez Canal** from the Egyptian leader, thus guaranteeing passage of its vessels to eastern waters.

As trade union membership steadily increases, a new **Trades Union Act** legalises peaceful picketing.

Trial By Jury, the first of the "**Savoy**" **operettas** written by **W.S. Gilbert** and set to music by **Arthur Sullivan**, is produced by **Richard D'Oyly-Carte** at the Royalty Theatre, London.

1876 Queen Victoria is proclaimed **Empress of India** by Disraeli's Conservative government in April.

In India, **Viceroy Lord Lytton** attempts to establish a protectorate in **Afghanistan** as **Russia** continues to exert pressure in Central Asia.

In August Disraeli is created **earl of Beaconsfield**. In September his political adversary **Gladstone** orchestrates an anti-Turkish campaign following a massacre of Christians by Turks in **Bulgaria**.

1877 The **Society for the Protection of Ancient Buildings** is founded by craftsman and artist **William Morris**, primarily in order to preserve medieval buildings from modern development.

1878 Following a Russo-Turkish war, Disraeli attends the **Congress of Berlin**. He returns to England proudly announcing "peace ... with honor." In return for providing limited military guarantees for a greatly diminished Ottoman empire, Britain gains control of Cyprus. Anglo-Turkish relations are soon soured, though, when Turkey develops an alliance with **Austro-Germany**.

The **Bicycling Touring Club** is founded.

> You have accused me of being a flatterer. It is true. I am a flatterer.
> I have found it useful. Everyone likes flattery; and when you come
> to Royalty you should lay it on with a trowel.
>
> —Benjamin Disraeli,
> speaking to Matthew Arnold c.1880,
> in G.W.E. Russell, *Collections and Recollections* (1898)

1879 In **southern Africa**, British forces set about subjugating the **Zulu** nation. Disaster threatens when 895 British troops are massacred at **Isandhlwana**, but 140 British troops resist an all-out assault by 4000 Zulu warriors at **Rorke's Drift** in March.

An uprising in **Afghanistan** in September leads to armed intervention by British Indian forces, but the results are inconclusive.

Campaigning in Scotland, **Gladstone** comes out strongly against the pursuit of imperial policies in **Africa** and **Afghanistan**.

The British government is dismayed by the formation of the **Irish Land League**, which openly calls for Irish independence.

The **telephone** is introduced into England from the USA.

John Henry Newman is made a cardinal by **Pope Leo XIII**.

1880 Following a Conservative defeat in a March **general election**, **Lord Beaconsfield** (Disraeli) resigns in April and Gladstonebecomes prime minister. **Gladstone** moves swiftly to pull British troops out of **Afghanistan**, but in December he is drawn into the **1st Boer War** in southern Africa when the Dutch Boers declare a **Boer Republic** independent of Britain's **Cape Colony**.

1881 Following a series of military defeats, Britain concedes Boer independence in the **Transvaal** and **Orange Free State** by the **Treaty of Pretoria** in April.

I would not be too much impressed by what the soldiers tell you about the strategic importance of these places. If they were allowed full scope they would insist on the importanc • of garrisoning the moon in order to protect us from Mars.

—Lord Salisbury
commenting on the continuing acquisition of African colonies,
in a letter to Sir Edward Baring, February 5, 1892

The arrest and imprisonment of the Irish patriot **Charles Stewart Parnell** creates a further surge of anti-English feeling in Ireland.

1882 In May **Parnell** is released from prison. Four days later the secretary of state for Ireland, **Lord Frederick Cavendish**, and his deputy are assassinated by Fenians in Dublin. As a result, the powers of the Irish constabulary are greatly extended, but "terrorist" activities revive on the mainland.

In July, British troops are deployed to defend the **Suez Canal** from Egyptian nationalists—the first step in a strategy that leads to the annexation of many further African territories in the hope that this will curtail any further threats.

1883 British forces begin a two-year campaign in **Burma** to suppress a "native" uprising led by **Ba Thone**.

The recently restored peace in Egypt is threatened by the Islamic leader **Mohammed Ahmed ibn-Seyyid Abdullah** (known as the **Mahdi**), who raises revolt in the Egyptian-controlled territory of **Sudan**.

1884 General Charles Gordon campaigns against the Mahdi on behalf of the Egyptian government, but without support from London becomes trapped in the Sudanese city of **Khartoum** in March.

In November, Parliament passes a **Third Reform Act**, doubling the size of the (male) electorate.

In London, the socialist **Fabian Society** is founded. Its members include the social reformers **Sidney** and **Beatrice Webb**, the author **H.G. Wells**, the future prime minister **Ramsay MacDonald** and the Irish playwright **George Bernard Shaw**.

Partly in response to pressure created by **Josephine Butler** and her "moral purity alliance," Gladstone's government passes a **Criminal Law Amendment Act** that raises the age of consent for girls to 16, outlaws brothels and introduces harsh penalties for homosexuals— though lesbianism remains legal as Queen Victoria supposedly refuses to acknowledge its existence when she comes to sign the Act.

1885 Because of the late arrival of a British relief force, **Khartoum** falls to the **Mahdi** on January 26. Gordon and his soldiers are massacred—an event that evokes calls for greater strong-arm methods in Africa.

The war in **Burma** ends with British suzerainty now extending into the upper reaches of the country. As imperial sentiments stiffen, Gladstone's Liberals are defeated in a June general election, and a new Conservative government under **Lord Salisbury** takes power.

The Mikado, the latest operetta by Gilbert and Sullivan, is premiered at the Savoy Theatre in London. Reflecting the fashionable vogue for all things Japanese, this astoundingly popular production will run for 672 performances in all.

1886 Salisbury's government falls in January, and **Gladstone** becomes prime minister for a third time at the beginning of February. In April he attempts to introduce a **Home Rule** (self-rule) bill for **Ireland**, but this divides his Liberal Party. **Joseph Chamberlain** resigns from the cabinet, the bill is defeated in July, and the Conservatives win a snap **general election**. **Salisbury** returns as prime minister, at the head of a coalition government, appointing his nephew **Andrew Balfour** secretary of state for Ireland.

1888 Local government is reformed with the passing of the **County Councils Act**, providing for elected local authorities.

The *Financial Times* newspaper is founded.

The **English Football League** is established.

"**Jack the Ripper**," a murderer of unknown identity, terrorizes London's East End prostitutes.

1889 A month-long strike by **dockers** in London beginning in mid-August threatens to bring England's economy to a halt.

1890 The **National Telephone Company**, with near-monopolistic powers, is established under license from the Post Office.

W.E. GLADSTONE (1809–98)

*G*ladstone, one of the great reforming statesmen of the Victorian era, was prime minister four times between 1868 and 1894. Born into a wealthy Liverpool merchant family, he trod the conventional path of late Victorian statesmen—education at Eton and Oxford, marriage into the aristocracy—and first became an MP in 1833 via the duke of Newcastle's patronage, representing Newark. He made an immediate impression with impassioned speeches about slavery, religion and Ireland. Within a year he was given a ministerial appointment in Peel's government, and in 1835 was promoted to undersecretary for the colonies. He was again given office by Peel in 1841, but resigned in 1845 after objecting to an offer of public funds to the Roman Catholic college at Maynooth in Ireland. It wasn't long before he was back in office, however, this time as colonial secretary. Having lost Newcastle's confidence, he also lost his Newark seat, but in 1847 became the member for the University of Oxford. He remained a Peelite until 1859 when he astonished everyone by crossing the floor to

1891 The Anglo-Irish aesthete **Oscar Wilde** courts notoriety by the publication of his novel *The Picture of Dorian Gray*, condemned by many for its ambiguous celebration of moral decadence.

1892 An August **general election** returns the Liberal Party to power. **Gladstone** becomes prime minister for the fourth time.

Keir Hardie, a Scottish socialist, is returned as MP for London's West Ham constituency.

1893 Led by **Keir Hardie**, the **Independent Labor Party** is formed

serve in Palmerston's administration as chancellor of the exchequer. After Palmerston's death he remained with the Liberals, serving first under Lord Russell and then becoming party leader.

Although Gladstone never abandoned his commitment to the Church of England—the inspiration of his markedly moral character—he modified his early conservatism to a more equitable (and ultimately more radical) politics. But although his own first administration (1868–74) was able to introduce the **disestablishment** of the Church of Ireland and the **Irish Land Act** of 1870, he failed in what became his dominant long-term objective—**Irish Home Rule**. Because of the entrenched interests of the mainland British establishment, Anglo-Irish landowners and the large Protestant community in Ulster, the Irish question remained intractable. Even his great adversary, **Benjamin Disraeli**, struggled to criticize the politician who did more than most to make Britain a fairer place—he said of Gladstone, only half tongue-in-cheek, that "he has not a single redeeming defect."

in Bradford specifically to represent and advance the interests of working-class people.

A second **Irish Home Rule Bill**, sponsored by Gladstone, is defeated in the House of Lords.

1894 **Gladstone**'s government falls in March following the prime minister's failure to promote Irish Home Rule, but the Liberals remain in power under the new prime minister, **Lord Rosebery**.

The first issue of *The Yellow Book*, a quarterly literary and art magazine, appears. Its notoriety as a "decadent" publication derives largely from the flamboyant drawings of its art editor **Aubrey Beardsley**, who had achieved notoriety with his illustrations for Wilde's Salomé a year earlier.

1895 In a June **general election**, Rosebery's Liberals are defeated, and **Lord Salisbury** forms a Conservative administration. Also defeated are every one of the **Independent Labor Party**'s 28 candidates.

Frederick Lanchester manufactures England's first four-wheel motor car.

The **London School of Economics** is founded by members of the Fabian Society.

The **National Trust** is founded to protect Britain's natural and architectural heritages.

Oscar Wilde, now a successful playwright and one of London's best-known artistic figures, is sentenced to two years in prison for homosexual offences after bringing an unsuccessful libel case against the **Marquis of Queensberry**.

1896 An Anglo-Egyptian force under the command of **Horatio Herbert Kitchener** begins the pacification of **Sudan**.

War between Britain and Germany is narrowly averted after **Kaiser Wilhelm II** sends a telegram to the Boer leader **Paul Kruger** congratulating him on a successful raid against Britain's **Cape Colony** in South Africa.

Alfred Harmsworth (later Lord Northcliffe) founds the *Daily Mail* newspaper, promising his readers that in it "four leading articles, a page of parliament, and columns of speeches will NOT be found."

England's first **cinema** opens in London's **Leicester Square**.

The Italian inventor-entrepreneur **Guglielmo Marconi** creates the world's first **radio station** on the Isle of Wight.

1897 Celebrating her Diamond Jubilee, Queen Victoria makes use of the **electric telegraph** to send messages to her subjects worldwide.

The physicist **J.J. Thomson** advances atomic theory by postulating the existence of **electrons** and a **nucleus** within every atom.

1898 Despite French interference, Kitchener completes the pacification of **Sudan**, following a brutal victory over Sudanese forces at **Omdurman** on September 2.

H.G. Wells publishes *The War of the Worlds*, a tale of alien invasion.

1899 Tensions between Britons and Dutch Boers in southern Africa escalate into all-out war in October—the beginning of the **Second Boer War**. Ill-prepared British forces are besieged at **Mafeking**, **Kimberley** and **Ladysmith**. At home, such affronts to national imperial pride are greeted with near-hysteria in the press.

The first performance of **Edward Elgar**'s *Enigma Variations* marks the emergence of the first internationally regarded English composer since Henry Purcell.

1900 Following the appointment of **General Frederick Roberts** as commander-in-chief against the Boers, **Kimberley** is relieved on February 15, **Ladysmith** on February 28 and **Mafeking** on May 17. Further British successes lead to the annexation of the **Transvaal** and **Orange Free State**. But the Boers prolong the war by adopting guerilla tactics. Roberts' replacement, **Lord Kitchener**, rounds up 120,000 Boer civilians in **concentration camps**, where one in six die of neglect and malnutrition.

In China, Britain leads its fellow European powers, Russia and the USA, in suppressing the "anti-imperialist" **Boxer Rebellion**. Largely as a result of "great power" reprisals, China's own imperial system will collapse at the end of 1911.

1901 On January 1 Britain's Australian colonies are formally amalgamated to form the **Commonwealth of Australia**.

On January 22, after 64 years on the throne, **Queen Victoria** dies. She is succeeded by her son **Prince Albert**, crowned as **Edward VII**.

As Boer resistance continues, **Kitchener** orders the construction of **blockhouses** (fortifications built to house small groups of troops) to defeat their guerilla tactics.

Seebohm Rowntree publishes *Poverty: A Study of Town Life*, based on a survey of York. His conclusion—that poverty is a social rather than a legal phenomenon—will have far-reaching consequences for 20th-century social and political planning.

An inexperienced naval officer, **Robert Falcon Scott**, sets out aboard *HMS Discovery* to conduct scientific research in Antarctica.

The **population** of the United Kingdom (including Ireland) rises to forty million, with London accounting for over six million people.

1902 Lord Salisbury resigns as prime minister in July, and is replaced by his nephew **Arthur James Balfour**.

In May the Boer War ends with the **Treaty of Vereeniging**, the Boers conceding British sovereignty in South Africa.

The first of **Beatrix Potter**'s illustrated children's books, *The Tale of Peter Rabbit*, is published.

1903 Allying herself with the Independent Labor Party, **Emmeline Pankhurst** founds the **Women's Social and Political Union** to lobby for the right of women to vote. Her followers swiftly become known as **suffragettes**.

Queen Victoria in the year of the Diamond Jubilee, 1897

Ramsay MacDonald, secretary of the newly formed Labor **Representation Committee**, concludes an anti-Conservative pact with the **Liberal Party**.

The **Conservative Party**, also known as the **Unionist Party** because of its opposition to Home Rule for Ireland, is damaged by the resignation of **Joseph Chamberlain**, after Chamberlain fails to persuade Balfour to safeguard the Empire by adopting protectionist **trade tariffs**. Balfour finds sympathy among Liberals, however, who contest that protectionism will only raise domestic food prices.

1904 Britain and France enter into an **Entente Cordiale**, a mutual defense pact aimed principally against **German expansionism** but also against **Russia**.

Scott's Antarctic expedition returns home with a new "furthest south" record, but having failed to reach the South Pole.

1905 Emmeline Pankhurst's suffragettes resort to hunger strikes, arson and other "public outrages" to publicize their cause.

Balfour resigns as prime minister, replaced on December 4 by **Sir Henry Campbell Bannerman**, who is committed to free trade.

Before the Boer war, we were spoiling for a fight ... Any government here, during the last ten years of the last century, could have had a war by lifting a finger. The people would have shouted for it. They had a craving for excitement, and a rush of blood to the head. Now, this generation has had enough of excitement, and has lost a little blood, and is sane and normal.

—**Foreign Secretary Edward Grey,
in a communication to
President Theodore Roosevelt, 1906**

THE EARLY LABOUR PARTY

Concerns within England's ruling elite that the electoral reforms of 1832, 1867 and 1884 would inevitably place government in the hands of the "great unwashed" proved to have little substance. Partly this was because the existing Liberal and Tory parties had already grasped the importance of electioneering; partly because the British working class was more diverse in its loyalties and opinions than upper-crust alarmists imagined; and partly because working men were slow to organize themselves politically. The Liberals had always claimed to represent the interests of labor, and the Conservatives did their best to assert likewise.

But the creation of an Independent Labour Party by Keir Hardie in 1893 began a process in which the political realities began—slowly—to change. The ILP's big strategy was to woo voters away from other parties by forging an alliance with the trade unions. Initially this failed— the unions had their own agendas, and in any case their restrictive practices made them less than ideal in the eyes of some wage earners. As a result the ILP performed disastrously in the 1895 general election. But Hardie and his followers persisted, and an agreement with the unions in 1900 (coupled with the formation of a Labour Representation Committee) consolidated the ILP's impact. Almost as important was the fact that the Liberals had begun to buckle, agreeing with Labour not to contest certain parliamentary seats in the hope of keeping out the Unionist Conservatives. In the long term, though, it was the two world wars of the 20th century that cemented Labour's place in British politics. The men who had fought and died for "King and Country" demanded a better deal when peace resumed.

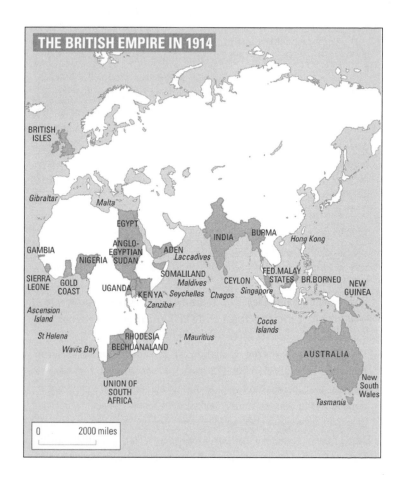

THE BRITISH EMPIRE IN 1914

BRITISH
ISLES

Gibraltar

Malta

EGYPT

ANGLO-
EGYPTIAN
SUDAN

GAMBIA

NIGERIA

ADEN
Laccadives

INDIA   BURMA   Hong Kong

SIERRA
LEONE   GOLD
COAST

SOMALILAND
Maldives

CEYLON   FED. MALAY
STATES   BR. BORNEO   NEW
GUINEA

UGANDA

KENYA   Seychelles   Chagos   Singapore

Zanzibar

Ascension
Island

St Helena

RHODESIA

Mauritius

Cocos
Islands

AUSTRALIA

Wavis Bay

BECHUANALAND

UNION OF
SOUTH
AFRICA

New
South
Wales

Tasmania

0   2000 miles

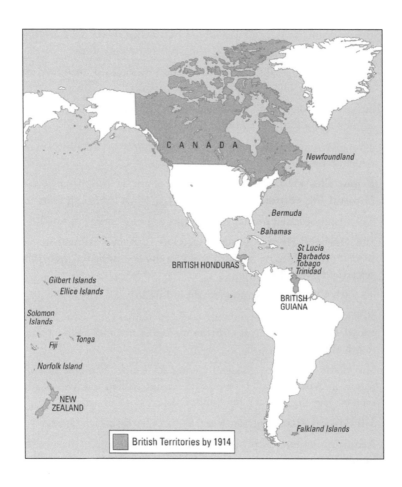

CANADA

Newfoundland

Bermuda

Bahamas

St Lucia
Barbados
Tobago
Trinidad

BRITISH HONDURAS

BRITISH
GUIANA

Gilbert Islands
Ellice Islands

Solomon
Islands

Fiji   Tonga

Norfolk Island

NEW
ZEALAND

Falkland Islands

British Territories by 1914

1906 In a January **general election** the **Labor Party** wins 29 seats in the Commons, but the **Liberals** are returned to power and **Campbell Bannerman** continues as prime minister.

Britain launches the first "modern" **battleship**, *HMS Dreadnought*. Germany responds by ordering its own fleet of battleships.

In England, the **Rolls Royce Company** is founded, dedicated to manufacturing advanced luxurious automobiles.

1907 As perceptions of a "German threat" grow, Britain and France admit **Russia** into the **Entente Cordiale**.

The government introduces **free school meals** as part of its social reform program.

Ernest Shackleton sets out for the Antarctic in command of the **Nimrod Expedition**, aiming like Scott to reach the South Pole.

The first motorized **public omnibuses** begin operating in London.

1908 Herbert Henry Asquith succeeds Campbell Bannerman as Liberal prime minister in April and introduces a **national pension scheme** for the elderly.

The **4th Olympic Games** are held in London.

1909 To pay for the government's social spending, chancellor **David Lloyd George** introduces a **surtax** on higher incomes and increases **death duties**.

Shackleton returns to England having set a new "furthest south" record in **Antarctica**. He is praised for not risking the lives of his men by pressing to reach the South Pole.

1910 Edward VII dies on May 6, and is succeeded by his son **George V**.

Asquith continues as prime minister after the Liberals win a fresh **general election**.

Captain Scott sets out on a second South Pole expedition, competing against the veteran Norwegian explorer **Roald Amundsen**.

1911 After prolonged public debate, Asquith's government brings about a major constitutional change by introducing a **Parliament Act** that curtails the powers of the **House of Lords** by abolishing its right of veto over legislation passed by the House of Commons, and by limiting its rights of amendment.

Lloyd George introduces a **National Insurance Bill**, affording selected workers state-funded benefits during sickness and unemployment.

During a year in which international tensions are heightened by German intervention in **Morocco**, traditionally a French sphere of influence, **George V** becomes the first British monarch to visit **India**.

1912 Attempts at an Anglo–German **arms limitation agreement** fail.

Scott reaches the **South Pole** on January 18 only to discover that Amundsen has reached it first. He and his four companions die on the homeward trek.

On April 15 the ***RMS Titanic***, a steam-powered ocean liner run by the White Star Line, sinks after colliding with an iceberg on her maiden voyage across the Atlantic. 1513 of its 2224 passengers and crew drown.

1913 A suffragette, **Emily Davison**, dies after throwing herself in front of the king's horse at the **Epsom Derby** on June 4. The movement attracts further publicity when **Emmeline Pankhurst** is imprisoned for urging her supporters to firebomb the dwelling of David Lloyd George.

1914 The peace of Europe is shattered on June 28 when **Archduke Franz Ferdinand**, heir to the Austrian throne, is assassinated by a Serbian nationalist in **Sarajevo**. A month later to the day Austria invades the **Balkans**. Austria's ally **Germany** declares war on **Russia** on August 1, and on **France** on August 3. On August 4 a German army invades **Belgium**, prompting Britain to **declare war** on Germany the same day.

CHAPTER TEN

England and the Two World Wars

{1914–1945}

THROUGHOUT THE 19TH CENTURY BRITAIN PURSUED A DUAL policy: outside Europe, large-scale imperial expansion; nearer home, the preservation of a "balance of powers." In India, the Far East and Africa, Britain's armed forces were kept busy maintaining order in the colonies and protecting British trade monopolies—the closest heavy fighting was in the distant Crimea. Domestically, the same period was one of comparative tranquility—the only major exception being in Ireland, where a vigorous independence movement began to take shape.

But in 1914, when Germany invaded Belgium, all that changed. The decline of the **Habsburg** and **Ottoman** empires and the emergence of a united Germany determined to rival England upset the European equilibrium in a way that Britain could no longer hope to deal with through diplomacy alone. The **Great War**, later called **World War I**, saw British troops committed directly across the English Channel for the first time since the fall of Napoleon in 1815. And a direct consequence of this conflict was that 25 years later Britain again found itself at loggerheads with Germany, now led by **Adolf Hitler** and the Nazi Party, in what would become known as **World War II**.

Though the second war was more wide-ranging than its predecessor—a truly global conflict—it directly confronted England with the prospect of invasion. During the summer of 1940 the German Luftwaffe relentlessly bombed British ports and cities. And yet invasion was averted: partly because of the courage of British, Canadian and

Polish fighter pilots who prevented German air superiority during the **Battle of Britain**; partly because Hitler turned his attentions instead to the Russian front. Yet until December 1941, when Germany's ally Japan attacked **Pearl Harbor**—and in doing so brought the United States into the war—Britain was largely isolated in its struggle against German and Italian fascism inside Europe itself.

In both World Wars American intervention proved decisive, which in turn brought about an alternative world order. In the years that followed 1945, Britain would find itself gradually displaced from the center of global politics. And even at this early stage, behind the facade of British imperialism there were counter-currents. Because of reforms to the electoral franchise and the introduction of salaries for members of Parliament, the House of Commons began to reflect an increasingly broad spectrum of opinion—not least the socialist aspirations of British labor, which was now strongly organized and eager to agitate for reform. In fact both wars resulted in significant political rewards for more people than ever before. Perhaps the starkest example is that of women: having proved their wage-earning credentials in the munitions factories of World War I, they were finally given the vote in 1918.

But it wasn't just war that accelerated political change. In the 31 years that separated the beginning of World War I from the end of World War II, there were a bewildering variety of events—many of them closely attuned to developments elsewhere in Europe. The **Liberal Party** met its demise as a political force, displaced by Ramsay MacDonald's Labour Party; Stafford Cripps advocated a **Popular Front** in alliance with the USSR; Oswald Mosley launched the **British Union of Fascists** in 1932; the "**Cliveden Set**," directed by Lord and Lady Astor, urged appeasement with Hitler after 1933; and when the **Spanish Civil War** broke out in 1936, hundreds of socialist-minded volunteers eagerly joined the International Brigade to resist General Franco's fascist Falange party.

True to form, however, Britain proved resistant to widespread reform. The dominant figure of the inter-war years was the unobtrusive Conservative prime minister **Stanley Baldwin**, who made a public virtue of his quietist instincts and middle-class moderation. The **Great Depression**, which followed the collapse of America's Wall Street stock market in 1929, brought down government after government abroad, but in Britain its effects were localized. Although unemployment reached a staggering 80 percent in some areas of the country (inciting the **Jarrow March** of 1936, when 200 unemployed workers walked from Tyneside to London to protest), little changed and Baldwin's government was never seriously threatened. Baldwin's hands were at any rate occupied later in the year by the "**constitutional crisis**" initiated by Edward VIII's eagerness to marry the American divorcée Wallis Simpson. The furor the abdication crisis caused (despite being officially held from the British press) demonstrates how little the political life of England had really changed in the opening half of the 20th century.

1914 On August 4 Britain enters **World War I**—known at the time as the **Great War**—by declaring war on Germany following that country's invasion of Belgium. At the end of the month Germany inflicts defeat on Russia at **Tannenburg**, shattering hopes of a swift conclusion to hostilities.

A **British Expeditionary Force (BEF)** is dispatched to the continent and only narrowly escapes encirclement after a breakdown in communications between British and French commands.

The German advance into France is halted at the **Battle of the Marne** in early September. As German forces withdraw beyond **Verdun**, both sides begin constructing networks of **fortified trenches** immediately opposite each other; by the end of the year these stretch from the English Channel to Switzerland. For four years the pattern of the war on this "western front" will consist of heavy artillery exchanges interspersed with desperate attempts to overrun the enemy's lines. In the opening months of this **trench warfare** the English officer corps is devastated, six peers and 85 sons of peers among the fallen, while the BEF as a whole suffers the loss of some 300 troops a day throughout 1914 and 1915.

On the "home front," war fever grips the nation as tens of thousands respond to a call to arms orchestrated by the charismatic secretary for war, **Lord Kitchener**. A minority protest against the growing carnage and, as the conflict develops, increasing numbers of **pacifists** are imprisoned.

Despite the carnage, the opening months of the war see some of the more bizarre camaraderie of warfare extended across the lines, as some of the English and German troops enjoy a **Christmas Day cease-fire** and an ad hoc game of soccer.

1915 In February German submarines armed with torpedoes, known as **U-boats**, begin a blockade of Britain, attacking merchant as well as naval shipping.

Following pressure put upon Prime Minister **Herbert Asquith**'s cabinet by the Admiralty later in February, Britain endeavors to relieve Russia and turn the German flank by opening a new front in the Turkish **Dardanelles**. The doomed campaign gets off to a disastrous start when four Royal Navy battleships and other vessels are lost to mines in the narrow straits.

Disaster continues in April, when an Allied landing force is held down by Turkish fire on the beaches of the **Gallipoli Peninsula**. Troops from Australia and New Zealand (known as the **ANZACs**) sustain particularly high casualties. The failure of the Gallipoli campaign leads to **Winston Churchill** being sacked as first lord of the admiralty in May. The senior naval officer, **Sir John Fisher**, resigns during the summer.

Poison gas (chlorine) is first used in trench warfare by the Germans. When the British and French protest that it is contrary to interna-

World War I recruitment poster featuring Lord Kitchener

tional military law, the Germans claim the Allies have already done so themselves. This is disproved, but by the end of the year both sides are using gas indiscriminately.

On May 7 the passenger liner *Lusitania*, rightly suspected of carrying military supplies, is torpedoed by German U-boats. Among the thousand or so dead are 128 American civilians, increasing pressure on the **United States** to enter the war.

On May 23 **Italy** joins the Allies by declaring war on **Austria**, raising (eventually unrealized) hopes for the creation of a fresh anti-German front.

Bombs are dropped on English cities from German airships, called **zeppelins**, named after their developer **Count Ferdinand von Zeppelin**.

In December the **Dardanelles** campaign is finally abandoned, Churchill being widely blamed for its failure. *The Rainbow*, a novel by **D.H. Lawrence**, is seized by police shortly after its publication on grounds of obscenity.

1916 Between February and July fighting along the Western Front is concentrated around **Verdun**, the defense of which costs the French army 350,000 lives.

On April 24 an insurrection against English rule in the Irish capital **Dublin**, known as the **Easter Uprising**, begins, but is swiftly crushed. Although some 250,000 Irish volunteers are fighting in the British army, the widespread resentment about British rule in Ireland is unmistakable, and the hanging of twenty ringleaders on August 3 only increases it.

On May 21 the two-day **Battle of Jutland** begins, the war's only major engagement between the British and German navies. The British lose more ships, but the German fleet returns to port and remains there for the duration of the war.

An Arab revolt against Turkish rule in **Arabia**, led by **Prince Faisal** with the assistance of the English army officer **T.E. Lawrence**, begins in June.

Under pressure from the French, the British commander-in-chief, **Sir Douglas Haig**, launches an all-out offensive known as the **Battle of the Somme**. On July 1, Britain loses almost 20,000 men, and by the end of the 140-day battle—during which the British army introduces the **tank**—Allied casualties from many countries climb to over 800,000. To replenish its losses, the British government introduces **conscription**.

In July, **Lord Kitchener** drowns on his way to Russia after his ship, *HMS Hampshire*, is torpedoed.

David Lloyd George becomes secretary for war in July.

On November 28 German warplanes begin bombing **London**.

On December 4 Asquith resigns, and **Lloyd George** takes over as prime minister at the head of a coalition War Cabinet.

1917 On February 3 the **USA** severs relations with Germany after British intelligence intercepts the "**Zimmermann telegram**," from the German government to its ambassador in Mexico, urging the latter to encourage Mexico to attack America. On April 6 the USA **declares war** on Germany, and begins transporting troops to Europe.

In May the **convoy system** for protecting merchant ships is set in place, and U-boats become gradually less effective.

On the **Western Front**, shortly after an unreported mutiny amongst British troops at **Étaples**, the **3rd Battle of Ypres**, also known as **Passchendaele**, begins on July 31. Again British and Allied troops fail to break through German lines, and the loss of a further 400,000 men undermines the British army's morale.

In September, as British forces take control of **Palestine**, foreign secretary **Arthur Balfour** declares Britain's support for the creation of a **Jewish homeland** there.

On November 20 the first massed tank attack is made at **Cambrai**; but although the assault achieves instant results, the Germany army repossesses all of its lost ground by the year's end.

The prolific novelist **P.G. Wodehouse** publishes *The Man with Two Left Feet*, a collection of stories that introduces his readership to the monied Bertie Wooster and his redoubtable valet Jeeves.

1918 On March 21, Germany launches the **Ludendorff Offensive**, a "big push" against Allied Forces on the Western Front that lasts until early April. British, French and American forces resist, and begin preparing a **counter-offensive**.

On April 1, Britain's Royal Flying Corps and the Royal Naval Air Service are amalgamated to form the **Royal Air Force**.

WORLD WAR I (1914–18)

*T*he Great War put paid to any lingering notions of warfare as a chivalric pursuit. New developments in weaponry—machine guns, airplanes, tanks, gas shells, specially designed barbed wire—were not accompanied by a revolution in communications technology, so commanders on both sides possessed neither the tactics nor the physical means to develop or control the fighting they initiated. Unable to achieve breakthroughs, armies were left with little choice but to dig in and pound each other with shellfire. Waves of infantry periodically went "over the top" to charge enemy positions or advance the front line, only to be mown down in no-man's-land. The sheer scale of this static conflict is apparent in the fact that by the end of 1914 the front lines extended from the Channel coast all the way to the Swiss border; in some places they were only thirty yards apart.

Nor did the rat-infested trenches themselves offer much in the way of comfort. They filled knee-high with rain, and attempts by the British army to limit lice, "trench foot" and a panoply of other infections were

In the early summer Britain is swept by a peculiarly virulent **influenza epidemic** (the "Spanish flu"), that kills twice as many people worldwide as die fighting in the Great War.

In August, as German defenses begin to crumble, British tanks again demonstrate their usefulness at the **Battle of Amiens**.

In September, **General Edmund Allenby** masterminds the climactic **Battle of Megiddo**, finally breaking the power of the 450-year-old **Ottoman Empire** and ensuring Western access to Middle Eastern **oil reserves** for the rest of the century.

ineffective. Some soldiers (many in "Pals' Brigades," recruited from one town to improve morale) named their trenches after landmarks in an attempt to humanize this new kind of war. Others went mad, or braved the death penalty for desertion and tried to escape. Most hoped to get a "Blighty"—an injury that would get them sent home. Huge numbers of survivors suffered for the rest of their lives from "shell-shock": by 1928 there were 48 mental hospitals catering for 60,000 long-term victims.

All told Britain lost some 960,000 servicemen. Whole villages saw their menfolk disappear, and universities were depleted of students as conscription was introduced for the first time. The "home front" also experienced a new threat, aerial bombardment—technology which had, ironically, been developed to control native populations elsewhere in the Empire. As more and more families lost relatives, the best hope was that this would indeed be "the war to end all wars." In reality it set the pattern for what was to come: the involvement of entire populations in a national war effort and their vulnerability to long-range assault.

After further Allied successes, the German army in Europe falls back on the **Hindenburg Line**. In October a German **naval mutiny** suggests the war may be drawing to a close. On November 7 **Kaiser Wilhelm II** abdicates, and four days later Germany and the Allies sign an **armistice**.

Partly in recognition of **Emmeline Pankhurst's** efforts to organize female labor during the war, a **Representation of the People Act** gives women aged 30 and over the vote.

The **Labor Party**, inspired by the 1917 Russian Revolution, calls for public ownership of "the means of production" in **Clause Four** of its revised constitution.

The pacifist **Lytton Strachey** publishes *Eminent Victorians*, a book that debunks the reputations of Florence Nightingale, General Gordon and other Victorian worthies.

Edward Elgar publishes his *Cello Concerto*, an autumnal work that reflects the composer's feelings about the tremendous futility of war.

1919 On June 28 the **Treaty of Versailles** formally concludes the Great War. Germany and its allies are stripped of their weapons, colonies and even raw materials. Britain immediately gains by the acquisition of territories in German **Southwest Africa**, and a mandate to govern **Palestine**, formerly part of the Ottoman Empire. Britain also takes a prominent role in the **League of Nations**, founded as a consequence of Versailles to safeguard future international security. Reservations about the treaty are felt by many, and are best expressed in *The Economic Consequences of Peace* by **John Maynard Keynes**, who warns that economic penalties can only lead to a resumption of hostilities.

The American-born **Nancy, Lady Astor** becomes the first woman to sit in the House of Commons.

1920 Following a nationwide manhunt, one of the leaders of the 1917 Étaples mutiny, **Percy Toplis**, convicted in his absence of a murder committed after the war, is gunned down outside **Penrith** in Cumbria.

> What passing-bells for these who die as cattle?
> Only the monstrous anger of the guns.
> Only the stuttering rifles' rapid rattle
> Can patter out their hasty orisons.
> No mockeries now for them; no prayers nor bells,
> Nor any voice of mourning save the choirs, –
> The shrill, demented choirs of wailing shells;
> And bugles calling for them from sad shires.
>
> —Wilfred Owen,
> "Anthem for Doomed Youth" (1917)

> The Great War is God's vengeance on the people
> who held women in subjection.
>
> —Dame Christabel Pankhurst

The **Cenotaph**, designed by the renowned architect **Sir Edwin Lutyens** as a tribute to Britain's fallen servicemen, is unveiled in Whitehall, and becomes the focus of an annual commemoration service.

1921 In the face of widespread disturbances in Ireland, Prime Minister **Lloyd George** concludes a pact with the Irish nationalist party **Sinn Féin**. As a result an **Irish Free State** is created, consisting of 26 southern "Catholic" counties. Six predominantly Protestant northern counties remain a part of the United Kingdom, however, and are known as **Northern Ireland**.

1922 In October, Lloyd George's coalition government disintegrates over fears that Britain may be dragged into a war between **Greece** and **Turkey**.

Following a general election in which the Labour Party gains an unprecedented 142 Commons seats under the leadership of **Ramsay MacDonald**, **Andrew Bonar Law** forms a Conservative government.

The **British Broadcasting Company** (later Corporation) begins making public service radio broadcasts.

The American-born poet **T.S. Eliot** publishes *The Waste Land*, a brilliant display of Modernist erudition that employs unsettling and self-consciously complex poetic techniques.

1923 Bonar Law resigns in May after being diagnosed with an incurable cancer of the throat. He is succeeded as Conservative prime minister by the eminently respectable **Stanley Baldwin**. In December Baldwin calls an election to secure his mandate, but the Conservatives suffer heavy losses and the result is a hung parliament. The Liberal and Labour parties decide to co-operate to oust the Tories.

1924 In January **Ramsay MacDonald** becomes Britain's first Labour prime minister, but his coalition government lasts only until November, when Baldwin resumes office.

E.M. Forster publishes *A Passage to India*, a novel that questions the cultural and social assumptions underpinning Britain's imperial ideology

1925 Chancellor **Winston Churchill** announces that Britain will return to the Gold Standard at a fixed rate of $4.80 to the pound. The move is designed to restore confidence in British industry, but is later criticized for prolonging the economic slump.

The popular professional cricketer, **Jack Hobbs**, overtakes W.G. Grace's record of 125 centuries scored in first-class matches.

1926 After the government refuses to renew a subsidy to Britain's **coal miners**, they come out on strike. Coupled with the slow pace of postwar economic recovery, the spread of trade union membership and the recalcitrance of many British managers, this leads to a **General Strike** beginning on May 3, which closes down many industries and virtually all public services. Amidst panic that the state might be overthrown, the **army** is drafted in to restore and maintain order on England's streets, and students and professionals are sworn in as **special constables**. Baldwin's cabinet holds its nerve, however, and the **TUC** (Trades Union Congress) capitulates on May 12. Only the miners remain on strike.

An **Imperial Conference** agrees that neither Britain nor its dominions should be expected to become involved in their own private disputes without the compliance of their own national governments.

1927 The **British Broadcasting Corporation** (formerly the British Broadcasting Company) is re-established by government charter with a monopoly in radio broadcasting and funded by license fees.

Revisions to the **Anglican Prayer Book** revive debate and ill-feeling between the Church of England's two most vociferous factions, the Anglo-Catholics and the Evangelical Protestants.

Virginia Woolf publishes *To the Lighthouse*, a novel that attempts to catalogue the moment-by-moment feelings and impressions of its characters.

1928 New legislation gives women full **electoral equality** with men.

D.H. Lawrence completes his final novel, *Lady Chatterley's Lover*, in Florence, where it is privately printed to avoid prosecution under English obscenity laws. It will not be published in full in England until 1960.

1929 Following the Labour Party's best performance yet in a general election, **Ramsay MacDonald** becomes prime minister for a second time on June 5.

The sudden collapse of the New York stock market, which becomes known as the **Wall Street Crash**, threatens to plunge the whole world into economic recession. In England unemployment soars, particularly in the steel and shipbuilding industries located in the north of the country.

1931 Stricken by financial crisis, Britain abandons the **gold standard**—the system for matching paper currency against actual reserves of gold. MacDonald resigns as prime minister, but returns immediately as head of a coalition **National Government**, stunning his Labour supporters. In an October **general election** the Coalition takes 556 seats, while Labour wins only 51.

In the Far East, the Japanese invasion of **Manchuria** in northeastern China threatens not only Anglo-Chinese commercial relations but Britain's oriental colonies.

THE BLOOMSBURY GROUP

*B*loomsbury" became the shorthand for a group of writers and artists associated with the Bloomsbury area of London, close to the British Museum and London University, from 1907 onwards. Although the group was influenced by the philosopher G.E. Moore—who argued for philosophy to be anchored to direct experience—and shared pacifist beliefs, it never really amounted to a distinctive movement. Rather it was an informal society of gifted individuals who had little interest in espousing a common creed but who decisively influenced cultural life in the early decades of the century.

At Bloomsbury's hub were the Woolfs: **Virginia**, the novelist and essayist whose "stream-of-consciousness" fiction explored new psychological ground; her husband **Leonard**, a left-wing commentator and novelist who set up the Hogarth Press (which printed many Bloomsbury publications); and Virginia's artist sister **Vanessa Bell** and her companion **Duncan Grant**. Orbiting closely round this inner core were the economist **John Maynard Keynes**, whose monetarist theories still influence economic policy; and the biographer–historian **Lytton Strachey**, who scandalized society with

1932 Britain abandons the **free trade** principle with regard to imported foodstuffs, in existence since the repeal of the Corn Laws of 1847. In an agreement reached at the **Ottawa Convention**, Britain's colonies—including the "commonwealths" of **Canada**, **Australia** and **New Zealand**—are exempted from newly imposed tariffs, strengthening what is already an imperial trading bloc.

Imitating Benito Mussolini, the leader of the Italian fascist party, the sometime Labour MP **Sir Oswald Mosley** establishes the **British Union of Fascists**.

Eminent Victorians, a no-holds-barred exposé of various Victorian worthies. There were also a galaxy of other associates, among them the philosopher Bertrand Russell, the society hostess Lady Ottoline Morrell, the orientalist Arthur Waley, the novelist E.M. Forster, the playwright Roger Fry, and Vita Sackville-West—a writer better remembered for the gardens she created at Sissinghurst.

But perhaps it was the gossip about what the Bloomsbury group got up to that proved its most memorable legacy. Its associates developed a reputation for experimental "free living" at Vanessa's farm at Charleston in Sussex, which she had taken partly to help Grant claim exemption from conscription by declaring himself a farm laborer. Strachey might turn up with his devoted companion Dora Carrington or one of a series of male lovers; Maynard Keynes could be accompanied by his Polish wife Lydia Lopokova or, more rarely, Clive Bell. This revolt against what the group saw as Victorian restrictions—whether artistic, sexual or social—reflected less extreme changes in English society, but the group's attitudes were beginning to seem outmoded in the political atmosphere of the early 1930s.

THE GENERAL STRIKE

*B*y 1925 the immediate economic problems thrown up by the war were beginning to abate. Unemployment was falling, and the prime minister, **Stanley Baldwin**, seemed in a good position to reap the political rewards. But all was not well. The coal industry, faced with competition from German and Polish markets, was struggling. Many thought it outmoded, and private mine owners showed little inclination to improve working conditions—indeed they even proposed lowering pay and increasing working hours so that they could keep up with the rest of Europe. It was in this climate that the mine workers walked out on strike in May 1926, joined shortly afterwards by the rest of the unions. In response to this **General Strike**, students and others rallied to make sure that essential services continued to operate, while in some areas strikers engaged in running battles with the police.

Despite expectations that this might prove the overture to the long-awaited "British Revolution," for the most part the strike proved far from radical. The union leaders discouraged its activists from attempting to take over local government, and in most places picketing was good-humored—strikers and police even taking part in games of football against each other. After little more than a week, the strike had collapsed and most returned to work, leaving the miners to continue their solitary protest.

This was to prove the pattern for industrial unrest in England before World War II. The **Jarrow Marches** of 1936—in which some 200 unemployed workers traipsed down to London with their local MP—have remained ingrained in the public imagination, but little was actually achieved by their protest. England was never to experience the kind of industrial and political turmoil seen in the rest of Europe.

In Cambridge, **John Cockcroft** and **Ernest Walton**, working with the New Zealand-born atomic physicist **Ernest Rutherford**, split the atom—an important step towards the creation of **nuclear energy** and **nuclear weapons**.

1933 Sir Owen Williams' Art Deco **Daily Express** building on Fleet Street opens, the first true curtain-walled building to be constructed in London. Other Art Deco buildings of this period include the **Firestone Factory** (1929) and the **Hoover Building** (1935), both by Wallis, Gilbert and Partners.

1935 George V celebrates his **Silver Jubilee**. The coalition National Government, now almost wholly Conservative, wins a substantial majority in a June **general election**. **Stanley Baldwin** replaces

A student volunteer manning a railway signal box during the General Strike of 1926

Ramsay MacDonald as prime minister and promotes legislation that gives **India** limited powers of self-government.

The foreign secretary, **Sir Samuel Hoare**, is forced to resign after the secret "**Hoare–Laval**" **pact** signed with his French counterpart is leaked to the press. The pact itself undermines the League of Nations' demand that **Mussolini** withdraw troops from **Abyssinia** (Ethiopia), which he seeks to make an Italian colony.

1936 George V dies on January 20, and is succeeded by his popular eldest son, David, who takes the name **Edward VIII**. The new king immediately creates a constitutional crisis by announcing his intention to marry an American divorcée, **Wallis Simpson**. The marriage is opposed by Baldwin, senior Church figures and other members of the establishment, and on December 11 Edward abdicates, his brother **George VI** becoming king.

In July **civil war** breaks out in **Spain**. Volunteers from all parts of Britain travel to the peninsula to join the International Brigade in its fight against the fascist leader **Francisco Franco**.

The financial crisis continues, and in October 200 unemployed workers from **Jarrow** in Tyneside—led by their local MP, **Ellen Wilkinson**—march over 300 miles to London to protest at their plight and those of the area.

The BBC launches the first high-definition **television broadcasting** service.

1937 In May, following Baldwin's resignation, **Neville Chamberlain** becomes prime minister.

In June, the ex-king **Edward** marries Wallis Simpson.

1938 In March the German chancellor **Adolph Hitler** seizes **Austria** and annexes it as German territory. He also makes it clear that he intends to incorporate the **Sudetenland**, comprising the German-speaking part of **Czechoslovakia**. During talks held in **Munich** in September Britain and France allow Hitler to have his way in

Czechoslovakia on the understanding he will not attempt further invasions. **Neville Chamberlain**, returning to London, proclaims that he has secured "peace in our time."

Belfast-born **Louis MacNeice** writes *Autumn Journal*, a poem cycle that captures the confused mood of England's younger generation during 1938 as the country is felt to be heading inevitably back to war with Germany.

1939 As the international situation deteriorates both in Europe and the Far East—where **Japan** enlarges its colony in **China**—mainland Britain is subjected to a terrorist campaign of bombings perpetrated by the **IRA** (Irish Republican Army), a group determined to join the "Six Counties" of Northern Ireland to the Irish Republic.

In January **W.H. Auden**, one of the most successful English poets of the century and a committed pacifist, emigrates to America. He is joined by the brilliant young composer **Benjamin Britten** and his companion, the tenor **Peter Pears**.

In the House of Commons, **Chamberlain** is attacked for giving recognition to **General Franco**'s fascist government in Spain.

On August 23 **Hitler** and the Soviet leader **Josef Stalin** conclude a **non–aggression pact**.

On September 1, reneging on its assurances given at Munich the previous year, Germany invades **Poland**. In response, on September 3 **Britain** and **France** jointly **declare war** on Germany, officially beginning **World War II**. On the same day **Winston Churchill**, who has consistently advocated re-armament against the German Nazi threat, returns as **first lord of the admiralty**.

In November, having agreed with Germany to partition **Poland**, the **Soviet Union** attacks **Finland**.

Despite long-overdue preparations for war in Britain, little seems to happen for the first few months of conflict, and this period quickly becomes known as the "**phoney war**." Over 827,000 children are

evacuated from major towns and cities to safety in rural areas, and **rationing** of essential foodstuffs and consumables begins.

In September a 150,000-strong British **expeditionary force** is dispatched to France, and in mid-December the German "pocket battleship" *Graf Spee* (one of several small German ships) is scuttled by its captain in the estuary of the River Plate off **Montevideo** rather than surrender to the Royal Navy.

1940 In April German forces occupy **Denmark** and **Norway**. On May 14 **the Netherlands** falls, and German armies begin marching on **France** and **Belgium**.

On May 7 Chamberlain, widely condemned for his policy of appeasement toward Hitler, resigns and **Winston Churchill** becomes prime minister.

On May 28 **Belgium** falls to Germany, and a day later the **evacuation** of encircled British forces and the remains of the French

My dear Neville, I shall always be an impenitent supporter of what is called the "Munich policy." No one who sat in this place, as I did during the autumn of '38, with almost daily visitations from eminent Canadians and Australians, could fail to realize that war with Germany at that time would have been misunderstood and resented from end to end of the Empire. Even in this country there would have been no unity behind it. We now know that it was inevitable sooner or later; but we owe it all to you that it was later rather than sooner and that we are assuredly going to win it ... Bless you for all you have done for this country.

—Geoffrey Dawson
writing to Neville Chamberlain,
November 1940

army from the port of **Dunkirk** begins, to be completed on June 4. In all 320,000 troops are ferried to safety across the Channel in a flotilla of boats (many of them civilian), but 30,000 men are killed and the French later accuse the British of leaving many of their own soldiers to their fate.

On June 10 Mussolini's Italy **declares war** on the Allies, but the USA remains neutral.

On June 14 German troops enter **Paris**, and eight days later France and Germany sign an **armistice**. To oppose the German occupation in France and other countries, **resistance movements** spring up, increasingly supported by Britain as the war continues.

In June, prior to a planned invasion of Britain itself, German **bombing raids** against England intensify. The raids initially focus on British airbases, but switch to major ports and cities in August. The attempt to defend Britain in the air becomes known, in Churchill's phrase, as the "**Battle of Britain**," in which pilots from the RAF's **Fighter Command** combat the **Luftwaffe**'s bombers and fighters over British territory.

Hitler declares a **naval blockade** against Britain, German submarines once again causing havoc amongst merchant shipping.

On August 23 **nighttime bombing raids** are launched against **London** and, later, other major cities including **Manchester**, **Belfast**, **Sheffield**, **Liverpool**, **Glasgow**, **Hull**, **Plymouth**, **Coventry** and **Sunderland**. These become known colloquially as the "**Blitz**," after the German word for "lightning warfare," *blitzkrieg*. In all some 60,000 civilians die as a result. Hitler's tactics mean that invasion is postponed, however.

In September the **USA** provides Churchill with 50 badly needed **naval destroyers** in return for military rights in **Canada** and the **Caribbean**.

On September 27 Germany, Italy and Japan form the **Axis** coalition, the three states agreeing to assist each other.

In November British forces occupy **Crete** in an endeavor to provide support for **Greece**.

On November 11 the Royal Navy incapacitates the Italian fleet at **Taranto**.

In December **General Archibald Wavell** campaigns successfully against Italian forces in **Libya**.

The *Queen Elizabeth*, the world's largest passenger liner, is launched and immediately requisitioned by the War Office.

1941 Germany invades **Greece** on April 6, and on May 22 British forces evacuate **Crete**.

On May 24 the German battleship *Bismarck* sinks the British flagship *Hood* in the North Atlantic, but is itself sunk three days later.

In **Palestine** Jewish nationalists, led by the **Stern Gang**, begin a terrorist campaign against British administrators.

On June 22 German forces invade the **Soviet Union**, which consequently becomes a British ally.

On December 7 **Japan** launches a surprise attack against the American Pacific fleet at **Pearl Harbor**, Hawaii. On the same day Japan **declares**

We shall not flag or fail. We shall go on to the end, we shall fight in France, we shall fight in the seas and oceans, we shall fight with growing confidence and growing strength in the air, we shall defend our island, whatever the cost may be, we shall fight on the beaches, we shall fight on the landing grounds, we shall fight in the fields and in the streets, we shall fight in the hills; we shall never surrender.

—**Winston Churchill,**
broadcast to the nation
from the House of Commons, June 4, 1940

war on Britain, and the USA **declares war** on Japan as Japanese forces move into British Malaya. On November 11 Germany **declares war** on the USA.

On December 25 Japan seizes **Hong Kong**.

In North Africa, Wavell's campaign flounders as the German **Afrika Korps**, commanded by **Erwin Rommel**, begins assisting the Italians; British forces are pushed eastwards toward **Egypt**.

1942 On February 15 **Singapore**, home to Britain's Far Eastern fleet, falls to **Japan**—an event described by Churchill as "the worst capitulation in British history" after 80,000 imperial troops are taken prisoner. As the Japanese Empire continues to expand, the British **Solomon Islands** are lost in March, and in May **Burma** is overrun. As Japanese forces threaten **India**, there is a resurgence of Indian nationalism, leading to the imprisonment of **Mahatma Gandhi** and other political leaders.

On May 30 British bombers bomb **Cologne**, the start of a continuing air campaign against German industrial centers and civilian targets, masterminded by **Air Chief Marshal Arthur "Bomber" Harris**.

Although Rommel takes **Tobruk** on June 21, a British bastion in **Libya**, his advance upon Egypt is decisively rebuffed by the British 8th Army under the inspirational command of **General Bernard Montgomery** at **El Alamein** during October and November.

On the Eastern Front, the German assault on **Russia** becomes bogged down in the brutal siege of **Stalingrad**, which begins in August.

In November Allied forces in **North Africa** are placed under the overall command of the American general **Dwight Eisenhower**.

The Oxford academic **W.H. Beveridge** completes a report outlining a program for far-reaching social reconstruction once the war is finished; in retrospect it will be regarded as the blueprint for the **"welfare state."**

Gilbert Murray founds the **Oxford Committee for Famine Relief** (later Oxfam), a charitable organization that will become a leading relief agency in the postwar fight against famine in developing countries.

1943 In the Pacific, US forces recapture the **Solomon Islands** and other islands from the Japanese.

On May 7 the capture of **Tunis** by the British 8th Army effectively ends Germany's African campaign, enabling African ports and cities

WORLD WAR II (1939–45)

*N*early sixty million people died as a result of World War II. The majority of them were civilians (unlike during the Great War) and many of them lived in Russia and the Far East, where nuclear weapons were deployed for the first time by the USA against Japan. The war was really a conflation of two separate conflicts—one against Hitler's "Third Reich," the other against an equally warlike Japanese Empire—but because Germany, Japan and Mussolini's Italy clubbed together to form the **Axis**, the war came to be seen (by the Allies at least) as a single struggle against a dark totalitarian menace.

In the long term there were two winners: the **Soviet Union** and its temporary ally, the **USA**. Only American intervention made victory possible, and this hard fact also confirmed that Britain's age of empire was drawing to a close. The **"cold war"** between the two superpowers dominated the world order after 1945, and America's huge investment in rebuilding Western Europe ensured that it would stay on the side of the USA. Many in Britain and America had regarded Stalin's totalitarian state as quite as much a threat as Nazi Germany, and the aftermath of the war saw their fears realized as Stalin extended his influence over a communist bloc covering most

to be used as bases for an assault on **Sicily**, which falls into Allied hands in July.

As British and American forces create bridgeheads in southern Italy, **Mussolini** resigns on July 28. Earlier in July, the Soviet army inflicts a defeat on Germany at **Kursk**.

On September 8 the Italian government formally **surrenders**, but fierce fighting against German forces in Italy continues.

of Eastern Europe, while other communist regimes secured power in **China**, **North Korea** and **Vietnam**.

Yet Britain's involvement in the conflict—whatever its original reasons for joining—was far from insignificant. British forces reversed the German–Italian occupation of North Africa, fought side-by-side with American troops in Italy and were a main component in the D-Day landings. In the Far East, having lost Malaya, Singapore and Burma, Britain fought back against Japan, saving its interests in India in the process. In the Atlantic, the Royal Navy countered German U-boats intent on destroying life-supporting convoys from America; and the Royal Air Force defended Britain with its fighters, and later helped to bring about the end of the Third Reich by its devastating raids on German towns and cities.

On the home front, too, there was a massive mobilization of resources—assisted by the government's tight control of information and an effective propaganda apparatus. In the face of devastating air raids on Britain's cities, many people performed their civilian duties, putting in long hours in weapons and munitions factories, coping with rationing by whatever means and "digging for victory" in an attempt to maximize agricultural production.

In late November, **Churchill**, **President Franklin Roosevelt** and **Stalin** meet in **Teheran** to co-ordinate strategy.

Barnes Wallis invents the "**bouncing bomb**," used by RAF "dambusters" to create floods in the **Ruhr Valley**, Germany's industrial heartland.

BLETCHLEY PARK

*I*n 1923 two publications shocked the defeated German military into reappraising their communications strategy. One was Winston Churchill's *The World Crisis*; the other was the Royal Navy's official history of World War I. Both revealed that the British had succeeded in breaking the Germans' codes regularly throughout the war. The Germans' response was the Enigma machine: a complex encrypting device that even in its simplest form necessitated a code breaker working through a possible 10,000,000,000,000,000 permutations before the hidden message could be deciphered.

When World War II broke out, the Allies discovered that they were totally unprepared to deal with Germany's new secret weapon. Fortunately, others had not been so complacent. The Poles had invested considerable energy into cracking Enigma in the 1930s, and thanks to the inspirational breakthrough of one of their most talented code breakers, Marian Rejewski, had invented a "bombe"—a mechanical apparatus—that enabled them to break the code. Shortly before the fall of Poland in 1939, the Poles shared their discovery with their British and French allies, and it was to Bletchley Park in Buckinghamshire, a rambling Victorian country house and home of the government's code and cipher school, that Rejewski's work (and one of the Polish replica Enigma machines) was sent.

1944 On June 4 Allied forces enter **Rome**.

On June 6—known as "**D-Day**"—the principal Allied counteroffensive against Germany (**Operation Overlord**) begins, under Eisenhower's overall command. An advance force of 175,000 troops, mainly British and American, are able to establish a chain of bridgeheads.

Bletchley quickly developed into an important—if eccentric—military center. The government recruited a bewildering array of "boffins" to its service, among them university dons, chess masters, crossword experts and linguists. One of the most outstanding was **Alan Turing**, a Cambridge mathematician who was put on the Enigma project. The problem he faced was not breaking Enigma, but doing it rapidly enough to cope with the fact that the Germans changed the machine's settings every 24 hours—meaning that each day the cryptographers had to start again. Like Rejewski, Turing turned to a "thinking machine" to save time, and invented his own "bombe" or "**Turing Machine**." Armed with this, the Allies were able to read the Germans' messages and anticipate their activities. Other brilliant machines followed, among them Max Newman and Tommy Flowers' "**Colossus**," which unpicked the **Lorenz** cipher.

The success of the Bletchley staff, though, created its own problems. The British government had access to more information than it could use without revealing that German codes had been compromised, so some British missions were deliberately allowed to fail. Less easy to excuse was the government's readiness to allow its former colonies access to Enigma machines after the war, knowing that in doing so their secret dispatches could continue to be monitored.

On July 23 Soviet forces, advancing westward, enter **Poland**. On August 25 Free French and American troops enter **Paris**, and on September 5 **Brussels** is liberated. As the Allies push eastwards toward the Rhine, however, German troops put up strong resistance during the **Battle of the Bulge**, and a British airborne division participating in Montgomery's **Operation Market Garden** is badly mauled at **Arnhem** in late September.

In September **long-range missiles** (V1s) are launched by Germany against Britain, causing civilian casualties in London and elsewhere.

An **Education Act**, introduced by the Conservative minister **Richard "Rab" Butler**, makes secondary education compulsory for all British children, and provides for the necessary schools to be built.

1945 The true extent of what becomes known as the **Holocaust** begins to become apparent when Russian forces arrive at **Auschwitz** in Poland on January 28 and discover that over a million people—the

Bomber Command had to be left out of the Myth of the Blitz, or mythology would have ceased to be efficacious. The heroism of the British under bombardment was quasi-Christian—its great symbol, after all, was St Paul's dome flourishing above the flames. The Myth could not accommodate acts, even would-be acts, of killing of civilians and domestic destruction initiated by the British themselves, however they might be justified strategically. Its construction involved putting together facts known or believed to be true, overlaying these with inspirational rhetoric—and leaving out everything known or believed to be factual which didn't fit.

—**Angus Calder**
on the Allied bombing of Dresden,
in *The Myth of the Blitz* (1992)

V-1 flying bomb over Southern England, 1944

large majority of them Jews—have been exterminated at a single prison camp.

In February Churchill, Roosevelt and Stalin hold a further conference at **Yalta**.

On February 13 the RAF destroys the cathedral city of **Dresden**, creating a firestorm in which an estimated 135,000 civilians die.

Allied forces cross the Rhine, occupying **Cologne** on March 10.

SIR WINSTON CHURCHILL (1874–1965)

*I*t is a curious fact that the man described in a famous footnote by the historian A.J.P. Taylor as "the saviour of his country" had, in 1939, a distinctly unconvincing track record both as a politician and as a military strategist.

The son of a cabinet minister, Lord Randolph Churchill, Winston was a descendant of **John Churchill**, the great 1st duke of Marlborough, victor of Blenheim and Ramillies, whose biography he wrote. Despite these starry connections, however, he never achieved much military success—having quit the army, the young Churchill managed to be taken prisoner in the Boer War despite his accreditation as a journalist. Elected a Conservative MP in 1900, he gained a reputation for deviousness, crossing the floor to join the Liberals in 1906. He became first lord of the admiralty during the Great War, but lost his job after the **Gallipoli** fiasco. Nor was his reputation enhanced when he rejoined the Conservatives after the war. He served without any great distinction as chancellor of the exchequer between 1924 and 1929 under Baldwin (his role in breaking the 1926 **General Strike** earned him the hatred of many), but after the Great Depression he spent the following ten

On April 21 Soviet forces reach **Berlin**. On April 29 German forces in **Italy** surrender, and the following day Hitler **commits suicide**. As Germany capitulates, May 8 is declared **Victory in Europe Day** (VE Day). On May 8 Montgomery formally receives Germany's unconditional surrender at **Luneburg**. Fighting continues in the Far East.

On July 17 Churchill joins Stalin and the new US President **Harry Truman** at the **Potsdam Conference** to determine how the spoils

years in the wilderness—a backbench MP going on 60 who irritated nearly everyone by his alarmist prophecies about the German menace. When war broke out, however, he was immediately reinstated as first sea lord, and in 1940 replaced Neville Chamberlain as prime minister.

Once in the job, he attempted to maximize Britain's chances of winning the war; during its course he would personally oversee every major campaign in which British servicemen were involved, sleeping in his underground bunker and once suffering an unreported heart attack. He was also active above ground, using radio broadcasts and his unmistakable oratorical gifts to chivvy and encourage the nation. After war was over he simply shifted his sights, warning of the new menace posed by Stalin's Soviet Union. Following the partition of Germany, he coined the phrase "iron curtain" to describe the growing rift between West and East, but failed to persuade President Truman to sponsor a pre-emptive strike. In 1951 Churchill became prime minister for a second time, but retired after four years in office. It is a mark of the esteem in which he was held that on his death in 1965 he was given the honor of a state funeral.

of war will be divided between the Western Allies and the Communist Soviets. During the conference, the results of a **general election** at home become known, revealing that Churchill's Conservative party has been heavily defeated. The new Labour prime minister, **Clement Attlee**, replaces Churchill at the conference.

With Britain's approval, the US Air Force drops **nuclear bombs** on **Hiroshima** (August 6 and **Nagasaki** (August 9), inducing Japan's **surrender** on August 10.

World War II finally ends on September 12, with the formal surrender of Japanese forces in **Singapore**.

George Orwell publishes *Animal Farm*, an allegorical novel warning of dictatorship in supposedly democratic societies.

Evelyn Waugh publishes *Brideshead Revisited*, an elegiac novel that charts the declining fortunes of a wealthy Roman Catholic family.

CHAPTER ELEVEN

Postwar England

{1946–2005}

IN THE JULY 1945 GENERAL ELECTION THE LABOUR PARTY gained 394 Commons seats to the Conservatives' 210—a landslide victory that took even Labour's leaders by surprise. "After this, what?" asked the minister James Griffiths. The answer would take time to emerge, but the results would be unmistakable. In the decades ahead England changed more rapidly, and more profoundly, than during any previous fifty- or sixty-year period of its history.

Much of the change followed global developments, particularly the growth of low-wage manufacturing economies in the Far East. From the 1960s onwards, Western markets began to be swamped with competitively priced electronic goods, automobiles, steel and other products that have steadily eroded Britain's once mighty industrial base. Nearer home, Britain also had to face challenges posed by the emerging **European Union**—originally a purely economic arrangement between six of Europe's war-ravaged nations but, from the late 1970s onwards, a pancontinental political grouping as well. In 1972 Britain joined an enlarging **Common Market**, as the Union was then called, but its membership has never been full-blooded, and skepticism revived sharply during the 1990s when the Union decided to introduce a **single European currency** in 2002. For many people, the prospect of replacing sterling pounds with euros meant (and means) nothing less than an abandonment of national sovereignty. Although the then prime minister **John Major** achieved opt-outs on certain issues at the Maastricht Conference in 1992, the issue of Europe has proved consistently hard to resolve.

Outside Europe, all Britain's recent prime ministers have had to contend with Britain's diminished status as a world power, dramatically brought home by the **Suez Crisis** of 1956. But the influence of history has proved powerful. For a variety of reasons—its imperial past, perhaps, or what some like to consider its "special relationship" with the United States—Britain has been reluctant to abandon its international profile. Through its leadership of a **Commonwealth** made up of its former colonies and its permanent seat on the **United Nations** Security Council, Britain has sought to exert an influence out of all proportion to its size and resources—a mindset that led to Britain playing significant roles in the **Korean War** of 1950–53, the **Gulf War** against Saddam Hussein's Iraq in 1991, in the **Bosnian** and **Kosovan** crises that followed and in the "war against terrorism" launched by President George W. Bush after the terrorist attacks in the US on September 11, 2001. From its voluntary participation in these conflicts the United Kingdom has emerged with some credit. Whether the same may be said of the **Falklands War** waged by Margaret Thatcher against Argentina in 1982—which has been called Britain's last imperial adventure—is more open to question.

As Britain steadily relinquished its empire after 1945, the development of separatism within the constituent parts of the United Kingdom became a conspicuous feature of domestic politics. Conflict between majority Protestant **Unionists** and minority Catholic **Republicans** in Northern Ireland spilled over into civil war between rival terrorist groupings. The **Scottish National Party** (SNP) and the Welsh **Plaid Cymru**, both founded before 1939, campaigned hard for greater autonomy in their respective countries. And though the situation in Northern Ireland still remains uncertain, following referendums in 1997 Scotland gained a Parliament of its own and Wales a National Assembly. The legislative powers of both bodies are restricted as yet, but many have speculated that the future of the United Kingdom lies in the balance.

Devolution has been accompanied by growing republican sentiment in all parts of the United Kingdom. While **Elizabeth II**—monarch since 1952—has proved to be a ruler of some tact and talent, in recent years the royal family has repeatedly experienced adverse publicity in the media. Some commentators have questioned the very survival of the monarchy. But no mainstream political party has taken a republican line, and no alternative to the existing system has gained popular credibility. Post-war, other British institutions began to show their age, not least a "first-past-the-post" electoral system, superseded elsewhere by the adoption of more inclusive systems of **proportional representation** (PR). But despite an attempt to place PR at the top of the political agenda by the newly formed **Social Democrat Party** in the 1980s, both Britain's main parties, Labour and the Conservatives, have resisted change in that direction. Indeed, after 1945, political life in England settled back down once more into adversarial combat between two main parties within the framework of a constitutional monarchy. Sometimes both Labour and the Conservatives have laid claim to the "middle ground," promoting a politics of consensus. At other times, far more radical programs have been advanced—notably by **Clement Attlee** in 1945 and by **Margaret Thatcher** in 1979.

Attlee's and Thatcher's administrations, probably the two most influential governments since 1945, have been seen as representing opposite poles in their views of how Britain should function. Attlee's Labour government created a powerful state apparatus extending all the way from the "cradle to grave" philosophy of state-funded health care and social security to nationalized industries such as coal, iron and the railways. Thatcher sought to reverse those policies one by one: **privatization** returned industries old and new to private ownership; the state provision of health care was steadily eroded and private insurance encouraged; financial stability, low taxation and low inflation were all-important. Whether Thatcher's reforms proved beneficial is still hotly debated: economically the results have been inconclusive, and it seems certain that her government renewed many of the inequalities between rich and poor that have dogged Britain in the 20th century. Especially hard hit were underprivileged immigrant communities, many of whose members had been encouraged to settle in Britain in the 1950s and 1960s.

Discontent with Thatcher's government (and that of her Tory successor, John Major) opened the door for **Tony Blair** and his "New Labour" party. Blair achieved a huge electoral landslide in 1997, it has been argued, by speaking the language of socialism—improved public services, renewed social justice—while adhering to Thatcherite economic precepts, creating a so-called "third way" centrist approach which won the endorsement of many. However, Blair's post-September 11, 2001 strategic alliance with American president George W. Bush lead directly to Britain's taking part in the unpopular 2003 invasion and occupation of Iraq, proved damaging to Labour's leftist credentials. Though Blair's government is designed to appeal to as many voters as possible, it remains to be seen whether the bold changes it has promised to deliver will appear.

Perhaps the most profound change England has experienced in the years following World War II has been the growth of sizeable "ethnic minority" communities. The arrival of the *SS Empire Windrush* in 1948, a cruiser carrying nearly 500 Jamaicans, was one turning point: in the decades to follow, large numbers of immigrants from former colonies were encouraged to settle in England to meet shortages in the labor force. Reactions to this influx were not generally positive, and tensions have escalated on numerous occasions—notably when **Enoch Powell** encouraged repatriation in 1968, more recently when the bungled investigation into the 1993 murder of the black teenager **Stephen Lawrence** exposed London's police force as institutionally racist. In the aftermath of the 2005 London terrorist bombings, perpetrated by Muslim British nationals, the society (rather belated) discovered the depth to which the **Muslim population**, some egged on by radical religious leaders, felt alienated from the society at large. Despite these and other flash points, though, Britain has not witnessed the development of a coherent far-right political movement (unlike some of its European neighbors), and political milestones such as the **race relations acts** of 1965, 1968 and 1976 have made a significant contribution to shifting attitudes. The 21st-century debate about the effects of pluralism on the nature of British identity seems likely to rumble on for many years yet, but in the historical perspective there is nothing new about that.

1946 As **Clement Attlee**'s Labour government struggles with the problems caused by massive postwar demobilization, Welsh-born **Aneurin "Nye" Bevan** creates the **National Health Service**, which aims to offer free health care to all. While Labour makes it clear that the NHS must be paid for by increased taxation, Bevan's revolutionary measures are broadly welcomed, although some doctors object to the idea of becoming state employees.

Britain becomes a founding member of the **United Nations**, an organization designed to promote both peace and democratic rights worldwide.

In **Palestine**, the Jewish terrorist campaign against Britain intensifies after the government announces its plans to **partition** Palestine into Israeli and Arab Palestinian states.

1947 An extremely cold **winter** paralyses Britain: the army is mobilized to transport basic supplies and prisoners are used to clear snowdrifts.

Notwithstanding a strike by **road hauliers** at the very beginning of the year, Labour presses ahead with its **nationalization** of key industries, including **coal**, **steel production** and the **railways**, in accordance with Clause 4 of the party constitution.

On August 15 Britain restores **independence** to **India**, the largest step in the break-up of the British Empire. In the years immediately ahead nearly all Britain's colonies are liberated, although many opt to join the **British Commonwealth**—an association of nations that acknowledges the British monarch as its titular head. India is partitioned, its northwestern and northeastern areas forming the new state of **Pakistan**, which is inhabited by Muslim majorities.

In November, **King George VI**'s eldest daughter and heir to the throne, **Princess Elizabeth**, marries **Philip**, son of the exiled Prince Andrew of Greece and a nephew of the last viceroy of India, **Earl Mountbatten**. The day before their wedding Philip is created **duke of Edinburgh**.

1948 A **Representation of the People Act** abolishes the two university constituencies of Oxford and Cambridge, which have allowed some electors to vote twice.

A strike by dock workers forces the government to declare a **state of emergency** in order to maintain essential food supplies.

The **11th Olympic Games** are held in London.

The *SS Empire Windrush* docks in Tilbury on June 22, carrying immigrants from Jamaica.

1949 In the face of severe economic pressures, the chancellor of the exchequer, **Sir Stafford Cripps**, devalues the pound, despite previous assurances that he wouldn't.

A **Housing Act** provides subsidies to landlords to improve rented accommodation where Labour's ambitious program of **public housing** is insufficient to meet demand.

Britain becomes a founder member of the **North Atlantic Treaty Organization** (NATO), a mutual-defense pact between the USA and western European nations intended to counter Soviet expansionism.

Laurence Olivier's film of Shakespeare's *Hamlet* wins five American **Academy Awards** (Oscars), the first British film to win any.

A year before his death, **George Orwell** publishes *Nineteen Eighty-Four*, a chilling futuristic novel depicting the helplessness of the individual caught between warring totalitarian governments.

1950 Labour narrowly holds on to power following a **general election** during which the Conservatives stage a significant recovery.

British soldiers are dispatched to **Korea**, which was partitioned in 1948, to fight alongside Americans and other United Nations troops against an attempted takeover of the whole country by the Communist North, supported by the **People's Republic of China**. But although a **Cold War** between the West and the Soviet Union is already well-entrenched, mainly as a result of a gathering **nuclear arms race**, and although China and the Soviet Union have a mutual defense pact, the military conflict fails to widen—averting fears of a third world war.

1951 The Labour government sponsors the **Festival of Britain**—an occasion for the nation to give itself "a pat on the back," in the words of the minister in charge, **Herbert Morrison**. Exhibits on London's South Bank include a temporary "**Dome of Discovery**" and, more permanently, the **Royal Festival Hall**. The cost of the Festival is criticized by Conservative MPs.

In October Attlee is obliged to call a fresh **general election**. The Conservatives win, and **Winston Churchill** returns as prime minister. His government promises to build 300,000 new houses a year to resolve an increasingly acute **housing crisis**—a target never actually achieved, although the availability of public housing continues to expand.

Two British diplomats, **Guy Burgess** and **Donald Maclean**, disappear after the double agent **Harold "Kim" Philby** warns them that their espionage activities on behalf of the Soviet Union have been detected. They subsequently resurface in **Moscow**.

1952 George VI dies of lung cancer on February 6 and is succeeded by his daughter **Elizabeth II**.

In October, following extensive tests with a British-made plutonium bomb developed mainly at **Aldermaston** in Berkshire, Britain becomes one of the few nations with access to **nuclear weapons**.

1953 In April the Cambridge scientists **Francis Crick** and **James Watson** announce their discovery of **DNA** (deoxyribose nucleic acid), the "basic building block of life" and the key to further genetic research.

In May the **Queen's coronation** coincides with the conquest of **Mount Everest** in Nepal by the New Zealander **Edmund Hillary** and Sherpa **Tenzing Norgay**.

An **armistice** signed on July 25 effectively ends the Korean War.

In London the recurrence of deadly **smogs**, caused by fossil fuel emissions and nicknamed "peasoupers," leads doctors to issue masks to those most vulnerable.

FILM, TELEVISION AND RADIO

*A*lthough during World War II the government censored media in ways that would seem utterly alien in today's cultural environment, the war provided a great fillip to the English film industry. Familiar names turned patriotism to their advantage by making new films—**Noel Coward's** *In Which We Serve* and **Leslie Howard's** *The First of the Few* attracted audiences by the hundreds of thousands. A more remarkable offering still was **Laurence Olivier's** film version of Shakespeare's *Henry V*—highly stylized, shot in Ireland at huge cost and, emphasizing the Battle of Agincourt with a score by **William Walton**, guaranteed to make collateral sense of the struggle against Germany. The film was a huge success and even pulled in England's first Oscars. Although seldom able to compete globally with the glamour and wealth of Hollywood, English cinema developed into an important industry during the 1950s and beyond, its products ranging from mannered "Ealing" comedies through the popular "Carry On" series to epics such as *Lawrence of Arabia* (1962) and *Doctor Zhivago* (1965), both directed by **David Lean**. From the 1960s it also supported an influential school of social realism from directors such as **Karel Reisz** (*Saturday Night and Sunday Morning*, 1960), **Lindsay Anderson**

1954 In May **Roger Bannister** becomes the first human on record to run a mile in under four minutes.

The government announces an end to **rationing**, introduced as a wartime measure in 1940.

An **Independent Television Authority** is established as the **BBC** (British Broadcasting Corporation) loses its monopoly of

(*This Sporting Life*, 1963), John Schlesinger (*Billy Liar!*, 1963) and Ken Loach (*Kes*, 1969).

British television also took off in the 1950s, receiving significant boosts with the televised coronation in 1953 and the launch of commercial services in 1954. TV soon became an integral part of British life and, despite commercial competition, is still largely shaped by one of the most influential institutions of the 20th century—the BBC. First floated in 1922, then incorporated as a public body in 1927, the corporation soon developed into a powerful arbiter of national culture through both radio and TV, striving to justify its peculiar method of funding (in effect compulsory taxation) by maintaining a balance between mass entertainment and responsible output. It has also played cat-and-mouse with political authority and, after further deregulation, with a host of competitors ranging from satellite and digital channels to independent radio stations eager to steal market share. The international face of the BBC has long been the World Service, funded by the Foreign Office. During the Cold War it offered radio broadcasts in over a hundred languages, though today that number has been drastically cut as its rationale has become harder to justify in the face of powerful international competition.

television broadcasting. It retains one in radio broadcasting for another twenty years, however.

J.R.R. Tolkien publishes the first two volumes of his trilogy, *The Lord of the Rings*, which is destined to become a cult novel among adults as well as children.

1955 Following Churchill's voluntary resignation in April **Anthony Eden** becomes prime minister and leads the Conservatives to victory in a May **general election**.

Hugh Gaitskell succeeds Clement Attlee as leader of the Labour Party.

The government announces plans to construct a network of **motorways**.

THE SUEZ CRISIS
(1956)

*B*uilt during the 19th century mainly by French engineers, the Suez Canal connected the eastern Mediterranean to the Red Sea and the Indian Ocean beyond, slashing journey times and therefore transportation costs. Such was its maritime and commercial importance that Britain acquired control of Suez under Disraeli when the British Empire was at its zenith.

It was in a very different political climate that the Egyptian leader, Colonel Abdel Nasser, announced his intention in 1956 to nationalize the canal. Already there were the beginnings of an Islamic resurgence seeking to limit Western influence in the Middle East, but more immediately Nasser was angered by an Anglo-American decision not to proceed with a project to build the hydroelectric Aswan Dam across the Nile. There was also considerable Islamic resentment at the West's intention to support the newly created Jewish state of Israel.

1956 On June 4 Egypt's **President Nasser** announces that his government will not renew Britain's concession on the **Suez Canal** when it falls due for renewal in 1968. Three weeks later Nasser seizes and mines the Canal, sparking an international crisis during which the newly formed state of **Israel** launches an attack on the **Sinai Peninsula** at the end of October and the Soviet Union threatens to use missiles against an Anglo-French force dispatched to recapture the Canal. Spurning a UN resolution, British paratroopers land at **Port Said** on November 5, but, after intense diplomatic activity that fatally damages Eden's reputation, withdraw on December 22 following the arrival of a UN peacekeeping force.

Rather than attempt a diplomatic solution, Prime Minister **Anthony Eden** opted for military action supported by **France** (perhaps mindful of Egypt's recent decision to purchase 200 million dollars' worth of Soviet weaponry). British troops were mobilized, and **Israel** was secretly persuaded to launch a simultaneous attack on Egypt across the Sinai desert. The campaign, however, ended in fiasco—the US rounded on Eden, as did the United Nations. Despite initial successes on the ground, Britain and France were forced to hand over captured territory to a UN peacekeeping force in November.

A new world order had been confirmed, in which the old imperial powers—most significantly, Britain—were demonstrated to be impotent without American backing. In some of its surviving colonies (notably Malaya, Aden and Kenya), Britain continued to apply force to get its way, and in 1982 Margaret Thatcher successfully countered Argentinian aggression in the **Falkland Islands**. But in the places that really mattered, Palmerstonian gunboat diplomacy was dead in the water.

John Osborne's controversial play *Look Back in Anger*, which ridicules middle-class values, is first performed in August at the **Royal Court Theatre** in London.

1957 In January Eden resigns in the wake of the Suez Crisis, and is replaced as Conservative prime minister by **Harold Macmillan**.

1958 The **Campaign for Nuclear Disarmament** (CND) is formed and holds a mass rally in London's Trafalgar Square, then marches on a weapons research center at **Aldermaston** in Berkshire.

Debutantes—"eligible" young aristocratic ladies presented to the monarch—make their way to Buckingham Palace for the last time before the tradition is discontinued.

During a partial Cold War thaw, the actress **Coral Browne** meets the missing diplomat and spy **Guy Burgess** while performing *Hamlet* in Moscow.

The first section of British **motorway**—a small stretch of the M6 around **Preston**—is opened to motorists.

1959 Campaigning under Macmillan's slogan "You've never had it so good"—supposedly reflecting a steady rise in national prosperity—and relying on "Super Mac's" patrician unflappability, the Conservatives easily win a **general election**.

The British Motor Corporation unveils its new compact motorcar, the **Mini**, which becomes an immediate bestseller and something of a fashion accessory.

There aren't any good, brave causes left. If the big bang does come, and we all get killed off, it won't be in aid of the old-fashioned, grand design. It'll just be for the Brave New-nothing-very-much-thank-you. About as pointless and inglorious as stepping in front of a bus.

—**John Osborne, from *Look Back in Anger* (1956)**

1960 Britain and France begin collaboration on **Concorde**, the world's first supersonic passenger airliner.

The queen's sister **Princess Margaret** marries a "commoner," the photographer **Anthony Armstrong-Jones**, who is created earl of Snowdon.

The **Royal Shakespeare Company** (previously the Shakespeare Theatre Company) is refounded under the direction of **Peter Hall**, with theatres in both Stratford-on-Avon and London.

Penguin Books successfully defends its decision to mass-market D.H. Lawrence's novel *Lady Chatterley's Lover* against charges brought under the **Obscene Publications Act**. The publisher's victory is heralded as a landmark in the relaxation of censorship.

1961 The need to provide greater opportunities in higher education in Britain is reflected in the opening of the **University of Sussex** in Brighton. Other new universities at **York**, **Canterbury**, **East Anglia**, **Warwick** and elsewhere soon follow.

The **birth control pill** goes on sale in Britain, but is only available for use by married women.

1962 James Watson, Maurice Wilkins and Francis Crick win a **Nobel Prize** for their discovery of the helical structure of DNA.

The BBC launches *That Was The Week That Was*, an irreverent weekly TV program that satirizes politicians. The similarly irreverent and satirical weekly magazine *Private Eye* is also launched.

The consecration of a new cathedral in **Coventry**—designed by **Sir Basil Spence** and decorated with stained glass by **John Piper**, a tapestry by **Graham Sutherland** and a statue by **Jacob Epstein**—is marked by the first performance of **Benjamin Britten**'s *War Requiem*.

1963 Britain's application to join the **European Common Market**—formed by France, West Germany, Italy, Belgium, Holland and Luxembourg in 1957 to provide a tariff-free trading zone within Europe—is **vetoed** by France.

The **Profumo Affair** dominates domestic politics. It centers on the minister for war, **John Profumo**, and his involvement with the "call girl" Christine Keeler and another of her lovers, the Soviet naval attaché **Evgeny Ivanov**. Profumo lies to the Commons before being forced to resign, and Macmillan himself is compromised, resigning in October. He is replaced as prime minister by the Scottish aristocrat **Alec Douglas-Home**.

Hugh Gaitskell dies, and **Harold Wilson** becomes leader of the Labour Party.

The **Beatles** form in Liverpool. Along with the **Rolling Stones** and other English bands, they start a shockwave of youth culture character- ized by throngs of screaming fans and the explosion of youth fashion.

1964 In an October **general election** the Labour Party narrowly defeats the Conservatives and **Harold Wilson** becomes prime min- ister. Wilson begins his premiership by introducing **comprehensive schools**, which are designed to replace what many see as the socially divisive system of fast-track grammar and slow-track secondary moderns. The private school system is left undisturbed, however, as is the unelected House of Lords.

In May **Brighton seafront** becomes a battleground as groups of rival "mods" and "rockers" engage in violent clashes.

1965 In July, **Douglas-Home** retires as Conservative leader. As the Conservative Party adopts a more open leadership contest system, he is succeeded by **Edward Heath**.

Britain's long-term economic prospects are buoyed by the discovery of substantial deposits of **North Sea oil**.

Partly to offset the influence of the TUC (Trades Union Congress) under Labour rule, the **Confederation of British Industry** (CBI) is founded to provide employers with a forum of their own.

Mary Whitehouse, outspoken in her criticisms of "permissive soci- ety," founds the **National Viewers' and Listeners' Association**— a watchdog body that campaigns for greater censorship.

A **Race Relations Act** is passed by Parliament, prohibiting discrimination in public places and the promotion of hatred on grounds of "colour, race, or ethnic or national origins."

Swinging Sixties icon, Twiggy, 1966

1966 In a March **general election** the Labour Party increases its parliamentary majority.

In football, England hosts the **World Cup** and, to the delight of the nation, wins.

1967 Unable to reverse a steady decline in Britain's manufacturing industries and confronted by an increasingly adverse balance of payments, Wilson is forced to **devalue the pound**. Amongst other emergency measures tight restrictions are placed on the amounts of sterling holidaymakers can take abroad.

THE SIXTIES

*T*he "Swinging Sixties" were part of a steady continuum of change in postwar Britain—less an era, perhaps, than a succession of small explosions that together shifted the basis of society. One revolution was the introduction in 1961 of the **birth control pill**: initially available only to married women, the pill was championed by campaigners for women's rights and by the end of the decade it had over a million UK users. It did more than perhaps anything else to alter attitudes to sex, and, with Britain's student population rocketing as the so-called "baby boomers" came of age, sexual liberation and feminist politics began to shape the lives of an entire generation.

Many young people were hungry for American culture, which became more and more powerful throughout the decade as the effect of international idols such as **Jim Morrison** and **Bob Dylan** took hold. This in turn triggered home-grown musical talent, which rapidly became exportable. The story of the **Beatles** is in some ways a representative tale: they climbed from church-fête origins, via a stint in Hamburg strip-bars, to national success then global stardom. Equally successful—and certainly edgier—were

Abortion is legalized.

Agriculture is hit by an epidemic of foot-and-mouth disease, which necessitates the slaughter of over 400,000 animals.

1968 An "**I'm Backing Britain**" campaign is launched by five Surrey workers who pledge to work an extra thirty minutes a day to help continuing economic difficulties.

In April the Conservative MP **Enoch Powell** heightens racial tensions (and gathers a great deal of popular support) by warning of "rivers of blood" unless immigrant workers from the Caribbean, India,

the **Rolling Stones**, a band whose 1964 hit "(I Can't Get No) Satisfaction" guaranteed them a number-one position on both sides of the Atlantic.

The music industry's later engagement with political themes echoed and amplified that of its target audience, and the protests for which the British Sixties became infamous—the student revolts of 1968, the peace protests against the war in Vietnam, the civil rights movement in Northern Ireland—revealed that many were eager to overturn what they saw as "establishment" values, whether that meant indulging in free love, plotting Marxist rebellion or experimenting with LSD (or just talking about all of those things).

But it was consumer culture that benefited most. English style—or a certain version of it—became marketable for the first time that century. James Bond movies starring the impossibly debonair (and certainly Scottish) **Sean Connery** were a worldwide hit; the designs of **Mary Quant** and **Ossie Clark** and London's fashionable Kings Road and Carnaby Street were making headlines; the sleek lines of Jaguar's **E-type** sports cars embodied English chic. In the end the "Swinging Sixties" might make little overall sense, but that is somehow their point.

Pakistan and other former colonies are repatriated. In the same year **South Africa** refuses to allow a touring English cricket team to enter the country if **Basil d'Oliviera**, the first black player to be considered for the English squad, is selected. The MCC later drops d'Oliviera.

Partly in imitation of militant student activities in **Paris** and other foreign capitals, Britain's students begin agitating on British university campuses. There are also demonstrations outside the **American embassy** in London's Grosvenor Square in protest at the USA's military involvement in **Vietnam**.

The growing civil rights movement in Northern Ireland erupts into violence when a march by the anti-Unionist **Northern Ireland Civil Rights Association** on October 5 in **Derry** is broken up by the Royal Ulster Constabulary. The RUC is widely criticized for its brutality in dealing with the marchers, further destabilizing the region.

1969 As student protests spread, the **London School of Economics** becomes a center for militant students demanding the overthrow of the "capitalist" state. Thirteen ringleaders are barred from the college after police are called in to end a mass sit-in.

In July **Prince Charles** is invested as **prince of Wales** by the Queen at Caernarvon Castle in Wales.

The first Anglo-French **Concorde** supersonic aircraft take to the skies.

A splinter group of the Irish Republican Army, the **Provisional IRA**, is formed towards the end of the year and initiates a high-profile bombing campaign in **Northern Ireland**.

The **Open University**, a distance-learning institution designed to provide tuition to students irrespective of their location or social background, is founded.

1970 Defying the predictions of most opinion polls, the Conservatives win a June **general election** and Edward Heath—who is committed to taking Britain into the **Common Market**—becomes prime minister.

Economic prospects improve as more and more **North Sea oil** comes on tap.

The **Gay Liberation Front** begins campaigning for an end to legal and other kinds of discrimination against gay men and women.

1971 Heath's government begins to be confronted by **industrial action**, often prompted by "militant" trade unionists. For the first time mail workers strike, demanding a 20 percent pay increase.

Decimalization simplifies the structure of Britain's currency, changing it from pounds (twenty shillings), shillings (twelve pence) and pence to just pounds (100 pence) and pence.

The **Rolls-Royce** group goes into receivership, before being split into engineering and automobile production components after the government intervenes.

1972 Following intense negotiations, the European **Common Market** admits Britain into its community, which now comprises nine members. Britain's membership is confirmed by Parliament in July.

A six-week strike by coal miners leads to the **rationing of power**, and there are subsequent strikes by rail workers and dockers.

Sectarian violence in **Northern Ireland** continues to escalate. In what becomes known as "**Bloody Sunday**," on January 30 members of the British Parachute Regiment open fire on a Catholic protest in **Derry**, killing thirteen people.

1973 The Northern Ireland Assembly at **Stormont** is suspended and the "six provinces" are brought under **direct rule** from Westminster.

Strikes and industrial disputes continue throughout the year, and the economy is further bruised by a decision by **OPEC** (the Organization of Petroleum Exporting Countries, centered in the Middle East) to quadruple **oil prices**—even though the effect on Britain is mitigated by its own oil production in the North Sea.

Chancellor of the exchequer **Anthony Barber** announces a pre-Christmas **crisis budget** that includes severe cuts in public spending, instigating the closure of one in five of Britain's schools. Industry and commerce are limited to five days' electricity consumption per fortnight, and public services are put on a three-day working week.

1974 As Barber's budget bites, power cuts become routine, some foodstuffs become scarce, coal miners go back on strike and unemployment mounts. Determined to force a showdown with the trade unions, Heath calls a **general election** on March 6 and campaigns under the slogan "Who Governs Britain?" He loses, and Labour is returned to power by the narrowest of margins. **Harold Wilson** becomes prime minister once more at the head of a minority government, but is obliged to contemplate a **"Lib–Lab" pact** with the minority Liberal Party. He calls a second election on October 11, and increases his Commons majority to 3.

As the **IRA** escalates its campaign of terror on the mainland, 21 people are killed in **Birmingham** by bombs that explode within minutes of each other. Six men—who become widely known as the **Birmingham Six**—are later convicted, but are freed on appeal 16 years later.

1975 A **national referendum** promised by Labour confirms Britain's membership of the European Common Market by a margin of two to one.

As trade unions press for wage rises of anything up to 30 percent, **inflation** worsens. In response Wilson attempts to negotiate a "**social contract**" with union leaders.

1976 Harold Wilson resigns, and **James Callaghan** becomes prime minister in April.

As Britain's underlying economic instability continues, the government is forced to turn to the **International Monetary Fund** for assistance.

An unusually hot summer leads to the first **drought** in living memory.

The **National Theatre** opens, housed in a complex designed by **Denys Lasdun** on London's South Bank.

A further amendment to the 1965 **Race Relations Act** is passed by Parliament, setting up a **Race Relations Commission** to promote "equality of opportunity and good relations."

1977 Queen Elizabeth II's **Silver Jubilee** is celebrated in June throughout England with street parties and other events.

The home secretary, **Roy Jenkins**, resigns his seat in Parliament to become Britain's first president of the EEC Commission.

1978 As Labour fails to resolve tensions with the unions and public sector strikes proliferate, Britain experiences a "**winter of discontent**": power cuts and fuel shortages become commonplace, the Army has to assume the responsibilities of the fire brigade, rubbish accumulates on city streets and even some dead are left unburied.

1979 At a **general election** held in May the Conservative Party gains a majority of Commons seats, and its leader **Margaret Thatcher** becomes prime minister, the first woman to hold the office. She will remain in power for thirteen years.

In January the country is troubled by a series of **strikes** by a number of public sector unions, but the following month the TUC and the government attempt to patch up a mutual co-operation agreement.

On March 30 the Irish MP **Airey Neave** is assassinated by the IRA, who plant an explosive device in his car parked underneath the houses of parliament.

Violent demonstrations break out at **Southall** in April against the far-right **British National Party**, in which one man is killed.

1980 Britain achieves **self-sufficiency in oil**, able to trade high-grade North Sea oil, of use particularly in producing aviation fuel, for lower-grade Middle Eastern oil, used for ordinary industrial and motoring purposes.

Inflation reaches a high of 20 percent, and Thatcher faces critics inside her cabinet (collectively known as the "wets") as she begins implementing a draconian program to revive the economy.

In October, **Michael Foot** replaces James Callaghan as leader of the Labour Party.

1981 Thatcher reorganizes her cabinet to sideline the "wets": **Lord Soames** is sacked as leader of the House of Lords and **James Prior** is moved to the Northern Ireland office. Among those promoted are **Nigel Lawson**, who becomes secretary of state for energy, and **Norman Tebbit**, who becomes secretary of state for employment.

The Labour Party, suffering weak leadership, continues to be divided between traditional and militant socialists, and those who wish to modernize the party. In an attempt to "break the mould of British politics" the "Gang of Four"—**Roy Jenkins**, **Shirley Williams**, **David Owen** and **William Rogers**, all former Labour cabinet members—split off to form the **Social Democrat Party**, dedicated to replacing Britain's "first-past-the-post" voting system with **proportional representation**.

On July 29 the queen's eldest son and heir, **Prince Charles,** marries **Lady Diana Spencer**, daughter of Earl Spencer—the first time a Prince of Wales has married an Englishwoman since the Black Prince's marriage to Joan of Kent in the 14th century. The wedding ceremony, held in St Paul's Cathedral, is broadcast worldwide.

In the summer, there are **race riots** in **Brixton**, following tensions between the police and Brixton's large black community. Later in the year further riots and violence occur in Liverpool's **Toxteth** area and Manchester's **Moss Side**.

1982 In April **Argentina**, under the dictatorship of **General Leopoldo Galtieri**, launches an invasion of the **Falkland Islands** in the South Atlantic, laying claim to an isolated sheep-farming territory under British control since 1833. Despite pressure from the international community to arrive at a diplomatic solution, Thatcher orders a combined-services **task force**, commanded by **Rear-Admiral Sandy Woodward**, to reclaim the colony. A swift campaign is ended on June 14 when British commandos enter the Falklands' capital, **Port Stanley**, but not without significant casualties on both sides. The frailty of Britain's warships is exposed when *HMS Sheffield* is sunk by missiles fired from an Argentinian aircraft, and British tactics are called seriously

Prime Minister Margaret Thatcher

into question when Argentina's **General Belgrano** is sunk on May 2 sailing away from the Falklands, with the loss of 400 lives. Although the *Belgrano* incident eventually forces the resignation of defense secretary **John Nott**, Thatcher reaps the full benefit of Britain's military success, and her personal popularity soars to new heights.

At home **unemployment** rises, seen by some as a deliberate ploy on the government's part to restrict demands for higher wages.

MARGARET THATCHER (B.1925)

A genuinely radical Tory, the "Iron Lady" took over leadership of the Conservative Party after widespread disappointment with Edward Heath's government of 1970–74. Elected prime minister in 1979, Margaret Thatcher retained power until 1990, when a party putsch brought about her downfall.

In power, she invited adoration and loathing in equal measure—largely because she had the strength of character to follow through her convictions. Abroad she was often better thought of than at home, forging a close personal bond with US President Ronald Reagan and impressing Mikhail Gorbachev of the Soviet Union. Both in the UK and internationally her policies were unashamedly capitalistic. An apostle of free enterprise, she curbed the powers of the trade unions, overhauled the civil service, and created tax breaks and other incentives for small and big businesses alike. Most famously, she carried through a wide-ranging program of privatization, returning nationalized industries such as steel, electricity, gas, water and telecommunications to private ownership. Although this led many to criticize her for favoring City "fat cats," her vision was wider than that. She was unashamedly populist in the Disraeli tradition—privatization went

1983 Buoyed by the Falklands campaign, Thatcher calls a **general election** in June and the Conservatives win a landslide victory. The **Social Democrats** gain a handful of seats, but fail to make a significant breakthrough despite opinion poll predictions. **Michael Foot** resigns as leader of the Labour Party. His successor, **Neil Kinnock**, immediately sets about rooting out Labour's militants.

hand-in-hand with a well-advertised concept of a "share-owning democracy." Everybody, her reasoning went, should have the opportunity to become a "stakeholder" in their own society.

How successful such policies have been is bitterly contested, however. Her celebrated dictum that "there is no such thing as society" has been taken by some to celebrate the spirit of free enterprise that saved Britain from its postwar decline; others blame it for creating an abrasive "get-rich-quick" society which benefited the few, not the many. Her erosion of funding for public services was widely criticized, and many felt that her increasing extremism (particularly towards Europe) left the government increasingly isolated. And indeed Thatcher herself was capable of startling inflexibility. If her decisiveness over the Falklands crisis early in her premiership did wonders for her popularity ratings, her autocratic decision to introduce the unpopular Poll Tax—a system of taxation which many felt to be grossly unfair—was badly handled. In the end, though, it was her party, not Thatcher, who panicked. When a cyclical recession took hold at the end of the 1980s, an alliance of Tory grandees and ministers, fearing that Thatcher's reputation as an "uncaring" leader would lose them the next election, decided to dump her.

> Walking into the hotel was the fulfillment of a dream, a fantasy that had filled all our thoughts for almost three months. "We never doubted for a moment that the British would come," said the proprietor Desmond King. "We have just been waiting for the moment." It was like liberating an English suburban golf club.
>
> —Max Hastings, syndicated press dispatch from Port Stanley in the Falklands, June 14, 1982

1984 A strike by **coal-miners** for higher wages beginning in March enables Thatcher to stage a showdown with the trade unions. Refusing to give way to the miners' demands, the government demonizes the leader of the National Union of Mineworkers, **Arthur Scargill**, as a militant subversive. After numerous running battles with police, in November the strike begins to collapse and miners return to work. Although Thatcher seizes the opportunity to initiate a legislative program curbing trade unions' powers and influence, the strikes highlight a wider industrial problem—that British industry is being priced out of the market.

In October the IRA executes one of its most high-profile attacks when it bombs the **Grand Hotel** in **Brighton** during a Conservative party conference. Five are killed and over 30 injured, but Thatcher herself narrowly escapes injury.

1985 Criticism of Mrs Thatcher resurfaces within the ranks of the Conservative Party. The former cabinet minister **Francis Pym** publishes *The Politics of Consent*, attacking the prime minister's lack of interest in views substantially different from her own. In the House of Lords, the former prime minister, **Harold Macmillan**, now earl of Stockton, rebukes Thatcher for her blind pursuit of monetarist policies. These rifts come to a head over the **Westland Affair**, which begins to make headlines in December. The proposed sale of Britain's only helicopter-manufacturing company to the American Sikorski corporation, backed by the Thatcherite trade and industry secretary **Leon Brittan**, is opposed by defense secretary **Michael Heseltine**, who favors the creation of a European consortium instead.

1986 Amidst gathering acrimony as to how the Westland dispute has been leaked to the press, in January **Heseltine** resigns from government, to become a dangerously popular rival to Thatcher. Brittan is also forced to resign, and discontented Tories begin contemplating a replacement leader.

A **strike** by prison officers indicates that Thatcher's muzzling of the trade unions is less comprehensive than she would wish.

The government's program of **privatization**—returning state owned industries to the private sector—gets properly underway with the offer of shares in **British Gas** to the public.

In some opinion polls, the minority **Social Democrat** and **Liberal** parties, joining forces as the **Liberal–SDP Alliance**, attract up to 30 percent support, while in others Neil Kinnock's reformed **Labour Party** attracts 40 percent.

In the winter, newspaper headlines are dominated by the government's attempts to prevent a former intelligence agent, **Peter Wright**, from publishing his memoirs, *Spycatcher*. Since the book is easily obtainable abroad, the campaign proves futile.

The explosion of the **Chernobyl** nuclear power station in the Ukraine causes panic in Britain, and in some parts of the country lamb grazed in contaminated fields is banned from the shops.

1987 Ahead of a June **general election**, Thatcher travels to **Moscow** for talks with **Mikhail Gorbachev**, whose twin policies of *glasnost* (liberalization) and *perestroika* (economic and political restructuring) are already transforming the Soviet Union. Returning to Britain, Thatcher pronounces that Gorbachev is a man she can "do business with," a critical step in the ending of the Cold War.

In the **election** itself the Conservatives are returned to power with a reduced majority, and Thatcher continues as prime minister.

A severe storm (rapidly nicknamed the "**Great Storm**" and the most destructive for many years) causes havoc, particularly across the south of the country, in October. It kills 18 people in all.

1989 Thatcher's decision to reform local government income by replacing rates, levied on the basis of property values, with a **Poll Tax**, levied on people, creates a furor inside the Conservative Party and in the country at large. Her proposals mean that a rich adult living alone in a very large house makes one-fifth the contribution to local services of five adults living in a very small house in the same local authority. Notwithstanding widespread objections, Thatcher proceeds with the legislation.

In April Neil Kinnock stages a "Red Rose Rally" in **Birmingham**, correctly predicting that forthcoming local elections will deliver an adverse verdict on "ten years of Thatcherism." The Conservatives are trounced, and in July Thatcher reshuffles her cabinet.

Further political divisions, affecting all parties, are created over the issue of whether or not Britain should join the **EMS** (European Monetary System), a first step toward the creation of a common European currency. Chancellor **Nigel Lawson** cautiously supports entry, but Thatcher's "special adviser" **Sir Alan Walters** dismisses the scheme as "half-baked." Lawson resigns, adding his weight to the Tories' backbench dissenters, and Thatcher again reshuffles her cabinet.

In November, a relatively obscure Conservative MP, **Sir Anthony Meyer**, challenges Thatcher for the party leadership. Although he is convincingly beaten, his ability to attract the votes of 33 fellow MPs, and the abstention of another 27, suggest that Thatcher's days may be numbered.

The Iranian leader **Ayatollah Khomeini** issues a *fatwah* against the Indian-born author Salman Rushdie after his Islamically "sacrilegious" novel *Satanic Verses* is published in London.

1990 Despite the building of Japanese-owned **car plants** in England's northeast (and continued investment from overseas companies), an **economic recession** begun in 1988 continues in Britain.

As disquiet over the Poll Tax grows, there are clashes between protestors and police in **Manchester** in February. On March 21 a national **anti-Poll Tax demonstration** is held in London's **Trafalgar Square**. The meeting becomes violent, some shops are looted and in the "Second Battle of Trafalgar" 450 are injured and 339 arrests are made.

Tension continues into the summer, when the Conservatives again lose seats in a second round of **local elections**.

In August, the invasion of **Kuwait** by **Iraq** under the leadership of **Saddam Hussein** creates an immediate international crisis.

In November the resignation of the Conservative deputy leader **Sir Geoffrey Howe**, accompanied by an uncharacteristically forthright speech in the House of Commons, heralds Thatcher's downfall. Forced to submit herself to a leadership contest, Thatcher runs against **Heseltine** in the first ballot. She wins, but fails to achieve an outright majority and is forced to step down. A second ballot contested by Heseltine, the foreign secretary **Douglas Hurd** and chancellor of the exchequer **John Major** sees Major win through; he becomes prime minister.

1991 On January 16 a military coalition—led by the USA, including British forces, approved by the UN and backed by an alliance of 28 Western and Arab states—begins operations **Desert Shield** and **Desert Storm**, designed to expel Saddam Hussein from Kuwait. The campaign, lasting 42 days, starts with a massive display of air power against Iraq, and ends with the humiliation of Iraqi forces.

At home, in February the IRA fires mortar shells into the **Cabinet Office** at Downing Street.

John Major scraps the Poll Tax, replacing it with a **Community Charge**—in effect a restitution of property rates.

1992 At a **European Union** (formerly EEC) conference in **Maastricht** in February, Major secures important concessions for Britain, including an "opt-out" clause with regard to entry into the **single currency**.

Despite opinion poll predictions, the Conservatives narrowly win an April **general election**, and Major continues as prime minister. Neil Kinnock, accused of premature triumphalism at a rally held in **Sheffield** on April 1, resigns as leader of the Labour Party, which elects Scottish-born **John Smith** in his stead.

As conflict between Serbs, Croatians and Bosnian Muslims develops in **Yugoslavia**, Britain agrees to deploy troops as part of a **UN peacekeeping force**.

Chris Patten, the architect of Major's surprise election victory, is rewarded by being appointed the last governor general of **Hong Kong** ahead of the colony's agreed handover to the People's Republic of China in July 1997.

On September 16, known as **Black Wednesday**, Britain withdraws from the **ERM** (European Exchange Rate Mechanism) amidst turmoil in the financial markets. Overnight the chancellor, **Norman Lamont**, raises base lending rates (already running at 12 percent) to 15 percent, but Major intervenes the following day to reverse his policy. Although it is from about this time that the economy enters a decade of sustained growth, the episode tarnishes the reputation of Major's government and hardens anti-European feelings.

The general synod of the Church of England votes to permit the **ordination of women** into the Anglican priesthood, provoking some traditionalists to join the Roman Catholic Church.

In October fire destroys part of **Windsor Castle**. In the ensuing wrangle over who should pay for repairs, the queen agrees to begin paying **income tax**, from which she had been exempt.

1993 As parliamentary by-elections continue to erode the Conservatives' slender majority, the party exhibits signs of being torn apart on the **"European"** issue. Neither pro- nor anti-Europeans are satisfied by the prime minister's "wait-and-see" policy over monetary union.

In April the black teenager **Stephen Lawrence** is killed in London in what appears to be a racially motivated attack; to date no one has been convicted of his murder. The "institutionally racist" Metropolitan police are later heavily criticized for their handling of the investigation in a report by **Sir William Macpherson**.

In November Major opens talks with the **Irish government** in a bid to end the sectarian violence in Northern Ireland, the beginnings of a **"peace process"** that continues to the present.

1994 The massively expensive **Channel Tunnel** between England and France opens in May—seen by some as a symbol of future European integration, by others as the possible harbinger of a rabies epidemic.

Sir Michael Rose, commander of the UN peacekeeping force in Bosnia, brokers a fragile **cease-fire** between the contending sides.

In May, **John Smith** dies of a heart attack. After a brief hiatus **Tony Blair**, who has made clear his ambition to modernize the Labour Party still further, becomes its leader.

The IRA announces a **suspension of hostilities** against the British government—the first agreed cease-fire in 25 years. Major promises that if it holds he will open negotiations with the IRA's political wing, **Sinn Féin**.

1995 As talks between the British government and Sinn Féin commence, Major and the Irish Taoiseach **John Bruton** issue a joint declaration outlining a "twin track" initiative to secure peace. The American senator **George Mitchell** is invited to oversee the **decommissioning of weapons** held by both Republican and Protestant militant groups in Northern Ireland.

As feuding within the Conservative Party escalates, in June Major **resigns** as leader and challenges his detractors to "put up or shut up." The secretary of state for Wales and hardline Euro-skeptic **John Redwood** takes up the challenge, but Major is re-elected by his party.

The **National Lottery** is set up, the first time that a weekly competition on this scale has been seen in Britain. Controversy greets its arrival, not least because the profit-making operator with the contract to run it, Camelot, will only give a certain percentage of its proceeds to so-called "good causes."

1996 The **cease-fire** in Northern Ireland breaks down following disagreements with Sinn Féin about the timing of arms decommissioning and other aspects of the peace process. The IRA resumes its **terrorist campaign** in mainland Britain. Bomb attacks leave two dead and scores of civilians injured in **London** and **Manchester**.

An outbreak of **BSE** (Bovine Spongiform Encephalopathy)—the apparent cause of the deadly **Creutzfelt-Jakob disease** in humans—leads to a **mass cull** of British cattle and a prohibition of **beef exports** being imposed by the European Union.

1997 Damaged by a series of scandals involving senior Conservatives, Major loses a **general election** held on May 1. With a Commons majority of 179 seats, **Tony Blair** becomes prime minister at the head of a "New Labour" government. Major resigns as Conservative leader and is succeeded by former secretary of state for Wales, **William Hague**. The government immediately acts to relocate control of **base lending rates** from the Treasury to the Bank of England, removing at least one temptation to manipulate the economy for political ends. Aware that "Europe" is potentially also a divisive issue for Labour, Blair announces that Britain will adopt the **single European currency**— scheduled to come into effect in the EU in 2002—only if certain economic tests are met.

In July, following a renewal of the peace initiative by Blair, the IRA announces a further **cease-fire**.

In the early hours of August 31, **Diana, Princess of Wales** (now divorced from her husband Prince Charles) is killed in an automobile accident in Paris along with her companion "Dodi" Fayed, the son of the Egyptian-born owner of Harrods department store, Mohammed al-Fayed. Immediately eulogized as the "People's

Prime Minister Tony Blair

Princess" by Prime Minister Blair, Diana's death leads to public mourning verging on mass hysteria.

In September, decades of lobbying by the **SNP** (Scottish National Party) and **Plaid Cymru** (Welsh Party) pays off when New Labour announces its intention to create **national assemblies** in Scotland and Wales. In referendums held in September, 74 percent of Scots vote for the creation of a Scottish Parliament, and just over 50 percent in Wales for a Welsh Assembly. While "**devolution**" is seen by some as a natural expansion of democracy within Britain, others foresee the eventual break-up of the United Kingdom itself.

1998 In April the British and Irish governments arrive at the **Good Friday Agreement**, calling for the restitution of a **Northern Irish Assembly** and provincial administration at **Stormont** in which the Catholic minority will be guaranteed participation.

At Westminster, in fulfillment of New Labour's election manifesto, Blair sets in motion legislation to curtail the voting rights of **hereditary peers** in the House of Lords. Critics on the left of the party, however, complain that such reform does not go far enough.

1999 British troops are sent as part of a UN peacekeeping force to **Kosovo**, a breakaway state of the "former" Yugoslav republic, to contain violence between **Serbs** and ethnic **Albanians**.

Ahead of planned celebrations to mark the advent of the coming Millennium, controversy surrounds the central **Millennium Project**, part of which involves a vast dome situated on cleaned-up industrial land in the London borough of Greenwich (and originally commissioned by Major's Conservative government). What it will contain—and what it will eventually be used for—remain uncertain.

In October 31 people die and over four hundred are injured in a **train crash** near London's **Paddington** station. As with a similar crash near **Southall** in 1997, safety failings are blamed on private operators—the train companies involved and the firm responsible for the rail infrastructure since privatization, **Railtrack**.

2000 The **New Year** is greeted by celebrations across Britain. Inside the Greenwich **Dome**, Elizabeth II, Prime Minister Blair and other notables attend an entertainment which is widely derided for its amateurishness. Other millennium projects encounter difficulties: a "**river of fire**" intended to sweep majestically up the Thames passes by unnoticed; a new **footbridge** over the Thames sways so badly it has to be closed; an (eventually successful) **Millennium Wheel** opens late and refuses to turn. The Dome itself opens as an enclosed technological theme park, attracting far fewer than the twelve million visitors needed during the course of the year for it to break even financially. Some millennium projects—such as the new Great Court at the **British Museum** in London, covered with a new roof by architect **Norman Foster**—are more enthusiasticallyreceived, however.

The **BSE scandal** resurfaces once more with the publication of a report analyzing its handling. The government is heavily criticized for covering up scientific evidence that pointed to the threats of the disease and the way it was managed.

Following an October train crash at **Hatfield** in which four people die, **Railtrack** imposes widespread speed restrictions while it attempts to repair the rail infrastructure. Delays paralyze the network for months to come, and are a major factor in Railtrack's slide into government-managed **receivership** a year later.

2001 Just as the threat of BSE seems to have evaporated, England's countryside is hit by **foot-and-mouth disease**. The government's policy of slaughter (encouraged by the farmers' unions) is widely criticized, and TV pictures of burning carcasses cause a crisis in British tourism, both domestic and international.

On May 1, worldwide "**anti-capitalist**" riots, orchestrated by increasingly well-organized international protest groups, dominate the news. As in previous years, protests in London turn violent, to widespread condemnation.

In a June **general election** Blair is re-elected with a parliamentary majority similar to his 1997 landslide (but turnout is significantly lower). William Hague resigns as Conservative leader, to be replaced by the little-known Euro-skeptic **Iain Duncan-Smith**. In the same election, the centrist **Liberal Democrats** (the rebranded Liberal-SDP alliance) gain an unprecedented 52 seats, and, under their Scottish leader **Charles Kennedy**, begin claiming that they and not the Tories are the real Opposition. Public anxiety about the continuing poor performance of the National Health Service, the education system, an overstretched

TONY BLAIR AND NEW LABOUR

*B*y the mid-1980s several things had made the "old" Labour Party of Wilson and Callaghan distinctly unappealing to the electorate. Many thought they embodied the worst of the 1970s—industrial unrest, political division, economic instability. More generally, though, there was a Europe-wide drift toward middle-ground, "consensus" politics: the product of more diversified economies, greater individual wealth and growing disillusionment with outright socialist precepts. In Britain the process was accelerated by Thatcherism, for all that Thatcher's government was scarcely centrist. By undermining the trade unions (Labour's traditional bankrollers) and offering greater scope for individual investment, Thatcher pulled the rug from under the feet of her opponents.

Successive leaders—beginning with Michael Foot and continuing with Neil Kinnock and John Smith—attempted to remold the Labour party, aligning it more closely with its continental Christian Democrat counterparts. But it befell Tony Blair to reap the rewards. In 1997, after 18 years of Conservative rule, the country wanted a change, and Blair provided it. New Labour won a huge majority in the House of Commons. On the hustings he

police force and Britain's privatized rail services (all areas New Labour has pledged to improve) continue to dominate headlines.

In June **riots** between different racial communities break out in several British cities, among them **Oldham** and **Bradford**.

On September 11, however, domestic concerns are temporarily set aside when two hijacked aircraft are piloted into the **New York World Trade Center**, whilst another hits the Pentagon in Washington. Among the estimated three thousand civilians killed are several hundred British people.

had promised a Britain that would be "fair to all," and he started in dramatic style, exiling hereditary peers from the House of Lords and offering limited autonomy to Scotland and Wales. There was, however, no significant alteration to the tax regime—jealously guarded by Chancellor **Gordon Brown**—and in the key areas of public health, education and crime control beneficial changes were slow to appear.

Press attention soon focused on the character of Blair himself. What the media reported was a prime minister determined to institute a presidential style of leadership, constantly in front of the cameras and surrounded by media-manipulating "spin doctors." Since he seemed unwilling to abandon much of Thatcher's legislation (until recently), critics also began to ask whether Blair—for all his claims to follow a "third way" politics—was in fact a neo-Conservative. Yet he has proved a complex figure to analyze. Some have picked up on his consciously Christian beliefs; others have inferred control-freakish tendencies; many have been bemused by his claims to be "just an ordinary guy." Perhaps the answer lies somewhere in the middle, like New Labour itself. Quite what "Blairism" will finally stand for remains an open question.

Amidst condemnation of the atrocities in Britain (particularly by many Muslim organizations), it becomes apparent that they have been perpetrated by an Islamic fundamentalist network centered on the Afghanistan-based **al-Qaida** group, headed by **Osama Bin Laden**. The American president, **George W. Bush**, declares a "**War Against Terrorism**" which Prime Minister Blair pledges to support. By November British special forces are participating in a ground war against al-Qaida and the **Taliban** Afghan government. Blair embarks on a series of alliance-building diplomatic missions to countries in the Middle East and elsewhere, while repeatedly assuring Britain's two million Muslims that a war on terrorism is not a war on Islam. But doubts are raised about the scope of hostilities, and Blair is criticized for ignoring his domestic responsibilities in order to cut a figure on the world stage.

2002 **Queen Elizabeth the Queen Mother** dies at Windsor on March 30, and is widely mourned.

In an April **budget**, the chancellor **Gordon Brown** announces that taxes will rise in order to fund increasing expenditure on the NHS— a decision cheered by many "old Labour" supporters as a return to the party's socialist roots. In the same month the government announces plans for **regional assemblies** in some areas of England.

Millions turn out for events across the country in June, celebrating the Queen's **Golden Jubilee**.

Europe-wide controversy over **illegal immigration** continues. At an EU summit held in Seville in June, Britain agrees to tighter border controls and a common policy on refugees.

2003 On February 15, as the threat of war with Iraq escalates, an estimated one million people **protest** in London against an invasion.

The House of Commons votes overwhelmingly on March 18 to support Tony Blair's decision to use military force, along with the US and Spain, to remove **Saddam Hussein** from power. The invasion begins on March 20. By April 6, British troops have taken Iraq's second-largest city, **Basra**.

On July 18, the body of weapons expert **David Kelly**—identified by a journalist as the source for a controversial BBC story claiming the government had "sexed up" a dossier of evidence on Iraq—is discovered; an apparent suicide.

2004 In January, the **BBC**'s top management resigns after mounting criticism of their handling of the David Kelly story.

In March, Tony Blair meets with **Muammar Qaddafi** in Tripoli, signaling a thaw in relations prompted by Libya's decision to pay $2.7 billion for its complicity in the 1988 bombing of an airliner over **Lockerbie**, Scotland which killed 270.

An inquiry set up by **Lord Butler** to examine the government's intelligence gathering efforts leading up to the Iraq invasion releases its report on July 14, having found some flaws but overall concluding the government acted in good faith.

Tony Blair announces on October 1 that if he is re-elected as Prime Minister, he will not seek a fourth **consecutive** term, quelling rumors that he was considering quitting.

2005 On May 5, Tony Blair wins re-election for an **unprecedented third term**, though Labour takes a hit due to the growing unpopularity of the Iraq war, earning only a little over a third of the popular vote.

London is declared on July 6 the winner of its bid to host the **2012 Olympics**. During the next day's morning rush hour, in an attack reminiscent of the March 11, 2004 Madrid commuter train bombings, **terrorists** set off three bombs in London's Underground and one on a double-decker bus, killing 52 (including the four bombers) and injuring hundreds in the single worst attack on British soil since the end of World War II. Three of the bombers were British nationals of Pakistani descent. On July 21 a **copycat attack** fails, with none of the bombs detonating.

The sixth book in J.K. Rowling's young-adult fantasy series, ***Harry Potter and the Half-Blood Prince***, is released on July 16 and makes publishing history, selling almost nine million copies within 24 hours in the UK and US.

The **IRA** releases a statement on July 28 declaring a formal end to its armed campaign. On September 26, the IRA announces that it "has destroyed all its arms."

London police officers in front of the bus hit in the July 7, 2005 terrorist bombings

BOOKS

THERE IS AN EMBARRASSMENT OF RICHES in all areas of English history, making it an impossible task to present a comprehensive list of all that is worth reading in the space allowed. What follows, therefore, should be treated as a thumbnail sketch of some books that will carry the story onwards.

Many of the titles listed below are in paperback and in print. Those that aren't (marked "o/p") should be available in secondhand bookshops, or via online retailers. Publishers are detailed with the UK publisher listed first, separated by an oblique slash from the US publisher where both exist. When a book is only available in one market, "UK" or "US" follows the publishing information; if the same publisher handles both, it is simply listed once.

GENERAL

John Cannon (ed.), *The Oxford Companion to British History* (Oxford University Press). This one-volume reference work is both handy and comprehensive, and is in general fairly reliable.

Margaret Drabble (ed.), *The Oxford Companion to English Literature* (Oxford University Press). Invaluable general reference guide to the essentials in English literature, recently updated.

J.R.H. Moorman, *A History of the Church in England* (Morehouse UK). A comprehensive survey of the development of Christianity in England, now in its third edition.

Kenneth O. Morgan (ed.), *The Oxford Illustrated History of Britain* (Oxford University Press). Don't be put off by the "illustrated" tag. This is a scholarly but readable introduction to British history.

J.E. Morpurgo (gen. ed.), *The Pelican History of England* (Penguin). This nine-volume series provides a set of good, manageable guides to the key periods of English history from the Romans to the present day. It includes titles by S.T. Bindoff (Tudors), J.P. Kenyon (Stuarts) and J.H. Plumb (18th-century England).

Leslie Stephen and **Sidney Lee** (eds), *The Dictionary of National Biography* (Oxford University Press o/p). Although superseded by the New Dictionary of National Biography, this 22-volume edition remains the first point of call for anyone looking for a concise life of any of the major figures of English history—more than that, it's a national institution.

CULTURE AND SCIENCE

John Brewer, *The Pleasures of the Imagination: English culture in the 18th century* (HarperCollins; Chicago University Press). Delightful—if weighty— study of the finer things.

Asa Briggs, *A Social History of England* (Penguin). A thoroughly worthwhile book to thumb through.

Linda Colley, *Britons: Forging the nation* (Penguin; Yale University Press). Controversial but rewarding assessment of what it means to be British.

Adrian Desmond and **James Moore**, *Darwin* (Penguin). A textbook example of science-as-autobiography, this study attempts to read Darwin's achievements through the prism of his frequently troubled life.

Maureen Duffy, *England: The making of the myth from Stonehenge to Albert Square* (Fourth Estate UK). Poet and dramatist Maureen Duffy's fascinating survey of the myths that have helped to create a sense of national identity in England.

Lisa Jardine, *Ingenious Pursuits: Building the scientific revolution* (Abacus; Anchor). Lisa Jardine is one of the most interesting literary and cultural critics around, and her books never fail to surprise nor intrigue. This study of early Enlightenment science in England is typically engaging.

Oliver MacDonagh, *Jane Austen: Real and imagined worlds* (Yale University Press). An imaginative analysis of Regency Society through the medium of Austen's books. Each chapter tackles a theme based on one or more of the novels: a marvellous way to become acquainted with Austen and the world in which she lived.

John Summerson, *Architecture in Britain 1530–1830* (Yale University Press). Seminal study of English architecture from the Tudors to the close of the Regency, now in its ninth edition.

Ian Watt, *The Rise of the Novel: Studies in Defoe, Richardson and Fielding* (Pimlico; University of California Press). Watt's study of the novel has become the standard point of departure for anyone wanting to know more about where this peculiar literary form came from. He examines a variety of causal factors—among them the rise of the middle class and the changing status of women.

Michael White, *Isaac Newton: The last sorcerer* (Fourth Estate; Helix Books). An engaging account of one of the founders of English science, which attempts to uncover the more mysterious (and far less "scientific") sides of Newton's work—his interest in alchemy and numerology in particular.

Andrew Wilton, *Five Centuries of British Painting* (Thames & Hudson). Part of the enormously popular World of Art series, Wilton's book is a reliable and informative guide to the major themes in British painting and their involvement in social history.

Classic Texts

The Anglo-Saxon Chronicle, trans. G.N. Garmonsway (Everyman UK o/p). An absorbing edition of this unique source, providing side-by-side translations of the main manuscripts that make up the Chronicle.

Asser's Life of King Alfred and other contemporary sources, trans. S. Keynes and M. Lapidge (Penguin). A fine volume of Alfredian sources. The principal one is a hagiography of Alfred written by the Welsh monk Asser, who later became bishop of Sherborne: a revealing piece about "British" attitudes to the "English" in the 9th century AD.

John Aubrey, *Brief Lives, ed. J Buchanan-Brown* (Penguin). Aubrey's character sketches were initially compiled as research material for Anthony Wood's histories of Oxford University, but they contain fascinating insights into Jacobean England in their own right.

Bede, *The Ecclesiastical History of the English People*, ed. J. McClure and R. Collins (Oxford University Press). Bede's most celebrated work, charting the history of the English and the spread of Christianity from the time of Julius Caesar to the beginning of the 8th century AD.

Thomas Babington Macaulay, *The History of England* (Penguin). Still the best general history of England from the reign of James II until the 19th century. Full of enjoyable anecdotes and wonderfully partial interpretation, and introduced in this edition by Hugh Trevor-Roper.

Thomas More, *The History of King Richard III*, ed. Richard Sylvester (Yale University Press; Vail-Ballou Press). One of the principal sources for Richard-as-monster. Brilliant—if factually skewed—character assassination of one of England's more unfortunate monarchs.

George Orwell, *The Road to Wigan Pier* (Penguin). Orwell's classic account of unemployment in the industrial north, commissioned by the Left Book Club and first published in 1937.

Samuel Pepys, *Diaries* (HarperCollins). The most famous of all English diaries, Pepys' candid account of a ten-year period at the end of the 17th century—detailing everything from the Great Fire to his numerous sexual adventures—makes for an involving and absorbing read, and it's an appealing insight into daily London life during an unusually hectic period. If you can't stomach the full eleven volumes, there is an abbreviated paperback version available.

BIOGRAPHIES

John Ehrman, *The Younger Pitt* (Constable UK). A life's work: John Ehrman's phenomenal study of Pitt may appear unwieldy at three volumes, but it's incisively written and a pleasure to dip into.

Amanda Foreman, *Georgiana, Duchess of Devonshire* (HarperCollins; Random House). Charming and provocative assessment of one of 18th-century England's most glamorous figures.

Martin Gilbert, *Churchill: A Life* (Park Lane; Henry Holt). Gilbert's book is detailed (perhaps overly so in parts) and does assume a certain amount of basic knowledge of the periods he covers, but this is nonetheless an engaging examination of Churchill, carefully researched.

John Grigg, *Lloyd George* (HarperCollins; Fontana). John Grigg's exhaustive three-volume study uncovers the mysteries of one of England's most enigmatic prime ministers, a man who attracted loathing and affection in equal measure.

Peter Gwyn, *Cardinal Wolsey* (Sussex; Barrie & Jenkins o/p). Gwyn's account is a welcome relief from the withering attacks Wolsey has suffered at the hands of some, though in attempting to right the balance this is perhaps too generous.

Roland Huntford, *The Last Place On Earth* (Abacus; Modern Library). Controversial dual biography of Captain Scott and the Norwegian who beat him to the South Pole, Roald Amundsen. Loathed by some for its uncompromisingly critical assessment of Scott, it is in places perhaps too quick to damn, but is nevertheless a scintillating examination not only of the rival explorers but of Edwardian society on the brink of World War I.

L.G. Mitchell, *Charles James Fox* (Penguin). The best account of this mercurial politician to date, and an engaging exposition of 18th-century Whig society.

J.J. Scarisbrick, *Henry VIII* (Yale University Press; University of California Press). Unsurpassed scholarly biography of one of England's most notorious rulers, revealing the extensive political and religious changes that his reign oversaw.

Hugo Young, *One of Us: a biography of Margaret Thatcher* (Macmillan). Exhaustive study of the transformation of Margaret Thatcher from research chemist to one of the most controversial of all British prime ministers.

PREHISTORY AND ROMAN BRITAIN

Nora Chadwick, *The Celts* (Penguin). Classic survey of this mysterious people, tracing the spread of the Celts through Europe until their transformation by the conquering Romans and Saxons.

H.H. Scullard, *Roman Britain: Outpost of the Empire* (Thames & Hudson/ Norton). Accessible guide to the major themes in Roman Britain.

Peter Salway, *Roman Britain* (Oxford University Press). Hefty but readable study of Britain and the Roman empire, recently reissued.

ANGLO-SAXON AND MEDIEVAL ENGLAND

James Campbell (ed.), *The Anglo-Saxons* (Penguin). Masterly thumbnail sketch of Anglo-Saxon England, lavishly illustrated.

Christine Carpenter, *The Wars of the Roses: Politics and the Constitution in England c.1437–1509* (Cambridge University Press). One of the best studies of the Wars of the Roses to have been published in the last few years.

M.T. Clanchy, *England and its Rulers 1066–1272*, (Blackwell UK). Valuable assessment of England from conquered nation beneath the Norman yoke to reinvigorated country with a renewed sense of identity, culminating in the accession of the warlike Edward I.

J.C. Holt, *Robin Hood* (Thames & Hudson). Enjoyable historical study of one of England's most famous myths.

G.L. Harriss (ed.), *Henry V: The practice of kingship* (Alan Sutton). A rewarding series of essays on—arguably—England's greatest king.

R. Horrox, *Richard III: A study in service* (Cambridge University Press). Scholarly reassessment of Richard III, for once placing the emphasis on his policies and followers rather than on speculation about his psychological motivation.

Michael Prestwich, *The Three Edwards: War and state in England 1272–1377* (Routledge). A fine study of three very different kings. Prestwich arranges his materially both thematically across the period, and by studying each individual—a satisfying combination.

TUDOR AND STUART ENGLAND

Geoffrey Elton, *England Under the Tudors* (Routledge). A classic assessment of the Tudor regime, now in its third edition.

Christopher Hibbert, *Cavaliers and Roundheads: The English at war 1642–49*, (HarperCollins; Scribner). A fascinating study of the English Civil Wars, including individual studies of some of the major players.

Christopher Hill, *The World Turned Upside Down: Radical ideas during the English Revolution* (Penguin). Hill's Marxist interpretation of the English Revolution. It's treated with a degree of skepticism now, but its thoroughly rewarding nevertheless.

Mark Kishlansky, *A Monarchy Transformed: Britain 1603–1714* (Penguin). Shrewd and lucid overview of this often turbulent and confusing period of English history.

D.M. Loades, *Politics and the Nation 1450–1660* (Blackwell). Part of the extremely valuable Blackwell "classic history" series. Detailed yet readable.

W.A. Speck, *Reluctant Revolutionaries: Englishmen and the Revolution of 1688* (Oxford University Press). Refreshing reappraisal of the "Glorious" Revolution.

David Starkey, *The Reign of Henry VIII: Personalities and politics* (Vintage; Trafalgar Square). Accessible and well-illustrated study of the court intrigue that surrounded Henry VIII.

THE 18TH CENTURY

J.C.D. Clark, *English Society 1688–1832* (Cambridge University Press). Controversial study of the "long 18th century"s propounding the view that England truly was an ancien régime society.

Douglas Hay, *Peter Linebaugh, John Rule, E.P. Thompson and C. Winslow, Albion's Fatal Tree: Crime and Society in 18th-century England* (Penguin). Important and eminently readable interpretation of the criminal underclass in 18th-century England. A classic Marxist appraisal of the "Black Acts"—the criminal code that maintained the property-owning interests of society in a position of dominance over the rest.

Geoffrey Holmes and **Daniel Szechi**, *The Age of Oligarchy: Pre-industrial Britain 1722–83* (Longman). A fine overview of the 18th century, which emphasizes only too clearly the difficulties inherent in marking cut-off points in English history.

Paul Langford, *A Polite and Commercial People* (Oxford University Press). A real gem—scholarly yet accessible. This weighty book is one of the best things to come out on the 18th century in the last few years.

Frank O'Gorman, *Voters, Patrons and Parties: The unreformed electoral system of Hanoverian England 1734–1832* (Oxford University Press o/p). Detailed study of the political culture of England before the Reform Act. Required reading for anyone serious about the subject.

J.H. Plumb, *The First Four Georges* (Penguin). Elegant study of the first four Hanoverians.

Roy Porter, *English Society in the 18th Century* (Penguin). Porter, one of the most popular historians of the "Enlightenment," here considers the full range of English culture and society. The result is a bold, comprehensive survey of England in one of its most controversial periods.

THE 19TH CENTURY

Paul Adelman, *Gladstone, Disraeli and Later Victorian Politics* (Longman). Part of the invaluable Longman Seminar Series. This provides a clear insight into the world of late 19th-century politics, and also includes a selection of interesting documents at the back.

Eric Evans, *The Forging of the Modern State: Early industrial Britain 1783–1870* (Longman). One of the most dependable surveys of this intricate period, which saw England recover from the loss of America and develop a powerful empire in the East and Africa.

Eric Hobsbawm, *The Age of Empire 1875–1914* (Vintage). Towering work by one of England's most influential historians, charting the downfall of the empires which dominated the world in the 19th century.

Lytton Strachey, *Eminent Victorians* (Penguin; Random House). Bitingly satirical reassessment of some of the great figures of Victorian England, written by one of Bloomsbury's leading lights.

THE 20TH CENTURY

Alan Clark, *Diaries* (Phoenix UK). These caused a minor sensation when they were published in 1994. Clarke's unashamedly un-PC and rude—but endearingly honest—reflections on political society in the 1980s have helped to shape the way we think of the Thatcher years.

Peter Hennessy, *The Prime Minister: The office and its holders since 1945* (Penguin). Hennessy's new study of central British political office charts its changing role in the years after World War II, and the pressures that have forced it to adapt.

Arthur Marwick, *British Society since 1945* (Penguin). Marwick's survey of the changing face of British society considers a variety of causes and trends (among them the "permissive society"), and asks important questions about the nature of Britain's relationship with the European Union.

Norman Rose, *The Cliveden Set: Portrait of an exclusive fraternity* (Jonathan Cape). Engaging and thoroughly balanced study of the politicians, academics and aristocrats who were demonized for advocating a more sympathetic response to Hitler's Germany.

A.J.P. Taylor, *English History 1914–45* (Oxford University Press). A provocative study of England from the outbreak of the first world war to the end of the second. As ever, Taylor's work is entertaining but scholarly history at its best.

A.J.P. Taylor, *The Origins of the Second World War* (Penguin). Taylor's work upset many who had made it their life's work to assault the appeasers and put the whole blame on Hitler for the catastrophe that overtook Europe in the 1930s and 1940s. Willing to challenge the conventional view, Taylor's marvelously skeptical book dares to examine the events leading up to the outbreak of war objectively.

INDEX

Entries in color represent feature boxes

PHOTOGRAPHY CREDITS

Art Resource, NY: The Pierpont Morgan Library: p. 52

Bridgeman Art Library: P. Brannon and T. Picken (color litho)/©Guildhall Library, Corporation of London, UK: p. 358

Corbis: p. 415; ©Archivo Iconografico, S.A.: p. 70; ©Bettmann: p. 98, 141, 154, 221, 231, 254, 262, 325, 331, 433; ©Werner Forman: p. 79; ©Hulton-Deutsch Collection: p. 379; ©Reuters: p. 441; ©Jim Richardson: p. 7; ©John Stillwell/Pool/Reuters: p. 451

Getty Images: ©Carl de Souza/AFP: p. 458; ©Adam Woolfitt: p. 24

Mary Evans Picture Library: p. 391, 403